Sister Saints

Sister Saints

Mormon Women Since the End of Polygamy

Colleen McDannell

OXFORD
UNIVERSITY PRESS

OXFORD
UNIVERSITY PRESS

Oxford University Press is a department of the University of Oxford. It furthers
the University's objective of excellence in research, scholarship, and education
by publishing worldwide. Oxford is a registered trade mark of Oxford University
Press in the UK and certain other countries.

Published in the United States of America by Oxford University Press
198 Madison Avenue, New York, NY 10016, United States of America.

Library of Congress Cataloging-in-Publication Data
Names: McDannell, Colleen, author.
Title: Sister saints : Mormon women since the end of polygamy / Colleen McDannell.
Description: New York : Oxford University Press, [2019] |
Includes bibliographical references and index.
Identifiers: LCCN 2018001321 | ISBN 9780190221317 (hardcover : alk. paper) |
ISBN 9780190221331 (epub)
Subjects: LCSH: Mormon women—History.
Classification: LCC BX8643.W66 M333 2018 | DDC 289.3082—dc23
LC record available at https://lccn.loc.gov/2018001321

1 3 5 7 9 8 6 4 2

Printed by Sheridan Books, Inc., United States of America

To my Friend Ann Braude, who always stands for women

CONTENTS

PREFACE

In the summer of 1989, my husband and I made the long trek across the country from Baltimore, Maryland, to Salt Lake City, Utah. We had just spent four years in Heidelberg, Germany, and I was on my way to start a new teaching position at the University of Utah. Our two cats enjoyed a relatively painless airplane ride, while we struggled with the heat and the boredom of the American interstate highway system. At our first meal in our new state, we ate something called a "Mormon scone," which bore little resemblance to its British cousin. While I had lived most of my life in the western United States, Utah was alien territory. That a scone was not quite a scone was a complicated harbinger of things to come.

I had come to the University of Utah as the holder of an endowed chair in Religious Studies, housed in the Department of History, and named after a feisty Latter-day Saint philosopher, Sterling M. McMurrin. According to the lore passed down to me, the donor who funded the chair wanted someone to teach "comparative religion" and thus introduce the students to something other than Mormonism. Before that point, my experience with the Latter-day Saints had been limited to dealing with the director of public affairs in the Europe Area Office in Frankfurt. I had been writing a book about heaven with a German colleague and wanted to include a section on the Latter-day Saint understanding of life after death. We contacted the Mormons to see if they had a library we could use, but then they told us that if we merely described which books we wanted, they would have them shipped from Salt Lake. Any books? Any books. Over the next few months we were loaned every book we asked for and extra ones that they thought might be helpful. Mormons, it seemed, were profoundly kind and—even better for a scholar—were organized bibliophiles.

Once settled in Salt Lake, I joined a group of women scholars from our University and Brigham Young University, all of whom were new to Utah. We were interested in women's issues and considered ourselves feminists, even the women from BYU. By the early nineties, however, Tomi-Ann Roberts and Cecilia Konchar Farr found their faculty positions at BYU to be increasingly tenuous. The critical Gender Studies that had become standard across the educational landscape was generating strife at BYU. None of this made any sense to me. These were excellent scholars and engaging teachers. In any other environment, they would have been valued colleagues. Why were these women not welcomed on their campus? What happened to the kind and book-oriented Mormons I knew?

Then, in 1991, I experienced more directly the fear of intellectual inquiry that was threatening Mormon women at BYU. I was working on a book about the objects and spaces people use in their religious lives and was conducting interviews with Latter-day Saints about their feelings about their priesthood garments—the special underclothing Mormons wear. We never talked explicitly about the temple experience, which I knew was sacred. That August I presented a few tentative results at a conference held in Salt Lake. Every summer average Latter-day Saints met to discuss the history, culture, sociology, and literature of their faith. A few of the speakers were faculty at BYU or other colleges, but most of the presenters were simply bright individuals who felt a passion to study their own religion.

Shortly after the conference, the highest authorities of the Mormon church told members that they should not attend such symposia. In spite of my careful attention to Mormon sensibilities, my paper and several others by Latter-day Saints were deemed to be offensive. I kept thinking: Why would Mormon leaders want to silence their intellectually engaged flock? Wouldn't Catholic bishops be overjoyed if average parishioners rigorously studied theology and church history and presented their findings to packed rooms? Soon after, I stopped writing about Mormons. The climate was inhospitable. Latter-day Saints were being silenced; a few were excommunicated. I would follow the desires of the funder of my endowed chair and concentrate on the religious world outside of Utah.

But I never lost the desire to understand the Latter-day Saint women who surrounded me—students, friends, and neighbors. *Sister Saints: Mormon Women Since the End of Polygamy* is my effort to explain what led up to the conflicts that Latter-day Saint women faced in the early nineties and how Mormonism has changed since then. As a historian of religion, I knew that the Church of Jesus Christ of Latter-day Saints was a vibrant, growing international religion claiming almost sixteen million members. It publishes church materials in 188 different languages and supports over 30,000 congregations. And yet, there is a lack of historical scholarship on the ordinary lives of the women who make up more than half of the Mormon population.

Much of Mormon history circles around the stories of men—those who founded the church, led it, fell from it, directed it, or defined it. *Sister Saints*, however, continues the movement by feminist Mormon historians to explore a different set of questions: What were the women doing while the men were doing what they did? If women were brought into the historical narrative, how might that change the story? What do women see as spiritually fulfilling in their lives? What new religious forms occur as one generation slides into another? Calling on my background in American religious history, I investigate what has sustained and motivated Latter-day Saint women and how that has changed over time.

When women *do* work their way into the story, they tend to be either polygamists or pioneers—often both. The nineteenth century looms large in Latter-day Saint culture, because it was then that the central concepts of the faith were laid out. Moreover, Mormons see the early years as overflowing with evidence of the supernatural and the extraordinary. Latter-day Saints treasure their history, building bridges between the present and the time of sacred beginnings. Even Mormon feminists look backward to the nineteenth century for evidence of a usable past of female agency and originality. They point to the women who went East and studied medicine or the ones who secured the right to vote in 1870. "Why can't the twenty-first century," they seem to be asking, "be more like the nineteenth?"

In the American imagination, Mormon women *still* have not left the nineteenth century. In the media, Mormon women silently support their men and say little about their own lives. Television shows tell tales of plural wives. Their clothing might be modern and the settings look familiar, but the themes recall the anti-Mormonism of a hundred years ago. The famed Broadway play *Angels in America* paints women as either addled wives on pills or bossy mothers. In 2002 news reports of the kidnapped Elizabeth Smart kept asking, "why didn't she fight back?" *The Book of Mormon* musical almost entirely erased Latter-day Saint women. The female lead, Nabalungi, is baptized late in the show and does not remain orthodox. Mormon women are cast either as helpless Victorian ladies or strange sexual beings. It is hard to break free of the Mormon nineteenth century.

The Latter-day Saint women of *Sister Saints* are modern. Most are not polygamists, they do not live on farms, they do not suffer in obedient silence. Yes, there are Latter-day Saint women who do—or have done—all of those things. But this is (for the most part) a book about monogamous women, who are members of a church that vigorously disavows polygamy. Although their grandparents or parents may have been pioneers who walked across the plains and produced their own domestic goods, the women I write about live modern lives.

One of the reasons that the story of modern women is rarely told is because it is much easier to imagine the nineteenth century as a time of unified sisterhood. Conflict, of course, exists in everyone's history, but during the twentieth century Latter-day Saint women more confidently asserted their differences with each other and with church leaders. *Sister Saints* pays close attention to the feminist stirrings within the church and the price that many women have paid for speaking out against inequality. At the same time, it explores how Mormon women have resisted being pushed out of traditional domestic roles. Antifeminism belongs in a book about modern Mormon women as much as feminism does.

The modern women of *Sister Saints* also value things that others would define as "not modern." Mormon doctrine resists the modern divide between sacred and secular. God's real presence is felt in everyday life. New revelations come all the time. Women in particular have a sacramental view of reality in which the transcendent intervenes regularly. Consequently, Latter-day Saints expect their inspired leaders to comment authoritatively on the private aspects of their lives. Members are not surprised to learn that their church earns profit from cattle ranches in Florida or shopping centers in Utah. Mormon women live in a fluid religious world that is structured by the informal and spontaneous—reflected in their Sunday "meetings"—as well as highly symbolic rituals conducted in temples, which they consider profoundly holy. Women's acquiescence to the authority of male prophets and church leaders can only be understood if one takes seriously the power of the sacred in their lives.

If the mark of the modern is the autonomy of the individual, then the mark of the modern Latter-day Saint woman is that her autonomy is exercised in relationship with others.[1] *Sister Saints* stresses the importance of community in the evolution of the modern Latter-day Saint. Individual agency and intelligence are valued, but the divine is not experienced in isolation. It is "sociality" or community that forms the foundation of both heaven and earth (D&C 130:1–2)—for women and for men. From the collection of plural wives, to the sisterhood of the Relief Society, to the female missionary traveling with her "companion," to the digital village built by bloggers, Latter-day Saint women express themselves through and with each other. Even God, as we will see, must be understood in the plural. Consequently, the family—and women's significant yet changing role within it—has intensely spiritual as well as emotional and economic dimensions. *Sister Saints* explores how women come to know themselves in conversation with friends, family, church leaders, and the writings of ancestors. It is these women that I am trying to make visible.

Finally, *Sister Saints* argues that Mormon women have always been active creators of Mormon culture, even if they do so within a given religious framework. Without women's support of polygamy, plural marriages never would have survived the attacks of the US government and of American popular culture. Latter-day Saint women not only shared in the building and sustaining of farming communities, but they developed an array of civic and charitable institutions that shaped a growing faith community.

Even the development of a Mormon style of self-restraint, chastity, domesticity, and hyperfemininity—a style that persevered through the counterculture years of the sixties and seventies—was able to survive because women were committed to that worldview. As more Latter-day Saint women graduate from college, serve missions, and seek to balance outside work with family life, a more intricate and varied Mormonism is evolving. Today, more Latter-day Saints live outside of the United States than inside of it. The "Mormon style" lingers, but global Mormonism is far too complicated for easy caricatures. Women now are a part of a vast array of cultures, classes, and political orientations. *Sister Saints* offers a social history built from these voices of Latter-day Saint women.

Sister Saints

CHAPTER 1

---◆---

Building Zion

In the winter of 1884 Mormon editor Emmeline B. Wells took time out from her busy schedule to meet with British reformer Emily Faithfull, who was on a speaking tour of the West. The two women shared much in common. Both were fully committed to the rights of women and their political equality with men. Both had founded magazines in which women wrote the stories, set the type, and marketed the results. Both were considered strong-minded women who moved easily in the world of ideas. And both were well known and respected for their passionate dedication to improving women's lives.

Wells wrote that she found Faithfull to be amiable and noble, with good sense and a superior education.[1] Faithfull's extensive travels made her a charming conversationalist. Her 1884 tour was actually her third such venture in the United States, having previously lectured on "The Changed Position of Women in the Nineteenth Century."

Wells was a woman with little or no patience for the mindlessness that marked many women's lives in the late nineteenth century. Born in 1828, she was raised in a serious Yankee household where her mother encouraged her intellectual spirit. In an era when most girls had limited education, the young Emmeline was sent away for schooling in various western Massachusetts villages. It was while she was away in 1841 that her mother and younger siblings joined a new religion. A traveling preacher told them about a young man from Vermont to whom God had given special prophetic authority and a new book of Scripture. This seer, named Joseph Smith, organized the Church of Christ in 1830, shortly after the publication of that Scripture: the Book of Mormon. The community would soon become known as the Church of Jesus Christ of Latter-day Saints, though outsiders called them "Mormons." Insiders knew each other as "Saints." Neither Wells's stepfather nor older siblings converted to the new faith, so as a teenager Emmeline had to choose her own path. Was the religion a true revelation or a dangerous delusion? Persuaded by her mother and others in her town, she was baptized on her fourteenth birthday.

Her life changed immediately and dramatically. By fifteen she had married a fellow Mormon and moved with her mother and some of her siblings to a utopian community being built on the banks of the Mississippi River. Life in the new town was a struggle. Emmeline began teaching school but soon suffered a string of tragedies: her prophet was murdered, her baby died, and her young husband abandoned her.

New forms of Christianity, youthful marriages, fleeing husbands, and infant death were nothing new in mid-nineteenth-century America. That a recent convert would turn to teaching to earn her way in the Mormon city of Nauvoo would have made sense to any Victorian lady. Nor would anyone have been surprised that in 1845 she married the fifty-year-old father of some of the children she was teaching. We do not know who initiated the marriage, but a surviving letter from Emmeline reveals her deep love for her new husband.[2] What would have been surprising to most people, however, was that she was one of several wives of Newel K. Whitney. She would bear him two daughters before his death in 1850. Then, after having walked across the plains and over mountains to Salt Lake City, Emmeline would propose marriage to Daniel H. Wells, a distinguished member of the growing Latter-day Saint community. In 1852, at the age of twenty-four, she became his seventh wife and mother to three of his thirty-seven children.

Emmeline Wells was a "new" Mormon woman—a city dweller, a woman of ideas who looked outward to the nation and the world, and a woman who managed her own household with little male help. Wells would also go on to own and edit a women's magazine, travel to the nation's capital to argue for women's right to vote, organize emergency wheat storage, and serve on a hospital board. She ran for public office and was active at the highest level in the Relief Society, a Mormon women's organization. Wells frequently acted as a hostess to important visitors to Utah while still managing a complicated extended family. She was an unusually active and outspoken Latter-day Saint, but she shared many traits with other Mormon women.

Emmeline Wells was thus perfectly situated to introduce Emily Faithfull to the Mormons. Brigham Young had imagined a vast empire in the intermountain West, beyond the reach of the federal government, which he initially named "Deseret" after the Book of Mormon term for honeybee (Ether 2:3). Like a beehive, Deseret would be a place of industry and community. Latter-day Saints also understood themselves to be the remnant of God's Chosen People, a Nation of Israel. They were in Zion, the land given to the righteous by God. By the time of Faithfull's visit, Deseret as a polit-ical entity had ceased to exist. It had become Utah Territory: much reduced in size, multireligious, multiethnic, and under the authority of the federal government. But Zion continued to endure in the minds of the Latter-day Saints. Women were praised for being "Mothers in Israel" or "Daughters of Zion," partners in constructing a promised land. From the moment the Mormons arrived in the Salt Lake valley in 1847, women created and maintained both the ideal and the reality of the American Zion.

Unfortunately, Emily Faithfull would have none of this. She ignored Wells's accomplishments and sneered at the Mormon women she met. Even attending a luncheon at the elegant mansion of the church president and conversing with some of its leading women did not impress Faithfull. In her memoir, *Three Visits to America*, she admitted that she was treated with kindness and courtesy, but she saw nothing worthwhile in the reli-gion the women practiced. Faithfull disparaged the structure of the Latter-day Saints church by comparing them to the much-maligned Jesuits and dismissed the notion of a sacred Zion as a land speculation scheme. The emigrants who settled the region were "ignorant people," she wrote, and the "hateful system of polygamy" caused "the cruelest subjection and the most hopeless degradation."[3] It seemed that no amount of accomplishment or refinement could sever the association of polygamy with degeneracy.

Wells, however, gave as good as she got. When the publisher of *Three Visits to America* asked Wells to review the book for her own magazine, she did not mince words. Wells began her comments in the *Woman's Exponent* by observing sarcastically that many authors seemed to think that writing a book "in forcible language and thrilling incident" detailing the "horrors of Mormonism" would immediately push Congress to end polygamy.[4] She then wondered how someone who lectured about the hypocrisy, extrava-gance, and shams of the modern world could pander so much to society's taste for the sensational. Why would the visitor "join in the hue and cry against those of whom she knew so little, before she had thoroughly investigated the subject?" Wells noted that Faithfull saw almost nothing of Zion because her asthma had gotten the better of her and so curtailed her visit. According to Wells, Faithfull had lied about attending the eightieth birthday party of Mormon notable Eliza R. Snow. Instead, she based *Three Visits to America* on her own imagination and the writings of other anti-Mormons. Faithfull, it turned out, was not very faithful.

Although we might point to polygamy as the dividing line between Mormon and non-Mormon, the foundational difference is much deeper. Wells and her sister Saints had converted to a specific *religious* system that shaped both their highest aspirations and the humblest aspects of their everyday lives. It was the intensity of women's religious experiences that enabled them both to endure the everyday struggles of pioneer life and to assent to the plural marriages that so disgusted Faithfull and other non-Mormons. What were the aspects of this religion that drew women together into a tight community that could withstand the ridicule of a whole nation? What were the consequences of adopting this new faith? What roles did women play in building Zion?

The Mormonism that Wells and the pioneer generation of women embraced was embodied, practical, and supernaturally oriented. The reluctance of Latter-day Saints to separate the spiritual from the material set them apart from most Protestants of the time, who were increasingly devoted to the Enlightenment values of reason and privatized faith. Latter-day Saints were more like the religious enthusiasts of antebellum America, who believed the current order of the world was ending and that new revelations required nontraditional worship and unconventional social arrangements. Like the Shakers, Mormons conflated spirituality, economic production, and communal living. And like the Methodists, they accepted the duty to seek out the power of the supernatural in everyday life. Eventually, Latter-day Saints would develop feelings for sacred space, liturgical rites, and sacred clothing not dissimilar from those of Catholics and Anglicans.

So while Latter-day Saints shared many characteristics with other Christians, there was one thing that truly set them apart: their conviction that their prophet, Joseph Smith, had received multiple revelations from God. For Mormons, the Bible was not the definitive testament of God's relationship with his people. Smith had translated from an ancient Egyptian script a book that, they believed, accurately described the history of a tribe of Israelites who had settled in the New World. The Last Days were near, and soon would come the millennial age with its renewed, transformed, and glorified earth. Until that time, these Saints of the latter days were called upon to construct a literal kingdom of God, to gather where they could build their own sacred nation: a New Jerusalem, an American Israel, a Zion. There they would experience God's continual revelation—to the presidents of the church for the group and to individuals for their own well-being. The divinely inspired leaders deserved the obedience and submission of their followers. Those who could not submit or obey were expelled; Zion was to be a place for Saints. The Saints insisted that they were not simply reforming Christianity but restoring religion to its pure and original form.

For early Latter-day Saints, religion was not a set of abstract beliefs. Mormons saw plowing fields, digging ditches, and constructing homes as fundamentally religious acts. For the first twenty-five years or so in Salt Lake, they held large religious services either outside or in a large assembly hall. During the eighteen-seventies, "meetinghouses" made of adobe or stone were built for geographical areas called "wards," but the Saints were sporadic in their attendance.[5] Since labor was perceived as a religious act, work could take precedence over worship. Some attended Sunday School or Sacrament meetings, but even Wells showed no guilt in writing "this morning we rose very late."[6] Churchgoing had not become a marker of piety. Constructing meetinghouses and attending services were more important outside of Salt Lake City, but Mormonism was more like an ethnicity than a denomination. Eventually meetings and organizations would come to define Latter-day Saint existence, but in the Nation of Deseret it was the immediacy of the divine and the prevalence of all-consuming labor that structured women's lives.

The intensity of a woman's religious commitment typically began with her conversion. The decision to be baptized and join the Latter-day Saints was usually a life-changing experience because conversion often meant separating from families and friends. When Helena Erickson Rosbery heard traveling missionaries preach in her village in Sweden, she "thought the two Brothers looked more like angels than men." After having a series of visions of the truth of their message, she was baptized. "I was so full of the Spirit," she recalled decades later, that "I thought if I was a man, I could go and preach the gospel and refute all the arguments the learned priests could bring to establish their doctrines." Her Catholic husband did not share her enthusiasm and refused to let her participate in the new religion. Eventually Helena escaped with her daughter to a Mormon community in Denmark. "I left all that was near and dear to me," she remembered, "for I loved the Lord more than anything on earth." Helena's husband pursued his wife and child but eventually he, too, converted, and in 1859 the family joined the Saints in Utah.[7] For many convert women, becoming a Latter-day Saint was an act of both commitment and defiance.

Not all men who followed their wives to the New World accepted the new religion. When Mary Bulkley converted in 1857 in England, her husband treated her cruelly and her neighbors threatened her. "I had to travel my journey all alone; a very thorny path," she recalled, "but thank the Lord I was blest with dreams to help me, and I got my children all baptized that was old enough and the others blessed but had to do it all in secret [and] not let my friends know."[8] Bulkley arranged for the family to immigrate to Utah, but her husband died unconverted in Iowa City, leaving her penniless. She and her seven children walked to "the valley," with Bulkley guiding an oxcart. Even if a whole family converted, a woman knew that her other kin would no longer be a part of her life. Between 1852 and 1887 over 73,000 European immigrants came to the Salt Lake Great Basin.[9] Deseret was built on a foundation of foreign and broken families.

Sometimes women who had once enthusiastically joined the church had their fervor transformed into anti-Mormonism. When Fanny Stenhouse's husband left the church, she became disenchanted and carved out a place for herself in the developing genre of anti-Mormon exposés. Ann Eliza Young infamously divorced Brigham Young and then set off to discredit her former family through writings and lectures. These women skillfully utilized the media at a time when most women's voices were not heard in the public arena.

Other women made the decision to remain Mormon even when their husbands left the church. William S. Godbe and William Jarman were famous excommunicated apostates, but their wives, Charlotte and Maria, remained orthodox Mormons. Both divorced their husbands and raised their children within the community of Saints. Women's enthusiasm for religion often took precedence over their commitments to family.

Women made such sacrifices because they believed they had seen with their own eyes the spiritual blessings God had given to the Saints. Other Christians believed that the extraordinary miracles of the New Testament ended with the early church, but Mormons preached that believers could experience the supernatural in their everyday lives—just as the apostles did in their day. The immediacy of these experiences fulfilled the promises made by Mormon missionaries. The physical manifestations of God were proof that the Book of Mormon was true and that Joseph Smith was a prophet.

Beginning in the eighteen-thirties, some Mormon women were caught up in a divine power so strong that they spoke and sang in unknown languages. For example, hearing Joseph Smith preach, Lydia Bailey felt the glory of God swell up in her: "She was enveloped as with a flame, and unable longer to retain her seat, she arose and her mouth was filled with the praises of God and his glory. This spirit of tongues was upon her."[10] Other women interpreted what was said. At times men were present; at other times only in intimate gatherings of women were heavenly sounds heard. Women experienced glossolalia (speaking in tongues) in the early temples of Kirtland and Nauvoo, at large conferences, in their local churches, at school openings, and in the most mundane circumstances. In 1895 at "Sister Stevenson's" birthday party, "Sister Sarah Phelps spoke in tongues with great power insomuch that the floor and the chairs and our limbs trembled."[11] In her diary, Wells often mentioned that her women friends spoke and interpreted in tongues—and at times she did as well.[12]

During the nineteenth century, hearing unknown languages was a common occurrence at both Latter-day Saint worship services and at informal home gatherings, to the point of becoming routine and unexceptional. The nature of this language was unclear. Wells thought the strange words could be a primordial Indian dialect or the pure language of Adam.[13] While glossolalia was typically translated, diaries rarely explained what actually was said. Communicating an explicit message was less important than conveying a general feeling of spiritual empowerment and comfort. At times of celebration, during periods of anxiety, or even during routine church meetings, women experienced the intense spirit of the Lord.

Speaking and singing in tongues was often accompanied by women blessing and prophesizing. In 1894 a Canadian couple asked the community's spiritual leader, Charles Ora Card, to bless the new home they had built. Card described in his diary how the couple had been fasting and praying, hoping that his wife, Zina Presendia, might speak in tongues. Zina did speak in tongues, but then she "put her hands on their heads as if to bless them. She did upon mine [Charles] more particularly and with longer duration." Atena, the woman who owned the home, interpreted what Zina had said. Then Atena herself prophesized, telling Charles he would eventually be free from debt. "This comfort[ed] me very much for I long to see the day," Charles wrote. "We had a spiritual feast and spent the evening in conversing," he concluded. "God blest us much."[14] The Gifts of the Holy Spirit were just that, gifts that came to some and not to others.

By far the most widespread spiritual gift experienced by women was the ability to heal. Healing was an essential part of Latter-day Saint life because illness and death were unavoidable, as they were everywhere in nineteenth-century America. No family could boast of being free from pain, suffering, and grief. Children contracted scarlet fever, chicken pox, and pneumonia. In 1880 Eliza Lyman observed that "to see a beloved child suffering the pains of Death without the power to relieve them in the least is almost too much for human nature to bear."[15] Adults fared little better. Most available medical treatments took place at home, and so women intimately interacted with the sick and disabled. Women managed the "gates of mortality," both introducing new souls into the world and smoothing their transition into the next.[16]

Two models of healing exist within Christianity in general and in Mormonism in particular. In the first, healing was one of several spiritual gifts given by God to believers, including women (I Corinthians 12:9). The father of Joseph Smith, recognized as the "patriarch" of the church, gave special blessings (Patriarchal Blessings) that recognized such gifts in women. In 1835 he told Elizabeth Ann Whitney (later Wells's sister wife in Nauvoo), "When thy husband is far from thee and thy little ones are afflicted thou shalt have power to prevail and they shall be healed."[17] In 1842 Joseph Smith himself chided those who questioned women's healing abilities. "Respecting the female laying on hands," he explained, "there could be no devils in it if God gave his sanction by healing—that there could be no more sin in any female laying hands on the sick than in wetting the face with water—that it is no sin for anybody to do it that has faith."[18] Women practiced healing throughout the nineteenth century.

In the second model, healing was tied to church offices typically occupied by men. In his 1831 revelations on healing, Smith explained how it worked: two or more elders should be called to pray and lay their hands on the afflicted person (D&C 42:44). In another revelation, William E. McLellin was told to "lay your hands upon the sick, and they shall recover" (D&C 66:9). These revelations echoed the epistle of James (5:14), who also mentioned that the *elders* of the church would anoint the sick with oil in the name of the Lord. For Smith, women could also be marked to heal, although it is unclear how he is using the word "ordain": "Wherein they are ordained, it is the privilege of those set apart to administer in that authority which is confer'd on them—and if sisters should have faith to heal the sick, let all hold their tongues, and let everything roll on."[19] Women might be "set apart" by others in the church for healing. In this version of the model, healing required the acknowledgment of authority figures.

Throughout most of the nineteenth century, these two models for healing existed simultaneously and peacefully. Women healed, and they called on men to heal. In 1878, after the deaths of four of her children and the near death of a son who had disemboweled himself on a pitchfork, Margaret Ballard's husband fell ill. First the elders were called and they attempted to heal him, but he did not seem to be recovering. According to Margaret, "a voice came to me and said, 'administer to him,' but I was very timid about this for the brethren had just administered to him." Then the voice came again, but "I felt that they would think me bold and I was very weak. The voice came to me this third time and I heeded to its promptings and went and put my hands upon his head. The Spirit of the Holy Ghost was with me and I was filled with a Divine strength in performing the ordinance." A few years later, her father had a serious case of pneumonia, and Margaret again healed after the elders left. She recalled her father saying, "Thank God for this blessing, I knew this power was in the church and I thank Him for it."[20] From Margaret's perspective, while it was her own divine gift that enabled her husband and father to recover, this did not negate the call to the elders, nor did they impede her efforts.

Only certain women were engaged in healing, blessing, speaking in tongues, and prophesizing, but many Mormon women reported uncanny dreams during which God gave them special insights and inspiration. Martha Cox had to flee to Mexico in 1889 to avoid being arrested for polygamy. Her life was difficult, and "I had bitter hatred in my heart against the officials in Utah and against the traitors who exposed the Saints."[21] One

night she had a dream that she believed gave her insight into what this hatred was doing to her. She dreamt that she had a chain around her neck
with bundles on it. Each bundle represented a wrong she had done, or a
complaint she had, or a debt she had accrued. Then, in the dream she slowly
lifted off each bundle, freeing herself from the burdens she had imposed
on herself. The dream told her that she needed to become free of her hatred and fears. Dreams were a key source of spiritual power. They reassured
women about lost loved ones, comforted them, and provided them with
hidden information.

Latter-day Saint temples, however, were increasingly becoming the place
where the divine touched the human. Utah's first temple was constructed in St.
George in 1877; one went up in Logan in 1884. The Manti Temple would be
dedicated in 1888 and the Salt Lake Temple finished in 1893. Until 1889 the
Saints in Salt Lake had conducted the special rituals in the small "Endowment
House" on the temple block. But steam-powered derricks enabled temple
walls to rise eighty feet into the air, complementing the massive nearby
Tabernacle (1864–67) and Assembly Hall (1877–82). The Logan Temple
sat atop a hill with painted white limestone walls. With their mansard roofs
and crenellated towers, the temples were dramatically different from the small
ward meetinghouses where the Saints worshipped during the week.

Within the temple, women found personal inspiration while cultivating
ritual authority. They decorated the space as they would their own homes,
expressing both their artistry and devotion in woven rugs, drapery, and
even hair wreaths. Women sewed special robes worn in the temple and then
dressed the dead in those priestly garments when they prepared the Saints
for burial. Female temple workers washed and anointed other women,
reciting prayers while touching their bare skin with oil. Wells recalled in
1880 that her friend Eliza Snow "ministered in that Temple in the holy
rites that pertain to the house of the Lord as priestess and Mother in Israel
to hundreds of her sex," and that women officiated earlier in the Nauvoo
Temple "in the character of [a] priestess."[22]

Groups of men and women then observed the plan of salvation dramatically portrayed by actors in various rooms. Women promised to obey
their husbands and special signs and words were given to them that enabled
married women to enter the highest kingdom of heaven along with their
husbands. Women often went to the temple prior to giving birth or when
they were ill. They also performed rituals for their dead ancestors to ensure
that they, too, had the opportunity to move into the highest realms of the
afterlife. "It gave me great joy to be an instrument in the hands of the Lord,"
Margaret Ballard explained, "in helping work out salvation for those who
died in darkness."[23] Only women could perform ordinances for women,
securing their role in temple rituals.

It would be incorrect to conclude, however, that women associated being a Latter-day Saint solely with otherworldly experiences. The kingdom of Zion relied on women's practical contributions not only to care for their families but also to attend to the needs of the community's poor, widows, and orphans. A "Female Relief Society," not unlike Protestant benevolent associations common at the time, had been founded in Nauvoo in 1842. Smith, however, told the assembled women that he had something more ambitious in mind for a select group of them. In addition to attending to the poor, they should correct the morals and strengthen the virtues of the community's women in order to "save the Elders the trouble of rebuking."[24] In speaking to the Relief Society, Smith employed terms that up until then had only been addressed to men: he would deliver "keys" to "this society and to the church," and he promised, according to notes taken at the meeting, that "he was going to make of this Society a kingdom of priests as in Enoch's day—as in Paul's day."[25] Smith would "ordain" officers to direct the Society. His wife Emma would "preside" as president, and he repeated the revelation that she would also expound the Scriptures and teach other women (D&C 25:5–8). Smith did not explain the Society's precise relationship to the male priesthood, and the meeting's minutes are tantalizingly obscure.

The prophet was never able to clarify his intentions. After Smith's death, Brigham Young was convinced that Joseph's wife Emma was stirring up women against the practice of plural marriage. Emma Smith was a forceful, intelligent, and well-regarded member of the Latter-day Saint community, and Young did not want to risk her—or any woman—disrupting his authority or the unity of the Saints. In March 1845, Young made one thing absolutely clear to influential Mormon men: women, when they got together in groups, were trouble. Not only would there be no more Relief Society meetings, but "I will curse every man that lets his wife or daughters meet again—until I tell them . . . I don't [want] the advice or counsel of any woman—they would lead us down to hell—." According to Young, women were weak like Eve and needed men to lead them into the Celestial Kingdom.[26] Moreover, Young claimed that Smith had not initiated the Relief Society, and if anyone said he did, "tell them it is a damned lie for I know he never encouraged it." Colorful, opinionated, and always confident in his judgments, Young preached that "when I want sisters or the wives of the members of the church to get up [a] Relief Society, I will summon them to my aid but until that time let them stay at home."[27] For a community struggling to find and uphold a God-appointed leader, women's diverse attitudes regarding plural marriage were seen as undermining hard-fought unity.

Emma Smith, who never wavered from believing her husband was a prophet of God, did vacillate in her support of his multiple marriages. She came to know of his wives at different times and seemed torn between her love for Joseph and her disgust at his sexual behavior. After her husband's death, when Young decided to lead the Saints into the Western desert, Emma and her children rejected his prophetic authority and stayed in Nauvoo. In that regard, Young was correct that women could be trouble.

Once in Utah, however, Young realized that if he wanted to create a stable, self-sustaining economy, he needed the support of women. Lingering in the background were Smith's talks to Latter-day Saint women, which were both obscure and empowering. In 1855 some of the ambiguous character of the prophet's injunctions to the newly formed Relief Society was clarified through the publication of a set of edited excerpts of Smith's sermons. While compiling a manuscript history of the church, church historian George A. Smith and Thomas Bullock altered the "original sermon" that Eliza R. Snow had transcribed. The new editing more clearly linked women's authority to that of men's. For instance, in the original minutes, Joseph Smith simply spoke of "delivering the keys to this Society and to the church," but the revision read: "He spoke of delivering the keys of the Priesthood to the church, and said that the faithful members of the Relief Society should receive them *in connection with their husbands*" [italics mine].[28] After the revisions were read to him, Young reportedly said he "was much pleased with them."[29] Upon hearing the alteration, Heber C. Kimball, Young's first counselor, explained: "heard Joseph's sermon read, liked it better as revised."[30] These changes surely made it easier for Young to permit Latter-day Saint women to meet for charitable activities. In 1867 Young approved the church-wide reorganization of the Relief Society under the authority of Eliza R. Snow.

Over the next decade, until his death in 1877, Young would call on the newly reorganized Relief Society to perform a great variety of tasks ranging from making clothing for poor Indians, to producing silk, to running cooperative stores. By 1888 there were almost four hundred local Relief Societies, each with an organization similar to that of the male priesthood.[31] Women raised funds to build and furnish their own buildings, where they not only conducted meetings but also dried fruit, wove rugs from rags, sold baby clothing and shoes, sewed temple clothing, braided straw for bonnets, and produced quilts. By the turn of the century, Relief Society property in Utah was worth more than $95,000.[32]

In 1876, after Young became frustrated trying to get men to save wheat for emergencies, he asked Wells to organize the women of the Relief Society to collect grain. Using the *Woman's Exponent* as a vehicle to generate enthusiasm for the project, Wells reported on how women sold the eggs they collected on Sundays and bought grain with the money they earned. Other women and children went into fields after wheat had been harvested and gleaned the leftovers. They put on dances and teas and used the proceeds to buy surplus wheat. Relief Society committees were organized in order to fundraise and coordinate building the storehouses. Like the Relief Society buildings and the cooperative stores, women owned both the wheat and the storage facilities. Church leaders warned local ward bishops that they had no authority over the stored grain.

Young also worked hard to convince women to produce their own silk fabric for clothing. In 1868 he imported mulberry seeds from France and planted them at an experimental farm in Salt Lake. Once the trees had grown, he made cuttings and distributed them to families around the Valley. On his own property he built a cocoonery capable of feeding and tending over two million silkworms, which would be fed with the mulberry leaves. Young believed that women could effectively do this work, and Wells's *Woman's Exponent* explained how the breeding and sale of silk eggs could provide a handsome income "with little trouble and less outlay."[33] Young gave the task of organizing silk production to his wife Zina Diantha, and even after he died she continued to organize Mormon women to produce silk.

Silk production was highly labor intensive because the worms required much space, constant monitoring of temperatures, and copious amounts of mulberry leaves cut in specific dimensions. Matilda Andrus was probably not alone in characterizing raising silkworms as a "nerve-racking, stinking mess."[34] Most production was done in homes, but in 1880 a silk factory was finally completed at the mouth of City Creek canyon, although it only functioned for ten years. Women had a difficult time making any profit from their efforts because they could not get loans to buy the equipment needed to weave the silk threads into material. In 1899 Zina "regretted the indifference of the people" toward these efforts in spite of the three hundred pounds of cocoons that had been raised in Provo.[35] The quality of silk was never very high, and most of it went into making token pieces like fringe decoration for the St. George Temple and souvenir scarves. By 1905 the experiment was officially over.

Even if storing grain proved successful while manufacturing silk did not, both activities helped meld together religious commitment and economic behavior. Not all Latter-day Saint women belonged to the Relief Society during the nineteenth century, but many who did belong did more than take care of the poor and the sick. The Relief Society responded to the diverse needs of the community and in doing so encouraged women to learn the skills of management, budgeting, compromise, and leadership. Relief Society buildings provided women with their own space separate from that of men. The *Woman's Exponent* documented and publicized their accomplishments, making it possible for Mormon women even in small towns to learn what their sisters around the country were doing. The

Relief Society provided religious instruction and aid for the needy, but it also constructed a practical framework for women to work toward common goals and to share their knowledge and achievements.

The Relief Society supported economic activities because Young felt that women should work at whatever jobs would build up Zion. He variously suggested they learn how to spawn fish in springs, manage a telegraph office, write schoolbooks, do men's tailoring, and study obstetrics.[36] Women doing such work would free Latter-day Saint men up to do heavy labor and to serve the church. "Our work, our everyday labor, our whole lives are within the scope of our religion," Young preached in 1869. The Saints should develop what "they are inclined to," and Young taught that women should use "the powers with which they are endowed" even if that meant becoming a mathematician or accountant. "We believe that women are useful, not only to sweep houses, wash dishes, make beds, and raise babies," he told the Saints assembled in the new tabernacle, "but they should stand behind the counter, study law or physic, or become good bookkeepers and be able to do the business in any counting house, and all this to enlarge the sphere of usefulness for the benefit of society at large." Women, by "the design of their creation," were expected take on diverse jobs in the growing Latter-day Saint community. [37] Family was not their only concern.

Working to build up the Kingdom of God was as much a religious act as healing or speaking in tongues. Women raised on Victorian notions of womanhood in Europe or on the East Coast may have had a difficult time imagining this expanded understanding of work and religion. But life in the intermountain West demanded physical strength, especially for women who continued to live on farms after the waning pioneer days. The "weaker sex" was expected to be strong. Young asked women to develop expertise in areas the community needed rather than assume that their sentimental nature limited what they could do. Pioneer life could be violent and brutal—and even city dwellers at the end of the century experienced a stream of illness, accidents, and death that made female "innocence" hard to maintain. Women were expected to be productive members of the community, and their sex did not exempt them from hard work.

After the continental railroad tied the Utah Territory closer to the national culture, Young worried about its impact on the Latter-day Saints. Would Zion be able to hold its own place as an alternative to worldly Babylon if the territory and the nation were yoked together by a growing transportation system? As Utah slowly moved to a cash-based economy, Young increasingly directed his concerns about consumerism to women. "We have hundreds of young men here who dare not take girls for wives. Why?" Young asked in 1872. "Because the very first thing they want [is] a horse and buggy, and a piano; they want somebody to come every day to give them lessons on the piano; they want two hired girls and a mansion, so that they can entertain company, and the boys are afraid to marry them."[38] An emerging class system was impeding the dream of a society in which all believers shared in God's blessings. It seemed that not all women wanted a life devoted exclusively to work and religion.

Women were blamed for turning families away from home manufacturing and for demanding an easy life. However, as the Utah Territory became increasingly linked to a national economy—newly oriented toward big business and laissez-faire capitalist values—women suffered. Eliza Lyman wrote in her 1878 diary that at Thanksgiving rich people feasted on roast turkey and plum puddings, but she and her family only had oyster soup, "which I despise." She poignantly observed that "we poor have not much enjoyment on such days." Rather, she could only look forward to "hard work and poor fare the same as any other day." Her friend "Sister Rogers" had to leave her children almost every day to wash and iron for others. "Today which is a grand holiday for the rich," Lyman reported, "she is out cleaning house and her children at home alone as usual. No rest for her."[39] If Mormonism meant work and religion, what would be the impact if one Latter-day Saint woman had leisure because another one did her work?

It was not only class differences that threatened Zion. The steadily rising number and proportion of non-Mormons in Utah made the territory far more multicultural than the Saints had ever imagined. In 1860, 88 percent of the territory was Mormon; by 1890 it was 66 percent and falling.[40] Mining had brought non-Mormon "Gentiles" into the Utah Territory and merchants followed. Protestant and Catholic clergymen arrived and set up churches. Catholic nuns and Protestant women staffed schools, hospitals, and orphanages. In 1870 Salt Lake City's total population of 12,900 was mostly Mormons; twenty years later it was a multireligious 44,800.[41] It was not simply Presbyterians and Catholics who bought goods manufactured in the East or imported from around the world. Latter-day Saints also read cheap magazines. Their newspapers advertised the latest fashions and labor-saving devices. Not satisfied with the likes of handmade straw bonnets, the daughters of the Latter-day pioneer generation increasingly looked to non-Mormon merchants to satisfy their fashion desires.

Even more threateningly, Mormon girls began looking at Gentile boys, Gentile religions, and Gentile notions of womanhood. A pluralistic Utah, in short, meant more options for young men and women. In 1880, after Jane H. Blood had attended a "mixed" wedding, she wrote disparagingly of it in her diary. "I felt sorry to see a good girl like her marry out of the church," she lamented. "I believe it is her mother's fault. I would sooner bury my girls then see them marry out of this church for I think I should have to bear part of the blame for not teaching them better."[42] In order to help families keep their children securely in the fold, the church centralized its youth organizations, and in 1889 Susa Young Gates founded the *Young Woman's Journal*. There, in story after story, girls learned of the disasters that followed when they did not heed the instructions of their Mormon mothers.

As the nineteenth century was ending, Latter-day Saints had many worries. The railroad had brought consumer goods, "worldly" values embedded in popular magazines and newspapers, and an increasing number of settlers who had no interest in the truths that the Saints held close to their hearts. Indeed, many of those who traveled to the Utah Territory thought Mormonism to be alien and un-American, not quite a religion. But what truly astonished the rest of the nation was Latter-day Saint women's continual refrain that their religion called them to accept plural marriages. With the end of the Civil War and the Northern victors declaring slavery abolished, attention turned to the other "relic of barbarism" that the country's politicians had vowed to uproot.

CHAPTER 2

Polygamy's End

Outsiders thought that Latter-day Saints had given their allegiance to a false and fanatical religion, and—like Catholics or, even worse, Muslims—promoted an immoral notion of family life. Just as Protestants condemned the celibate lives of Catholic clergy and fantasized about debased life in "Mohammedean" harems, they could not understand how plural marriage could be defended as "celestial." Since the Reformation, Protestants had embedded eternal values within the structure of family life. "True" Christian men and women knew how to keep house, raise children, have proper sex, and structure married life. Domesticity was not detached from religion but derived from it. Marriage reflected eternal Christian values. Consequently, from the perspective of outsiders, a false religion—like Mormonism—would naturally produce a false family.

From the perspective of the Latter-day Saints, however, plural marriage was divinely ordained. Mormons had moved from place to place in the United States, and then left it entirely, at least in part to be able to fulfill God's commands. Emmeline Wells lived as a plural wife because she believed that the revelations of Joseph Smith came from God. For women like Wells who converted when they were young and underwent the struggles of pioneer life, plural marriage was but one aspect of a vast array of controversial religious practices. In order to understand the nature of plural marriage and women's complicated responses to it, we must first grasp Smith's innovative ideas about heaven and of divinity. Although Mormon women had diverse experiences with plural marriage, they were unified in their assertion that they had a constitutional right to worship according to the dictates of their own conscience. By the end of the nineteenth century, antipolygamy polemics and legislation had made life intolerable for the Saints in Utah. Yet women's efforts to justify plural marriage had laid the groundwork for them to demand their rights as citizens.

Smith's revelation on plural marriage both accompanied and relied on a substantial reconceptualizing of the structure of heaven. In 1843 Smith told his closest male followers that God had given him a glimpse into the nature of eternal life. The highest degree of heaven could only be reached "if a man marry a wife and make a covenant with her for time and for all eternity" (D&C 132:18). Heaven had "degrees" (D&C 131:1), and at the highest level, a woman and man needed to be linked together under the authority of the Latter-day Saint priesthood. For the dead, heaven did not end marital relations in favor of focused contemplation of the divine. Instead, Latter-day Saint temple marriages would be eternally durable and perfect. If men and women were properly married in the temple, the spiritual progression begun on earth continued after their death. Their eventual exaltation and glory would enable them to produce spirit children, "a fullness and continuation of the seeds forever and ever" (D&C 132:19). Such heavenly development had no end: "Then shall they be gods, because they have all power, and the angels are subject unto them" (D&C 132:20). Only a united female and male could experience the highest realm of glory.

Also residing in the highest heaven were the divine parents. Heavenly Father, who created and rules over our world, is the same as the biblical God the Father. But the early Mormon understanding of the Heavenly Mother is underdeveloped. The first published account of a Heavenly Mother was not made by the Prophet but by one of his plural wives.

After Smith's death, Eliza R. Snow mourned not only the loss of a prophet but also that of a man to whom she was secretly married. An accomplished poet, Snow used verse to make sense out of her grief. In 1845 she published "My Father in Heaven," which laid out the Mormon plan of salvation. In it, Snow begins by reflecting on her "primeval childhood" when she resided in a "glorious place" and was nurtured by the side of "my Father." She then comes to earth where she is but a stranger from "a more exalted sphere." However, when the "key of knowledge was restored" she learned the answer to her question: "In the heav'ns are parents single?" Developing the idea of the eternal couple, Snow responds: "No, the thought makes reason stare!/Truth is reason; truth eternal/Tells me I've a mother there." The poem ends with another rhetorical question: "When I leave this frail existence/When I lay this mortal by/Father, Mother, may I meet you/In your royal courts on high?"[1] For Snow, who would become the plural wife of Brigham Young and a formidable force in early Mormonism, there was no question that there was a divine female presence awaiting the righteous Saints in heaven.

When two volumes of Snow's poems were published in 1856, the "Invocation, or The Eternal Father and Mother" appeared on the first page.[2] The poem was also put to music, first to a popular song by Stephen Foster and then to several other tunes. The *Deseret News* reported that the poem set to Foster's tune was Young's favorite hymn.[3] The hymn became known as "O, My Father," and when it was sung at Young's funeral in 1877, the words (but not the melody) became the classic statement of the hope of eternal life. At countless funerals, when Saints sought to be uplifted by the promise of celestial glory, they sang about meeting their divine Mother.

Snow's poem imagines dwelling with her Mother and her Father "in the heav'ns." However, she herself knew that if (as Christianity taught) the human world was a hazy reflection of the celestial, then "the heav'ns" might be far more complicated than traditionally portrayed. As early as the mid-eighteen-thirties, Smith had married an additional wife, and plural marriages were being conducted in Nauvoo ten years later. In the same 1843 revelation that reordered heaven, God reminded Smith of the social structure of the ancient world. Sarah, the wife of the biblical patriarch Abraham, had given her handmaid to her husband to wed when she herself had not borne children. King David also "received many wives and concubines," as did Solomon and Moses (D&C 132:34–39). Consequently, if a man desired to marry again and his first wife consented, then a second marriage under the authority of the priesthood would be "justified" (D&C 132:62). The goal of these marriages was to "multiply and replenish the earth," enabling the exaltation of the faithful who would eternally bear more souls (D&C 132:63). For Smith, the celestial cosmos was an ever-enlarging community because men—on earth and in heaven—could marry multiple women. Celestial marriage created an eternally expanding and intimate bond between people, what one historian has termed a great "Chain of Belonging."[4] Both sexes, connected by the authority of the priesthood, were necessary for exaltation. Without women, there could be no marriage, no eternal network of linked souls. Marriage was not simply an economic necessity or a romantic compulsion; it was a religious act that prepared one for a revealed divine eternity.

While Smith's understanding of plural marriage developed throughout the eighteen-thirties and eighteen-forties, it was not until after his death, when the Saints were firmly established in Utah, that the practice was made public. In 1852 Apostle Orson Pratt, with Young by his side, publicly announced why God had revealed the principle of the plurality of wives. Pratt began with a specifically Mormon revelation, that eternal marriage produced spirit children who assumed earthly bodies ("mortal tabernacles")—everyone on earth had previously existed, in spirit form, in heaven. He then reasoned from the Bible, as had Smith. Drawing from the

Old Testament, Pratt explained that God promised Abraham as many seed as a seashore full of sand (Genesis 22:17); therefore, "It would have been rather a slow process, if Abraham had been confined to one wife, like some of those narrow, contracted notions of modern Christianity." Pratt went on to conclude that it was monogamy rather than polygamy that was unnatural and often led to sin. Men limited to one wife fell into whoredom, adultery, fornication, and prostitution. On the other hand, into celestial marriages would come the noblest spirits of the preexistence, those who had waited thousands of years to descend to earth. These spirits would become the children of the faithful Saints, "the most righteous of any other people upon the earth."[5]

Expanding on plural marriage a year later (and probably in response to Snow's poem), Pratt speculated on the nature of "a heavenly Mother." Because Christian tradition held that earthly things were a dim likeness of heavenly things, "God associated in the capacity of a husband" with his heavenly wife. Heavenly Mother, however, should not be worshiped: the New Testament described how Jesus prayed to his Heavenly Father, not Mother. In addition, Pratt explained that given the patriarchal order, Heavenly Father was the head of his household of wives and children. Without elaboration, Pratt had introduced the notion of multiple Heavenly Mothers. Once the church ended polygamy in 1890, the possibility that Heavenly Father had several wives faded from church writings, but Heavenly Mother remained. In 1895 church president Joseph F. Smith asserted that the "great truth" of a Heavenly Mother and Father came not from Snow but directly from Joseph Smith.[6] Then in 1909 the First Presidency affirmed that "All men and women are in the similitude of the universal Father and Mother and are literally the sons and daughters of Deity."[7]

In their public writing, women did not contradict the reasoning behind polygamy. Helen Mar Whitney explained in her essay "Why We Practice Plural Marriage" that God had revealed to Smith a cosmic plan by which heavenly parents produced children who needed to live on earth to be tested and prepared for eternity. "There were thousands of spirits, yet unborn," she wrote in 1884, "who were anxiously waiting for the privilege of coming down to take tabernacles of flesh, that their glory might be complete." The more children who were brought into the world, the more souls could continue their eternal progress. "Their greatest punishment," Whitney explained, "is not having bodies." The point of plural marriage was "for the purpose of raising a righteous seed."[8]

As the federal government attempted to rid the nation of polygamy, Mormon women steadfastly proclaimed their support of plural marriage. In 1870 five thousand Latter-day Saint women gathered in Salt Lake City to rally against proposed antipolygamy legislation. Nine years later, the women of the village of Fillmore met to send their protests to Washington. Eliza Marie Lyman penned a fiery address, asserting women's right to live as they pleased:

> We are happy with our husbands and children and do not need the sympathy of the outside world nor do we thank them for it. Let those who would destroy our institutions travel through the cities of the United States and see if they cannot find some of their fallen sisters who would gladly receive the sympathy they are so anxious to bestow upon us.

Lyman pointed out that the Latter-day Saints had been persecuted and driven out of their homes even before outsiders knew about plural marriage. She knew that her religion was true and that the "puny arm" of opposition could not stop its growth. "Every person should have the privilege of serving God according to the dictates of their own conscience," she ended her speech, "and as citizens of these United States we claim that privilege."[9]

Wells also upheld the benefits of polygamy in the *Woman's Exponent*. In 1876, in a column about the importance of women speaking and writing, she countered the common belief that polygamy made women inferior to men. "Polygamy gives women more time for thought, for mental culture, more freedom of action, a broader field of labor," she asserted. Polygamy "inculcates liberality and generosity, develops more fully the spiritual elements of life, fosters purity of thought and gives wider scope to benevolence." Most importantly, this true principle of marriage "leads women more directly to God, the fountain of all truth."[10] Plural marriage, by releasing an individual woman from continual childbearing and by allowing her to share her domestic life with other women, offered women more possibilities for exercising their talents.

Privately, however, women held diverse opinions about the practice and experience of polygamy. When Rose Shepard asked her mother why she married into polygamy, her mother first cited her faith and then suggested that "she would much rather marry a man she knew to be righteous and kind then to throw herself away on some young man who might turn out to be worthless."[11] Mrs. Orson Smith believed that she was always cut out for polygamy because it was how she was raised. She waited until she found a family in which "I loved the woman as well as I loved the man."[12] Then, living as a second wife, she taught school while her sister wife did the bulk of the housework. A child of polygamists, Esther Huntsman, learned about a different kind of parental love. "I used to ask father if it was possible for a man to love more than one woman," Huntsman told an interviewer. "He always answered by asking me if a woman could love more than one child."[13]

Lucy Walker Kimball believed that her husband, Heber C. Kimball, "was capable of loving more than one woman as God himself is capable of loving all his creations."[14] True love, celestial love, was not exclusive because it was modeled on divinity.

As can be imagined, the everyday experience of plural marriage was highly dependent on wealth, social status, and personality. Anthon L. Skanchy, for instance, was baptized in Norway in 1861 and married a widow with four children. After his conversion, he left his family several times to do missions in his country, and then in 1868 the household moved to Utah. For the first few years, Anthon, his wife Christina, and their multiple children and stepchildren occupied a four-room house. Skanchy eventually married a second and a third wife. After the second marriage, Anthon built a few smaller rooms for the new wife, but the accommodations remained exceedingly cramped. For fifteen years, the three wives lived together. Ultimately, Anthon did provide a small adobe house for Christina, the first wife.

According to the son of the second wife (Caroline II), Christina's drinking problem was exacerbated by polygamy, and she would "go off on a toot," sitting for hours staring at the irrigation ditch in front of the house. "Once when it was especially bad," he told an interviewer, "she went out and threw a shoe through a window in Caroline II's house." Skanchy, a bishop and a prosperous lumber merchant, remonstrated his wife, who reportedly promised to do better. Christina was well liked and a leader in the ward, so neighbors blamed her husband for not putting a stop to her drinking. Eventually, Christina divorced Skanchy, but she died shortly after.[15]

By the eighteen-eighties some families had kept "the principle" for two generations. Scholars estimate that around 25 percent of the Latter-day Saints of that time lived in plural families, although that number varied by region and the practice was declining.[16] Just as women had varying degrees of success living in monogamous relationships, so they did with polygamy. Some women found comfort and support among their sister wives while others experienced jealousy and contention. Some men were fair and generous with their attention while others left their wives emotionally and physically destitute. Because Young wanted stable and productive families, he enabled couples whose relationships had broken down to end their marriages. Utah Territory had some of the most liberal divorce laws in the nation. The assumption was that the divorced would quickly remarry and establish new, happier families. Although the age gap between husband and wife did increase as men married additional wives, antipolygamists exaggerated the level of discontent among polygamist women. Far off in the Western desert, the Saints had created families both radically different from and surprisingly similar to those of the rest of the country.

It is difficult, however, to describe how women experienced plural marriage per se because of the pressures placed on the institution by anti-Mormon reformers and the federal government. Those who practiced or promoted polygamy were always doing so within a context of criminality. In 1856 the Republican Party platform termed polygamy and slavery the "twin relics of barbarism."[17] According to this logic, just as Africans had been unjustly enslaved, so too were white women imprisoned by depraved Mormon men. After slavery had been abolished, the nation's reformers turned their attention to polygamy. They insisted that the Morrill Anti-Bigamy Act (1862), which criminalized "spiritual marriage" and limited the church's wealth, be vigorously enforced. In addition, reformers supported the Cullom Bill (1870), which called for greater federal control over Utah Territory. It was the possibility that this new legislation would become law that mobilized the protests of Latter-day Saint women. While the Cullom Bill did not pass, the 1874 Poland Act transferred local legal authority of Utah Territory over to the federal government and banned polygamists from sitting on juries.

Latter-day Saints responded with loud cries that practicing plural marriage was constitutionally protected under the freedom of religion clause of the First Amendment. In addition, local communities should be self-governing and the power of the federal government limited. In November 1878, the US Supreme Court heard such arguments for plural marriage—and rejected them. The Court concluded that Congress *did* have the right to prohibit certain types of marriage when those marriages contravened acceptable standards of decency and civility. Chief Justice Morrison Waite maintained that Congress must not legislate religious beliefs, but the government could regulate religious activities when they violated social duties or were subversive of good order.[18] Waite agreed with the antipolygamists and deemed that Mormon marriage patterns were as uncivilized as those of "Asiatic" and African people. Congress had a moral responsibility to enact legislation that would end the unreasonable control that Mormon men held over women.

The intensified campaign to destroy plural marriage motivated church leaders to renew their support of it. Young died in 1877 and the new president, John Taylor, was an adamant polygamist. At a special priesthood meeting during the spring 1884 general conference, he told all ward bishops and stake presidents who were monogamists either to marry an additional wife or resign from church office.[19] Annie Clark Tanner remembered that ambitious men "felt a compulsion to accept and practice this principle. Prominent men were counseled by the church leaders to enter this practice as qualifications for leadership."[20] Having seven wives himself, in 1885 Taylor went into hiding to escape prosecution. He died two years later.

The decision in *Reynolds v. United States* and the defiant attitude of the Latter-day Saints laid the groundwork for increasingly harsh legislation. The Edmunds Act (1882) was devised to ban Mormons from voting and cripple the political and economic power of the church. Everyday life in Utah became increasingly difficult as federal marshals hunted down men suspected of living with multiple women. Sheriffs broke down doors, dragged men from hiding spots, and demanded to know the intimate details of a couple's sex life. Men left their homes and families in order to escape from the authorities. Children on their way home from school were questioned about their neighbors, so parents taught them to avoid strangers. Women who married did so in secret, often not acknowledging their change in status to family and friends until after they got pregnant. Although only men were accused of polygamy, women—including wives—were expected to testify in court. In 1885 Lucy Devereux was put in prison for two months along with her infant for refusing to reveal who had fathered her baby. Two years earlier, Belle Harris, also with a nursing infant, had been imprisoned. Elizabeth Starkey, Eliza Shafer, Lydia Spencer, Annie Gallifant, and Nellie White all spent months in prison because they refused to "remember" all the members of their family.[21]

The most forceful attack on Mormonism came on March 3, 1887, when the Edmunds-Tucker Act became law. The act disincorporated the church and the fund that it used to bring converts to Utah. No longer would the church be able to own banks, mines, farms, or factories. The federal government seized all church property valued at over $50,000. Where once the church controlled the marriage process, the Edmunds-Tucker Act required couples to secure civil marriage licenses, and it prohibited illegitimate children (e.g., children of plural wives) from inheriting money or property. No longer could a wife avoid testifying in court about her marriage. The legislation increased the fines and sentences for polygamy convictions. It also required men to take oaths against polygamy in order to vote, serve on juries, or hold public office. With passage of the Edmunds-Tucker Act, only Gentiles would have political power in Utah Territory. By 1889 nearly one thousand Latter-day Saints had been convicted of violating federal law.[22]

The strains of living "the principle" became increasingly unbearable as the federal government stepped up enforcement of its antipolygamy laws. While Wells put a shiny gloss on celestial marriage in the *Woman's Exponent*, in private she was well aware of the sacrifice that plural marriages demanded of women like herself. In 1879 her husband Daniel was held in contempt of court for refusing to answer questions about the marriage ceremonies he had performed. Tried, sentenced, and fined, he spent two days in prison. By then, Daniel Wells was a member of the Mormon elite: a prosperous businessman who at various times was the director of Utah Central Railroad, a counselor in the First Presidency, the mayor of Salt Lake City, and the chancellor of the University of Deseret. He also was the husband of seven wives and father to thirty-seven children. In 1884, in order to prevent further arrests, church leaders sent Wells to London to take charge of its European mission. Wells had the position and the financial means to live in Europe, unlike the many Latter-day Saint men who hid from federal marshals or ended up in the territorial penitentiary. Wells was gone for three years.

During his absence, Wells's finances failed. In 1887, in order to liquidate his assets, he decided to sell the home in which Emmeline had been living for thirty-seven years, never consulting her. He also sold the large homes of his other wives and built them smaller ones away from the center of town.[23] Emmeline never got over the sale of her home, even when she was living comfortably elsewhere. In January 1890 she confessed to her diary that she had walked by her old home and saw "the dear old garden so neglected now and so forlorn. . . . Heaven help, and I am homeless." A few months later she wrote, "my tears fell like rain when I gazed upon my former home now taken from me, strangers fill the rooms once ours only and I have not the privilege of entering them."[24] She was inconsolable.

While many nineteenth-century men made domestic financial decisions without consulting their wives, plural wives who lived on their own had a sense of independence. On a day-to-day level, they managed their households, budgeted their money, disciplined their children, and basically lived as single mothers. When a husband arrived for a visit or to spend time in their bedroom, wives acknowledged his love, authority, and often whims. Then he would leave, and the space was theirs again. Until, that is, he decided differently. Even the formidable Emmeline Wells could not save her home.

The federal attacks also made it difficult for the church to regulate community life because plural marriages had to take place in secret, leading to confusion and, at times, disaster. In November 1884, while Daniel Wells was safely ensconced in London, a scandal broke in Utah.[25] The local anti-Mormon newspaper, the *Salt Lake Tribune*, published a story that accused Emmeline Wells's daughter Louie of having become the plural wife of her sister Annie's husband. The article reported that the pressure on up-and-coming Latter-day Saint men to take plural wives had motivated John Q. Cannon to flirt with and then to secretly marry Louie in the Logan Temple. Beautiful, talented, and just twenty-two, Louie had many suitors. The *Tribune* asserted that the most eligible of them had been shuttled off to a mission in Europe in order to pave the way for her brother-in-law's courtship. Emmeline Wells demanded a retraction of the story as contemptible slander. Cannon physically attacked the article's author and was thrown briefly in jail. The article was not withdrawn.

Two years later, however, Cannon publicly confessed to having committed adultery, although he did not name his partner. Maybe that secret temple marriage had not taken place. Cannon's admission of guilt and speedy excommunication shocked the community. Privately, Cannon told his brother he had earlier gotten Louie pregnant, and she had miscarried. It seemed that Emmeline's daughter was now pregnant a second time. None of the women involved knew that Cannon was going to publicly confess his indiscretions. The *Tribune* had a field day, accusing Cannon not only of polygamy but also of adultery with yet another woman. Cannon then divorced Annie and married Louie. In the meantime, federal deputies served Cannon with a warrant for violation of the Edmunds Act, on the more serious charge of polygamy rather than cohabitation. Both Emmeline and Annie received subpoenas. Louie tried to hide to avoid arrest, but the deputies found her and all three women were held until $1,500 in bond was posted to ensure they would appear as witnesses. They all testified at the initial grand jury hearing, with both Annie and Emmeline saying that they had approved of John's divorce and marriage to Louie.

By the time of the actual polygamy trial, Louie was five months pregnant and living with relatives in San Francisco. Most likely she had left for California in order to avoid another court appearance, as the stress of the legal procedures had made for a difficult pregnancy. In early April 1887 Louie gave birth to a stillborn son and became gravely ill. Her mother Emmeline immediately caught a train to California. For the next six weeks, Emmeline watched a bloated and delirious Louie slowly die. The nights were particularly unbearable: "Can never forget the fearful night never, never." Emmeline wrote in her diary, "Alone with my darling in a far off city away from home. . . . The look on Louie's face was the look of death and the pain was unbearable. Never did I pass such a night, no fear, but sorrow for my darling."[26] Louie died the next day.

Historical research does not reveal whether Cannon and Louie were sealed in the Logan Temple or were having an affair. What the history does reveal is that the federal criminalization of family relationships shattered existing patterns of plural marriage. In an earlier time, it would not have been unusual for two sisters to marry one husband or to divorce if they were unhappy. After Louie's death, for instance, Cannon remarried Annie and they had nine more children together. Although he never recovered his leadership position in the church, Cannon was rebaptized and integrated back into the community.

Plural marriage tried the faith and the patience of Latter-day Saints, but it was the imposition of antipolygamy legislation that made their lives unbearable. Emmeline Wells's family's wealth and position could not shield her from the emotional trauma of watching her daughter die or losing her beloved home. Many more Mormon women had to manage homes, farms, and businesses when their husbands went into hiding. Poor women were accustomed to coping with the reality of men leaving to find work, but the shame of their husbands being in prison could not easily be forgotten. Financial struggles, loneliness, secrecy, disappointment, prosecution, and imprisonment all tested the endurance of the Saints.

In many ways, the persecution of Mormons in the late nineteenth century can be understood as a type of collective trauma. Even if a couple were monogamous, they observed the harassment of their neighbors and the debasement of their religion. Such experiences brutally disrupted the stable structures of family and community life. In order to make sense out of such suffering, Latter-day Saints understood their pain in religious terms. Obedience and authority became highly valued as evidence of one's willingness to sacrifice for the faith. Secrecy took on spiritual meaning as the means of preserving a threatened truth. While one might privately harbor doubts about church activities, members needed to publicly display unity in order to withstand the attacks of non-Mormons. Only if the Saints persevered would their trials and sacrifices eventually be transformed into blessings and comforts.

One unexpected "blessing" of polygamy was that Utah women were granted the right to vote. American reformers had begun advocating for women's rights in the eighteen-forties, but the antislavery movement took precedence. Following the Civil War, women's rights advocates agitated for voting rights for both women and free blacks, but neither the Fourteenth nor Fifteenth Amendments gave women the right to vote. The movement, however, was rekindled. Some men also began to promote women's suffrage, albeit for less egalitarian (often anti-egalitarian) reasons. In the Western territories in particular, male political leaders saw female enfranchisement as a way to draw attention to the needs of their sparsely populated wilderness. Would not women want to settle on the frontier if they had the vote? Male voters also believed that giving the wives of the Eastern settlers the vote would help keep political control in the hands of whites. Several territorial legislatures attempted to enfranchise women, but it was not until December 1869 that Wyoming Territory became the first government to grant women the right to vote.

Hamilton Wilcox, a female suffrage advocate, appeared before the House Committee on Territories and asked for female suffrage in Utah. If female voters were granted suffrage, Wilcox and others reasoned, they would then throw off the chains of polygamy. [27] Given that federal legislation was not ending plural marriage, surely empowering the victims would be more successful. In March 1869, Congressman George Washington Julian from Indiana introduced "A Bill to Discourage Polygamy in Utah" in the House of Representatives. A Quaker and a women's rights advocate, Julian also believed that having the vote would embolden Mormon women to reject plural marriage. Senator Samuel C. Pomeroy of Kansas introduced a similar bill in the Senate.[28]

To the surprise of the bills' sponsors, both the Utah Territorial representative and the press in Utah spoke favorably about the bills. The church-owned *Deseret News* went so far as to call itself an "earnest advocate of Women's Rights" and a supporter of the right of suffrage for "the ladies."[29] Such Mormon enthusiasm dampened the antipolygamists' zeal and the bills never came up for a vote. However, at the same time Latter-day Saint women also were thinking about enfranchisement. At a January 1870 planning meeting for the upcoming protest against national antipolygamy legislation, Bathsheba Smith proposed "that we demand of the Gov the right of franchise." Her resolution was approved by her fellow Relief Society sisters. Another influential Saint, Lucy Kimball, remarked in the meeting that she felt "we had borne in Silence as long as it was our duty to bear, and moved that we be represented at Washington."[30]

The Relief Society women believed that voting would strengthen—not deter—plural marriage. Undoubtedly, they also believed that they were intellectually and morally fit to vote. From their ownership of Relief Society buildings to their struggles on family farms to their accomplishments in medicine, Latter-day Saint women clearly demonstrated that they would be informed voters. However, it was the preservation of their religious principles that made female enfranchisement critical to women.

Although it might seem obvious that male church leaders would have supported female suffrage because it would have more than doubled the Mormon vote in the territory—thus maintaining church authority—Latter-day Saints already far outnumbered non-Mormons. More likely, church authorities recognized that a suffrage victory might improve the image of the Latter-day Saints among women's rights advocates and their supporters on the East Coast. In turn, those reformers might pull back from so enthusiastically promoting antipolygamy legislation. Apostles such as George Q. Cannon and Franklin D. Richards vocally endorsed women's franchise in part because they believed that women's natural moral authority would serve to uplift civic life. The women's vote would not only hasten statehood for Utah, women's political involvement would make it a more righteous state.

Significantly, Young also approved of such reasoning. On February 9, 1870, the Utah Territorial Legislature introduced a suffrage bill; three days later it was passed with no dissenting vote. The acting governor, Stephen A. Mann (a non-Mormon), signed it into law. A few days later, Utah women voted in a municipal election in Salt Lake City, thus beating Wyoming women to the ballot box. Although Utah women secured neither the right to hold political office nor to sit on juries, they did exercise their right to vote long before the Nineteenth Amendment was ratified in 1920. Utah suddenly became famous for something other than polygamy.[31]

East Coast women who had been organizing for women's rights since 1848 were now faced with a dilemma: Should they embrace Mormon women as fellow reformers, or would the marital practices of the newly enfranchised voters continue to set them apart? One wing of the suffrage movement, the American Woman Suffrage Association (AWSA), led by Lucy Stone, refused to associate with the Mormons. From the AWSA's perspective, in the name of religion Mormonism had degraded women. How could voting alter that fact? The other wing, headed by Elizabeth Cady Stanton and Susan B. Anthony, thought differently. A more radical group of thinkers, these women had refused to support the enfranchisement of freedmen because women were left out of the legislation. Their organization, the National Woman Suffrage Association (NWSA), pushed for a broader agenda of women's rights than simply securing the vote. This more extreme wing of the suffrage movement had room for Mormon women in their organization.

Excited about women voting in Wyoming and Utah, Stanton and Anthony took the recently built railroad to visit the Western territories. In June 1871 they gave a series of well-attended lectures in Salt Lake City. They immediately learned that Utah women who supported women's rights were not unified. One small faction of pro-suffrage women were the wives of men who were challenging the economic and political power of Brigham Young. A far larger group encompassed women who supported the tight unification of religion, politics, and economics. Stanton and Anthony first addressed large crowds in the Tabernacle and then the next day an equally large group in the Liberal Institute, the hall built by the dissenters.

In both venues, the famous women's rights advocates laid out their criticisms of male–female relations, motherhood, exploited female labor, and unfair divorce laws. The reformers urged women to keep up with men intellectually and to establish coeducational colleges. They shocked the assembled Saints by encouraging them to have fewer children so that they could raise them properly. Stanton imagined a day when a woman could hold "her place in the world of work, educated to self-support, with land under her feet and a shelter over her head, the results of her own toil, the social, civil, political equal of the man by her side." It would be at that point that "she will not clutch at every offer of marriage, like the drowning man at the floating straw."[32] Of course polygamy was an unjust system for women, Stanton and Anthony argued, but so was monogamy. All religions, not just Mormonism, created structures that oppressed women. Securing the vote was just the first step toward enabling women to reconfigure both society and religion to their own advantage.

Emmeline Wells was committed to the overall vision laid out by women's rights advocates, but she pointedly ignored Stanton and Anthony's criticism of religion and warnings about family size. Wells understood suffrage to be both a constitutional right and a basic form of justice. The vote would enable Latter-day Saint women to defend their religion, protect their homes, and uplift their society.[33] If only the radical wing of the suffrage movement was willing to associate with the Latter-day Saint women, so be it. Wells was convinced that men had no right to keep women from their God-given privilege of freedom and that only through organizing nationally would those rights be secured.[34]

By 1879 Wells had edged out the wives of the dissenters to be Utah's representative to the NWSA meeting in Washington, DC. She and Zina Young Williams were welcomed at the conference and permitted to sit on the speakers' platform. The meeting rooms filled up when they spoke. The Latter-day Saint women's pleas for religious tolerance fell on deaf ears, but they did find sympathetic friends among the other women reformers.[35] Inspired by her time in Washington, Emmeline Wells added a dedicatory banner to the *Woman's Exponent*: for "The Rights of Women of Zion and the Rights of Women of All Nations."

Wells's enthusiasm was somewhat dampened by a more cautious Eliza R. Snow. Snow, the influential widow of Joseph Smith and Brigham Young, had been the president of the Relief Society since it was reconstituted in 1867. Although she had no doubt about women's capabilities, and had encouraged the sisters to explore their talents in medicine, education, and writing, Snow was fundamentally a religious leader. Her intense experience with Mormonism in its earliest days had convinced her that it was only through faithfulness, order, and obedience that the lot of women could ever be improved. Progress came from religion, not from political equality.

Shortly after Stanton and Anthony finished their 1871 lectures, Snow spoke to the Saints at a Pioneer Day celebration in Ogden. Her goal was to lay out the limits of women's rights. "Although invested with the right of suffrage," she observed, "we shall never have occasion to vote for lady legislators or for lady congressmen." The land of Zion, led by an inspired priesthood, "will never be deficient in a supply of good and wise men to fill governmental positions, and of brave men for warriors." Having the vote was fine, but Snow wanted Latter-day Saint women to realize that the desires of non-Mormon women were irrelevant. "Our standard is far above theirs," she preached. "We have already attained to an elevation in nobility and purity of life, which they can neither reach nor comprehend, and yet they call us 'degraded.' "[36] For Snow, who had experienced the brutal violence of men who hated Mormons, working with the nation's women had distinct limits.

It was, however, the outward-looking perspective of Wells that prevailed. Especially after Snow's death in 1887, national suffrage became a cause of the elite women of Utah. The antipolygamy Edmunds-Tucker Act (1887) had taken away the voting rights women had exercised for seventeen years. In 1889 Relief Society leaders, with the approval of church authorities, organized the Territorial Woman Suffrage Association. They utilized the networks developed by efficient Relief Society women to organize branches throughout Utah. By 1891 there were seventeen county associations, numerous auxiliary branches, and a membership of 1,500.[37] The suffrage supporters assembled in Relief Society buildings and Mormon meetinghouses. During their gatherings, they studied American history and political science. They held mock trials and conducted symposia on parliamentary procedure. Uniting politics and pleasure, they held picnics where they wore pro-suffrage yellow dresses.

For these reformers, voting convinced them that involvement in politics would enhance, not contaminate, family and community life. Whereas many women (and men) across the country viewed the NWSA as extremists, Latter-day Saint women who were suffrage supporters were the influential members of their communities.[38] "Let no man or woman be mistaken as to what this movement for suffrage really means," explained the minutes of the Beaver Suffrage Association: "None of us want to turn the world upside down, or to convert women into men. We want women, on the contrary, above all things, to continue to be womanly—womanly in the highest and best sense—and to bring their true, honest, just, pure, lovely and of good report to bear upon conduct of public affairs."[39] With the full support of their church leaders, Latter-day Saint women joined one of the most radical movements of their day—on their own terms.

It was clear that the US government would continue to vigorously prosecute both individuals and organizations that engaged in plural marriages. Utah's women were disenfranchised, and many feared that the next antipolygamy law would take the vote away from all men, not just those who practiced plural marriage. At that point, with all Latter-day Saints unable to vote or hold public office and with church finances in ruin, the Utah Territory would be fully under the control of non-Mormons. Perhaps the Gentiles would even take over the temples. Influential church authorities held a range of opinions on how to proceed, but those discussions came to an end with an announcement by church president Wilford Woodruff on October 6, 1890: "Inasmuch as laws have been enacted by Congress forbidding plural marriages, which laws have been pronounced constitutional by the court of last resort, I hereby declare my intention to submit to those laws, to use my influence with the members of the Church over which I preside to have them do likewise."[40] The "Woodruff Manifesto" officially ended the practice of plural marriage.

Woodruff gave no indication of what should happen to existing polygamous families. Polygamy was officially over, but it continued to shape the lives of Latter-day Saint women for generations. Church leaders, for instance, continued to cohabit with their wives.[41] Dr. Martha Hughes Cannon, who had left her hospital position in 1885 to go underground, had begun a political career in 1896. She had defeated both her husband and Emmeline Wells to become a state legislator. Then, in 1899 she resigned her position because she became pregnant by her husband, Angus, who had five other wives. Martha was forty-two and Angus was sixty-five. Angus had been president of the Salt Lake stake since 1876 and would continue in that position until 1904. Between 1890 and 1898 more than half of the Quorum of the Twelve and the First Presidency took an active part in post-Manifesto polygamy.[42]

It was not only the wives of polygamous church leaders whose lives were transformed. Some women found that their husbands had left them in Utah and taken other wives to Canada or Mexico. The Manifesto upheld American laws, but other countries were quiet about polygamy. Women who went abroad had to face difficult lives in foreign lands. In Utah, not all men followed the practice of recognizing only their first marriage as the legal one. Norwegian immigrant Anthon Skanchy, whose alcoholic first wife had divorced him, decided to legally marry his third wife rather than his second. They had been sealed together in 1885 when he was forty-six and she was seventeen.[43] Skanchy followed the pattern of many men who decided to civilly marry their youngest wife so that they could have more children and be assured of a healthy caregiver when they were old. Most men tried to support their families, but as they aged this became increasingly difficult.

With many children in a family and unclear inheritance, resentments often festered. The children of polygamous households often blamed the church for their difficult lives. Loving their mothers, they directed their anger toward the institution that pressured their fathers to take on additional wives.[44] While mothers may have been willing to sacrifice for their beliefs, children resented not having "normal" lives. "We've always been like a family of illegitimate children turned loose," Josephine Spillsbury Vance told an interviewer. The daughter of a second wife, she left home early because it made "us all nervous and affected us all our lives. I couldn't stand it." Decades later she would confess, "I don't want to think of it or to talk about it. I never can get over the feeling I have towards them all."[45] Families would talk among themselves about their polygamous ancestors but not in celebratory terms.

Well after the Woodruff Manifesto, Mormon men continued to marry additional wives and to cohabit with those married before the Manifesto. To attempt again to end the practice, in 1904 the church issued a "Second Manifesto" stating that those members who entered into new marriages would be excommunicated. In 1918 Joseph F. Smith, the symbol of patriarchal polygamy, died. His successor, Heber J. Grant, made it a point to eradicate plural marriage, delivering stern messages denouncing the practice. Plural marriage became a taboo topic in church materials, and those still enamored of the practice were marginalized as apostates. In 1933 a sixteen-page "Final Manifesto" denouncing polygamy holdouts was read aloud in every ward of the church.[46] While the document's historical narrative has been challenged by modern scholars, its point was utterly clear: those who continued to practice plural marriage challenged the authority of the church and would not be tolerated.[47]

In anticipation of a sustaining vote by Latter-day Saints at the 1890 fall conference following the first Manifesto, Emmeline Wells wrote in her diary that "there are some who will be very much tried over this affair; but we must wait and see what the Lord has in store for us—we do not always know what is for our better good here and hereafter."[48] At sixty-two years of age, Wells might have imagined that she would not see much of what the Lord had in store for her and her church. Wells would live, however, an additional thirty-one years. In 1896 she saw the territory become a state and the old political parties of Mormon/non-Mormon dissolve. The new state constitution secured both the vote for women and their right to run for public office. As the citizens of Utah embraced national parties, Wells became an active Republican. She often threw her weight behind legislation that affected women's lives, but her goal of becoming a state legislator went unrealized. Although lingering tensions over polygamy—especially on the national level—continued to divide the Saints from the Gentiles, Mormon women worked with non-Mormon women on suffrage and other progressive causes.

The end of polygamy was slow and uneven. The absence of reflection in women's diaries on how their families coped with the rearrangement of marriage patterns points to the traumatic impact of the last decades of the nineteenth century. Victorian sensibilities led people to deny and bury their pain rather than to express it. Although women were silent on what it meant to have their prophet end the controversial practice, it is clear that

Latter-day Saint women gained a public voice through their support of polygamy. If Mormon women had not vigorously supported their religion's
understanding of family life, polygamy would not have survived as long
as it did. Just as women were necessary for building the Lord's kingdom
in Zion, they were critical in demonstrating that plural marriage was not
simply a justification for male lust. It made sense, then, that male church
leaders would have facilitated women's public voice. Suffrage simultaneously upheld the values promoted by women like Emmeline Wells and
supported church goals.

CHAPTER 3

———— •◆• ————

Uplifting Humanity

The dawn of the twentieth century brought a series of challenges to Mormonism. Much of the energy of the previous century had been directed toward physically building the Kingdom of God, articulating and defending celestial marriage, and managing relations with a hostile federal government. As Utah became increasingly integrated into the nation's social, economic, and political order, those tasks became less urgent. The immediate problem was the financial situation of the church. The Edmunds-Tucker Act had confiscated church wealth and although much of it had been returned, the 1893 Depression decimated Utah's economy. In addition, the Saints were accustomed to supporting their local religious communities through donating farm goods and manual labor—not cash. By 1898 the church was $2.3 million in debt, mostly to bankers outside of Utah.[1]

Ann Cook, who lived in the village of Paris, Idaho, observed another problem: when the bell was rung for the Saints to go to a Thursday fast meeting, "so few came that they did not have the meeting. So many people getting their hay put up."[2] Busy building the Kingdom of God, Latter-day Saints were not concerned with consistent churchgoing. Indeed, being Mormon was a communal identity and not dependent on attending worship services. If the church was to survive as a religious institution in the industrial world, however, Latter-day Saints were going to have to change their attitude about what it meant to be "righteous."

Nineteenth-century Mormonism was a fluid mixture of spiritual enthusiasm, practical labor, controversial marriage practices, and theocratic politics. Organized worship services were not a high priority. While Protestants and Catholics dutifully attended services on Sunday mornings, Latter-day

Saints developed a less predictable religious schedule. Ward bishops decided when to hold "Sacrament Meetings," the time to commemorate the Last Supper by blessing and distributing bread and water. In Salt Lake City during the nineteenth century, the sacrament was administered not in wards but in the Tabernacle during a Sunday afternoon preaching service. (The sacrament might also be given once a month on a Thursday morning at a testimony meeting that occurred after fasting.) Children, young men and women, adult male priesthood holders, and married women all met at different times for their own religious meetings. At times, the sacrament would be given at those meetings. Eventually Sacrament Meetings came to be held in the early evening or late afternoon and with Sunday School (for all ages) on Sunday mornings. In 1913 slightly more than 14 percent of Latter-day Saints attended Sacrament Meetings.[3]

Women's attendance at Relief Society meetings was also sporadic. More like a women's club than a congregation, women paid dues to belong to the Relief Society. Even in Salt Lake City, women were not particularly active. In most wards, only about half of adult women were dues-paying members, and only a third of those regularly attended meetings.[4] During the late nineteenth century, Relief Society meetings were held sporadically, sometimes only once a month. Each ward could decide what materials (if any) to study and what activities to perform. The all-encompassing duties of rural life and large families consumed much of each woman's day, leaving little time for Relief Society work.

For Mormonism to flourish in the twentieth century, it needed to realign the commitments of its members so that attendance and financial support became more regular. Latter-day Saints came to this critical juncture of their history during a period of modernization within the wider nation. Americans believed that by knitting together science, Western cultural values, and Christianity a new era of progress would be born. Polygamy's end had left the Saints in a cultural crisis. To rebuild their religious community, they drew from national trends that were liberal and progressive.

While both Protestants and Catholics were also adopting Progressive Era attitudes, Latter-day Saints embraced reform, efficiency, and centralization with striking enthusiasm. Mormon women in particular looked to the activities of middle-class, white, Gentile women to model modern religious and social behavior. Leaders of the Relief Society—drawn from the Mormon elite in Utah—were inspired by their connections with the suffrage and the women's club movements to embrace civic activism and rational religion. Although not all women welcomed this turn away from the spiritual enthusiasm of the nineteenth century, a decidedly modernist orientation took hold among Latter-day Saint women.

Compared to previous decades, the Progressive Era was a secular time in American history. Industrialization and urbanization were already providing many Americans with abundant consumer goods and more leisure time. Social reformers believed that if the scientific analysis that enabled the economy to expand was applied to other aspects of life, then progress was inevitable. Experts were to adhere to professional standards so to shape a rational and progressive nation. To instill the values of efficiency and rationality, local organizations were disempowered and authority was placed in centralized bureaucracies. Under this regime, science and business flourished.

The energy that moved secular reformers had religious origins. Religious reformers intended to throw off the chains of denominational theologies, which they thought inhibited social change, but those beliefs proved difficult to dislodge. The quest to rationally perfect society reflected Protestant notions about the godly nature of order and the ability of people to overcome sin. Reformers pursued change with evangelical zeal as they sought to work hand in hand with God to bring about a better world. Optimism, efficiency, and consistency came to be valued as highly as faith, hope, and charity. Protestantism birthed progressivism and then the mother was disciplined by the daughter.

Religious organizations submitted to the gods of productivity. More than other Christians, Mormons believe that human beings could slowly make their way toward divine perfection. God placed them in the world to be tested and improved, if not fully in this world then certainly in the next. Perfectibility was possible because there was no Original Sin holding humanity back from realizing its full potential. A pragmatic people, Latter-day Saints readily saw the benefits of study, efficiency, and order. If young men had the opportunity to study at the nation's best universities, for example, they would return home and uplift Utah's own colleges and professions. Members were accustomed to obeying leaders they considered inspired. If their duties were more clearly defined, wouldn't that make for stronger leadership? The traditional values of obedience, unity, and charity needed to be maintained, but in the early twentieth century church leaders did not perceive modernity as a natural threat. Individual expertise and organizational efficiency would elevate life for all.

Under the influence of President Joseph F. Smith, Mormonism modernized. Head of the church from 1901 to 1918, Smith's private life was firmly rooted in the nineteenth century. With six wives, forty-eight children, and a long white beard, he was the quintessential pioneer Mormon patriarch. Publicly, however, he was firmly rooted in the twentieth century. During his tenure as president, church administrative offices were organized, a budget was established, and the male priesthood quorums were rearranged. With clear lines of authority in place, men who continued to marry plural wives could be easily disciplined.[5] From Salt Lake City came requirements for weekly Sacrament Meetings, systematic recordkeeping, and centralized publications. Bishops of local wards lost authority as the church bureaucracy became stronger. The Saints also heard frequent calls to tithe regularly. These early efforts to make Mormonism more organized (perhaps at the expense of individual expressions of piety) were effective. By 1907 the debt was paid off and the church owned property worth $10 million, with additional investments in business.[6] The church did not merely become another denomination, like other Protestant churches: instead, it mixed religion with business, sexuality, entertainment, gender roles, and politics.

As church leaders in Salt Lake pursued financial and social stability, they increasingly asked bishops to oversee the affairs of women and children. During the nineteenth century, the president of the Relief Society coordinated women's activities and the Relief Society owned and managed its own property. But during the twentieth century, male leaders decided that the church would function more effectively if men did not have to negotiate with women. The ability to direct and supervise the behavior of women, youth, and children increasingly became an intrinsic part of priesthood authority. The pursuit of a strong church organization through efficient use of resources and personnel would profoundly alter how and when women could exercise authority.

At the same time, the Relief Society General Board, headquartered in Salt Lake City, sought both to increase national membership and to have more authority over local wards. Women were not immune from the centralizing and bureaucratizing pushes of the twentieth century. Some on the General Board wanted to give churchwide guidance, coordinate women's activities, and own property just as women did in their wards. As the influence of the General Board grew, it came into direct conflict with the growing authority of male church leaders in Salt Lake.

In 1896 the General Board decided it wanted to purchase land "in the shadow of the temple" on which to construct its own building.[7] Board members felt that with their own space they could better discharge their administrative responsibilities. Considering that local Relief Societies owned and managed real estate, halls, and granaries, this was not an unreasonable desire. But the church owned the land around the temple, and so the General Board was told that if it raised $20,000 church leaders would give them the land.[8] In 1900 the Board launched a fundraising campaign, appealing to Relief Society women across the country to donate to the building fund. Women saved a dollar here and a dollar there from their meager household finances. The money slowly accumulated, and by 1907 the women had raised $14,000.[9]

Yet the General Board heard a rumor that no building of its own was forthcoming. The rumor proved to be true. Without consulting the General Board, the First Presidency decided to construct a building for the offices of the Presiding Bishopric, the three men charged with organizing the temporal affairs of the church, on the land the Relief Society sought. For a church striving for institutional stability, the Presiding Bishopric was crucial because it oversaw tithing as well as ward chapel design and construction. At best, the General Board would be allotted a few rooms in this new building. Upon hearing this decision, Relief Society President Bathsheba Smith was "overcome with grief."[10] From her point of view, Latter-day Saint women had scrimped and saved to come close to raising the required $20,000. They had had to convince members to support a building in Salt Lake City that would enable more efficient global—not local—leadership. From the men's point of view, the women had dithered for seven years and raised only $14,000. What the larger church needed was administrative offices. Two years later, in 1909, the Presiding Bishopric building was dedicated.

The story of the Presiding Bishopric building is emblematic of declining Relief Society independence during the twentieth century. Once efficiency and standardization are established as virtues, the customary ways of ordering a community are challenged. Improvement and innovation are valued over consistency and tradition, and too often only men have access to the tools of modernization. Mormon women, for instance, did not engage in wage labor as men increasingly did. Women thus had no efficient means of raising the capital needed to construct a modern building in a growing city. On the farm, women's expertise was not all that different from men's. With some help, women could manage. This was not the case in the modern city where professional and mechanical training was reserved for men. Building a ward Relief Society hall in 1880 was not the same as building a national headquarters in 1907.

Consequently, it is not surprising that by 1913 the First Presidency directed ward bishops to take over all real estate belonging to the Relief Society.[11] By this period, the Relief Society had property and buildings worth over $149,000.[12] However, the granaries and halls were falling into disrepair, and it was increasingly difficult to provide proper upkeep. Women may have wished to continue to own and manage their buildings, but modern standards could not be met without impinging on masculine forms of knowledge. The Relief Society had supported women's independence, and its leaders had always upheld women's intellectual capabilities. However, the Relief Society did not establish institutions that would have given women the professional training needed to flourish in the twentieth century. Latter-day Saint women were not unlike Protestant and Catholic women who went to college in increasing numbers but, once married, left the workplace. Men and women both assumed that men would build the buildings and women decorate them.

Consequently, when new ward meetinghouses were planned, rooms and not separate buildings were set aside for the Relief Society—in the same way they had been set aside in the Presiding Bishopric building. Women were expected to direct their fundraising efforts toward communal spaces rather than their own separate halls. Slowly the Relief Society stopped setting its own agenda and making its own decisions and became an auxiliary society under the direction of the male priesthood. Latter-day Saint women were unable to maintain their authority in a world that had moved away from agriculture and small-scale communities. In this they followed the pattern of most American women.

It was not only the expectations of Latter-day Saint men that changed in the early decades of the twentieth century. For women, the process of finding authority and identity in the new century was proving difficult. Emmeline Wells observed the development of generational tensions. In 1904 she candidly admitted in her diary that the pioneer era of female unity had ended. "Today is three years since Aunt Zina D. H. Young died," she wrote about one of the leading sisters of Zion, "it seems much longer. How awful the change has been for the Society—never peace or union scarcely at all. Vexation and annoyances all the time. Perhaps it is well for us to know the extremes."[13] Wells noticed that factions were forming on the General Board. Some members preferred to continue as an explicitly religious organization that occasionally provided local charity. Others wanted to increase Relief Society membership by recruiting younger women.

What were the interests of the new generation? As a twenty-one-year-old, Wells's daughter Annie knew that she wanted more out of life than domestic tasks. In 1880 she confessed in her diary that she worried that her household duties might cause her to "carry my kitchen and cookery into the parlor as some women do." Would she, like others, "entertain Senators and such dignitaries with these subjects: How to make puddings, soups, & etc.?" No, Annie thought, "it was more necessary than ever that I should educate myself and be a cultivated and refined woman." The young wife promised herself "to read and have parlor subjects for the parlor and leave the kitchen subjects in the kitchen."[14]

Although Annie Wells was no doubt influenced by the orientation of her mother, women everywhere were looking to develop their interests in "parlor subjects." Women's clubs were sprouting up across the nation. In the privacy of their homes, members were learning how to speak confidently, gracefully give and take criticism, and generate cultural uplift through study.

Even before women received national suffrage in 1920, clubwomen effectively lobbied for progressive causes. By joining together in federations, middle-class women mobilized for the right to vote, to prohibit child labor, and to secure safe working conditions for women. They also joined together to alter male behavior in ways we now think of as conservative, not progressive—such as eliminating "red light districts" of prostitution and regulating the use of alcohol. Clubwomen also pushed for women's education and for the acceptance of women in the professions. Just as they expected their homes to be safe and beautiful, they sought to create cities that all could enjoy. Through women's efforts, parks, hospitals, schools, and preventive health measures were funded and constructed. National women's clubs organized to eliminate lynching and raise the minimum wage. Since it was generally believed that women were naturally more nurturing and less corrupted by worldliness, women's reform activities were seen as "above" the divisiveness of politics. Women combined the evangelical push for moral reform with scientific optimism to create a formidable force for social change. Women's clubs were not just about reading books; they were the engines that pushed progressive legislation.

White women reformers and club members made certain assumptions that betrayed their privileged positions in society. They would work to eliminate poverty, but distinctions needed to be made between the worthy and unworthy poor. This focus on determining who in a community deserved help limited their ability to see the structural causes of poverty. It also assumed that certain class cultural markers—like what people ate or how clean their homes were—indicated who was "worthy." Such convictions could lead to condescension and even arrogance about one's own superiority. Moreover, reformers assumed that married women's economic dependence on men was the ideal goal. White women reformers, unlike black women reformers, were less interested in working for childcare or maternity leave policies that might facilitate a woman's permanent entrance into the workforce. Respectability was never far away from reform.

Another popular pastime for the younger generation of women was participation in hereditary associations like the Daughters of the American Revolution (1897) or, in Utah, the Daughters of the Utah Pioneers (1901). Like other women's clubs, membership was multireligious (though not multiracial). Hereditary societies sought to preserve a particular (generally exclusive) understanding of American history during a period of increased immigration. Like other clubs, their goal was to instill proper values through study and historical awareness. For Emmeline Wells, membership also provided a good excuse for a party: "The parlor is decorated in buff and blue and the front portion draped with bunting," she wrote about a DAR meeting to be held in her home. "In the library we have a large flag and smaller ones in the parlor." Not as many women attended as she expected, but they all ate ice cream cake and macaroons after singing *The Star-Spangled Banner* and hearing Annie recite her poem, "When the Flag Goes By."[15] Indeed, Latter-day Saint women often demonstrated their citizenship by celebrating their patriotism. Rather than be bitter about past persecutions, women used hereditary organizations to situate themselves squarely within the American mainstream rather than on its edges.

Wells's daughter fully embraced the new generation's commitment to community improvement. Women might not be permitted the skills to build a new Relief Society building, but they did have the skills to organize within the edifice men built. The new generation of Mormon women was committed to personal uplift, civic improvement, and religious involvement. Annie Wells Cannon had graduated from the University of Deseret in 1879, experienced the tensions of divorce and remarriage due to her husband's plural marriage (or perhaps adultery) with her sister, and then found her place in Salt Lake's civic society.[16] For twenty-three years she sat on the city's public library board. She was a president of the Daughters of the Utah Pioneers and a member of three other clubs. While helping her mother write, edit, and publish the *Woman's Exponent*, she sat on the board of the Red Cross. She also served two different terms in the Utah State Legislature. After World War I, Herbert Hoover asked her to head up the European Relief Drive in Utah in order to gather funds for those displaced by war. Annie Cannon had her first child in 1884 when she was twenty-five and her twelfth (and last) in 1904 when she was forty-five. One baby died, and twins were born when she was forty. Her diary depicts a woman ironing in the morning, attending political meetings in the afternoon, and worrying about her sons in the evenings. Another Annie, Annie Clark Tanner, mused that if joy in living could be measured by "the number of interests one has in life, the Mormon people should be one of the happiest on earth." She summarized her view of Mormon philosophy in two words: "Keep Busy."[17]

In such a busy life, where would religion fit? Some men worried that club work distracted women from home and church. In 1900, Mary Fowler, from the rural farming community of Huntington, decided to organize a literary club. She and her friends would write essays on literature, read them aloud, and then discuss their themes.[18] With the support and approval of her bishop, the literary society joined the State Federation of Women's Clubs. However, shortly after, Apostle George Teasdale came to visit the Huntington Ward. Fowler wrote in her diary that the apostle did not heartily approve of the ladies' club, but he told her that if the bishop permitted their meetings, they could continue.

Teasdale's first response reflected nineteenth-century Mormonism in that local activity was the concern of local leaders. However, Fowler was worried, writing: "unless we get a warmer consent than that, I am not in favor of continuing." The very next Sunday a letter from Teasdale was read at a Sacrament Meeting stating that anyone who belonged "to any but church societies would not be considered [a member] in good standing." Fowler knew the letter was addressed to her club, although she was confused: "I don't know why he should give his private consent and then send a letter to be read in public," she wrote. "Those who are against us are rejoicing. I am glad for once that I was not at meeting." We do not know what motivated Teasdale to reconsider his attitude toward the club, but his actions are consistent with declining local authority accompanying the rise of centralized control over church affairs. Without further complaint, Fowler disbanded the club and used the ten dollars it had accumulated to buy a Bible for the ward meetinghouse.[19]

Teasdale's reaction to the Huntington women might have been inconsistent, but his final decision was not surprising. At the 1907 October conference, Apostle George F. Richards tied together many aspects of modern society that he and others worried about. "When you go into the homes of some fashionable people of the world today," he observed, "instead of finding children there, as you find in the homes of Latter-day Saints, you see poodle dogs, pussy cats, canary birds, things which can be tethered to a string and left in a corner." With no children to care for "the ladies are at liberty to attend clubs and society meetings, and go to the resorts and public places of pleasure as often as they wish."[20] For some church leaders, declining birth rates, increased leisure, the rise of mass entertainment, and unattached, independent women were a worrisome part of modern American culture. If Latter-day Saint women were joining women's clubs, would they next want to limit the size of their families?

Mormon women knew that they participated in clubs for cultural enrichment, not as an excuse to avoid family life. Influential members of the Relief Society General Board were supportive of Progressive Era values that sought to combine education, civic reform, and sociability. In 1909 Relief Society President Bathsheba W. Smith made an appointment that would stimulate the modernization of women's work in the church and bring it more in line with the desires of younger women: she invited Amy Brown Lyman to join the General Board.

At thirty-seven, Lyman was a college graduate with several years' teaching experience at Brigham Young Academy. Married to the son of an apostle (who would become an apostle himself), she had traveled widely with her husband. Although she had been one of twenty-five children in a polygamous household, she herself only had two (although she also raised her infant granddaughter). Lyman had served as a leader in the Young Ladies

Mutual Improvement Association of the church and was an active member of the "Author's Club," a small group of literary-minded Latter-day Saint women. During one summer, Lyman had taken classes at the University of Chicago. Her classroom studies inspired an appreciation of the new discipline of sociology, and her conversations with reformer Jane Addams stimulated a commitment to the profession of social work. Rational and efficient means of improving society made sense to Amy Lyman; she was remembered as being straightforward, precise, outspoken, quick paced, and determined.[21] When Relief Society General Secretary Emmeline Wells wrote Lyman of her election to the Board, Wells speculated that the "work will doubtless appeal to you as it has to most of us, who have enlisted in this worthy cause of uplifting humanity and that you will in the not far-distant future find it a joy and a blessing."[22] Lyman would be a daunting presence in the Relief Society for thirty-six years.

A year after Lyman became a board member, Bathsheba Smith died, and Emmeline Wells became Relief Society president. At the age of eighty-two, Wells knew that she needed an energetic secretary to carry out the Society's increasingly complicated business. Lyman first became the assistant and then the general secretary of the Relief Society. In that capacity, she began to modernize its administrative procedures. She convinced the General Board to employ bookkeepers and to buy typewriters in order to make their office run more smoothly. Motivated by church president Joseph F. Smith's encouragement to collect accurate data on membership, she helped create standardized ward minute and record books. Like many reformers around the country, Lyman believed that efficient administration and accurate statistics produced effective organizations.

Lyman also pressured Board members to convince Wells to standardize the curriculum used in Relief Society meetings. This was not an easy task because it entailed convincing the aging president to give up her own longstanding personal voice on women's issues, the influential *Woman's Exponent*. In 1915 the General Board decided that a cycle of lessons should structure Relief Society meetings and that a new publication, the *Relief Society Magazine*, would publish materials for the lessons. With the exception of summer months, all Relief Society members across the world would meet weekly (typically on a Tuesday afternoon) to study the lessons laid out in the magazine. One week the topic would be theology, the next literature, and the third social studies. One meeting a month would be devoted to producing goods for charity: making quilts, sewing baby clothes, putting together rag rugs. Up until 1945, the sophisticated lessons contained in the *Relief Society Magazine* were probably written by the editors and General Board members. Like the *Woman's Exponent*, the *Relief Society Magazine* also contained short stories, poetry, and nonfiction. Some articles were original compositions by the General Board, but most of the lessons were written by appointed committee members. Other essays were excerpts from male secular experts or church authorities.

Weekly Relief Society meetings encapsulated the spirit of modern Mormonism. Religion should be systematized, educational, and practical. Studying theology (the explications of church doctrine, the complexities of biblical history, the recent writings of church leaders) was the focus of the religion lessons. Educated, cultured women read serious literature and the considered writing of religious experts. In her spare time, for example, Annie Tanner read the works of popular Protestant ministers.[23] The temple remained a place of spiritual power but it, too, took on more prosaic functions. Women performed temple "work," which included keeping meticulous track of the ordinances they performed for the dead. The increasing importance of temple rituals motivated Latter-day Saint genealogists to develop charts and record books in order to systematize family history.

As spirituality assumed a rational character, women's writings no longer contained examples of speaking in tongues or demonstration of supernatural powers. In 1904 Wells reflected in her diary that she "had a singular dream, cannot recall it all but would like to know its meaning. Aunts Presendia & Zina used to interpret dreams for us but now there is no one to do it."[24] As the pioneer generation of women died, their connection with the spiritual power of Joseph Smith and early Mormonism faded away. Wells at times gave blessings to women who were sick or pregnant, but frequently Annie noted in her diary that her mother was too weak to perform such duties. Older women continued to heal and bless into the twenties, but they healed at home and not at Relief Society meetings. Healing in the temple (frequently by women) was ended in 1921 and church leaders (both male and female) sought to place healing solely in the hands of male elders.[25] Slowly, the acts of women blessing, anointing, and healing each other became more and more rare.

Younger women seemed not to lament the loss of female healing rituals; at least, they did not comment on the loss in their diaries or later life histories. The constriction of women's roles in healing accompanied the expansion of male priesthood activities. Eliminating the intimate and physical gestures of healing also paralleled the modernizing that was occurring in other parts of the women's lives. "Modern" women were less interested in those activities that could be negatively labeled "magic." Hospitals, not homes, became places of healing. The miraculous certainly occurred, but it was not common. Healings and blessings by women became a part of the Mormonism of the past.

Religion was not the only aspect of women's lives that was becoming more intellectual and predictable. In 1915 John A. Widtsoe, president of

Utah State Agricultural College in Logan, pressured the Relief Society to include home economics in its weekly lessons. Under the Smith-Lever Agricultural Extension Act, the federal government was making funds available for domestic science. A proponent of modern farm living, Widtsoe wanted to ensure that Utah women understood the benefits of scientific housekeeping. Widtsoe's wife Leah had studied home economics in New York, and in 1897 she started a similar department at Brigham Young Academy. Because Utah had more electricity, piped-in water, and motorized equipment than other states, emerging domestic technology was increasingly available.[26] Likewise, if managing a modern farm family became easier, perhaps women would not migrate to the cities, thus making it harder for men to find suitable wives. Through his mother-in-law, General Board member Susa Young Gates, Widtsoe threatened to organize home economics clubs for women if domestic science did not find a place in Relief Society meetings.[27]

Finding support for domestic science was not difficult; the new science of home economics was already spreading across the country. Unlike some earlier reformers who imagined a future of communal living in which women were freed entirely from the kitchen, home economists believed that the house was precisely where women naturally belonged. Like any workspace, however, the home needed to be transformed into a safe and productive environment by making it cleaner and more efficient. As with other aspects of Progressive Era reform, domestic science had religious overtones that dovetailed well with modernity: domestic efficiency had a moral character because it uplifted routine aspects of homemaking that could be demeaning and demanding. An ordered home reflected God's ordered universe.

During the first half of the twentieth century, discussions of home-making in the *Relief Society Magazine* were technical and pragmatic. Lessons brought scientific knowledge into the home via articles on sanitary cooking, parenting, and the latest consumer products. The editors of the magazine freely reproduced specialized articles written by respected non-Mormon authorities. Healthy recipes, rather than complicated ones, were reproduced. Articles on domestic hygiene were in the same *Relief Society Magazine* monthly issue as articles on theology; cleanliness actually *was* next to godliness. While male leaders romanticized motherhood in their conference talks, women taught mothers how to use science to make their homes efficient and healthy.

Creating healthy saints—in body and mind—became a major concern of Amy Lyman. Lyman wanted to continue the Relief Society's focus on caring for the poor and the sick, but she sought to do so in a modern manner. Her experiences outside of Utah had convinced her that the casework method of social work was a more productive way of caring for those in need than simply giving them charity. Church president Joseph F. Smith also wanted to cultivate more efficient ways of helping the Saints. With his support, Lyman was able to attend a Red Cross workshop to learn how this organization used modern methods to support families after World War I. Shortly before President Smith died in the 1918 flu epidemic, he appointed Lyman to direct a new division of the Relief Society, the Social Service Department. Her appointment took effect in 1919, three years before the state of Utah developed its own division of social welfare.

Lyman developed a twofold strategy to efficiently care for the poor. First, a small number of women would be trained in the casework method and paid to be professional social workers. "It wasn't a matter of the bishops telling the caseworkers what to do," recalled Hilda Harvey, "or the caseworkers telling the bishops. They just all worked together."[28] Caseworkers contacted members, assessed their problems, and then strategized with the local bishop about a plan for the family. Social workers recorded their visits on a tape recorder and a stenographer typed up transcripts. Everything was held strictly confidential.[29] The social workers drew on a small Relief Society emergency fund, a milk fund, and the Relief Society's storehouse of used clothing, quilts, and furniture. Before the thirties, however, the Relief Society Social Service Department was more likely to provide counseling than actual direct relief. Caseworkers learned how to combine support from a variety of Mormon and non-Mormon sources to help their clients. By 1929 the Relief Society's Social Service Department employed a supervisor and five caseworkers, an employment counselor, and an office secretary. This staff oversaw the care of 330 families per month in Salt Lake City.[30]

The second strategy Lyman developed reflected both the Latter-day Saint zeal for volunteer labor and Progressive Era commitment to "demystifying" science and making it relevant to society. The General Board put together workshops for Relief Society members on how modern science could help promote stable family life. Utilizing her national connections, Lyman invited experts to come to Utah to lecture on social problems. After attending an institute, a woman was qualified to become a "social service aide." By 1925 almost 1,800 local workers had been trained, and that number rose to 3,000 by 1930.[31] Social service aides were a distinctive position within the ward, and women were to give up their other church callings when they accepted that responsibility.[32]

The Relief Society's Social Service Department also assumed other responsibilities that enabled it to directly address modern problems. In 1922 it established an employment bureau for women and girls, and by 1929 it had secured over 12,000 placements. These positions were mostly in domestic service, but some women did find jobs as stenographers or nurses.[33] Rather than continue its own nursing program, the Relief Society provided loans for women to study at colleges and hospitals. Infant adoption also came under the purview of Relief Society social workers. Traditionally, if a woman giving birth was not married or could not care for her baby, a local midwife or doctor quietly arranged for the child to be adopted by another family. By 1922, believing that it could more effectively care for pregnant women and their babies, the Relief Society took over the adoption process.[34]

The creation of institutes to train social service aides continued the longstanding Latter-day Saint practice of voluntary service. However, the employment of women as caseworkers and office staff, as well as its support of nursing education, indicated a new attitude toward modern wage labor. The General Relief Society Board was expanding its outreach. Receiving professional training and a salary from church funds was new and often controversial. "My mother and dad did not want me to be professionally employed," recalled Evelyn H. Lewis, an early social worker. Her father told her, "I have one living daughter and I ought to be able to support her. Stay at home. Get a master's degree, get a doctor's degree, anything you want to, but stay at home." When Lewis's family refused to support her social work training, Lyman located a place for her to live where she could do house-work to pay for her room and board.[35] Latter-day Saint women had always worked outside the home, supporting family farms and businesses or in un-paid positions for the church, but now they were becoming professionals.

Lyman found that maintaining continuity in the department was diffi-cult because the young women she hired quit when they got married. Helen Ross stopped working as a social worker in 1936 because her new husband told her, "I don't want to be married to a working woman." As a pediatri-cian, he expected her to manage their active social life. "That was the end of my contact with social work," she told an interviewer. "My whole life changed after that."[36] Keeping busy with unpaid church work—even the so-phisticated labor that Lyman performed—was not perceived as a threat to domestic stability; being paid for one's efforts was. Yet, even if they were few in number, Lyman had introduced paid, professional women into the church bureaucracy.

Managing a modern office during an era when working women were sus-pect required Lyman to develop a forcefulness not always appreciated by other Relief Society Board members. In 1921 Annie Cannon complained in her diary after one Board meeting that she was "bored to death" because an executive committee (with Lyman at the heart) made all the real decisions. Even though her mother was Relief Society president, Cannon believed that she had "no opportunity of initiative or expression on my questions what-ever. The way I am discriminated against in matters of appointment etc. and treated generally is very apparent and unpleasant."[37] Cannon believed that her friend Susa Young Gates shared her sentiments: "she is greatly exercised over Mrs. Lyman's authority and feels that things are in a bad way."[38] At the age of ninety-three, Emmeline Wells was finally showing her age and could do little about how power was exerted. Lyman was modernizing the Relief Society and the older Board members felt they were being pushed aside.

Susa Young Gates's own diary concurred with Annie Cannon's perspec-tive. After recalling how her editorship of the *Relief Society Magazine* had been demoted from a lifetime calling to a rotating appointment, she prayed hard to "see the light" about Lyman. Her conclusion was a severe one and reveals the pain that modernization brought to many Relief Society women. According to Gates, Lyman did not respect those men who held the priest-hood, and she suffered from a "real ignorance of the fundamentals of the Gospel." Because of Lyman's lack of testimony, she was "willing to make the Church a tail to the Gentile kite."[39] Susa Young Gates, the child of Brigham Young's twenty-second wife, had penned a stinging insult: Lyman lacked personal spirituality, and she was robbing the Relief Society of religion. Gates would have agreed with Annie Cannon, who thought it a "dreadful statement" that some called their organization the "Club of the Church called the Relief Society."[40]

For Annie Cannon and her mother, Emmeline, the modernization of the Relief Society would take a particularly tragic twist. Although neither woman could admit it, Wells's failing health made it difficult for her to carry out her Relief Society duties. It never occurred to Cannon that her mother might retire from her position and thus allow a more vigorous woman to take the lead. Like every male church president to date, each female Relief Society president had died in office. The presidency was not simply a job that needed to be competently executed; it was a lifelong calling from which one was only released by God. Wells even lived in the church-owned Hotel Utah, located near both the temple and her office, to facilitate her work. What Wells and her daughter did not fully recognize was that the modern church valued effectiveness more than tradition.

In March 1921 church president Heber J. Grant informed John Q. Cannon (Emmeline Wells's son-in-law and Annie's husband) that he was going to release Wells from the presidency and that she would have to leave her rooms at the Hotel Utah. John told Annie that she would have to prepare their home for her mother. "How am I to break the news to her I do not know," Annie Cannon worried. "It will just break her heart."[41] On April 2 President Grant and his counselor Anthony Ivins met with Wells and informed her of their decision to appoint Clarissa Williams in her place. "I was quite hysterical," Cannon wrote in her diary, "mother was calm but courageous, and told them her opinion. She did not accept the condition at all well, but resented it."[42] Wells did not change her opinion over the next few weeks as her health steadily declined. When Cannon asked her why she was crying, she responded, "I should think I would cry when they have taken away my position."[43] Cannon watched helplessly as her mother slowly retreated into herself. At the end of that year's diary, Cannon summarized: "On April 3rd she was released from presidency of R. S. The shock killed her. She died on April 26th, beloved, honored, adored but nevertheless heart-broken."[44] The officials of the church paid for her funeral and spoke glowingly of her long and admirable commitment to her faith. Cannon continued on the Relief Society Board, but Susa Young Gates was released a year later.

Although Wells failed to fully understand the impact that modernization was having on the Relief Society, other Mormon women embraced the opportunities offered to them by a changing American society. As soon as Utah became a state and women were granted the right to hold public office, Mormon women entered the state legislature. Regardless of political party, the elected women supported a progressive agenda. For instance, during her two terms as Democratic state senator (1896–1900), Dr. Martha Hughes Cannon pushed for the creation of a Department of Health. Another Democrat, Elizabeth Hayward, served for four sessions from 1915 to 1921 and worked to limit women's labor to an eight-hour day. Annie Wells Cannon became a Republican state legislator in 1921 when she was fifty-three and still sitting on the Relief Society General Board. She resented the First Presidency telling her not to involve the Relief Society in politics without their approval. "I am very unhappy," she confided in her diary, "because I had not thought that anyone could think it wrong when it was for the protection of women and children, however, so long as men place business before morals these things will happen."[45] Cannon only served one term, seeing public office as a civic duty, not a lifelong career.

Lyman's longtime friendship with the new president, Clarissa Williams, solidified her position in the Relief Society's leadership to the point that in 1922 she felt comfortable enough to run for the state legislature. As a Republican legislator, Lyman continued the progressive orientation of previous female politicians. In 1923 she introduced a bill to fund programs created by the federal Sheppard-Towner Maternity and Infancy Act. Two years earlier the US Congress had approved federal matching funds directed toward improving the health of women and children. States that participated might use the money for health clinics and visiting nurses, classes on nutrition and hygiene, or literature for pregnant women and new mothers.

The Sheppard-Towner Act was a landmark social welfare program and directly resulted from pressure put on Congress by women after they received the right to vote. Women's clubs, magazines, church societies, and heritage associations like the DAR all supported the Act. Male politicians sought to curry favor with the newly granted female vote and so they, too, were supportive. Only the American Medical Association and a few antisuffrage groups spoke out against it. Writing in the *Relief Society Magazine*, Board member Jeannette A. Hyde asked rhetorically: " 'Would not the men in the legislature have done the same?' I shall only answer you by asking: 'Have they done it in the past?' "[46] The Utah legislature passed Lyman's bill without a dissenting vote.

Even before the state of Utah approved funding, Relief Society president Clarissa Williams had proposed that interest from wheat profits also go toward funding child and maternal health. In 1876 Wells had been given the responsibility from Brigham Young to glean, buy, and save wheat for emergencies. By 1911 stored grain was rotting in its silos, so the Presiding Bishop offered to store the wheat in modern facilities (for a 5 percent storage fee). [47] Some local Relief Societies moved their wheat; others kept it in their communities. A few years later, Wells agreed that church authorities could distribute the wheat.[48] During World War I, the federal government asked to buy the wheat to supply US soldiers and their European allies. Without consulting the Relief Society, male church authorities agreed to sell the wheat and asked ward bishops and Relief Societies to ship the wheat to the government. Wells was not happy that the General Board was not consulted. Eventually the men apologized and promised that nothing like that would happen again.[49] The $412,000 sale generated interest and church authorities permitted the money to be spent by the Relief Society. By 1922 the General Board had decided that wheat interest should only be spent on healthcare for mothers and children.[50] Local Relief Societies then partnered with non-church government agencies (each using their own monies) to cosponsor projects that benefited the whole community.

Relief Society and Sheppard-Towner monies supported an array of maternity and health programs. Between 1925 and 1929, over four thousand volunteers assisted public health officials to establish 133 health centers, sponsor 274 dental clinics, and organize 2,203 health conferences.[51] In Burton, Idaho, the Relief Society arranged for doctors to examine and vaccinate the community's children. Some had their tonsils removed and others were given eyeglasses for the first time. To help establish standards of proper diet, nutrition courses and food demonstrations were held.[52] Such care was provided to whoever needed it, but Mormon women supplied the volunteer labor. Lyman and her Relief Society members could rightly be proud: in 1926, when Grace

Abbott, the director of the Children's Bureau, came to visit Utah, she reported that the state had "achieved the honor of having at the present time the lowest maternal death rate of any state in the Union, and is also among the four or five states having the lowest infant death rate."[53] On a grassroots level, Latter-day Saints were seeing what a partnership between church and state could accomplish.

By embracing modernism, women traded their specifically religious expertise for more rational pursuits. Rather than speak about miraculous healings in their diaries, the elite women of Zion were encouraging Mormon women to learn social work skills and volunteer at health clinics. As they had done in promoting women's suffrage, Latter-day Saint women joined with women from diverse religious backgrounds to enact civic improvement and uplift "their sex." Such partnerships improved the well-being of Mormon and non-Mormon alike. Around the country women were attempting to join the traditionally male world of politics, science, higher education, and community organizations. Modernization in both religion and society appeared to be precisely what was needed in order to enhance women's position in the world.

CHAPTER 4

⸱◆⸱

Edged Out

Modernization was not the only critical shift in American culture and politics during the early part of the twentieth century. The 1917 Russian Revolution and the carnage of World War I had made Americans fearful and suspicious. Anxieties over radicalism in the United States and the explosion of bombs set off by anarchists in April 1919 provoked the government to conduct raids, deportations, and arrests. Female suffrage had become the law of the land in 1920, but conservative women who had predicted negative repercussions were not quieted. They and their supporters amplified the fears of a collapsing moral order after the disastrous events in Europe. The female "antisuffrage" movement became an "antiradical" movement.

The fact that women were divided over political issues just as much as men was revealed in the 1924 national elections. There was not, it seemed, any "women's vote." Consequently, women's issues became less of a concern for vote-counting men, and male politicians could return to business as usual and ignore women's concerns without suffering any consequences. Conservatives then adapted the lobbying strategies of progressive women reformers and founded national organizations to advance their political goals. Labor organizers, immigrants, and Progressive Era reformers were all seen as potential enemies of the country. National feminist reformers like Grace Abbott were dubbed "radicals" and unjustly accused of trying to inflict a socialist agenda on the United States. One by one, women's organizations like the DAR turned away from progressive legislation.

When Congress initially debated the Sheppard-Towner Act in 1921, there was a strong dissenting voice: William H. King, the Democratic senator from Utah. When the Act came up for renewal six years later, he killed it. The rapid change in the fortunes of the bill reflects the nation's larger shift away from progressive reforms. Mormons and the rest of the country had become fearful of changes in both American society and the world. Modernization had not led to a peaceable kingdom of God on earth but a chaotic reordering of values and priorities. Senator King and eventually other Latter-day Saint male leaders would see the salvation of their people not in their partnering with other progressive reformers but rather in growing independence. While Amy Brown Lyman and her supporters would try to maintain a progressive stance throughout the Great Depression, the cooperation between government and religion facilitated by Latter-day Saint women would be short-lived.

William H. King was born in the small town of Filmore, Utah (the first capital), in 1863. He served in the territorial legislature and then studied at the University of Michigan, from which he graduated with a law degree. After returning from a mission to Great Britain, in 1889 he married the daughter of an apostle, Ann Louisa Lyman, which placed him within the circle of prominent Latter-day Saints. Ann was the sister of Richard Lyman, the apostle husband of Amy Brown Lyman. After serving as an associate justice for the Utah Supreme Court between 1894 and 1896, King entered national politics. A traditional Jeffersonian Democrat, King was an outspoken proponent of individual freedom, limited government, and local rule. First as a member of the US House of Representatives (1897–99, 1900–01) and then in the Senate (1917–41), King rejected any expansion of the federal government and became well known for his anti-imperialist stance during an era of American colonial expansion. He believed that self-rule, "private ownership, the inviolability of contract, and the primacy of individual liberty" were ordained by biology.[1]

King opposed Sheppard-Towner when it was introduced because, most simply, he opposed all new federal programs. In addition, he considered the measure socialist. King reached this conclusion after his service on the Overman Committee. Established by the Senate to investigate domestic pro-German activity during World War I, by 1919 the committee had expanded its reach: King and the other members now were investigating the possible overthrow of the US government by radical sympathizers of the Russian Revolution. King accepted without question the reports of chaos and unrelenting violence emanating from Russia. In addition to Bolshevism's centralized and far-reaching government, King also feared its antireligious orientation, which rejected God and sought the "destruction of Christianity."[2] Democracy, capitalism, religion, and the family no longer seemed safe. The Red Scare had begun.

Americans feared that left-wing social agitation was going to unravel fundamental national institutions. On January 13, 1927, when King began his filibuster against the renewal of the Sheppard-Towner Act, the country was much more attuned to his ideas than it had been six years earlier. Antiradical women joined with the American Medical Association and the Catholic church to resist government involvement in healthcare. King gave voice to their fears when he warned of the impending doom of American democracy if the government continued to involve itself in the daily lives of its citizens. It was time, he argued, that the country stopped "listening to these social workers and professional patronizers of the poor."[3]

King's filibuster laid out a set of fears echoed by Mormon conservatives up to the present day. Renewal of Sheppard-Towner would "shackle the individual, devitalize the States, destroy local self-government, and vest in the Federal Government unlimited power."[4] It would promote the evils of bureaucracy, paternalism, and the role of the expert over everyday families. The Act was not for "the babes and the mothers of the country"; it actually was for "the conscious purpose of setting up State control of maternity and childhood."[5] The women of the Children's Bureau were "fanatics and uplifters" who sought "standardized, federalized recreation for children."[6] King bound together the integrity of the home, the belief in God, and the endurance of capitalism. "The Bolshevists told me when I was in Russia that the first thing to do is to destroy belief in God," King explained. Once this is accomplished, the people "will not care for marriage, they will not care for homes." Not caring for homes meant not valuing private property, so "in order to destroy capitalism in all the world, a belief in God must first be destroyed. With its extirpation, the family unit will disintegrate."[7] The gauntlet had been thrown.

Grace Abbott contacted her friend Amy Lyman to ask her to try to persuade King, her fellow Mormon and brother-in-law, to recognize the good that Sheppard-Towner had done.[8] Lyman complied, but King probably had no difficulty ignoring this "professional patronizer of the poor"—the very type of woman he was railing against. Although a compromise bill extended Sheppard-Towner funding to 1929, it also stipulated that funding would then cease. A renewal bill was proposed again in 1931, but it failed to pass either house. Some states replaced lost Sheppard-Towner money with state funds, but Utah did not.[9] When King came up for reelection in 1928, Relief Society General Board member Jeannette Hyde paid for a full-page advertisement in the *Salt Lake Tribune* denouncing King as "Against the Welfare of Utah Mothers and Babies,"[10] but King was easily reelected. That same year, Clarissa Williams was released from the Relief Society presidency and the more conservative and less dynamic Louise Robison put in her place.

The Relief Society General Board, however, was not deterred. Even after government funding ended, the members continued to spend the Society's wheat interest on child and maternal health projects. Mormon women established a maternity hospital. The women who headed Primary (the church's children's organization) renovated a home in which sick children could be treated. During the twenties, the Social Service Department, with Lyman as supervisor, was at its peak. Relief Society women were partnering with county welfare agencies, the Red Cross, the American Legion, the Chamber of Commerce, and other businessmen's clubs to secure health-care. The *Relief Society Magazine* was filled with dense articles on the benefits of vitamins and pure milk, advertisements for automatic refrigeration, and reports on the National Conference of Social Work.[11] The Relief Society's leaders were committed to civic involvement that combined national and local expertise.

Shortly after King's reelection, the Great Depression shook the nation's economic and social stability. The women who worked for the Relief Society soon realized that the crisis was unprecedented. Agriculture, which continued to engage the majority of Utahns, had declined by 66 percent. Mining fell a staggering 85 percent. Soon almost 36 percent of the state's workforce was unemployed.[12] Banks foreclosed on homes and farms. There had always been vulnerable people in their communities, but now hunger was widespread. Fathers, who knew they were strong workers and who took pride in supporting their families, could no longer do so. Like widows and the infirm, they had to ask for handouts.

Social worker Evelyn Lewis remembered the desperation of one un-employed man "from one of the better parts of town" who came for help. "Asking hurt him badly," she recalled. "He wept. The family lived on flour, salt and water before applying."[13] Hilda Harvey saw the same thing among her clients: "Among them were wonderful men who had jobs all their lives and suddenly everything went to pieces."[14] Relief Society social workers realized that their previous strategy of creating a family budget was not an adequate solution. In 1932 the *Relief Society Magazine* reported on the shift that the Social Service Department was experiencing:

> Whereas formerly they [men] were weak or sick or unfortunate, now many of them are strong and determined and defiant. There are young men clean looking, perfectly built, well dressed, *demanding* [italics hers] that their dependents shall not suffer; and there are sturdy men of middle age who weep because of rents unpaid and credit houses threatening.[15]

That same year, on behalf of the Relief Society Social Service Department and the Salt Lake County Welfare Agency, Lyman went to the state legislature with a set of case studies that suggested that the state needed federal help. By March 1933 almost a third of Utah's citizens were receiving aid through the Reconstruction Finance Corporation.[16] Existing charity organizations were utilized to distribute funding, with families being divided by religion. For Latter-day Saints, Relief Society social workers continued what they had done in the past: determined eligibility, assessed the family's needs, filled out paperwork, and located food and clothing. Monthly coordinating conferences were held in Salt Lake City, where Latter-day Saints worked with Catholic Social Services, the Salvation Army, and Jewish Social Services.[17] The Relief Society was comfortable working in a modern welfare mode that equally engaged government agencies and non-Mormon private charities.

Nonetheless, 1933 was the year that would radically alter the Relief Society's role as a modern welfare organization. The first change came in March when the successful Democratic candidate, Franklin Delano Roosevelt, took his presidential oath of office, observing that, "the only thing we have to fear is fear itself." A majority of Latter-day Saints had voted for this president, although their leaders had supported his Republican rival. Roosevelt's New Deal helped the unemployed but with increased federal involvement came a shift in who could dispense the tax dollars. That August the Federal Emergency Relief Administration informed the states that public employees must administer its programs; states could no longer use private and religious charities to distribute federal monies. However, since religious groups organized much of the nation's charity, this mandate could not be immediately met. In Salt Lake, because of a shortage of trained social workers, Relief Society women were permitted to reorganize themselves as District 7 of the Salt Lake County Department of Public Welfare. When District 7 was dissolved in 1934, it was handling 775 cases per year.[18]

Across the country, a pattern was repeating itself. Private charities, typically run by women, were being sidelined by the government. When charity organizing was just a small part of a woman's domestic activities, then it did not threaten traditional gender roles. Even the professionalization of social work in the early twentieth century was dominated by women. But the Great Depression was so large a crisis that male leaders felt women could not handle it. As both the money involved and the administrative apparatus expanded, men assumed leadership in what had once been "women's work."

The month after Roosevelt became president, Latter-day Saint president Heber J. Grant called J. Reuben Clark as his Second Counselor. Clark would be the key player in redirecting the mission of the Relief Society. Clark's appointment was unusual because he had lived much of his adult life outside of Utah, working as a government employee, often in legal affairs or in the State Department. He had never been a bishop of a ward or served as an apostle, which meant he had no experience working with Latter-day Saint women. An ardent Republican who took pride in his political appointments, Clark had no sympathy for Roosevelt's New Deal. Although he was in the opposite political party from William King, Clark shared the senator's preference for local autonomy. Both men longed for a nineteenth-century pioneer past of self-reliance, isolation, independence, strength, and cultural purity. Neither supported the Relief Society's willingness to partner with non-Mormon welfare agencies.

In the spring conference of 1933, while acknowledging the immensity of the world's economic problems, Clark argued that the real culprits were the traditional evils of idleness, ambition, and greed. Clark called on the Saints to rekindle the "old time virtues" of "industry, thrift, honesty, self-reliance, independence of spirit, self-discipline, and mutual helpfulness." Once doing so, "they should be on their way to returned prosperity and worldly happiness." The world's problem was not "primarily one of finance," but rather it had been "on a wild debauch, materially and spiritually." Clark suggested that "it must recover in the same way the drunken reprobate recovers; by repentance and right living."[19]

At the very time in 1933 that Clark was gaining support for a new approach to the ills of the Depression, Lyman was coping with a personal tragedy. Almost a decade earlier, her daughter-in-law had died suddenly. Amy's son Wendell could not cope with his young wife's death, and so he and his newborn baby moved in with his parents. He not only left the care of his child to his mother but also took to smoking and drinking, and he refused to remarry. Even his business dealings were unsuccessful. Then, on a spring day in 1933, Amy Lyman came home for lunch and found her son in the garage under his car with its motor still running. He had been asphyxiated by carbon monoxide fumes. Newspaper reports called the event an accident, noting that the son still held a wrench in his hands, but suicide seems probable. Whatever the cause of his death, family tragedies certainly distracted Lyman from the shifting political winds.

During the next few years, Clark attacked the government's approach to the Depression and pushed for an alternative Latter-day Saint response. As church leaders considered their options, they asked the Relief Society for statistics on government relief disbursements for church members. They also wanted an evaluation of whether or not the people on relief really needed it. After reviewing the Relief Society's numbers, an unnamed church official penned a summary across the top of the report: "If the Church were to undertake to take care of this amount, it would bankrupt us." The Relief Society also informed the leaders that 95 percent of those receiving aid needed it.[20] Clark's desire for Latter-day Saint autonomy and the conclusions of the Relief Society could not have been more at odds.

Despite the unnamed official's fiscal warnings, the church decided that welfare was too important a function to be handed over to the government. As the US Congress debated what would become the Social Security Act of 1935, Latter-day Saint leaders decided to follow Clark's advice and develop their own welfare system. No representative of the Relief Society (or any woman) sat on the planning committee. A year later, the Church Security Program was launched. Managing director Harold B. Lee explained that "There is no new organization necessary to take care of the needs of this people. All that is necessary is to put the priesthood of God to work."[21] The hope of what eventually became known as the Church Welfare Plan was that the church would take care of all needy Saints. Church members were discouraged from participating in federal relief programs. Rather than receiving money or a government-funded salary, the poor were to be given food and clothing produced by other church members. Men would receive help finding work.

The Welfare Plan ended the "scientific charity" of casework that Relief Society social workers had been practicing for sixteen years.[22] Cooperation with private organizations and governmental agencies was ended. The Social Service Department still existed, but it was no longer in charge of organizing relief. Although it might have been a coincidence of timing, two months after the Church Security Program was publicly announced, Amy Lyman's husband was called to be the president of the European Mission. Even if she had been tempted to resist the reorientation of church welfare, she was not in a position to do so from Europe.

The structure of the Church Welfare Plan would profoundly shape the religious activities of Latter-day Saint women long into the twentieth century. The holders of the priesthood would help men find jobs in the difficult times of the Depression, but the production of clothing and food fell to women. Ann Esplin remembered bottling gleaned peaches at a cannery in Cedar City until four or five in the morning. She also bought corn, husked it, picked off the kernels, and spread it out to air dry in her home. The process took up so much space her boys had to sleep in the barn.[23] A Mormon woman living in New Jersey admitted that most in her ward had never canned anything before, but women enthusiastically learned how to put up peaches, tomatoes, beans, and corn.[24] In 1937 the Deseret Clothing Factory was established to produce priesthood garments; traditionally sewed by women, they would now be manufactured by men. Unemployed men were also hired to renovate old chapels and build new ones, but it fell to women to raise the money to equip the new facilities. If, after all this, a woman had an hour or two of spare time, she could make goods to sell at the Mormon Handicraft store, which opened in 1937 so that women could earn money without working outside of the home. The Church Welfare Program did not decrease women's involvement with charity, it only placed the high-level decisions in men's hands.

As with most Americans, Latter-day Saints hated being "on the dole." Most stoically accepted what they were offered. Still, some individuals thought that receiving government money was less stressful emotionally than accepting commodities from their church. Cash distributed by federal or county agencies could be rationalized as something that "everyone was getting." Hilda Harvey recalled that "some people preferred to be on county welfare, because they didn't want their bishops to know too much about them."[25] Mormon women who distributed boxes of food or clothing at times found the intimacy of the exchange taxing. Some Saints got so frustrated by the process that they misbehaved. Ann Esplin remembered asking the recipients of aid to bring back the glass jars that their fruit came in, but "they'd take them out in the backyard and throw rocks at them." Another time she told a father that he could not have the order he put in for coffee (coffee drinking ran counter to the Word of Wisdom). "Then we found out," she reported, that "he traded some flour or some other commodities that his family needed for his tobacco, so we had to put a stop to that."[26] Social worker Evelyn Lewis found that "relief in kind" was inadequate and demoralizing. It might work as a supplement, but "to try to meet a family's needs from the warehouse and what the bishop gives out at intervals, I can't approve of. I think if a family is needing relief over a period of time, they need the security they are given in federal relief."[27]

In theory, Latter-day Saints' faith in church leaders, pioneer self-sufficiency, and Christian love should have made the Welfare Plan a success. In reality, the situation was so dire that Mormons needed support from *both* the church and the government. From 1933 to 1939 Utah ranked twelfth among all states in per capita expenditures by New Deal agencies.[28] Federal nonrepayable expenditures in Utah for the period 1936 to 1940 were ten times the value of churchwide Welfare Plan transactions.[29] Clark's desire to return to pioneer autonomy made for good public relations during a time when the country was desperately looking for creative responses to the Depression, but it was insufficient to meet the needs of the people.

When Amy Lyman returned from Europe in 1938 and became Relief Society president in 1940, she had high hopes for the organization. While an associate recalled that she was "a little defeated" by the direction of the Church Welfare Plan, Lyman was dedicated to church authority and prophetic inspiration. "She could have very well been heartbroken," speculated her secretary Vera Pohlman, "but she wouldn't have complained. She would see the direction things were taking I'm sure."[30] Buoyed by her new position, Lyman dismissed all of the women who had served on the Board for more than ten years, including Annie Cannon. She had the *Relief Society Magazine* redesigned to visually emphasize its new motto of "Looking Forward." The Relief Society launched a membership drive to commemorate its hundredth anniversary.

In July 1940 in an address at Utah State Agricultural College, Lyman called on women to renew their commitment to political and civic involvement. Recognizing that some women had turned away from community affairs and others did not even vote, she lamented that "men in general have so obstinately opposed the activity and development of women, but stranger still that many women have also joined the opposition."[31] Women should run for public office, she held, and women's organizations should be interested in city, county, state, and national administration and finance; in industrial problems and economics; in personal health, both mental and physical; in public health and health education; in the schools and school programs; in recreation; and in housing. Lyman repeated a familiar call: women should uplift all of humanity, not simply their own families.

Lyman may have become more strident in advocating for women's public life because she was facing more intense pressure from church leaders to curb the activities of the Relief Society and to focus women's concerns on the home. Earlier in the spring, Clark had gathered the leaders of the church auxiliaries, including Lyman, to discuss a "Memorandum of Suggestions" regarding the "simplification" of church programs, with simplification typically referring to shifting authority away from auxiliaries like the Relief Society. Clark, worried about church finances, wanted to make sure that programs did not proliferate. He asked the Relief Society leaders to confine their social service work to the welfare program and their cultural work to promoting "faith and testimony."[32]

Clark had become more powerful in the church since becoming first counselor. The illnesses of both church president Heber J. Grant and second counselor David O. McKay limited their activity. At the Relief Society conference in October 1940, Clark told the women that they were to serve as a "handmaiden to the priesthood."[33] He expanded on that idea when he addressed the full Latter-day Saint community, explaining that auxiliaries like the Relief Society may provide "aids and helps," but the priesthood was "responsible for a due and proper instruction of Church membership in the way of life and salvation." The women of the church were to be "first aid to the priesthood" by supporting men in their trials and tribulations through their loyal devotion. The duties of women included maintaining the modesty and chastity of youth, creating a righteous home, and keeping the world from sinking into a "welter of sin and corruption."[34] Absent from his address was any specific mention of women's contribution to public life as workers, as volunteers in civic organizations, or as elected officials. Women's role in social service was appropriate only when it duplicated what they already did in the home.

The slow edging out of women from the administration of social welfare by World War II was not unique to Mormonism. During the nineteenth century, Catholic sisters and lay organizations had cared for immigrants who found themselves poor and sick. In order to care "for their own," Catholic women built and organized a vast private system of hospitals, orphanages, and homes for "wayward" women. However, by the thirties, male bishops and clergy had established diocesan social service bureaus to manage services for families and children. Like Progressive Era Latter-day Saints, they sought to centralize, coordinate, and professionalize, thus making efficient what they believed to be the premodern, disorganized efforts of women. Catholic sisters would continue much of the work of charity but, increasingly, it was male clergy who were making decisions.

However, unlike Latter-day Saint male leaders, Catholic clergy strengthened their relationships with governmental agencies rather than diminishing them. Diocesan charities secured access to state funds, agreeing to eliminate certain religious markers of Catholicism in exchange for better resources for the poor and sick. Both Catholic and Mormon women found their public influence curtailed, but only Mormons turned away from partnership with the government. By the end of the New Deal, poor Catholics were receiving assistance primarily through public agencies, but Latter-day Saints assumed that relief should come from the church.[35]

Two events of the forties signaled the end of the Relief Society's involvement in modern social service. Shortly before Lyman became Relief Society president, her predecessor, Louise Robison, had agreed to the sale of 190,000 bushels of old, stored wheat.[36] Church leaders then combined the income from that sale with the previous wheat fund and bought new wheat. That left nothing to generate future income to fund Relief Society social service initiatives, and healthcare projects ground to a halt.

Then, in September 1944, Lyman and the General Board decided to stop collecting donations for charity. For many years, Relief Society members visited their neighbors' homes, said a prayer, exchanged pleasantries with the lady of the house, and asked for a small donation for local charity projects. With the Depression over and the Welfare Plan caring for poor Saints, there seemed no reason to continue such collecting. In January 1945, the Relief Society rolled its charity fund balance of over $150,000 into its general fund.[37] No longer directly providing commodities, funds, or services to those in need, local Relief Societies could only act under the bishop's direction.

When Lyman released Annie Cannon from the General Board in 1940, she was eighty-one years old. As her mother had been, Cannon was bitter about the transference of power to younger women. "I have been extremely lonesome and at times very sad," she admitted in her diary. "Not happy over the reorganization of the Relief Society. It does seem to me that I deserve more consideration than I have received and I have found true friendship is very rare."[38] Cannon would have a heart-to-heart talk with Lyman, but she still felt she had been shoved aside.[39] She particularly resented the fact that she was not issued a personal invitation to attend the dedication of the new church grain elevator, built to store all the wheat purchased with Relief Society funds. "All through the years I stood by mother in this great activity," she recalled, "and today when the $400,000 worth of wheat is placed for keeping I was not even invited to the exercises."[40]

Miffed by the personal affront, Cannon could not see the wider implications of building the grain elevator. The position of the Relief Society itself had been altered. No longer would it partner with the government, raise money for charity, or throw its weight behind progressive reforms. Its members would not be encouraged to run for public office. Rather than help women develop professional skills as social workers or nurses, they were asked to intensify the tasks they were already doing: cooking, preparing food for storage, sewing clothing, and raising money for projects initiated by men. Women should engage in Christian charity, but church leaders were silent on working with non-Mormons or mastering the increasingly complicated systems of modern social service. The new Welfare Plan, along with the addresses and talks that extolled the spiritual dimensions of motherhood, accentuated the religious nature of women's domestic labor and ignored all else.

Cannon died in 1942, and a year later Lyman's influence among the Latter-day Saints vanished. On November 13, 1943, a notice of only a few lines appeared on the front page of the *Deseret News* announcing that Richard R. Lyman, Amy's husband and church apostle, had been excommunicated for "violation of the Christian law of chastity."[41] A few days earlier, church authorities and the police had found him in a compromising position in the apartment of a woman who was not his wife. After admitting his guilt to his fellow apostles, he was speedily removed from his leadership position and his church community. He had been an apostle (as both his father and grandfather had been) since 1918. However, his church responsibilities did not stop him from falling in love with a Danish immigrant, Anna Sofie Jacobsen, in the early twenties. The couple may have seen their relationship as a form of plural marriage. When their clandestine affair was discovered, they were both in their seventies.

It soon became clear that her husband's transgressions made Lyman's own position within the church's hierarchy untenable. Simply ignoring the problem and carrying on became impossible. Whereas second counselor David O. McKay personally escorted her back to her office and hoped that her work would keep her mind off her troubles, first counselor J. Reuben Clark was far less supportive. Lyman did not divorce her husband, but she did submit her resignation from the Relief Society presidency and in March 1945 was released from her calling. She asked Belle S. Spafford, who would become the next president, to pray "that I won't grow bitter and just pray that the depth of my understanding of the gospel will carry me through."[42]

The circumstances surrounding the end of Lyman's Relief Society presidency are particularly dramatic, and we can only speculate about the extent to which she was blamed for her husband's indiscretions. It would be difficult, however, to imagine that there was no gossip about the strong-willed and outspoken Amy whose husband wandered off into the arms of another woman while she was busy with professional activities. A year earlier, in 1942, Clark had read an address written by ailing President Heber J. Grant that clearly laid out the virtues of modesty, the horrors of adultery, and the holy calling of motherhood. "Motherhood is near to divinity," the First Presidency explained. "It is the highest, holiest service to be assumed by mankind. It places her who honors its holy calling and service next to the angels." Nurses, public nurseries, or hired help could not provide the "divine service of motherhood." Quoting the Bible, the highest authorities of the church warned about women who had worked during the Depression and now during the war: "The mother who entrusts her child to the care of others, that she may do non-motherly work, whether for gold, for fame, or for civic service, should remember that 'a child left to himself bringeth his mother to shame' (Prov. 29:15)."[43] Ensuring that motherhood assumed its place next to the angels must now be the goal of all Latter-day Saint women.

CHAPTER 5

A Style of Our Own

The scaling back of the Relief Society's activities put an end to conflicts between reform-directed, nationally connected Latter-day Saint women and tradition-oriented, inward-looking men. The new president of the Relief Society, Belle S. Spafford, embraced the Relief Society's new support role and its emphasis on women's domestic responsibilities. Women were to carry out policies designed by men and not insert alternative agendas into church life. If a national organization needed the help of Latter-day Saint women, they were to ask the male church leaders, who would then pass the request along (if they approved) to the Relief Society General Board.[1] With women's activism at a low point across the country after World War II, it would have taken tremendous energy and skill for the next generation of Mormon women to maintain the reforming spirit of their mothers. Given the value that Latter-day Saints placed on communal harmony, consensus, and obedience, it was downright impossible. After the disorienting period of the Great Depression and World War II, most Americans preferred security over change.

The centennial membership drive of 1942 did increase the number of women who attended Relief Society meetings. And after the war, Relief Society membership became almost mandatory. With public engagement no longer encouraged by the Relief Society leadership, the Tuesday afternoon literature and social science lessons became important avenues for women to learn about the world. As with other women's clubs, Relief Society meetings offered training in public speaking and leadership, all within the acceptable confines of church. Cultural enrichment, local charity, and sociability came to be the hallmarks of the Relief Society.

With both male and female leadership united, Latter-day Saints crafted a well-defined image of the faithful Mormon woman. The postwar Mormon culture constructed between 1945 and 1970 was so secure and vibrant that it flourished throughout the tumultuous years of the sixties and provided a workable ideal until the end of the century. Caring for large families and participating in ward activities became so all-encompassing that most Latter-day Saint women had little time or energy for anything else. Even when women detailed their struggles in private letters and diaries, they expressed no desire to fundamentally change their culture. Mothers could be severely tested by their home lives, but they sought strategies for improvement, not radical restructuring. Women might leave the church altogether or, like the historian Fawn Brodie, be excommunicated, but until the early seventies most women accepted a particular Latter-day Saint "style" to be their own.

Latter-day Saints constructed this formidable culture during two decades of profound national unrest. The notion that the fifties were a halcyon era is outdated; the postwar years profoundly transformed how many Americans understood their place in society and culture. Women in particular were living in worlds markedly different from their mothers'. Even though the white, middle-class family was idealized, married women increasingly worked outside of the home and expected their husbands to help—at the very least—with childrearing. African American women demanded civil rights. In 1963 Betty Friedan's *Feminine Mystique* helped catalyze a renewed feminist movement. By 1970 some women embraced the sexual liberation of a "counterculture" while other women mobilized to fight communism, abortion, and sexual liberation. As women increasingly moved into the workforce, into politics, and into education, defining appropriate gender roles became more difficult. Many American women were asking "Who am I?" Often, there was no clear answer. For Mormon women of this era, there was.

The nation's religious women were also experiencing upheaval. The push for the ordination of women, which some Protestants had called for since the nineteenth century, became more forceful. In 1956 the Methodist church in America began ordaining women, and that same year Margaret Towner became the first woman minister in the Presbyterian Church (USA). Sally Priesand entered Hebrew Union College in 1964 and eventually became the first American female rabbi. Southern black women called on the liberating message of the gospel as well as the organizational capacities of their churches to challenge segregation. Changes resulting from the Second Vatican Council brought average Catholic women into the liturgical life of their parishes. Catholic nuns were active in movements for racial justice, and Protestant women protested the Vietnam War as unethical. Evangelical women joined the John Birch Society and campaigned for Barry Goldwater, believing that society needed stronger values. On the left and on the right, women believed that their religious commitments required rethinking the faith of their mothers. The home was not the only place where women could be influential. Religious commitments did not isolate women from social change but intensified its impact.

Before 1970 Latter-day Saint women ignored or resisted the "Who am I?" question and the movement of women into politics and the professions. They also turned away from the social movements that both inspired and frightened the nation. In partnership with men, Latter-day Saint women promoted values traditionally associated with women: domesticity, engaged churchgoing, and bodily purity. These traits became the defining characteristics of postwar Mormonism. Women tempered the modern trend toward consumerism and individualism by marrying early, having large families, and intensifying their religious activities. While some Latter-day Saint women worked and had fulfilling careers, this was the exception and not the rule. Latter-day Saint women gave their full commitment to their religious community and its values, which enabled distinct elements of Mormon culture to flourish despite the upheavals of postwar America.

In August 1945, Japan surrendered to the Allied forces, and American soldiers slowly began to come home. Families were expected to go back to normal. However, exactly what was "normal" was not clear. Two powerful and conflicting forces tore at America's women. Americans embraced the familiar and comforting image of a father earning a living for his family, nurtured by a loving mother. Insecurity, felt by individual traumatized soldiers or by Cold War fears, would be relieved through family stability, womanly graces, godly piety, and capitalist consumption. Almost every aspect of American culture taught that when women crossed into the male sphere, disaster ensued. Mental breakdowns, children transformed into juvenile delinquents, and political disorder inevitably would ruin the nation.

At the same time, during World War II, millions of women had answered the call to join the labor force—often doing traditionally male jobs—in spite of the pressures it placed on home life. Work was patriotic; women took pride in their accomplishments and often enjoyed their newfound independence. At the war's end, female workers quit (or were fired) to make room for returning soldiers. The growing economy, however, needed more workers. Since women were marrying earlier and quickly having babies, employers looked to older women. Companies abandoned their rules against hiring mothers. During the fifties the number of working married women grew by 42 percent.[2]

Many white women worked in order to secure a higher standard of living that enabled rather than challenged the postwar domestic ideal. The GI Bill made homeownership a reachable dream for more families, and women wanted to be partners in achieving that dream. Advertisers targeted female consumers, hoping to convince them to buy their products and thus make their homes modern, efficient, and beautiful. In order to sell consumer goods, advertisers labeled housework a chore that could be quickly dispatched if you used a new electric stove or vacuum cleaner and purchased supermarket (often frozen) foods. The focus on children and home meant more money was needed for family vacations, station wagons, outdoor barbecues, and do-it-yourself crafts. Middle-class families wanted to save for their children's college education. To safeguard familiar gender roles, women understood their outside employment to be simply a job; being a mother was their career. Husbands helped more at home, but women still did the bulk of housework and childcare. "Pink-collar" work was not perceived as a revolt against domesticity but rather as a means to improve home life.

Latter-day Saints also benefited from the expanding postwar economy. Utah's population expanded 25 percent during World War II as people migrated to the state to work in war industries.[3] Rural Utahns also moved to the cities for work. Before the war, the state's per capita income was 20 percent less than the national average; by 1943 it was almost 3 percent greater.[4] Like much of the American West, Utah benefited from the growth of the federal government. Cold War fears brought contracts for missile systems, facilities for chemical weapon storage, and the expansion of military bases. Utah women participated in this burgeoning economy.[5] In 1950 Utah had a female workforce of 57,294, and half of those were married and living with their husbands—an 87 percent increase over a ten-year period.[6] By 1970 half of Utah's women over age sixteen were employed.[7]

Access to education also altered the social lives of Latter-day Saints. Immediately after the war, Utah men took advantage of the GI Bill by attending college, enabling many to move more quickly into the middle class. In 1947 Brigham Young University (which would, over the next two decades, become the flagship Latter-day Saint college) enrolled 2,000 veterans out of a total student population of 4,403.[8] Lillie Day, who had not graduated from high school, married one of those BYU graduates. "I had always thought I would be a farmer's wife," she recalled, "and I was a little frightened for I did not know how to be a teacher's wife."[9] Other Latter-day Saint women moved out of state with their husbands when opportunities arose. Moving up the social scale or away from the community of the Saints was both exciting and terrifying.

In 1951 Relief Society president Belle S. Spafford recognized this social transformation. Women were being lured into the workforce by "vocational opportunities . . . increased living standards and high living costs, requiring greater income than one member of a family can provide." More perceptively, Spafford recognized that Latter-day Saint women, like other women, had "desires for independence, yes, and in some instances a sense of discontent and fear of missing something in the seclusion and the unrecognized activities of household routine." Still, she concluded, women should resist such enticements because employment came "at too great a cost to their children, at the too costly sacrifice of a full realization of the joys and blessed privileges of motherhood."[10] Barely into the decade of the fifties, Spafford was well aware of the challenges that a changing American society posed to Latter-day Saint women.

Although Spafford's warning would make sense to many religious women of the fifties, Latter-day Saints' belief in the eternal character of the family was alien to other Christians and Jews. For Latter-day Saints, the purpose of establishing a home was to enable embodied spirits to learn how to be righteous individuals and to facilitate their participation in temple ordinances. By participating in rituals conducted by a male priesthood, family members could guarantee that eventually they would live with each other in eternity. Mormons could be "sealed" together so that their marriages would persist. If a temple marriage occurred on earth, in the Celestial Kingdom spiritual perfection could be achieved. Children born of temple-married parents would be automatically sealed to their parents, and any children born before a temple marriage (or who were adopted) could be sealed later. Latterday Saints could also perform ordinances for dead ancestors who could then continue with their eternal progression. Existence was not limited to this earth because life existed before birth and would continue after death. The church thus promised families that they could defy the limits of earthly life and expand their happiness into eternity. A husband would never permanently leave his wife. Children and relatives would be bound together. Each year, more temples were built to make it easier for the Saints to conduct the rituals that would begin their eternal progression.

Latter-day Saint men and women had separate duties because gender differences, like the family itself, were eternal. In 1914 Latter-day Saint scientist, theologian, and church apostle James E. Talmage articulated a religious understanding of family life and its implications for women. He explained in the *Young Woman's Journal* that prior to birth all children lived as "male or female in the primeval world," where they had distinguishing characteristics. In the far future, gender differences would also exist: in the "glorified state of the hereafter, husband and wife will administer in their respective stations, seeing and understanding alike, and co-operating to the full in the government of their family kingdom." However, such equality and cooperation would not be possible on earth because it is imperfect. A woman's mission in this life was "to occupy a secondary position of authority in the activities of the world, both in the home and in the affairs of public concern."

Talmage justified his claim by pointing out that every organization needed a centralized form of authority and that "secular law recognizes the husband as the head of the household." That men might oppress women or be weak themselves did not negate the general principle that home and society must be ordered. Talmage called woman "the associate of man" who has her own "duties and functions, which the other is less qualified to discharge." Together, the "two should form the governing head of the family institution."[11] Earthly home life was a dim reflection of the glorified family. "Homemaking is a joint enterprise," Spafford would explain over a half-century later, "with divinely ordained division of labor for forming, maintaining, and protecting the family unit." The husband was the head and presiding officer and the wife his companion and helpmate.[12]

Fleshing out the "duties and functions" of mortal women became a preoccupation of postwar church leaders, who articulated what might be thought of as a theology of gender for a growing Latter-day Saint community. For instance, in 1950 Vesta Crawford, an associate editor of the *Relief Society Magazine*, wrote a memorial essay about her friend Virginia Clark. In it Crawford described Clark as the ideal Mormon mother, an image frequently employed throughout the fifties and sixties. Clark was the mother of six and had experienced the death of one son. She had been a missionary and went on to marry a former missionary who became a ward bishop. Clark served as a Relief Society teacher and made sure her children were active in church. As her family's historian, she collected the talks her husband had given and prepared a "Book of Remembrance" scrapbook for each child. Filled with the spirit of the gospel, Clark faced her impending death with comfort and peace. While she was ill, she embroidered needlepoint seat covers for fourteen chairs, faultlessly sewed a "Doctor's academic robe" for her husband, and knitted sweaters for her children. She accepted the help of her sister and her eighty-three-year-old mother ("of the best pioneer lineage"), who were living with the family. Clark confided to her friend that her life "had been satisfying and complete, full of joy and fulfillment."[13]

The ideal Latter-day Saint woman willingly accepted all the children God sent her and followed her church's warnings against limiting family size. Focusing exclusively on her home meant accepting limits on her personal freedom and desires. Sacrifices made for others enabled her to create a strong home life by modeling Christ-like behavior. Productive and practical, she was skilled at housework and expressed her creativity through the domestic arts. Household efficiency and enthusiasm for the gospel moved her to accept the "callings" asked of her by church leaders.

Clark stood in sharp contrast with another woman described that same year by David O. McKay, soon to become church president. McKay told the story of a woman who had been married five years, worked, went skiing and skating, and enjoyed dinner out followed by a movie. She and her husband did not want a family as children would be "a foreign element in this little world that is so perfect and so all our own." Such childless women, however, would eventually "lose their beauty, their alertness, their interest in life. Their faces are so often empty and vacuous, even if pretty." These women were not a credit to their sex. "Wifehood is glorious," McKay concluded, "but motherhood is sublime."[14]

In both of these examples, women neither have careers nor are involved in civic activities. Clark's life circled around the traditional triad of home, children, and church. The childless woman, in contrast, focuses exclusively on herself and excludes all that does not give her pleasure. In neither caricature do we see a glimpse of the Progressive Era woman who sought to improve the community, promote cultural refinement, or broaden the intellect. Both the ideal woman and the frivolous one look inward and not outward.

Latter-day Saints were especially suspicious of modern forms of leisure or consumption that detracted from the home's centrality. McKay had little respect for women who preferred skiing to childrearing. By the end of the sixties, the high birth rates of the fifties had declined and more Americans came to worry about global overpopulation. In 1960 the US Food and Drug Administration approved the sale of an oral contraceptive, and by 1965 one out every four married women under forty-five years of age had used the Pill.[15]

Mormon teaching, however, still stressed the familiar theme that families should take precedence over other concerns. Apostle Ezra Taft Benson pithily observed in 1969 that "The Lord did not say to multiply and replenish the earth if it is convenient, or if you are wealthy, or after you have gotten your schooling, or when there is peace on earth, or until you have four children." Reproduction enabled spirits to come to earth, increased the community of the Saints, and was essentially an act of worship. "God is glorified by having numerous children and a program of perfection for them," Benson explained. And, because Latter-day Saints believed that blessings come to those who are faithful, "So also will God glorify that husband and wife who have a large posterity and who have tried to raise them up in righteousness."[16] Church leaders worked against the understanding that children's material, educational, or emotional needs demanded a small family.

Women's fiction provided drama and color to such admonitions of church leaders. The *Relief Society Magazine* routinely cautioned its readers not to exchange productive domestic work for superficial consumer goods. In Sylvia Probst Young's short story "The Lasting Joys," the heroine (who could only afford a cheap dress) yearned for her friend's perfectly decorated home. Eventually she came to realize that "the warmth of boyish arms" of her sons was far superior to material possessions. Blanche Sutherland wrote a story about a working woman named Kay whose husband reminded her that now that they had paid off the car, she could quit her job. Kay countered by reminding him about the mortgage, the secondhand furniture, the "ragged" stove and refrigerator, and her hope for an automatic washer. A patient husband, Don waited. Eventually Kay saw how, when an earache tormented her toddler, he could not say "Mummy" but instead called out for his caregiver. Bills would get paid, her husband reassured her, as Kay gave her notice to her employer.[17]

A productive and well-ordered home did not require newly purchased appliances but rather the traditional values of strength, perseverance, obedience, and faithfulness. Whereas other women might feel conflict between modern desires and long-established roles, Latter-day Saints emphasized that true happiness came from recognizing and maintaining the eternal truths of the past. Mormons had always linked together religion and work. For the home to have a spiritual focus it also had to be the center of meaningful labor. Rather than mutely stand by and let the mass media erase household industry, Latter-day Saint women stressed the meaningfulness of women's homemaking.

Finding and articulating the deeper meaning in housework became a goal of much of women's writing. In her memoir *A Daughter of Zion*, Rodello Hunter vividly remembered how her work produced "rows of canned peaches, their lids pinging as they seal, a cake swirled in frosting, standing on the cake rack, a stack of ironed linens, a full cookie jar, or a table of brown-crusted bread, hot from the oven." As late as 1965, church magazine *The Improvement Era* claimed that no French perfume could "possibly compete with the captivating power held by the aroma of bread baking in the oven when a hungry man enters the door of a home."[18] Canning, bread baking, quilting—these activities held symbolic value that connected modern Latter-day Saint women to the foundational era of their religion and the efforts of their pioneer foremothers. Female writers concentrated on what they knew best and minutely detailed the beauty and rewards of home life.

In addition to fiction and memoir, women engaged with history to assert their critical place in Mormon life. The Daughters of the Utah Pioneers assembled a vast collection of quilts, furniture, needlework, carriages, and farm equipment that physically embodied the productive spirit of the past. Aggressive fundraising enabled the construction in 1950 of a neoclassical style museum to house this material culture of early Utah. Kate B. Carter, president of the Daughters of the Utah Pioneers from 1941 to 1976, published a multivolume historical series of books and pamphlets that preserved the stories of the past, purged of anything that would be injurious to the church or that would discredit the pioneers.[19] Carter stood in sharp contrast to another female historian, Juanita Brooks, who in 1950 published the first critical history of the 1857 Mountain Meadows massacre. In the early sixties, Young Women's Mutual Improvement Association president Florence S. Jacobsen fought to keep Brigham Young's home from being demolished to make way for an office building parking lot.[20] She later oversaw the houses' restoration as well as the renovation of many other historic buildings. Women were critical in both creating and preserving Mormon history during a period when church leaders were more concerned about future growth than past legacies.

By returning to the preindustrial nineteenth century, these women underscored the importance of women's work without the problematic inclusion of modern wage labor. The drama of beautiful buildings and the uplifting stories of ancestors countered the increasingly bureaucratic orientation of Mormonism. As mothers stitched Victorian clothing for their children to make Pioneer Day celebrations more realistic, they physically joined the modern world to the past. Just as the pioneer woman was essential to the economic, social, and spiritual success of the home, so were contemporary Mormon mothers. No one could take the place of a mother who was an "economist, a psychologist, a chauffeur, an efficiency expert, a nurse, and I don't know what all."[21] Women's work, whether it was driving oxen across the plains or a carload of children across town, was irreplaceable.

The irreplaceable character of women's work was particularly evident in ward life. As the church grew and became increasingly global, it sought to secure the commitments of new converts and prevent the fragmentation of a Mormon culture through a myriad of ward activities. While the Saints assumed that men would direct the undertakings of their communities, they also assumed that women would provide the labor. Ward life thus became both an extension of the home and a respite from its demands. Women's ward activities were critical in shaping a Mormonism that looked largely the same in Salt Lake, Boston, and Cape Town.

President David O. McKay oversaw a postwar expansion of missionary activity. In 1940 there were 862,600 Saints living mostly in the intermountain West, but by 1970 church membership had more than tripled to three million.[22] Rather than encouraging converts to gather in

Utah, foreign converts had been encouraged to build up their Latter-day Saint communities where they lived. In 1950 the church constructed eighty-seven meetinghouses; by 1959 that figure increased to 180.[23] During McKay's presidency, over two thousand ward chapels were built. Temples were dedicated in Switzerland (1955), New Zealand (1958), and England (1958). By 1964 more than 60 percent of all church buildings had been constructed within the previous ten years.[24]

The increase in baptisms created a challenge: how to keep new converts active in the church. A parallel problem was faced by "cradle" Latter-day Saints who wanted to keep their children within the fold as they moved away from home. As usual, Mormons thought the solution was to keep busy. Latter-day Saints, male and female, were given "callings" in their wards: to teach Sunday School classes, be visiting teachers, or work with youth. Those who lived near temples, especially if they were older or retired, were asked to volunteer as temple workers. Trips were organized to bring the Saints to temples. Welfare farms needed to be tended and foodstuffs prepared for the needy.

Wards and stakes put on a dizzying array of social events that engaged every age group: dances, dinners, holiday parties, roadshows, pageants, musicals, speech contests, rummage sales, and summer camps. While men may have overseen or even initiated such events, women provided most of the labor. A woman from Alhambra, California, remembered that "the Gold and Green Balls in those days were very important because the girls were presented, and there was always an orchestra, and girls wore formals—a very elegant affair." There were, she recalled, "always two things going on."[25] In addition to social activities, large-scale fundraising for important Latter-day Saint institutions like the new Primary Children's Hospital (founded by women in 1952) was mostly the job of mothers. Women organized food for funerals and arranged music to be provided by the ward's "Singing Mothers." In places without Latter-day Saint mortuaries, Relief Society women prepared bodies for burial.

Women coordinated ward activities and had their Relief Society lessons in their own room within the meetinghouse complex. In many wards, the space resembled a corner in a comfortable home. Rodello Hunter remembered meeting in a room "serviceably decorated in shades of cream and rose, carpeted and draped, and furnished with walnut tables, covered by crocheted tablecloths, a piano, and sturdy folding chairs."[26] Women who were expected to spend their days at home met in rooms that felt familiar— at least to a certain class of American women. When in 1956, after years of fundraising, the Relief Society General Board dedicated its new building, it looked like an elegant home rather than an office building. The domestic values that the church promoted and that women embraced were inscribed physically on the places where they met.

Relief Society women had a say over how the rooms would look because they gathered their own dues, set their own purchasing goals, and managed their own funds. During this period of growth, wards were expected to contribute a portion of the construction costs, so women raised money both for the building fund and their own Relief Society activities. Goods to be sold at bazaars were often made during Tuesday afternoon Relief Society "work meetings." Women's efforts were creative and relentless. They raised money by selling crafts, foods, and services to other members of their ward or stake. Zina Burr, from Alberta, Canada, described in her diary how for one Relief Society bazaar she made more than fifteen pounds of chocolates, a doll cradle (out of a grape basket), two nylon dress slips, and two aprons. Other women in her ward made lampshades and ice cream. Burr was proud of her accomplishments, but she admitted, "My eyes are suffering from so much strain. Lot of fine hand work to [sew] those doll dresses."[27] Bazaars encouraged women to be imaginative. A woman from Cape Town, South Africa, remembered having an "ankle beauty contest" where, dressed in their favorite shoes, woman stood behind a curtain and modeled their feet. Relief Society sisters sold tickets to vote for the shapeliest ankle.[28]

Relief Society president Belle Spafford insisted that moneymaking was only one goal of the bazaars. She understood the primary purpose was to encourage women to make beautiful items for families. In the process of doing that, women would come together to socialize and have fun.[29] Raising and spending money also helped women learn successful budgeting principles. "Activities keep people together," another Relief Society woman remembered, "they give people a purpose and a definition; a desire to learn, and to go, and to do. In the process, the side effect is knowing the other sisters that [you] work with. And learning to love them, which to me is the ultimate goal anyway."[30] For women busy with family life, ward activities broke the isolation of the home and encouraged them to make friends with their Latter-day Saint sisters. The ward also served as an instant community for Latter-day Saints who had either recently converted or moved out of the intermountain West.

Relief Society meetings also introduced women to more intellectual undertakings. Hazel Lamoreau, from St. Anthony, Idaho, was not fond of housework and appreciated the fact that three out of four meetings had nothing to do with home and family. During the week on Social Science she was able to study the Constitution and, another week, "great literature."[31] In 1963, for instance, Relief Society women read lessons about *Moby-Dick*, Walt Whitman, and Willa Cather.[32] Rodello Hunter preferred the Theology week; she felt that it had the highest attendance because "it gave these ladies a chance to participate in the testimony-bearing after the lesson." From her perspective, women were willing to speak about their religious commitments to each other but "would never do on Fast Sunday in front of the Priesthood."[33] Women were able to see themselves as thinkers in addition to doers.

Not all women were enthusiastic about the intellectual orientation of the Relief Society lessons. A California woman remembered that she studied classical works of literature but didn't understand what they had to do with the Relief Society. "In my mind," she observed, "I felt that Relief Society should be teaching us to do good things rather than to learn about good things."[34] In 1966 the heavy emphasis on American history, literature, and culture was modified. Theology would now be called "Spiritual Living," thus stressing the practical rather than scholarly dimension of faith. The more fashionable term "Homemaking" replaced the more direct term "Work Meeting." Social Science became "Social Relations" and Literature became "Cultural Refinement."[35] It could no longer be assumed that Mormon women knew about (or cared about) Melville and Cather. Making lessons less specifically American and less academic was intended to better engage a global membership.

For a few Latter-day Saint women, working for the church evolved into full-time, lifelong careers. Longevity in their callings gave these women influence within a male-dominated church hierarchy. Belle Spafford rose from stake Relief Society president, to be a member of the Relief Society General Board, to editor of the *Relief Society Magazine*, to, finally, president of the Relief Society, a position she held for nearly thirty years. Spafford oversaw not only a staff but also approximately forty-five General Board members. She remembered, "I went in the morning and stayed until the building closed at night." She rarely took a day off and often had meetings on Saturdays.[36] LaVern W. Parmley served as Primary president from 1951 to 1974, and she also had a grueling work and travel schedule. Leaders like Spafford and Parmley cultivated sophisticated forms of influence over their long careers. They understood and respected the authority of male leaders, but they also knew how to present their ideas in ways that would get heard. Their names were known to Latter-day Saint women across the globe, who recognized their service.

However, working for the church, much like working for the family, was not considered "work." Church service might take as much time as a full-time job, but everyone understood that if a calling interfered with home life a woman was justified in asking to be released. Still, whether a woman was organizing a dance pageant of five hundred Latter-day Saint girls or chairing the Primary Hospital Board as Parmley did, church activities were intense and demanded nondomestic skills. Ward activities stretched women's emotional, intellectual, creative, and social capacities while both reinforcing Mormon practices and avoiding wage labor.

"I am the world's worst housekeeper!" an exasperated woman wrote to the *Deseret News* in the late forties. "I am a mother of five children, and hard as I may try, three days is the longest my house ever stays even in a semblance of order." The letter writer explained that she was thirty-one years old and had been married for sixteen years to a truck driver husband who was away from home most of the week. While she did not give her name, she did explain that she was a Latter-day Saint woman who believed that cleanliness was next to godliness and so "our homes should be clean, and well run, and an example to all who may see them." The writer took pride in her ability to style and sew children's clothing, make cute things, and "do quite a superb job at carpentering, both with electric machinery and hand tools." However, when it came time to do housework, run a home, and manage children, "I feel (and act) like someone lost in a strange city, and I get just about as far." She sometimes cried for hours, seriously considered seeing a psychiatrist, and contemplated divorce ("but my church teaches against that"). She ended her letter with the plea, "I'd like to know if you, or anyone knows of a school where I could go and learn to keep a home."[37]

The letter writer was not alone. Many women wrote to "Mary Marker," the advice columnist for the *Deseret News*, to detail their thorny domestic problems. Their letters give us a glimpse of Mormon home life outside of the rosy world of fiction and memoir. Mary Marker was the pen name of Ramona Wilcox Cannon, the daughter of Elizabeth Wilcox (a member of the Relief Society General Board) and Dr. Charles F. Wilcox, a prominent Salt Lake City physician. Ramona was a "half sister-in-law" of Annie Wells Cannon. In 1943 Ramona started the "Women's Sphere" page in the *Relief Society Magazine*, which cited the public achievements of women—both inside and outside of the church. Ramona's husband, Joseph J. Cannon, was the managing editor of the *Deseret News* until he died in 1945, leaving his fifty-eight-year-old wife to support their seven children. To help out the widow, the *Deseret News* began "Confidentially Yours," a column where "Mary Marker" responded to letters sent to the newspaper. Ramona Cannon wrote as Mary Marker for the *Deseret News* from 1947 until 1974, retiring at age eighty-six.[38]

Much of the correspondence sent to Mary Marker contained painful descriptions of everyday life, unmitigated by a family or church. "I hate everything about baking bread," observed a letter writer from the late forties, "but I was so sold on the idea that any good wife and mother baked bread for her family that I forced myself to do it." It was only after electric shock treatments, six months in a psychiatric hospital, and "an awful lot of therapy" that this woman began to "not feel guilty about not liking housework."[39] In 1951 Madelene Scott found an apt image of her life with three young children: a "mechanical rabbit being chased around and around by the greyhounds."[40] A mother from Ely, Nevada, wrote about spending a tedious evening with other young mothers. She marveled at the change in her life: a few years earlier she and the same friends were at college reading Proust in the original French, but now after a day of caring for babies, "we're almost dead at night." "We're losing interest in ourselves," she observed, "and we're becoming real bores. What can we do?"[41] A writer from Hurricane, Utah, signed a 1955 letter "Lazy Susan." "I have stomach ulcers and other nervous disorders," she confessed, "which I feel like I can never overcome until I learn to either become more efficient or not to let my undone work bother me." She ended her letter by revealing that "I pray about this all the time, but I guess I lack faith. Can you help me?"[42]

When Mary Marker published letters like these, she lent a sympathetic ear and added her own suggestions and remedies for homemaking improvement. Often, after reading Marker's advice, other women wrote in to the *Deseret News* to offer more traditional perspectives. While they recognized that domestic life was difficult, most had little sympathy for exhausted mothers, echoing church president David O. McKay, who had written, "Motherhood is just another name for sacrifice."[43] Like other Christians, Mormons held that Christ's life exemplified how pain and suffering had ultimate value. Life was for testing, and a mother's selflessness would lead to a strong home life and eventually to an eternity of happiness in the Celestial Kingdom. "We are here to learn obedience," Alberta Banks wrote to Mary Marker, "and [to] become acquainted with sorrow as well as joy."[44] Motherhood was not the problem; the problem was individual mothers.

Many women who wrote in to the *Deseret News* were convinced that the struggles of motherhood and housekeeping could be kept under control if women took the right approach. Their letters reflected decades of practical advice on housekeeping contained in the pages of the *Relief Society Magazine*. The Progressive Era understanding of the home as a factory that needed to be run with efficiency and knowledge resonated in the advice from Mary Marker and her readers. It did not help mothers to become overly concerned with achieving perfection; flawless motherhood was an unobtainable goal. Writers offered to the readers of "Confidentially Yours" not the hope of eliminating sorrows but of limiting them.

Mrs. O. H. Lamoreaux responded to "Lazy Susan" by expounding on her system for conquering domestic woes: "I scrub and wax [the floor] once a week and wash and iron weekly and have stopped worrying about whether the house is neat or not." If not every pillowcase was ironed or every toy picked up, so be it. Lamoreaux had found a method for housekeeping and a way to keep her life in equilibrium, even though she admitted that "I still get on 'nerve jabs' when I go to pieces and have fits of depression and crying spells but the times are getting farther and farther apart and I have my emotions under better control."[45] Elise E. Hart suggested ripping up the carpet and putting in linoleum.[46] Mrs. E. F. Kehl told another mother that she awoke an hour before her babies in order to iron, sew, and mend. "Have a <u>system</u>," she stressed with underlines, "made to your order but have <u>one</u>."[47]

Integral to any homemaking system was prayer. In 1953 a "A Tired but Happy Mother" wrote to "Harassed Mother in Need" that she should ask her husband for help doing the supper dishes, bathing the children, and even occasionally hanging the wash. "And most important," she concluded, "do you know of the strength and comfort a tired and discouraged mother can receive by kneeling and asking the help of God? Bear in mind they are His children, too, and surely He can help you find a way to provide for them—I know!"[48] Prayer kept one woman who struggled with an alcoholic husband "sane."[49] A pregnant mother of four urged a woman whose husband had been unfaithful to pray for strength and also to forgive him because "God expects us to forgive all men—not once but forever."[50]

Both Mary Marker and well-respected Latter-day Saint housekeeping expert Daryl Hoole argued that good housekeeping was a means to an end. Successful home management enabled women to have more time to play with their children and to cultivate personal hobbies. Church callings and even special evenings with their husbands could be indulged in once housework was under control. Since motherhood itself was a manifestation of the divine, if a woman was profoundly unhappy it was because her life was disordered. Once she had a system, mothers would have time for themselves, which was their right. Mild disorganization merited careful study of Hoole's *The Art of Homemaking* (1962). For more serious problems Mary Marker suggested marriage counseling or even psychotherapy, both of which were popular in postwar America. Perfection, however, was not possible for earthly mothers.

And yet, Mormon women who took up pen and paper to complain to Mary Marker described how difficult it was to let go of the ideal of domestic perfection. In 1952 "A Mother" wrote in to agree with another letter writer who fantasized about abolishing Mother's Day. The two women were fed up with sitting in church hearing "all the beautiful, sentimental songs and poems about other dear, sweet, superior mothers." One actually felt that "I seemed to do everything wrong about nine tenths of the time and feeling that sometimes my children even secretly hated me." When she looked at her children on Mother's Day she asked: "What have I done wrong?"[51] In 1955, Mrs. Floyd I. Galway argued, "It is not true that one can do or become anything he likes if he only tries hard enough." She dubbed this conviction "The Great American Pipe Dream." Galway was convinced that such ideas were simply "a breeder of frustration, guilt, neurosis." Although she lived for years battling shame about not getting "trivial things done," she concluded that in order to stay sane "sometimes it is right to take a job away from home, or earn money at home, or hire household help even if one earns no money at all."[52]

Real Latter-day Saints of the fifties, not the imaginary ones of fiction or the subject of church leaders' stories, clearly saw the dark side of motherhood. Vulnerable to their religion's emphasis on perfectionism, women's response to homemaking was an ambivalent one. They recognized perfectionism as unhealthy and offered remedies to recalibrate expectations, but they also measured themselves against the perceived accomplishments of other women. Although the church was expanding around the globe, women in the Mormon communities of the intermountain West still experienced the "small town" feel of living close to each other. When all your neighbors looked just like you, it was hard not to compare.

In 1955 Ruth Chapman wrote to Mary Marker that she lived as if Christ was in her home at all times. "It helped me keep my house cleaner," she explained, "and say only the things that he would be able to hear."[53] That same year, "Fed Up With Smoking" also conflated physical cleanliness, moral cleanliness, and the presence of Christ. "We are taught to keep our homes clean so that the spirit of the Lord will be our constant companion," she advised. "We are also taught that He will not dwell in unclean places. I can't for the life of me, imagine the Savior's presence in a lot of filthy cigarette smoke or a place where alcoholic fumes are."[54] A clean house meant having spaces free from dust and clutter, as well as living with a husband who did not swear, teenagers who did not drink, and friends who did not ask to come over for coffee. Cleanliness meant modesty and chastity. If Latter-day Saint women of the Progressive Era had extended housekeeping outward to include clean streets and water, then women of the postwar era had moved "being clean" inward into the body. An obsession with purity became a concern for many Americans during the fifties.

"Being clean" did not always refer to keeping the Word of Wisdom. Two years before Joseph Smith revealed what came to be known as the Mormon health code (D&C 89), he presented a broader understanding of cleanliness. In 1831 Smith heard the Lord speak of the corrupt, wicked, and unpurified, who were contrasted with "righteous people, without spot and blameless" (D&C 38:31). At the end of the revelation, God called for the appointment of men who would take care of the poor and needy, govern the affairs of the church, preach, and "accomplish the things which I have commanded" (D&C 38:34–41). To these men the Lord ordered, "And go ye out from among the wicked. Save yourselves. Be ye clean that bear the vessels of the Lord" (42).[55] The men who were to lead the church and bring in new converts needed to be above reproach. The general message of the revelation was that the Saints must separate from sinful people and cultivate a just society. Early Latter-day Saints were not concerned with the details of drinking tea or coffee, smoking, or imbibing wine or beer; they had larger worries and grander goals.

By the early twentieth century, the generalized binary between Saint and Gentile, pure and impure had begun to be reconfigured. With polygamy and the theocratic Mormon state confined to the past, Latter-day Saint leaders concentrated on the other distinguishing characteristics of their religion. Prohibition and an awareness of the importance of diet among America's Progressive Era reformers caught hold among leading Latter-day Saints. Section 89 of the Doctrine and Covenant (the text that started "A Word of Wisdom . . .") detailed Smith's 1833 revelation on wine, strong drinks, tobacco, and hot drinks. What had once been understood as encouragement for health and good living became a sign of Mormon identity. By 1921 keeping the Word of Wisdom became a requirement for entrance to the temple. An influential book written by John and Leah Widtsoe in 1937 used science to clarify why alcohol, tobacco, coffee, and tea were unhealthy. It also elaborated on the lesser-known injunctions to eat meat sparingly, consume grains and herbs, and eat seasonal fruit (D&C 89:1–21). Keeping the Word of Wisdom became a mark of a good Mormon, and righteousness became associated with what one did not smoke or ingest.

Even before the postwar years, cleanliness and purity had come to be associated with modesty and chastity. In the nineteenth century, Brigham Young had believed fashion to be costly, distracting, and frivolous but not necessarily overtly sexual. By the twentieth century, the reasons for criticizing fashionable clothing had shifted. President Joseph F. Smith lectured in 1913 that he had never seen such "obscene, uncleanly, impure, and suggestive fashions of women's dress." Female attire was on its way to reducing women "to the level of courtesans on the streets of Paris, from whence these debasing fashions come."[56] Women's clothing may have also been expensive and silly, but increasingly it was perceived to be a threat to the sexual purity of Latter-day Saints.

The linking of immodesty and fashion accelerated in the fifties. In a 1951 devotional address to BYU students, Apostle Spencer W. Kimball warned that "unchastity is the great demon of the nineteen-fifties" and would lead to societal destruction as it had in Pompeii, Sodom, and Babylon. By wearing too-short dresses, too-tight sweaters, or too-revealing gowns, women risked their chastity by tempting men. Without mincing words, Kimball told college coeds that if they wanted to be respected they should not let their boyfriends "fondle" or "touch" them. Boys were tempted to break the law of chastity because girls flaunted their bodies. "Evening gowns can be the most beautiful thing in the world," but "the Lord never did intend that they should be backless or topless. I want to tell you it's a sin." Kimball appealed for a "style of our own."[57]

Some BYU women remember rushing out and buying matching sweaters for their fancy dresses, but Kimball was not satisfied.[58] Three years later, he gave another address to the BYU student body called "Be Ye Clean." The address was eventually published and distributed to young male missionaries. Kimball told the story of a couple who had come to him for counseling and for forgiveness of a terrible act. The boy explained that they engaged in "necking" and "petting" following a junior prom. Eventually, the couple "continued on and on and the terrible thing happened." They had come to Kimball to seek forgiveness because the girl in particular was tormented by sleepless nights and horrible dreams. After listing the sexual sins cited in the New Testament (Colossians 3:5), Kimball explained, "Today we call these same sins: necking, petting, fornication, sex perversion, masturbation, included are every hidden and secret sin and all unholy and impure thoughts and practices." Forgiveness certainly was possible, but it was equally important for Latter-day Saints to control their instincts, strive to become perfect, and "control and master the self."[59] Kimball, who became church president in 1973, spoke relentlessly about the impure tendencies of youth and inspired other leaders to do the same.[60]

During the fifties, Latter-day Saints developed a rich set of metaphors for cleanliness and freshness, enabling them to talk quite imaginatively about inappropriate sexual behavior. "You wouldn't expect to wear your best party dress to scrub the floor," wrote Mary Marker, "and still have it nice enough to make a big impression on your beau at a party. And neither can you expect to indulge in indiscriminate kissing . . . and still have it mean anything when you finally do meet the boy you really care for."[61] Latter-day Saints developed an elaborate inventory of metaphors for sexual defilement: a piece of gum chewed and then passed around, a licked cupcake to be shared. "If you had an exquisite rose and you pulled off a few of the fragrant petals," Mary Marker observed in 1952, and passed them around to friends, "you could never restore that rose or have a complete and beautiful flower again." Her message was clear: "Keep it intact for marriage."[62] Since everyone supposedly knew what "it" was, the object lesson was clear.

Mormons were hardly unique in assuming that girls were responsible for unruly male desire or that women should be virgins before they married. Female sexual purity has been a longstanding cultural value. Where Latter-day Saint attitudes differed from those of most Americans was their insistence that purity was a requirement for both women *and* men. Mormon men were not given the benefit of the "double standard" whereby their sexual activity was dismissed as "boys will be boys." During the fifties, hypermasculinity infused popular culture. In 1953 Hugh Hefner began publishing his cosmopolitan entertainment magazine *Playboy*, making sexual accomplishments semilegitimate for the middle-class male and linking them to upward mobility. The rugged Marlboro Man helped push Philip Morris tobacco sales from $5 billion in 1955 to $20 billion in 1957.[63] This trend continued into the sixties, when the men of the counterculture moved on to illegal drugs and men became much more open about casual sex. "Liberated" women took on mannerisms and behaviors once primarily practiced by men. But even in the revolutionary sixties, men might have worn paisley shirts but not granny dresses. Men may have valued "feelings" more, but they were rarely full-time homemakers.

Mormon men, on the other hand, were expected to uphold virtues typically associated with "ladylike" women and "good girls." Not only were men to be chaste, they were not to smoke, drink, swear, lose their tempers, or be disinterested in home life. They were to be fully involved with their ward callings and with family prayer and instruction. As priesthood holders, Latter-day Saint men were held to the standards articulated by the 1831 "be ye clean" revelation given to Joseph Smith—to care for the poor and needy, govern the church, preach, and separate from the wicked. Eternal gender differences did not include different levels of purity or piety. "There is but one standard for men and for women," Joseph L. Wirthlin told Relief Society women in 1950, "and rather than lose one's virtue, better one lose his life, for at least he will die clean in the sight of God."[64] Domesticity, purity, piety, and even obedience—female virtues from a past era—were valorized because Latter-day Saint men were also expected to uphold these values.

A key figure in this "degendering" of purity was David O. McKay, who was church president from 1951 to 1970. In 1935, when McKay was a second counselor to church president Heber J. Grant, he delivered a conference address stressing the connection between preserving the Constitution and keeping well-ordered homes. McKay quoted freely from *Home: The Savior of Civilization*, a 1924 book written by James E. McCulloch, a Methodist minister. McCulloch railed against the man who put business, pleasure, or "the club" above his home. These men, he preached have "flunked . . . the final test of true manhood." McKay would often quote the next sentence: "No other success can compensate for failure in the home."[65] McCulloch would soon be forgotten, but Mormons treasure this phrase.

McKay, who was born in 1873, brought into the postwar years the chivalrous values of an earlier America. He was a young man when fraternal societies, "muscular" Christianity, and proponents of Theodore Roosevelt's strenuous life were at their peak. In these years, gentlemen were to exercise their manliness by controlling their emotions and guiding the development of the weak (women, children, the "dark" races). True men of the turn of the century—the white men of the middle class—had a measured and appropriate sexuality. McKay never abandoned such virtues. In a 1963 conference address given when he was ninety (seven years before his death), McKay urged men to guard their behavior: "No member of this church—husband, father—has the right to utter an oath [swear] or ever to express a cross word to his wife or to his children." Men were told to contribute to the ideal home via their character and by "controlling your passion, your temper, guarding your speech." McKay specifically told fathers to do whatever they could "to produce peace and harmony, no matter what you may suffer."[66] While the non-Mormon world may have assumed that only women had to endure in silence in order to preserve peace in the home, McKay told Mormon men they needed to do the same thing. The Mormon style required men to adopt practices and virtues that much of American society attributed to the "ladies."

The construction and promotion of this Mormon style of manliness had two important effects on women. At the very least, women could expect church leaders to denounce poor male behavior. Clearly it was wrong for men to be unfaithful to their wives, to push for sex before marriage, or to waste money on alcohol, coffee, and tobacco. Letter writers to "Confidentially Yours" frequently complained about the men in their lives, and Mary Marker felt no hesitation in telling a wayward husband to "throttle [the] desire to be a tyrant."[67] In 1963 Wander Lifferth wrote to Mary Marker responding to a previously published letter about a nagging husband. Lifferth explained that she, too, had such a husband, but after McKay said in his conference address that "a man should never say a cross word to his wife and children," her home life changed. She was grateful to McKay because "almost instantly, my husband ceased to find fault with my housekeeping."[68] This is not to say that Mary Marker and her readers assumed men set the tone and character of the home; over and over, Marker told women that they needed to use charm, tact, and tenderness to bring their erring men around to their virtues.[69] Like many other Americans, Mormons assumed that it was easier for women to simultaneously change their behavior and to exert subtle power over men. Men, however, were expected to comply.

Mormon women thus had considerable spiritual authority in dictating the behaviors of husband and children. Women had more experience understanding the significance of cleanliness and purity, which gave them more familial responsibility and influence. Fathers, of course, were expected to provide good examples and education for their children but less directly. On a daily level, it was the mother who controlled what families ate, drank, and wore. Mothers could legitimately expect their sons as well as their daughters to conform to Mormon behavioral standards. Wives had the backing of their church to assert their wills—subtle or not—when purity was at stake.

Along with this spiritual authority came a practical responsibility: preserving sexual purity. Mormon and non-Mormon women alike took it upon themselves to prevent sexual misconduct—and to take the blame when it occurred. In 1951, for example, a mother wrote a cautionary tale about premarital sex to Mary Marker. She was engaged when she got pregnant but her fellow "stuck by me." The couple had a lovely daughter, but the mother felt the girl "must bear the shame I've brought upon her." In spite of their repentance, people "never never quite forget & someday it will be whispered about the baby—the result of our mistakes." This experience was so intense for this mother that she wanted all to know that "outside of marriage it [sex] is a dirty, filthy, thing. Don't give in & learn that the stolen moment is only a hurt & heartbreak."[70] When "Words of Wise Advice" got pregnant, her lover left her after six months. She felt she understood why: "Because I lost his respect. He thought, if I gave myself to him, why not to others?"[71] Men must have also felt shame about their behavior, but only women and girls asked Mary Marker about how to relieve their guilt and to prevent others from making the same mistake. Maintaining purity standards—either as warning mothers or cautious daughters—was squarely their responsibility.

Women were also in charge of making the practical arrangements when an unplanned pregnancy occurred. Although the Relief Society no longer directed most Latter-day Saint welfare, until 1969 they administered the church's adoption program. Relief Society social workers were in charge of situating unwed mothers in "wage homes" and, after they gave birth, placing their babies in Latter-day Saint households. Lauramay Nebeker Baxter, director of Relief Society Social Services from 1948 to 1956, explained to an interviewer that because of the "stigma around pregnancy out of wedlock . . . girls would leave their communities to protect themselves." Other Latter-day Saint families would take them in, and they would do light housekeeping and tend children. The families received no compensation. Baxter made it clear to the interviewer that the women were not domestic workers and that the homes where they stayed were carefully chosen. The women were given obstetric care, and then approximately 85 percent of the infants were placed with Latter-day Saint couples who had been married in the temple. Typically, the adoptive couple had no other children and the child would eventually be sealed to the parents, binding the family together eternally. The Relief Society Social Services' intention was to give "the girls . . . a certain anonymity so that after the birth they could return to their own homes and go on with their lives." Baxter estimated that by the mid-fifties between 100 and 150 mothers were cared for in this way.[72]

"When I was growing up," Bonnie L. Dalton told an interviewer, "there was a different climate in the world than there is now. . . . It never occurred to me to take a career in place of family and marriage. That just wasn't even an alternative."[73] Dalton was typical of many Latter-day Saint women who received a college education, trained in gender-specific careers like elementary school teaching or home economics (just "in case"), married, gave birth, and spent their energies on home and church. Life in the postwar Mormon ward provided women a chance to form friendships, express their creativity, explore the world of literature and theology, and develop leadership skills. At every turn, both male and female church leaders praised the spiritual importance of women's work within the home. Motherhood, in and of itself, was divine and therefore irreplaceable. Mothers who lost their way within the morass of housework and children were encouraged to find a system for improvement.

Each year, more American women entered the workforce and sometimes those jobs turned into satisfactory, long-term careers. Latter-day Saint women, however, consistently heard and embraced a forceful domestic message. "I think Betty Friedan and the [other] women who are telling our women that they should be dissatisfied have just done us a great disservice," Dalton reflected. While a woman should not be a martyr, "her life is to guide others and to sacrifice for them and help bring them along. If she forgets this and is only worried about her own fulfillment and what she's going to become herself, she is really copping out on her role."[74] McKay's conflation of motherhood and sacrifice made sense to postwar Latter-day Saint women. Family life certainly might be frustrating, but it was the way to eternal rewards. Ward life, with its busy schedule of events, callings, and charitable activities, fully engaged Latter-day Saint women, reinforcing the standards of the church. It almost seemed as if nothing could ever possibly change.

CHAPTER 6

————— •◆• —————

Not All Alike

At the dawn of the seventies, a mother of four reflected on her life in a letter to Mary Marker. After stressing her love for her children and husband, the mother had to admit she was "touchy, irritable and angry with them all much too often." Such complaints were common among women who wrote to the columnist, now in her fourth decade of writing "Confidentially Yours." If the initial problem sounded familiar, the further disclosure from the letter writer was unexpected: "I used to be against Betty Friedan's *Feminine Mystique* idea," she explained, "but now I am like her housewife figure." This mother went on to observe that her family was "not very thoughtful of me and I seem only to fill the role of a servant in the house . . . an unappreciated one at that." Echoing Friedan's bestseller from the previous decade, the mother wrote that she was asking herself, "'Is this all?' Just housework, chauffeuring children, attending PTA?" As a college graduate she felt she had "a good mind, which has become almost atrophied for lack of time to develop it." Mary Marker knew well the challenges of motherhood, but she may have been surprised at the next observation: "I think I want myself back. I want to be really an individual again, with other people thinking me worthwhile and interesting—respecting me." Yes, the woman confessed, she was beginning to understand the "empty feeling" of the "feminine mystique."[1]

A decade earlier, Marker would have straightforwardly told this mother to organize her household better in order to free up time to read or to prepare lessons to teach in Relief Society. But attitudes were shifting. Latter-day Saint women faced the same struggles at home as all women did, but by 1970 some Mormon women no longer were satisfied with advice meant to improve their housekeeping and mothering. Even if they had not read

Betty Friedan's bestselling book, they had heard about "women's lib" and its questioning of traditional gender roles. What was unique about the seventies was that the interpretative framework of feminism was being used to make sense of personal problems and to craft new solutions. Yes, there was a broken "system," but fixing it was not as simple as ripping up carpeting and putting in linoleum. Thinkers like Friedan suggested that the patriarchy circumscribed a women's identity so as to justify discriminatory practices that disadvantaged her in education, in employment, and in the home.

A year later, in 1971, Apostle Thomas S. Monson posed a question about this new framework: "The Women's Movement: Liberation or Deception?" Monson never directly answered his question, but he associated the women's movement with a host of ills: free abortions, free childcare, equal employment of men and women, the philosophy of Engels and Marx, women who refuse motherhood, pornography, crime, delinquency, and materialism. "Have such mothers become liberated?" he asked rhetorically. "Have they achieved freedom? Equality? No they have not been liberated. They have been deceived. They have lost their true identity."[2]

Feminism was not merely the latest in a series of postwar social and cultural upheavals. For Monson and the leaders of the church, feminism was a fundamental threat to the plan of salvation. The new identities that women were cultivating undermined both the divine role of womanhood and the central power of the church, the priesthood. Throughout its history, church leaders had spoken out against frivolous women who concerned themselves with fashion, preferred poodles to children, and threatened patriarchal authority. However, what was unique about the era was that the "bad" Mormon woman now had a name—she was a "feminist."

Since the forties, male and female church leaders had been unequivocal in their celebration of motherhood, to the exclusion of almost every other role for women. While pioneer women had been admired for their faithfulness and determination, their political feistiness and spiritual authority had largely been forgotten. The progressive history of the first decades of the twentieth century was ignored as postwar women were told to concentrate on home and ward life. Consequently, even though a discontented letter writer could articulate her desire to "be an individual again" and believed a job would help, she feared that "I would worry constantly about my family."[3] Latter-day Saint women looked to the women's movement to expand their world, but how they could embrace it without endangering their family and their faith was uncertain. What was clear was that their church leaders would not help them with that negotiation.

By the seventies, Latter-day Saint men and women had achieved levels of education and financial stability that brought them squarely into contact with non-Mormon ideas and culture. More and more young Saints went to college, and though women gravitated to female-dominated fields like education, home economics, and nursing, college deepened their understanding of the world and stimulated their curiosity. The dynamic exchange between students and teachers was unpredictable, even at church-run Brigham Young University. It was assumed these women would marry, but they were still interested in the critical questions posed in their classes. Most women left their professions after the babies arrived, but even a few years of working introduced them to the benefits of wage labor. By the seventies, Latter-day Saint women were not unlike those women discussed in *Feminine Mystique*.

An increasing number of their husbands were going on to graduate school outside of Utah. Such families helped build a "Mormon diaspora"—a Latter-day Saint community far away from the normative control of Salt Lake, in which men and women created close-knit relationships with fellow Saints while simultaneously exploring their scholarship. The intensity of those experiences often deepened their commitment both to Mormonism and to serious thinking. "We will never forget our experience in New England," recalled Bonnie Dalton. Born in Seattle, Dalton had met her husband at BYU. She and her young family then moved to Cambridge, Massachusetts, where her husband attended Harvard Business School. "It was broadening to [my husband] Gene scholastically," she reflected, but it was also broadening to learn "how the Church operates in the mission field in different situations than where I grew up."[4] Although the Daltons eventually moved back to Utah, their time on the East Coast gave the couple a more cosmopolitan orientation toward the world and toward their religion.

Latter-day Saints who moved to Palo Alto, California, to attend Stanford University found a shared desire to explore their faith more deeply than they typically could in their home wards. In 1966 a small group, including one woman, established the journal *Dialogue* to address current affairs from a Latter-day Saint perspective. Completely independent from the church, *Dialogue* contained essays on religion, fiction, poetry, and social criticism. In its first issue, for instance, a professor of political science and member of a stake high council wrote a piece called "The Separation of Church and State in Mormon Theory and Practice." The editors hoped that the journal would present views from multiple perspectives. However, the very fact that *Dialogue* existed outside of the official church and tackled complicated and controversial topics set it apart as liberal.

The editors of *Dialogue* published articles on the most controversial topic in church society of the time: the refusal of the church to ordain African American men to the priesthood. In 1967 Stuart Udall, then Secretary of the Interior and a practicing Mormon, directly criticized church policy in a letter published in *Dialogue*. He then released it to the national news media. "My fear is that the very character of Mormonism is being distorted and crippled," he wrote, "by adherence to a belief and practice that denies the oneness of mankind."⁵ Articles in *Dialogue* used sociology and history to argue that nothing existed in Mormon Scripture to support an all-white priesthood and that modern explanations for the ban were racist interpretations based on folklore and mid-nineteenth-century sources. As civil rights organizations and the national media intensified criticism of the church for its racial policy, Latter-day Saints learned that serious arguments could be made for inclusion that stayed within their religious borders.

Most Latter-day Saints did not subscribe to *Dialogue*, but for those who wanted deeper reflections on Mormonism the journal helped shape and consolidate understanding of difficult topics. Perhaps more importantly, reading essays in *Dialogue* alerted geographically dispersed Latter-day Saints that there were others who shared their perspectives. "Just about the time I felt that I was really going down for the count as far as the church was concerned," recalled one woman, "I became a 'Dialogue Mormon.' I started just living for what I was reading from one issue to the next of that fine new journal . . . I felt that there were people out there who were really thinking like I was."⁶ *Dialogue* created a place for those who wanted to think about, not simply to participate in, Mormonism.

On a hot July evening in 1970, Eugene England, one of the editors of *Dialogue*, was traveling on the East Coast. As he strolled on the Harvard campus with two Latter-day Saint friends, Claudia Bushman and Laurel Ulrich, the group talked about the future of the journal. Both women were members of the Cambridge Ward, a tightknit community made up mostly of Boston professionals and students who attended the area's elite universities. Bushman was married to a contributor to *Dialogue*. As the trio passed the Widener Library, she remembered blurting out that "there should be a women's issue of *Dialogue* and that we had a group who could put it together."⁷ A month earlier Bushman and Ulrich had begun meeting with other Latter-day Saint women to explore issues of concern to women. "The women's movement was much in the air at the time," remembered Ulrich. "We just wanted to see what, if anything, it had to do with us." Having heard about *Feminine Mystique* from her ward organist, Ulrich believed reading it had changed her life.⁸ *Dialogue* confronted difficult topics, but it had been silent on the women's movement. Ulrich and Bushman wanted to remedy that.

The "pink issue" of *Dialogue*—known as such because of the color of its cover and the subject of its essays—appeared in the summer of 1971. As Bushman wrote in the introduction, the women who worked on the issue were not feminist militants, and "some of us are so straight as to be shocked by their antics."[9] Most of the writing concerned the everyday lives of women struggling to manage both their homes and their interests in the outside world. Essays focused on the textures of woman's experiences, not on political issues or controversial topics. Indeed, the lead article was a lyrically written portrait of a day in the life of a mother caring for her eleven children. Even Ulrich's essay on the implications of having four children in a world concerned about overpopulation had a personal flavor. Articles reflected the new feminist attention to history from below: the unacknowledged roles that women played in society and the silence of women's voices. The one male author in the collection, Leonard Arrington, documented the history of nineteenth-century women's self-reliance, resourcefulness, intelligence, and, at times, violence. Arrington, well known in the field of historical economics, introduced readers to Mormon women who dug irrigation ditches, traveled back East to go to medical school, and held political offices—all while caring for their families. The confidence of those women diverged sharply from the candid story told in the essay by historian Juanita Brooks. While writing her best-selling book *Mountain Meadows Massacre* (1950), she hid her typewriter and pretended to iron when an unexpected visitor arrived at the door.

With honesty, humor, and insight, the issue explored the first-hand knowledge that women acquired in their own lives. Tensions and difficulties were not solved or papered over; unlike articles in church publications, they were left standing. For many women, reading about each other sparked an "ah-ha" moment when life's experiences began to make sense. *Dialogue*'s pink issue was a literary form of "consciousness raising," a technique developed by feminists to become aware of and analyze their status as women within society. This feeling was exhilarating. There was, however, one strong message that all the authors appeared committed to: Mormon women were not all alike. "We argue then for acceptance of the diversity that already exists in the life styles of Mormon women," Bushman wrote on the behalf of the *Dialogue* authors.[10] Women should be respected within the Latter-day Saint community whether they were raising eleven children, studying to become lawyers, or doing both. Commitment to the gospel and to Mormon culture could take on many different forms.

In Salt Lake City that same summer of 1970, church leaders embarked on a contrasting project. The heads of the church auxiliaries were informed that they would no longer be allowed to raise their own funds. The several million dollars in the Relief Society general fund needed to be transferred to church coffers, and future funding would come from the church via the ward's bishop.[11] Dues paying would cease, and all Latter-day Saint women would automatically be enrolled as Relief Society members. A year earlier, the Social Service Department was removed from under the control of the Relief Society and placed under the authority of the priesthood. And, in December 1970, the *Relief Society Magazine* was suspended. Church leaders decided to have only one publication for adult Latter-day Saints, to be called the *Ensign*.

Since the early twentieth century, church authorities had attempted to create an efficient Latter-day Saint organization that consolidated power, standardized doctrine, and coordinated the various programs. In the early sixties, the hierarchy reinvigorated and intensified such "correlation" activities. One result of modern correlation was to place all programs under the authority of the male members of the church (the priesthood). Multiple opinions or agendas coming from the auxiliaries were distracting. Church leaders intended to reestablish the priesthood as the center of the church, with the auxiliaries placed in a subservient relationship to it. Curriculum once written independently by the auxiliaries would now either be produced or closely reviewed by the Correlation Committee.

Female leaders were suddenly relieved of their duties. Belle S. Spafford, who had served as Relief Society president since 1945, was released in 1974. That same year, LaVern W. Parmley, who had headed the children's auxiliary since 1951, was also released. From that point onward, auxiliary presidents would never serve longer than ten years. In 1975 Primary Children's Hospital (of which Parmley had been chairman of the board) was divested; the First Presidency determined that hospitals were no longer central to the mission of the church. Women lost control over manufacturing temple clothing and garments, they rarely prepared bread for sacrament meetings or bodies for burial, and in 1968 church members were informed that only priesthood holders could give prayers in Sacrament Meetings.

Under the influence of correlation, church leaders insisted that the ward and the home were a single entity under the guidance of priesthood bearers. Consequently, there was a renewed emphasis on men as the spiritual and temporal leaders of their families. Ward activities, which previously had taken up much of members' time, were now perceived as a distraction from home life. If the home was the cornerstone of religion and the nation, then Latter-day Saint fathers needed to devote time and attention to their domestic leadership. To facilitate that goal, church leaders reinvigorated the home teaching program. Ward bishops assigned pairs of men to visit with families, working with fathers to create strong Latter-day Saint homes. From Salt Lake came newly designed instructional and support materials to encourage fathers to direct Monday night "family home evening" programs of prayer, instruction, and entertainment. When illnesses or crises arose, fathers were told to give their families blessings using consecrated oil. "My husband has made the priesthood a real vital force in our home," Bonnie

Dalton observed. "He regularly gives the children father's blessings. They have come to rely on these, to the point that when a crisis develops or something important happens they'll come and ask him before it occurs. He'll give them a blessing."[12] Church leaders required Mormon men of the seventies, even more than their fathers, to act as domestic religious leaders.

Correlation decisions were made without consulting female church leaders. Spafford accepted the new policies because she trusted the divine nature of priesthood leadership and the inevitability of change.[13] Women who saw Relief Society funding as a time-consuming burden or who were not interested in its socializing functions welcomed the new funding. "We were barely getting by," explained a California Mormon. "The Relief Society then had one less thing to be responsible for."[14] More Mormon women were working outside the home, and many felt they needed to spend more time with their children. "Our leaders are teaching us to be more frugal, more spiritual and leave off the things that are frills," explained a Utah woman. While she found the array of ward activities fun and the camaraderie priceless, "that can't be any more because our church is just too large."[15] Latter-day Saint women believed in the inspiration of their leaders. "They'll live to see the wisdom of it all," Spafford concluded, "they'll adjust to these changes. Relief Society women know how to accept priesthood-directed change."[16]

Other women, however, recognized that the end of self-funding meant a decline in Relief Society autonomy and thus of women's independence and influence. Claudia Bushman remembered how the Cambridge Ward Relief Society used its earnings to pay for an educational program for children to be held the same time as Relief Society meetings. Mothers could then attend the weekly gatherings knowing their children were enjoying themselves as well. Once funding was taken out of Relief Society hands, however, the ward's bishop informed the women that "we don't need to spend money on that."[17] In the future, Latter-day Saint women would have to negotiate with the bishop and ward council to fund their activities rather than set their own goals and budget their own money. Even Spafford recognized that the new funding model would mean the Relief Society would no longer be a place where women learned financial management.[18]

In later interviews, women reminisced about the ways they used their Relief Society bank accounts before sending the balances on to Salt Lake. One president bought her ward some new tablecloths, a good wheat grinding mill, and a catered lunch.[19] In Honolulu, Relief Society women dressed up in colorful muumuus, put hibiscus flowers behind their ears, draped their necks with shell leis, and "spent every dollar" they had earned at a fancy buffet. One woman joked that the sisters stacked their plates so high with food that she feared it would fall off, but "they ate every bite."[20]

Relief Society women followed the injunctions coming from Salt Lake, but some did so on their own terms. The promotion of Latter-day Saint sisterhood remained important to them.

From the perspective of church authorities, correlation strengthened and unified the organization, helping it prosper during a period of time when both American society and Mormonism itself were undergoing rapid change. President David O. McKay had been church prophet for almost twenty years when he died in 1970. During the next decade, three different men led the church as prophet. Correlation smoothed out any instability that might have resulted. Church expansion could have meant a greater variety in ward culture, but, with centralized funding, wards in poor countries or in less established parts of the United States could afford the same activities as those in wealthier wards. Teaching materials distributed globally asserted a common, if more simplified, Latter-day Saint culture. On any given Sunday, members from Salt Lake to Houston to Buenos Aires would be discussing the same gospel topics. Standardization of church architecture throughout the world created a common Mormon "look." Church employees drawn from the business world fashioned a recognizable "brand" that stood for clear principles. Correlation tightened the control of the church. It placed authority in fewer hands (although within a growing bureaucracy) and thereby resisted the tendency toward fragmentation during a time of growth and social change.

Mormonism's centralization and its push to reinvigorate male leadership ran against the general trend in American Christianity. The Second Vatican Council, for instance, stressed diversity over uniformity. Catholic bishops agreed to replace Latin, which had been the universal liturgical language for millennia, with "the vernacular," the multiple languages spoken by the people of a place. Catholics living in Asia or Africa developed their own styles of worship from a core liturgy. The emphasis on the full participation of the laity, coming out of Vatican II, combined with a declining number of priests and women religious reduced the power of clergy in parish life. Theologians did criticize the devotion to the saints—to which many women were committed—but in their parishes women now distributed Communion and read from the Bible to the congregation at Mass. As Catholics promoted spiritual equality between the sexes, women assumed fuller roles in the ritual life of the church. Only the priesthood remained a male preserve.

American Protestantism was also experiencing a period of decentralization. Diverse perspectives on theology, as well as varying attitudes toward race relations, the war in Vietnam, gender roles, and worship styles, heightened differences between and within Protestant denominations.

Indeed, the movement towards a postdenominational America, in which powerful ministers ran their churches independent of church bodies, intensified. As more women became ordained as ministers or assumed places as theologians and professors, they broadened perspectives on Christian history and thought. Even evangelical women, who believed that the Bible limited their authority as clergy, developed forms of biblical feminism that supported women's religious leadership. Although Americans were less concerned with theological differences, social and political divisions fueled the fragmentation of Protestantism. Religious individualism expanded as traditional forms of religious authority diminished.

In contrast, correlation was intended to strengthen the Mormon church by focusing on its core mission and tightening its organization. However, as parts of the institutional church contracted, space opened up for other Latter-day Saints—those not employed by the church—to assert their individual perspectives. Mormons, like other Americans, possessed diverse understandings of what it meant to be a Christian in the modern world. While church leaders sought to reinforce the unifying value that the priesthood stood at the center of Mormonism and to assert that there was a vital difference between men and women, it would take a Latter-day Saint woman to fully sketch out *what* that difference should look like.

Helen Andelin was not unlike the many women who wrote in to the *Deseret News* at the end of the fifties about their domestic woes. "I was," Andelin declared, "the taken-for-granted, neglected housewife who was often ignored." Raised in Arizona, she went on a mission in 1940 and then married. She followed her husband around the country while he pursued various business ventures. After years of trying to make a happy home for him and their six children, she was at her wits' end. A chance meeting with Andelin's former mission companion, Verna Johnson, changed her life. Johnson shared with Andelin eight little booklets written in 1922 called "The Secrets of Fascinating Womanhood." Reading them, Andelin recalled how "a light turned on in my mind, the precious life of truth." God had given her a special knowledge into the "celestial world" that could be partially reproduced on earth. Through the booklets, Andelin believed she had received divine insight into "the man-woman relationship."[21]

Andelin began to adopt the advice in the booklets to her own marriage and labeled the result "tremendous." Her husband became a different man: he paid attention to her and became "more loving and tender."[22] The whole family was happier. Because Andelin felt that the booklets were a gift from God meant to improve all marriages, she wanted to share her experience with other women. In 1962 she first met with a small group of women from her ward and—not unlike a Relief Society class—taught lessons in what she called "Fascinating Womanhood." The response was overwhelming and within a year, she needed to rent space at a local YMCA to accommodate all of the women who wanted to attend her workshops.

Andelin believed she had a religious mission to uplift families, and the success of her classes brought her in contact with hundreds of women, Mormon and non-Mormon alike. Soon she was training teachers in her methods and putting her ideas down in writing. After hiring full-time housekeeping help, an editor, and a printer, in 1965 Andelin and her husband self-published *Fascinating Womanhood*. Andelin always wanted her system of marital happiness to be blessed by church leaders and integrated into church education programs, but she was consistently rebuffed. Correlation had made it difficult for innovations to percolate from the bottom up. Convinced of the importance of her revelation, Andelin went on to create a successful business and influence the lives of countless women.

The demand for *Fascinating Womanhood* was extraordinary. The church-owned Deseret Book ordered batches of one thousand copies at a time. The couple packaged books on their kitchen table and shipped them out in large grocery boxes.[23] By 1975 over 450,000 women had taken Fascinating Womanhood workshops and a million copies of the book had been sold. Two hundred letters were arriving each week, many thanking Andelin for insights that saved their marriages. A copycat book, *Total Woman* (1973), written by Protestant evangelical Marabel Morgan, made the cover of *Time* magazine.

Andelin had tapped into the growing discontent of women around the country, but she wasn't riding the wave of feminism. At the very time that feminists asked women to assert their independence, reject assumptions about their childish nature, and foster a mature sexuality, Andelin developed a self-improvement program based on just the opposite. Andelin's solution to "the problem that has no name" was for women to cultivate a feminine character distinctly different from that of men and to encourage men to take up their positions as leaders in the family. And she stressed the importance of romance. Andelin maintained that if women created an environment where their husbands found them desirable, then their marriages would become satisfying and uplifting. Such satisfying marriages resulted in happy women who would create stable families. Women did not need to learn how to be better housewives; they needed to learn how to be better wives. At the same time that correlation told men to assume leadership in the church and home, Andelin explained to women how to get their husbands to do so.

Andelin's notion of womanhood took the Latter-day Saints' understanding of gender to the extreme. The church taught that God created two different sexes with complementary characteristics, but Andelin filled in the details by describing the highly distinctive ways of men and women. By divine design, men were leaders and women followers. Female competition with men upset that natural order and produced unhappiness in the family. It was thus doomed to fail. Women needed to resist the urge to work outside the home and focus their attention solely on domestic affairs. "When you work," Andelin wrote, "you rob your husband of his right to meet ordinary challenges, and to grow by these challenges. And, as you become capable, efficient, and independent, he feels less needed, and therefore less masculine. This weakens him. As you lift, he sets the bucket down."[24] Andelin asserted that if women went out to work, their men would not.

Instead, women should cultivate their adorable, childlike natures and present themselves as charming, helpless, and dependent. This did not mean that women could shirk household duties—dinner needed to be on the table and the children under control when the head of the house arrived home. It did mean that the evening's focus needed to be on him and not her. Women must praise their husbands and admire them as providers, even if they were not. The wife needed to be happy with anything her husband did: adjusting her likes to his, her hobbies to his, her pleasures to his. Wives ought to smile and be ever beautiful, and Andelin provided a well-defined picture of what this beauty entailed. Women must only wear light or bright colors and patterns. Delicate and silky fabrics would encourage "her to act more feminine in the way she walks, her gestures, the way she sits and conducts herself."[25] As a good Mormon, Andelin never departed from valuing modesty. Being feminine did not mean being overtly sexual; women were to be alluring, not lusty. Obviously, anything that looked masculine, Andelin rejected. Expressing strong opinions or displaying flashes of intelligence were unbecoming of a lady. Fascinating women were saucy, not sarcastic.

Critics derided Andelin for reducing women to the status of helpless children and turning men into easily manipulated narcissists. Fascinating Womanhood became emblematic of antifeminism. But Andelin's influence on Mormon womanhood was undeniable. Prior to 1970, writers for the *Relief Society Magazine* presented official representations of "the" Mormon woman. Even during the fifties and sixties when domesticity was the dominant theme of the magazine, articles rendered women as competent achievers. Efficiency and usefulness, values cultivated in the Progressive Era, were lauded. Likewise, stories of women's efforts organizing bazaars or baking bread for Sacrament Meetings reinforced notions of Mormon women's abilities. Pioneer women, celebrated in fiction and at church, were unique because of their very associations with manliness.

The end of *Relief Society Magazine* and the alteration of ward activities left a vacuum. There was no longer a strong women's publication to remind

Latter-day Saints of the accomplishments of their female ancestors. *Ensign* magazine had to address everyone, not just women. When the general authorities spoke to women at the semiannual conferences, their ideas needed to make sense to an increasingly global church. The idea of "the pioneer" made sense in Utah but not necessarily in Uganda. Correlation also reinforced a patriarchal system that put men in charge as authorities in the home and the church, regardless of their level of competency. Latter-day Saints were told over and over to honor and sustain the priesthood, but how exactly should that be accomplished?

Andelin provided an answer: men would only become leaders when women were not. Although the Progressive Era virtue of competent womanhood did not die, it did gain a competitor. Fascinating Womanhood urged women to be satisfied with decisions made by men. Feminine smiles would uplift male confidence and make men easier to live with. Just as the church taught, when people acted properly within the guidelines set by God, they would be blessed. Andelin could point to her own life and the lives of thousands of other women who testified that her system produced loving husbands and stable families. Fascinating Womanhood dovetailed with an increasingly powerful American advertising culture that stressed the importance of appearance. And it certainly gained energy by serving as a foil for feminist anticonsumerism. However, its greatest impact on Latter-day Saint women was in establishing a feminine style that differentiated them from men—and from women who sought to resemble men.

Andelin practiced what she preached. Although she had eight children, she kept her girlish figure and dressed in polka dots and pastels. Since being a productive housewife was not the highest value, she hired help to clean and care for her children. A commercial press reissued her self-published book, and she wrote sequels. Appearances on popular television shows and interviews with Barbara Walters and Larry King presented her as a delightful "traditional woman." Evangelical Protestants flocked to Fascinating Womanhood workshops not realizing that Andelin was a devout Mormon. Indeed, by the mid-seventies Andelin was the most famous Mormon whom no one knew was Mormon. She also handed over to her husband the task of running the financial side of Fascinating Womanhood and she listened to him, even though he had a long track record of making poor business decisions. In 1977, exhausted from extensive publicity trips and following the desire of her husband for a quieter life, the Andelins moved to a farm in Missouri where Helen, in effect, retired from public life.

One of the reasons that she retreated to the farm was her weariness with the debates over marriage and womanhood. By the mid-seventies, the women's movement was spreading. Postwar wage growth, which once had enabled millions of women to stay out of the labor market, had stalled. Inflation, high unemployment, deindustrialization, more competition from emerging foreign markets, and an energy shortage pushed women into the workplace. At the same time, antidiscrimination legislation made salaries more equitable. Better-paying jobs opened up for educated women, enabling them to support themselves without male help. Female college graduates typically looked for employment, rejecting the notion that marriage required them to stay home. Contraceptives and legal abortions allowed women to plan their pregnancies, thus giving them greater control over when, and whether, they would have children. With more women working outside of the home, media and advertising reoriented their approaches to the family. *The Mary Tyler Moore Show* (1970–77) made television history by making a never-married, independent career woman its lovable central character. Feminism was no longer a radical philosophy.

In 1974, four years after the termination of the *Relief Society Magazine* and the publication of the women's issue of *Dialogue*, Claudia Bushman, Laurel Ulrich, and several New England friends launched their own women's publication, the feminist-inflected *Exponent II*.[26] Bushman volunteered to be *Exponent II*'s first editor and gathered a collection of her friends to work on it. Following the eclectic character of Emmeline Wells's *Woman's Exponent*, the new magazine sought to bring together reflections on the social issues of the day with local news, poetry, and hints on housekeeping. Bushman insisted that the magazine be "faithful but frank" and not shrink from either feminism or Mormonism.[27] Articles explored the ways that Latter-day Saint women tried to integrate careers with family obligations. They tackled difficult topics like depression and the place of widows in church life. Through history, humor, and personal essays, *Exponent II* connected its readers to each other. Writers for *Exponent II* vigorously rejected the notion that Mormonism required distinctly separate spheres for men and women. However, they did insist that women had unique voices and talents that should not be subsumed under men—and that these capabilities and capacities had not been fully exploited. As persuasively as Andelin argued that strong women were ruining America's marriages, *Exponent II* presented the opposite case.

Beginning in the mid-seventies, Mormon women began to turn to history for examples of faithful women who had expansive roles in society. Especially in its early years, *Exponent II* reprinted excerpts from the original *Woman's Exponent*. Both Ulrich and Bushman would go on to earn graduate degrees in (respectively) history and American Studies. Ulrich's research on New England women would culminate in her Pulitzer Prize–winning *A Midwife's Tale* (1990). Bushman's edited volume *Mormon Sisters: Women in Early Utah* (1976) made the round of publishers for a year and then was turned down by church-owned Deseret Book as very good but "dangerous."[28] Bushman and her authors then decided to publish it themselves; they called their imprint Emmeline Press.

The historical essays in *Mormon Sisters* profoundly influenced many. Kristine Haglund's father gave her a copy when she was nine and she had a "visionary experience one day when reading it." The stories of the pioneer women anchored her adolescence. "I had this sense that this is who you belong to," she remembered. "I had a heritage of feisty, strong Mormon women."[29] Within the church, women's history had an influential supporter. In 1972 Leonard Arrington was appointed as church historian and named several women to his staff. History would now be used by Latter-day Saint women to legitimate their ambitions and as evidence that crossing into the male-dominated world could be fruitful and faithful.

Latter-day Saint women thus responded to feminism in a variety of ways. For some, feminism provided an insightful way of analyzing their situation, connecting with other women, and seeking empowerment. Other women also knew that home life could be debilitating, but they came up with different explanations for the problem. Andelin insisted that liberated women were the cause of marital woes and that feminism was simply making a bad situation worse; only by cultivating gender differences could families be saved. Still other women sought to remedy the "problem with no name" by continuing the Progressive Era focus on domestic efficiency promoted by contemporary advice writers like Daryl Hoole.

Initially, church leaders tacitly maintained this plurality of perspectives. Correlation had expanded church bureaucracy but streamlined its message, leaving more space for individual expression. While Andelin was unhappy that the church education department refused to sponsor Fascinating Womanhood, readers of *Exponent II* did not have to worry about the church teaching them how to color coordinate their clothes in order to achieve better marriages. The Relief Society did not have to directly respond (at least in print) to the historical fact that nineteenth-century Mormon women had practiced medicine and supported the radical wing of the women's rights movement. Women living in Japan or Ecuador could read church magazines in their own languages that were not laden with pictures of quilts or instructions on how to make glass grapes. The *Ensign* might be bland, but at least it did not overtly promote middle-class American domesticity.

The tentative peace between various proponents of Mormon womanhood was short-lived. It met its end with the national debate over the Equal Rights Amendment (ERA). The ERA was one of America's most divisive "culture wars," and Latter-day Saint leaders would, in effect, pick a side in the battle. In 1972 the ERA passed both houses of Congress. (This notion of amending the Constitution to guarantee women's legal rights was much older; it was born in 1923 as an effort by former women's suffrage supporters to counter lingering discrimination.) The amendment read simply: "Equality of rights under the law shall not be denied or abridged by the United States or by any State on account of sex." In order to be enacted, the proposed amendment would have to be ratified by three-fourths of the nation's state legislatures. By 1973 thirty states had quickly ratified the proposal, and by the end of 1974 only five more states were needed.

Feminists provided the energy behind the ERA. In its first issue, *Exponent II* laid out "What the ERA Will Mean to You." Kate Gardner explained that government legislation that addressed one sex and not the other would become unconstitutional. For instance, in Wisconsin beauticians were only permitted to cut women's hair, while male barbers faced no restrictions. An Arizona law stipulated that the state's governor, secretary of state, and treasurer all had to be men. Most of Gardner's article, however, was spent refuting what critics of the ERA argued would happen if it were ratified. Tongue in cheek, Gardner reassured her readers that the family would not be abolished or women's basic personalities changed. Fears about "horribles" like changes in rape laws or the legalization of same-sex marriage were "specious."[30]

Directly below that 1974 article was another story, hinting that other Latter-day Saints were taking those "horribles" seriously. The story reported on a talk by Jaroldeen Edwards, a featured speaker at a three-day Boston stake event. Edwards had written the lead article in the women's issue of *Dialogue* three years earlier (and now was the mother of twelve children). Edwards was typical of Latter-day Saint women who rejected feminism. She warned that Satan had disoriented women, and that unless an eternal perspective was secured, "much harm can be done." Wifehood and motherhood were intrinsic to the female body, she argued, and "there is no way of throwing off that mantle." Women had different hormones, "and, say what you will, her personality, her nature, her inner desires are going to be different because she is chemically and physically created different. And the same with a man." Latter-day Saints needed to realize that the Lord had a plan for wholeness. Edwards then went on to encourage women to have the courage to bear as many children as they were capable of having and to condemn abortion.[31]

Edwards did not explicitly reject the ERA, but Relief Society president Belle Spafford did. In July 1974, shortly before being released as Relief Society president, Spafford delivered a lengthy and sophisticated address on "The American Women's Movement" to a group of New York businessmen. Spafford drew a detailed picture of the "rise of American women" beginning in the colonial era. She placed Joseph Smith's establishment of the

Relief Society within this progressive trajectory, which included the 1848 Women's Rights Convention, women's suffrage, and the expansion of work opportunities made possible by World War II. Spafford expressed sentiments that could have easily been found in *Exponent II*: nineteenth-century Mormonism was supportive of nineteenth-century feminism.

Contemporary feminism, however, was a different matter. "Recently we have been passing through a period of upheaval," Spafford observed. "Liberal advocates" had introduced controversial views such as that monogamous marriage "is the most male-dominated institution of all," that the overproduction of babies needs to be "throttled," and that women's volunteerism needs to be replaced by paid labor. "Certain new philosophies" ran counter to the character of home and family life. With more sophistication than either Edwards or Andelin but with equal conviction, Spafford "deplore[d] the far-out views" that men and women were physically and emotionally the same. "I am not in accord," she concluded, "with those who believe that current problems and needs of women may be answered by adoption of a constitutional amendment on equal rights."[32]

An influential church leader had chosen a side. The ERA, brief as it was, symbolized "certain new philosophies" that Spafford could not countenance. Spafford, of course, failed to acknowledge the historical fact that the earlier women's rights movement was also perceived by most Americans to contravene the God-given character of family and womanhood. It, too, was socially divisive. Nevertheless, Spafford believed that the ERA would not just reduce discrimination but would usher in a much wider societal reconfiguration. Sex discrimination, she argued, could be handled by normal legislative channels. Rather than a limited legal document, Spafford understood the ERA as a referendum on the nature of men, women, and the family. It would be more than two years before Mormon feminists realized that a line had been drawn, and that they were on the wrong side of it.

In October 1974 Barbara Smith replaced Belle Spafford as president of the Relief Society, and a month later Phyllis Schlafly, the head of STOP-ERA, came to visit the new president in her Salt Lake office. A Roman Catholic, Schlafly played a key role in the antifeminist movement (and remained an outspoken traditionalist until her death in 2016). Schlafly wisely recognized the importance of the Latter-day Saints in the burgeoning alliance of conservative American religions. Smith remembered telling Schlafly that while she agreed with her position, she did not think that the church as an organization would take a stand against the ERA "because they only took a stand against moral issues."[33] Schlafly insisted that this was one of the great moral issues of the day and that passage of the ERA would be destructive to the family.

Stimulated by the visit, Smith did more research and then contacted Apostle Thomas S. Monson about her concerns. Monson informed her that he thought the church would take action against the amendment. In early December, Smith was called into the office of Apostle Gordon B. Hinckley, where she met with James E. Faust, Assistant to the Quorum of the Twelve Apostles. The men explained that if she "felt so inclined" as "leader of the women of the church" she could announce "my stand against the Equal Rights Amendment." Smith agreed, and it was arranged that she would deliver an address just before the Christmas holiday. The announcement was meant to be heard by both Mormons and Gentiles. "I've never had such an experience with lights and cameras and microphones," Smith observed.[34]

It was clear that the church wanted to make a strong statement about where it stood prior to the Utah state legislature's upcoming February 1975 vote on the ERA. Throughout the ERA debate Smith remained firmly opposed. She discussed it on national television and at Latter-day Saint events. Like Spafford, Smith believed that the ERA would rearrange fundamental structures in family life. By stressing equality rather than difference, the ERA would eliminate the requirement that a father support his family and the preferential treatment given to mothers in divorce cases. "We would find ourselves locked into a system," she explained, "that did not provide for the emotional, physical, or biological differences between the sexes." That system would in turn weaken the moral and social values that built strong people, homes, and nations. "I felt that the Equal Rights Amendment," Smith elaborated, "would give those who had deviant lifestyles and a very different way of thinking than we do as Latter-day Saints a legality to practice immorality that would be destructive to society."[35]

A line had been drawn between "us" and "them." General debate over the amendment was providing a convenient way to sort American women, who held a variety of positions and ideas, into two contrasting groups. A few weeks before the Utah legislature met, the *Deseret News* published an editorial in its "Church News" section reiterating the problems with the ERA and thus signaling to Latter-day Saints the church's position.[36] *Dialogue* remained silent on the Utah ERA vote, as did *Exponent II*. In October 1976 the First Presidency ended any confusion by issuing an official statement: they predicted that if passed, the ERA would "strike at the family, humankind's basic institution" and "stifle many God-given feminine instincts." Whatever injustices existed for women would not be remedied by the amendment. Rather, the ERA would "nullify many accumulated benefits to women in present statutes" and fail to recognize the differences between the sexes.[37] While the First Presidency did not explicitly tell the Saints which side they should be on, it was clear where the leaders of the church stood. Not surprisingly, the Mormon-dominated Utah legislature voted overwhelmingly against the amendment.

After the church made its position clear, some Mormon women took up the cause of antifeminism. Like many of her fellow Saints, Dianne Fife Kay felt that the women's movement did not share her values. Married in 1952 when she was twenty-one, Kay had given birth to four daughters—all delivered, with difficulty, via cesarean section. Her own mother had worked as an administrative assistant at a California university and "didn't like being a mother and I knew that she hated being a housewife."[38] Kay, on the other hand, cherished both. When she first held her newborn, "I realized this great love that only a mother feels for her child . . . it was indescribable, this feeling that swept over me and overcame me and made me realize that I wanted to do everything I could to raise this child and my other children to make them as happy and well-adjusted as possible." After moving with her lawyer husband to Hawaii, Kay tended to her family but also earned a master's degree in American Studies. She valued her sacrifices as well as her commitment to church and education.

By the time she was forty-seven, Kay had become active in speaking out against the ERA and in favor of right-to-life causes through her grassroots organization, Hana Pono. In a panel discussion sponsored by the Junior League of Honolulu, Kay expressed feelings shared by many Mormon women: feminism demeaned their chosen role in the family. The word "housewife," she explained to the audience, had "become a dirty word now because of the feminist movement." From her perspective, the feminist "radical revolution" asked women to abandon their responsibilities to husbands and children and seek fulfillment elsewhere. Feminists labeled "romantic love and sacred motherhood and egalitarian marriage" as "myths" and women's "unremunerated service in the home or community" as "degrading." While she and other women lived with men who "love and respect us," feminists promoted a philosophy of selfishness and "a paranoid hatred of men." Kay resented the fact that feminists portrayed those against the ERA as "unenlightened obsequious housewives, obeying our men's orders to defend their superior patriarch positions."[39] She *did* believe in rights for women, but like the Relief Society presidents, she thought those rights could be best secured through specific legislative changes.

While her willingness to speak out publicly was rare, Kay was typical of Mormon women who found deep satisfaction in domesticity, resented the arrogance of those who assumed they were the victims of men, and worried that the state was trying to impose on women "the same obligation to support the family as her husband."[40] Mormon women like her had given much to their families, their communities, and their church, but now they felt denigrated and misunderstood. They resented the notion that they needed to be "liberated." Rejecting the ERA became one way of reasserting their satisfaction with their roles as wives and mothers. Standing with their church leaders was certainly an act of religious commitment, but it also was a way of claiming that their lives already had significant meaning.

Almost a year before the First Presidency's statement, Jan Tyler, a BYU professor and administrator as well as an ERA supporter, was appointed by the governor of Utah to chair the coordinating committee for celebrating the International Women's Year (IWY). The federal government had supplied funds for states to organize meetings where women would discuss a diverse set of issues pertinent to their lives. In June 1977, attendees would vote on a slate of proposals and elect delegates to attend a national conference to be held in Houston. Tyler assembled an organizing committee made up of Mormon and non-Mormon women and went about the complicated task of choosing topics, securing speakers, and arranging space. Seemingly unperturbed by Barbara Smith's anti-ERA stance, Tyler and Kathleen Flake visited with the Relief Society president and asked her to help generate support for the upcoming summer meeting. From the perspective of the IWY organizers, the meeting was nonpartisan and would be a rare opportunity for Utah women to honestly discuss issues of concern to all women.

Organizers were naïve about how closely the IWY was associated with the ERA in the minds of church leaders. Consequently, the IWY committee was totally unprepared for the church's active undermining of the conference. Barbara Smith rejected the organizational committee's suggestion that the church produce a "fact sheet of information," but she did support sending letters from Apostle Ezra Taft Benson's office suggesting that ten representative women from each ward attend the three days of meetings. Smith felt that it was important that Latter-day Saint women attend because the ERA and abortion were being discussed, and "we needed to make sure that Utah voiced its honest opinion" about issues that "the First Presidency had spoken out against."[41] Church leaders looked the other way when Dennis Ker, a bishop from Kearns and head of Utah's "Conservative Caucus," instructed women to vote down every platform presented at the meetings.

The IWY organizers for Utah had planned for 2,000 women to attend the June meeting; 14,000 turned up at the Salt Lake convention center. Twice as many women came to Utah's meetings as attended in the far more populous state of California. Crammed into hot conference rooms, the atmosphere was tense and apprehensive. Organizers, who assumed a rational conversation would be held addressing a variety of noncontroversial issues, faced women who voted down every proposal. Opponents even vetoed propositions that would have supported traditional family activities like caring for the elderly. Conference organizers watched months of careful planning disappear into chaos and hostility. Of the fourteen delegates and five alternates chosen to attend the Houston national meeting, all but one was Mormon, and all opposed the ERA.

The Salt Lake IWY meeting was a startling eye-opener for church leaders, conservative activists, and Mormon feminists. Those opposed to the ERA and the feminism it represented became aware of the organizing potential of the Saints. Women, comfortable working together on Relief Society and ward projects, easily shifted into political organizing. With the blessing of ward leaders, they contacted people via phone trees, wrote and distributed literature, and collected contributions. Small amounts of work by many people demonstrated the power of church networks and the resonance of anti-ERA ideas. Grassroots conservative organizing by the nation's women had increasingly become important for political causes, but the authority structure of Mormonism made pursuing a singular goal more attainable. Latter-day Saint women effectively directed the agenda of other state IWY conferences and successfully pressured legislatures to vote against the ERA—even in states where their numbers were limited.

Exponent II finally addressed the brewing culture wars, albeit gingerly. Reflecting on Utah's IWY debacle, Rebecca Cornwall rhetorically asked whether Mormon women had packed the conventions "voting blindly as their leaders told them, trampling on the rights of minorities in Utah, and attempting to thwart the will of less organized majorities in other states?" She concluded that Mormon women lived in a culture of denial, failing to admit that "historically we've been denied opportunities and considered weaker, less able then men, not really adult, and that this is just as true in Mormon history as in American society."[42] Cornwall failed to admit two critical points: an essential aspect of Mormonism was to follow church leaders, and many Latter-day Saint women believed that feminists, not men, denigrated their commitments to home and family.

Three years after the Utah legislature failed to ratify the ERA, a group of Mormon women in the Washington, DC, area met together and formed Mormons for ERA.[43] Ratification of the amendment had stalled, and a few states were actually voting to rescind their previous assenting votes. The initial 1979 deadline for approval was rapidly approaching. During Senate subcommittee hearings considering a possible deadline extension to 1982, Mormons for ERA president Sonia Johnson clashed with Utah senator and Mormon Orrin G. Hatch. Although the extension passed, Johnson and Hatch had dramatically and publicly demonstrated the level of antagonism between pro- and anti-ERA Latter-day Saints. Johnson and her supporters turned away from explaining why the ERA would be good for women (since no one was listening anyway) and toward documenting how their church was involving itself in politics.

At the end of the decade, Helen Candland Stark wrote a letter not to the advice columnist of the *Deseret News* but to Spencer W. Kimball, the church president and prophet. Stark believed that she was being marginalized by her own community. "In a classic example of guilt by association," she observed, "Mormon feminists are being linked to the destruction of the family, homosexual marriages, and abortion. We are accused of rejecting family responsibility and of abandoning moral values." From Stark's perspective, an "ultra-conservative squeeze" was deliberately trying to push women like her out of the church. "Suddenly," she concluded, "many devoted Mormon women are being treated like apostates."[44]

Perhaps Stark exaggerated. Social changes in the country as well as geographical and educational differences among Latter-day Saints had produced a variety of ways to be active and faithful. And the push for unity under male leadership failed to curb this growing diversity. Some Latter-day Saints attended the antifeminist Fascinating Womanhood workshops, but others read the feminist-leaning *Exponent II*. Some mimeographed materials for anti-ERA rallies and others protested with Mormons for the ERA. Many women, busy with their families, ignored the whole controversy. Each group called on Mormon history and theology to legitimize its claims, and neither had much to say to the other. Women continued to enact sisterhood on the ward level—coming together for worship and shared welfare projects—but many held on to beliefs they did not discuss at Sacrament Meetings.

Feminist Mormons were not the only women who felt they were being excluded and misunderstood. The church leaders' decision to speak out against the ERA brought Latter-day Saints in contact with other activist religious groups. At least in the realm of burgeoning "pro-family" politics, Latter-day Saints demonstrated their ability to organize their members, thus gaining respect among evangelical Protestants and conservative Catholics. Flexing that organizational power, however, alienated Mormons from secular feminists and liberal Christians. Stake Relief Society president Eleanor Ricks Colton remembered that Bella Abzug (chair of the national IWY committee) labeled those who did not support her "subversives" and accused Mormons of trying to disrupt the Houston meeting. Colton was surprised when IWY organizers canceled planning activities so as not to listen to opposing viewpoints. In the Washington Capitol, pro-ERA supporters refused to ride in the same elevator with Colton when they saw her "Stop ERA Extension" button.[45] Once again, Mormon women were being accused by non-Mormons of being the dupes of their controlling leaders. Now, however, some of those doing the accusing were Latter-day Saints. When the ban on blacks in the priesthood ended in 1978, gender would replace race as the topic that the media just could not understand about the Mormons. Latter-day Saint women had moved into the limelight.

Sonia Johnson and Orrin Hatch's public sparring occurred in August 1978. A few months later, Elaine A. Cannon, the new Young Women president, delivered an address at the first churchwide broadcast of a meeting that included all Latter-day Saint women over the age of twelve. On one level, Cannon represented the new Mormon woman who sought to balance professional life with home life. She had been the women's page editor of the *Deseret News* while raising six children. Yet Cannon's talk echoed the traditional ways that the church dealt with what leaders understood to be destructive diversity. She first reminded women that when President Spencer Kimball addressed them, "it is as if the Lord Jesus Christ himself were addressing us." Their leader's authority was divinely mandated, and they came together as a community "under the mantle of the mouthpiece of the Lord." While individual women might be separated by cultural differences and, she joked, might even clash over how to bake bread, there did exist a set of unifying sacred traditions. "Personal opinions may vary," Cannon insisted. "Eternal principles never do. When the prophet speaks, sisters, the debate is over." Division was to end and a unified church would be restored. The Latter-day Saint commitment to family, chastity, accountability, service, proselytizing, and genealogy would bring together diverse cultures.

Cannon saved the most important unifying virtue to the last: "And, sisters, we emphatically and happily declare, 'I will be obedient! I will help strengthen others that they may be so too!' "[46] For those Mormon women who felt satisfied with their positions at home, in society, and in church, such a request would be easy to follow. For others, it would provoke wrenching decisions.

CHAPTER 7

———— •◆• ————

Bullying the Saints

When Sonia Johnson spoke to the American Psychological Association in September 1979, she directly challenged Elaine Cannon's call for obedience to the Latter-day Saint prophet. While she didn't mention Cannon by name, Johnson condemned the "male trick of enlisting women to carry out men's oppressive measures against women, hiding the identity of the real oppressors and alienating women from each other." Taking control of the Relief Society away from women had "made us bootlickers and toadies to the men of the Church and destroyed what little freedom of choice we had." Calling up the ghosts of nineteenth-century theocracy, Johnson told the story of two male BYU students, former missionaries, who had accosted some women carrying a "Mormons for ERA" banner. As they argued, the students "solemnly vowed that if the Prophet told them to go out and shoot all Black people, they would do so without hesitation." Such experiences led Johnson to conclude that the Latter-day Saints were experiencing a "mass renunciation of individual conscience." Powerful men were financially and emotionally manipulating dependent women into being obedient. A "tiny minority" of Mormons was attempting to impose their prophet's "moral directives upon all Americans."[1]

Aware of her audience, Johnson further informed the assembled psychologists that the result of this unthinking obedience was mental illness. "Their church experience," Johnson recounted, "is making them sick." Citing media reports, Johnson explained how low self-esteem and lack of fulfillment outside of the home produced high numbers of teen brides, alcohol and drug abuse, as well as an increase in divorce, depression, rape, and suicide. Even attendance at church-sponsored Relief Society and Young Women meetings was on the decline. But, according to Johnson, not all

Latter-day Saint women were sick. Anger and frustration also resulted in a "sea of smoldering women" who were "waking up and growing up." Such women were "goddesses-in-the-making." They were beginning to speak of their "Mother in Heaven" and to demand the priesthood. "The time has come," Johnson heard these women call, "for women to insist upon full religious enfranchisement."[2]

Johnson's address challenged Mormon women. Whereas her earlier testimony to the congressional subcommittee had celebrated the independence and competency of the pioneer Saints—even citing Brigham Young's appeal for women to study law and physics and not just keep house—a year later she told a different story: Mormon women were "bootlickers and toadies," terms that probably sent many running to their dictionaries.[3] Johnson echoed the writer Marilyn Warenski, who argued in *Patriarchs and Politics: The Plight of the Mormon Woman* (1978) that the historical sisterhood Latter-day Saints so treasured was built on a faulty foundation. Nineteenth-century Mormon feminism was a myth because women were only given voting rights, access to education, and nondomestic employment in order to support a male culture of polygamy.

Johnson had ratcheted up the debate over women's rights to a new level. No longer were Latter-day Saint feminists simply speaking to each other: they now addressed the nation.

By the late seventies, Johnson had ceased agonizing over the ERA and her church's involvement in politics. She understood the problem as a theological one: patriarchal Mormonism required obedience that destroyed the individual's freedom of conscience. Latter-day Saint women would only be able to regain that freedom if they embraced—indeed demanded—the spiritual powers embedded in their religion. Johnson celebrated her Mormon heritage and believed in the truth of Joseph Smith's revelations, but she also insisted that Latter-day Saint women claim the reality of a Heavenly Mother and the power of the priesthood.

Three months after her New York speech, Johnson's bishop informed her that he was convening a church court to consider whether she had committed apostasy. For a month, he shifted dates for the trial, used officious legal language, changed the nature of the charges, and set strict standards about what witnesses would be permitted to say in court.[4] Although Mormon men may have read handbooks that delineated court procedures or even served on ward or stake trials, women had no familiarity with such processes. Bishop Jeffrey H. Wills eventually determined that Johnson had broken her temple covenants in three areas: (1) her actions influenced members and nonmembers to oppose church programs; (2) she advocated diminished support of church leaders; and (3) she presented false doctrine that damaged others' spiritually.[5] Wills insisted that the hearing had nothing to do with Johnson's ERA activism.[6] Johnson believed her fate had been determined long before her questioning began.

Johnson was excommunicated shortly before Christmas, and church leaders denied her appeal. Excommunication meant that her temple sealings—ties that connected her eternally to her family—were revoked. Although she could attend Sunday services, she could not partake of the sacrament or any of the other ordinances. She could not hold church callings or attend the temple marriages of her children. At death, her grave would not be blessed by a priesthood holder.

Johnson's excommunication began two decades of struggle within the church. Women who were feminist-leaning, those who were conservative, and church leaders all sought to use cultural and religious power to establish their perspective on Mormonism as "normal." Johnson and Warenski were particularly polemical in their criticism of the church and Johnson's excommunication was severe, but the strong assertion of righteousness—almost bullying—was widespread and multidirectional. Intellectually inclined women used secular scholarship to bolster their arguments and to gain influential allies outside of the church. This orientation enabled feminist thinkers to enjoy an exceptionally creative time as they explored Latter-day Saint history and theology.

On a more theatrical level, Mormons for ERA perfected publicity stunts to get press coverage. Johnson arranged for planes to fly banners over Latter-day Saint conferences boasting "Heavenly Mother Loves the ERA."[7] After her excommunication, Johnson and several other women chained themselves to the Seattle Temple gates and even went on a protest fast.[8] In response to the excommunication, conservative Latter-day Saint women took up pen and paper and wrote colorfully critical letters to her. Meanwhile, the church sharpened its public relations program to articulate its message to the national media and counter the attacks of angry ex-Mormons and Protestant evangelicals.

In order to preserve its teaching authority, church leaders were disciplining members, blacklisting their research, and blocking their church employment. Suspicion, judgment, condemnation, and fear colored the post-ERA period. Perhaps the most innovative decade of scholarship on Mormon women's history and theology ended in a climate of fear and profound pain.

This power struggle was just one of many religious conflicts occurring throughout the world. By the eighties, flaws in theories predicting religion's continual retreat into the private sphere were readily apparent. Indeed, revitalized religious ideologies were stimulating international upheavals. From the rise of an Islamic fundamentalism, to the lobbying of the evangelical "Moral Majority," to the labors of an anticommunist Polish pope, religious people were asserting their right to shape the public sphere. Religious experiences energized and legitimized behaviors that threatened long-established secular patterns. As believers became political actors, conflict was inevitable. The media scrambled to understand the willingness of people not only to follow religious authorities but also to utilize modern technology and social theory to explain why they did so. Controversies among Latter-day Saints over individuality, obedience, and religious power had parallels across the globe.

Sonia Johnson's rise to prominence as spokeswoman for Mormon feminism was nothing short of meteoric. Only three years prior to her excommunication, she and her family had finally settled in Virginia after almost two decades of crisscrossing the globe: Utah, Samoa, Minnesota, Nigeria, California, Malawi, Korea, Malaysia. Johnson even spent a year dragging a motor home across twenty-one US states. Although she had a doctorate in education and had taught on college campuses, it was not until 1977 that her friend Hazel Rigby introduced her to feminist writings. A year later Johnson had organized Mormons for ERA. It was the banner of that organization that caught the attention of congressional staffers who eventually arranged for Johnson to testify on behalf of Mormon women at the ERA extension hearings. Her sparring with Senator Orrin Hatch captured the interest of the media.

In December 1979, a week after Johnson's excommunication letter arrived, she appeared on *The Phil Donahue Show*, a popular television interview program. Donahue's producers had invited Relief Society president Barbara Smith to speak for the church. Smith declined but suggested Beverly Campbell, another Mormon woman from Virginia. Campbell owned a public relations firm and was being groomed as a church spokeswoman in the ERA controversy. Johnson, however, refused to appear with Campbell. She later explained that because women held no power in the church it was futile to debate them.[9] The *Donahue Show* producers decided to proceed with Johnson alone. Somehow this backstory did not get conveyed to Phil Donahue, who opened the show by announcing that "no woman from the Mormon Church would appear with Mrs. Johnson."[10] In newspapers and on television, the church quickly denied the statement. Relishing the increased publicity, Donahue secured both Barbara Smith and Beverly Campbell for future shows.

The interview drew attention to the question of what it means to be "religious." When Donahue asked Johnson why she belonged to a church whose rules she did not want to obey, she raised the larger issue of who constituted the church. "Well, I think they think it is their church," she observed. "But I felt as if it was my church too, you know." The exchange cut to the heart of a debate over the nature of religion. Donahue and others in the audience assumed that faith was an individual choice based on one's agreement to a set of beliefs established by religious authorities. Johnson, however, claimed a more communal understanding: religious commitment was embedded in collective heritage and practice. For Johnson and many Latter-day Saints, Mormonism was a tightly wound, complicated network of families and customs, in addition to being an intimate experience of the divine. Church was the spirit of God moving through a group of people, in the past and in the present.

Donahue, not understanding the distinction, asked why she didn't just leave her church; his assumption was that one religion could be easily exchanged for another. After emphasizing that Mormonism was good and that her Latter-day Saint community helped make her who she was, Johnson reflected: "And I feel that you don't just run away from something that was good to you, you don't just leave it when it's in trouble. And the church is in a moral crisis right now. It's not time for people to leave it." Johnson saw her excommunication as the result not of her departure from her Mormon beliefs or heritage but from her disputing the hierarchy's involvement in politics. She felt she was being unjustly punished.

Religious communities are bound together not only through a set of beliefs but also because members accede to the power of their leaders to regulate behavior. In order to form community, leaders sometimes discipline their followers. Excommunication breaks down spiritual, familial, and social networks by removing an individual from the religious group. Church leaders have referred to excommunication procedures as "courts of love," but Johnson's autobiography told the opposite story. For her, excommunication proved that what the institution said it valued and what it *really* valued were two different things. Johnson continued to attend Latter-day Saint services for a year, but after that she began to cultivate a different spiritual community for herself. She said goodbye to the church but admitted that in many ways she was "irrevocably Mormon."[11]

Johnson rejected the popular notion that faith was a private, sentimental affair—a perspective that religious people around the world were discarding. Audience members thought that Donahue's guest should have kept her opinions to herself, but Johnson defied attempts to silence her even as she admitted that speaking publicly was dangerous. Church leaders, she asserted, were afraid of women: "And they don't understand what to do with women like me. [. . .] That's why they excommunicated me. Because I was having some political power." Mormon men put women on pedestals, but pedestals where they could not move, could not connect with other people, and could not grow. Johnson and women like her were refusing to stay on them. "Things that are usually on pedestals are statues," Johnson declared, "and statues are less than human. Right?" In front of a national audience, during a time before cable had splintered the television audience, a Mormon woman had challenged the private and limited roles of both women and religion.

Hundreds of women wrote to Johnson about their concerns.[12] In their letters, we get a glimpse of how the faithful perceived the ERA controversy as well as the impact that the controversy had on shaping women's spiritual orientations. Of those Mormons who wrote to support Johnson, many described their struggles with the church and the liberation they felt when they finally stopped attending. Janie Budd, from Huntsville, Alabama, wrote that she had battled with the male priesthood until the struggle "broke the inner coil of my very faith." She then stopped and took "a very long and hard look at myself and at the church. Oh how painful! It was one of the hardest things I have ever done—but once I did—there was no going back."[13] Letter writers stressed their disgust with organizational conformity, hypocrisy, and chauvinistic policies.[14] However, these women often noted that, even after they stopped going to church, they did not discard their distinctive Latter-day Saint beliefs. Janie Budd avoided saying, "I am no longer a Mormon."[15] Officially, these inactive Mormons were still members of the Church of Jesus Christ of Latter-day Saints. Until 1989 members could not voluntarily leave the church.[16] Only excommunication via a court procedure removed one's name from membership rolls.

Johnson's criticism of the church and her very public excommunication crystalized many women's feelings, motivating them to actively reject their previous passive membership. Johnson's troubles gave them a chance to codify their own positions on churchgoing. "I have fought for years the Patriarchal attitudes of our Church," wrote Viann Anello from California. "Any intelligent woman with any initiative does not want to be treated as second-class, mindless, or ineffective. As of this date, I am informing my Stake President that they [sic] may feel free to cancel my membership, excommunicate me, or whatever." For many women, quietly drifting away from the church no longer was sufficient; Johnson drove dissatisfied women to act. Anello and others saw their requests for excommunication as a protest against Mormon "attitudes and treatment of women everywhere."[17]

Just as some women wrote to Johnson telling of their movement out of Mormonism, conservative women sent letters stressing their commitment to Latter-day Saint principles. As with supporters, critics believed that the ERA battle had morphed into a conflict with serious spiritual dimensions. Letter writers who defended Johnson's excommunication believed that a cosmological battle was raging in which good and evil fought for the souls of the Saints, and Johnson's behavior was proof that a real devil could lure people away from God. Writing from Visalia, California, Catherine Foster explained, "When a person becomes eligible for Excommunication, they [sic] have already dismissed the Holy Ghost from their lives and have accepted Satan's ways. Otherwise, they would not flaunt such a terrible thing before the world to accomplish their own selfish purposes."[18] Although men also wrote to Johnson, the excommunication particularly energized women who imbued Mormon ideas about evil with contemporary relevancy. "You are a liar," one Utah woman wrote. "Satan is the father of lies and if he's on your team and [the] ERA's, then I'm against it."[19] Another Utah woman echoed that opinion, suggesting that Johnson was obviously "blinded by the work of the devil."[20] Critics understood Johnson's acts in theological, almost apocalyptic, terms.

Individuals intensely committed to a political or religious position often understand the world as sharply divided between good and evil. However, the language used in these antifeminist and anti-Johnson letters reflected a specifically Mormon understanding of evil. For Mormons, as for many Christians, the devil is a real character who has existed since the beginning of creation. In Latter-day Saint theology, Lucifer pridefully rebelled against God and sought to rob humans of their God-given ability to freely choose between good or evil. God "cast down" those spirits who followed the rebellious "father of all lies." Now Lucifer would be called "Satan" and would endlessly "maketh war with the saints of God" (D&C 76:29).

Consequently, when Mormon women wrote that they saw the devil behind Johnson's excommunication, they both employed and reinforced the Latter-day Saint understanding of evil. According to their interpretation, Johnson responded to the call of Satan, who was promoting his own disordered plan for humanity. Like Satan, Johnson asserted her individual will over God's. Just as Satan seduced humankind through pride and lies, so letter writers accused Johnson of glorying herself through self-promotion. "You are a phoney [sic], Mrs. Johnson," accused Eleanor Leonard. "You know it and I know it and what is really pathetic is that you are sacrificing all that is good and should be precious and you will make no mark at all—you will not even be remembered." For Leonard, once people realized Johnson was only shedding "crocodile tears," she would "be despised."[21] A victim of the fallen and rebellious Satan, Johnson rejected God, chose the path of evil, and assembled a band of wicked followers. "Too bad," Norma Geiger chided. "You could have been a 'Queen on High' now you are just ERA's martyred mascot."[22]

Johnson must be following Satan because she clearly refused to follow the Prophet. "I am very angry with what you have done," wrote a woman from Edmonds, Washington. "You are not understanding the fact that our Prophet does speak and communicate with God."[23] Writing to Johnson became a way for women to assert their continued willingness to equate the leadership of the prophet with God's plan of salvation. Through their obedience, they underscored the absolute relevance of continuing revelation to modern Mormonism. Women followed the prophet because they believed in the truths of church teachings. "Disobedience to the prophet," declared Ethel Atkins, "is the same as telling our Heavenly Father that you're not willing to obey *his* will." Atkins informed Johnson that "the sisters here in Chico III ward don't agree with you and will not back you up."[24] With a rhetorical flourish as passionate as Johnson's, Xana Hansen promised that "If President Kimball were to say that the Lord wants all of the women in the Church to wear red skirts for the rest of our lives, then I would go to the store as quickly as I could to buy the fabric to make them."[25] A virtuous Mormon woman would both sew the skirt and wear it.

Such unambiguous loyalty to the president of the church was not always the norm in Mormon history. During his lifetime, Joseph Smith had to fight to maintain his authority among the Saints. Smith's death triggered a crisis because he had presented no clear plan of succession. Fellow Saints challenged Brigham Young for presidency of the church, causing other Mormon communities to break from the "Brighamites." During the nineteenth century, those who followed Young to Utah used the appellation "the prophet" to refer specifically to Joseph Smith. Members referred to Brigham Young, or whoever was the head of the church at the time, as "the president." At times his associates even called Young "Brother Brigham." Although Young had considerable authority, it had to be negotiated with other formidable men, and everyone knew that the president was not infallible. In 1890, however, another crisis shook the church. Not everyone agreed with Wilford Woodruff's prohibition of polygamy. To assert his authority to end plural marriage, Woodruff told the Saints that "The Lord will never permit me or any other man who stands as President of this Church to lead you astray."[26] The president was an oracle, the vehicle through which God speaks.

Increasingly the presiding president became referred to as a "prophet, seer, and revelator" (D&C 21:1, 107:92). Joseph Smith was not the only prophet; every church president was a living prophet. However, it would be the charismatic David O. McKay, who served from 1951 to 1970, who secured the emotional loyalty of church members and thus imbued the office with sentimental—as well as official—power. His kind smile, patience with modern culture, and iconic white suits drew members to him as a person. A world traveler, he brought the office of the prophet to the people. Still, he adjusted Mormon racial policy only slightly and continued the general prohibition against black men holding the priesthood. Those Latter-day Saints who thought this policy wrong, yet remained in the church, reinforced the salience of obedience to the prophet.

If McKay's personality secured the people's commitments to the prophet, other church apostles transformed those emotional bonds into doctrine. Shortly after Johnson's excommunication, Ezra Taft Benson accentuated the importance of obedience in his fourteen "fundamentals" for following the prophet. At that point, Benson served as the influential President of the Quorum of the Twelve Apostles and was next in line to become church president. Benson's fourth point reiterated Woodruff's: the prophet will never lead the church astray. Benson asserted that a living prophet was more important than a dead prophet and more vital than Scripture, and that the prophet can receive revelation on both spiritual and temporal matters. In his fourteenth point, Benson warned, "the living prophet and the First Presidency—follow them and be blessed—reject them and suffer."[27]

Latter-day Saints speak of "obedience" to the prophet or "following" the prophet but not "submitting" to the prophet; submission implies a too severe loss of personal choice and agency. Consequently, women who criticized Johnson for not listening to the prophet's teaching on the ERA did not suggest that Johnson submit to male authorities. Obedience to the prophet was not generalized to husbands. Maribeth Forrey, from Salem, Oregon, chided Johnson for making "it appear that the women of the Church are imbeciles controlled by their husbands or other male 'authority' like robots. What have you been reading and hearing and learning during all these years that you have been a member of the church?"[28] Antoinette Bush, from Montgomery, Alabama, agreed: "I believe men and women are equal," she wrote, "which means that as a group we are equally intelligent, responsible, gifted and loved by God." In case Johnson did not quite understand how authority worked in the family, Bush clarified: "I am not ignorant or subservient because my husband accepts some (half) of the responsibilities which includes leadership and direction of the family, which I override if I feel [it] is not going in a spiritual direction."[29] From Utah, Shelley Brook pointed out that Mormon women were busy with Relief Society, school, and community activities. "Women who stay at home and do not work," she reminded Johnson, "do not become stagnant idiots."[30] An obedient woman was not a lesser woman.

These letter writers found Johnson's portrayal of Mormon women misguided, but they also would not have approved of Helen Andelin's portrait; there was no echo of Fascinating Womanhood in any of the letters sent to Johnson. Although critics accepted the cosmological binary of good and evil as well as the notion that women and men had different roles, they did not accept the gender asymmetry that Andelin predicted would make for happy marriages. Latter-day Saint women did not act like coy and obedient children. Hyperfemininity may have made sense to evangelical Protestant women who found power in submission, but it had less staying power in Mormon culture.

"When we speak of marriage as a partnership," President Kimball taught in 1978, "let us speak of marriage as a *full* partnership. We do not want our LDS women to be *silent* partners or *limited* partners in that eternal assignment! Please be a *contributing* and *full* partner." The genders were different, but this did not negate women's "eternal intelligence."[31] "I am not put on a pedestal," wrote Karen Leeper from Missouri. "I am an equal partner with my husband."[32] Jaine Johnson from Idaho embraced her pedestal: "Me, I'm a woman, proud of it! I think I'm special and want to be treated as so."[33] LaRayne Day, the wife of a Utah dairy farmer, agreed. She preferred doing feminine activities: "I really don't need or want the right to work side by side with my husband in the field, hauling manure or working on construction or, etc."[34] Men and women had their own unique natures.

However, it was Nancy Graham, from Albuquerque, New Mexico, who explicitly laid out the divine "separate but equal" belief held by antifeminist Mormons. "In the Celestial Kingdom," she explained, "there will be Gods and Goddesses and no matter how much a Goddess wants to become a God (of course, this would not be her desire) it would not happen." Graham then made an earthly analogy: no matter how much Johnson or even Gloria Steinem might want to baptize someone, "it would never happen." Graham asserted that gender determined sacred power. Because gender distinctions were eternal, ordinances performed by women would not be valid. Only men held the authority of the priesthood. However, Mormon antifeminists also embraced this key precept: in the secular world, when women entered the male sphere, they should expect to be treated as men would. If Johnson or Steinem or "I wanted to become a nuclear physicist (that's what our bishop is)," Graham wrote, "we should all have both the opportunity and the pay that he has."[35] For her, the cosmos was divided between the celestial and the earthly, the sacred and the secular. Men possessed sacred authority, but in the profane world they had no natural rights over women.

Some Latter-day Saint women were troubled by the divide between feminists and antifeminists. Female faculty at BYU, for instance, sought to mediate between the various factions that had arisen in the Mormon community. Toward that end, in 1976 a small group of BYU faculty women established a "Women's Conference" to explore the choices facing Mormon women. The annual conferences were built around academic papers given by BYU faculty, but they also aimed to reach a nonacademic audience. Each conference featured a keynote address often given by the wife of a prominent apostle, and students were encouraged to invite their mothers and other community members. In 1980 four thousand people came to hear Relief Society president Barbara Smith's plenary address.

Similar changes were occurring at the ward level. In 1978 bishops were informed that Scripture did not prohibit sisters from offering prayers in Sacrament Meetings or any meetings they attended, reversing a decade-long policy.[36] Then, in 1979, church president Spencer W. Kimball specifically encouraged women to educate themselves in the Scriptures. Now eighty-four years old, the frail Kimball was in the hospital, so his address was read by his wife, Camilla, and broadcast around the world. "The Role of Righteous Women" cited John Widtsoe: "the place of woman in the Church is to walk beside the man, not in front of him, nor behind him" because "in the Church there is full equality." Although there were eternal role differences, women—like men—should become "scriptorians," scholars of the Scriptures, in order to uplift themselves and others. As always, Kimball praised motherhood, but he also called on women to "sharpen the skills you have been given and use the talents with which God blessed you."[37]

Women needed to become *religious* actors. Consequently, during the eighties, the *Ensign* slowly dropped women's poetry, fiction, and household hints.[38] *Ensign* articles sought to be gender neutral and stressed that gospel principles and Mormon doctrine were equally applicable to all. Beginning in 1980, the female presidents of the Relief Society, Young Women, and Primary auxiliaries were seated on the rostrum during the twice-yearly conference meetings, and four years later Elaine Cannon addressed the full general conference session—the first time a woman had done so since 1930.[39]

In his later years, Kimball moved the church toward more inclusivity and openness. His 1978 revelation opened the priesthood to Mormon men of all races, and Kimball signaled his willingness to have women take on expanded roles. He also wanted to make sure that the Saints placed their trust in God and realized that the prophets were inspired, yet human. After Young Women president Elaine Cannon had stressed the importance of obedience to the prophet, Kimball intervened and gently asked her not to use the phrase "when the prophet speaks, the debate is over." He felt that the message could be too easily misunderstood.[40]

Kimball had a long-term connection to Cannon, and his openness to larger religious roles for women may have been stimulated by their interactions. Beginning in the early sixties, Cannon had lobbied for more religious instruction for young women. Unlike Mormon young men, who did weekly activities with the Boy Scouts and then studied the gospel during their Sunday priesthood meetings, young women pursued mostly "secular" activities during their meetings. They did not meet together on Sundays for religious instruction. As Young Women president, Cannon pressed for increased focus on spirituality and not "just doodaddie stuff." Cannon believed that young women were the spiritual equals of young men. If girls were accorded the same time to study gospel principles as boys, girls would be able to fully recognize their divine identity. Having worked closely with high-level church leaders for many years, Cannon knew how to be subtly persistent. "If I lose a round," she told an interviewer, "I don't resent it. I just assume that I didn't explain things well enough." Cannon consciously sought power by being a "proper woman," not "too masculine . . . to sound authoritarian" but also not to "look like a non-brain."[41]

Her strategy paid off. As a part of a general rearrangement of ward life in 1980, the various meetings held throughout the week were consolidated into one, three-hour Sunday block. Young women were given their own time for spiritual instruction. The Relief Society met at the same time as the priesthood.[42] Initially, Sunday Relief Society meetings continued the curriculum of spiritual living (including testimonies), "mother education," social relations, cultural refinement, and occasionally home management. However, in 1984 the homemaking lesson was moved to a monthly weekday meeting and in 1987 cultural refinement lessons were eliminated. More and more lessons were on purely spiritual topics. Finally, 1996 church leaders decided to have one set of lessons for both the women of the Relief Society and the men of the Melchizedek Priesthood. Craft making and discussions of household issues were segregated to a few special nights during the year but notably not on Sundays.[43]

The end of Tuesday afternoon Relief Society meetings and the inclusion of specific religious instruction for young women indicated an important realignment of women's religious activities. Domesticity still held symbolic power, but correlation made the curricula for men and women look similar. Church materials increasingly were silent on the intimate connection between spirituality and homemaking, which had been so heavily cultivated in the years after World War II. It would be family relationships and not the mechanics of cooking, decorating, and sewing that would preoccupy church leaders. Marriage and motherhood were critical, but the church relinquished its control over the details of Mormon domesticity. Mormon women continued to take pride in efficiently and creatively running their homes, but they also found more openings for expressing deeper thoughts on spiritual matters.

When President Kimball encouraged women to become scriptorians, he most likely meant that they should increase their devotional reading of the Bible and Book of Mormon, but the statement was also taken as support for more rigorous religious study. By the late seventies, church historian Leonard Arrington had put together a team of researchers who applied modern scholarly methods to Latter-day Saint history, including women's history. The women he recruited—Jill Mulvay Derr, Maureen Ursenbach Beecher, and Carol Cornwall Madsen—met for Wednesday lunches with other Salt Lake City friends interested in Mormon history. Their questions ranged widely: Were Marilyn Walenski's conclusions in *Patriarchs and Politics* correct? What were pioneer women doing while their men were running the wards? Was Heavenly Mother only a line in a hymn? Armed with graduate degrees and inspired by both feminism and their prophet, women researched and wrote.

In the next two decades, Latter-day Saint women eagerly explored the unique aspects of Mormonism: Heavenly Mother, embodied divinity, the positive role of Eve, women's miraculous healings and blessings, and symbolic temple rites. Using methodologies drawn from secular history, Christian theology, and literary studies, women pushed the boundaries of Mormon scholarship. Topics that male historians had ignored became the subjects of serious study. Active Saints, the women believed that their research and publications would both highlight women's unique history and deepen Mormon understanding of spiritual principles. Like the female faculty at BYU, they were convinced that scholarship could bridge the divisions between the Saints and help leaders make more informed decisions about women's roles in the church.

In 1980 Linda Wilcox, who was part of the Salt Lake coterie of historians, published a history of the concept of Heavenly Mother. Although Latter-day Saints sang about Heavenly Mother in a popular hymn, Wilcox was the first to document her history in Mormon thought. Her essay demonstrated that Heavenly Mother was a legitimate, if not a shadowy, divine entity. Wilcox concluded by noting that there had been "no encouragement" by church leaders to pray to a Heavenly Mother, "but whether one can worship or adore her without the mechanism of prayer and/or meditation is an open question."[44] Women began to reflect on her spiritual importance in their poetry.[45]

A year later, another of the Salt Lake historians published an article about the forgotten spiritual powers of women. Linda King Newell documented how, in the early church, Latter-day Saint women washed, anointed, and blessed the sick. She maintained that spiritual authority and power were cultivated in the Relief Society, making it more than a charitable organization. Joseph Smith had taught that through temple rituals women would come to possess significant spiritual power. Following Smith's death, Newell argued, church leaders slowly took away women's spiritual authority. After 1880 healing and blessing by women became increasingly rare, and by the first decades of the twentieth century only men who held the priesthood were given the authority to heal. Significant spiritual power transferred from women to men. Female historians reminded their readers of a lost past of female authority.

Going a step further, BYU instructor Margaret Merrill Toscano examined newly available archival texts from Smith's Nauvoo discourses. Trained in comparative literature, Toscano became convinced that women were joint holders of the priesthood along with men. In August 1984, she gave a lecture later published as "The Missing Rib: The Forgotten Place of Queens and Priestesses in the Establishment of Zion."[46] Going beyond Newell's summary of early Mormon writing, Toscano sought to make theological sense of Smith's religious vision for women.

Toscano saw Smith as a radical and profound religious innovator whose ideas about men and women differed starkly from those of modern church leaders. Only by taking seriously the words of the first prophet could one see the truly revolutionary nature of Mormonism. Toscano believed that Smith understood priesthood power as coming to members in stages. In addition to the Aaronic and Melchizedek priesthood orders, Toscano reported that in Nauvoo, Smith created a third or "full" priesthood level. As the highest stage, those who had received this priesthood made up a special "Quorum." On September 28, 1843, Smith was ordained president of the Quorum; his wife, Emma, was also anointed and ordained to this highest order of the priesthood. With this ordination, Emma Smith could transmit priesthood power to other elect women. Toscano understood the ritual acts of Joseph Smith as indicating that women needed the priesthood as much as men because it was a requirement for full salvation.

Smith directed the Relief Society to establish an order of priestesses, not just a female charity organization, although he failed to define what he meant by "priestess." Toscano understood Smith as intending that the Relief Society was to be "a school to prepare women for the holy order."[47] Just as men had their priesthood quorums and offices, so would women. Women's priesthood enabled them to bless and heal, and eventually, when they had attained the highest holy order, women might cast out evil forces, receive special knowledge and wisdom, hear the voice of Jehovah, and be ministered to by angels. Toscano pointed out how the original Relief Society minutes had been altered to erase Smith's intention for women to be "a kingdom of priests."[48] Men like Brigham Young were unable to accept Smith's promise of priestly equality or that women might command heavenly powers.

By returning to accounts of the early church, Toscano showed that Smith had given women authority unheard of in nineteenth-century America. However, his innovation had nothing to do with what Toscano believed to be the current managerial system of the church. Smith "saw priesthood as raw spiritual power."[49] Struggling for power in a worldly way—to be the top manager in the corporation—missed Smith's emphasis on the sacrificial love of Christ. For Toscano, the essence of priesthood was "the power of life, the power of divine love, the power that restores, unites, harmonizes and balances extremes." To enact that form of mystical energy, men and women had to jointly hold the priesthood and work together on "the leading councils of the church."[50] In a later book, Toscano argued that because the godhood is male and female, Latter-day Saint women along with men could participate in that priesthood. Like deity, the priesthood resembled the interconnection of polarities into unity.[51] A critical element of Mormonism was to bind together opposites into wholes: spiritual and material; heaven and earth; humanity and divinity; individual and community; public and private. Consequently, it only made sense that through priesthood, gendered hierarchies and differences would be reconciled and unified.

In 1984 Linda King Newell and Valeen Tippetts Avery published *Mormon Enigma*, a biography of Smith's first wife, Emma, a leader in early Mormonism. She had been all but written out of Latter-day Saint history after she refused to follow the Saints to Utah, and her son would become the prophet-president of the group of Mormons who did not recognize the authority of Brigham Young. Rather than cast her as an apostate, however, Newell and Avery presented her as a complicated historical character. A force in the Nauvoo community, Emma fully embraced her religious and social roles as the first Relief Society president. Carefully evaluating the rumors and myths surrounding the prophet's wife, Newell and Avery argued that she struggled to accept plural marriage. They did not shy away from detailing Joseph Smith's multiple marriages and his lying to Emma. Nor did they hesitate to detail the conflicts that flared among the wives. Far from being an obedient helpmeet, Emma was a force in her own right. She claimed that Joseph made her an Elect Lady with autonomous, spiritual authority. Brigham Young encountered a formidable presence in the wife of the prophet.

The book revealed to the general reading public a strong Latter-day Saint woman who was spiritually engaged yet conflicted about love and men. With their respectful and insightful portrayal of polygamy, Newell and Avery introduced to many Mormons the idea that their prophet had indeed married multiple women. It won prizes and reached a national audience. The book's first two printings sold quickly, and by 1992 it had gone through six printings, selling 30,000 copies.[52]

And yet, during the summer of 1985, the *Los Angeles Times* broke the story that authorities in Salt Lake City told the bishops in charge of Newell and Avery's wards that the authors were not to speak about Emma Smith (or any church history) at Sacrament Meetings or church-sponsored events.

Without reading the book or consulting with its authors, the bishops agreed to silence the two Latter-day Saints. The ban continued for ten months. Eventually, Newell's stake president managed to convince Salt Lake church leaders to reconsider their position, and the restriction was lifted. The public controversy spiked book sales, but it unsettled Newell and Avery.[53] People gossiped. Rumors spread that, like Sonia Johnson, they had been excommunicated. After church authorities rescinded the ban, national newspapers carried the story, but the church-owned *Deseret News* did not. A slightly disreputable air hung over the book and the women.

No one had been excommunicated, but the silencing took an emotional toll. Newell received phone calls from around the world asking whether she had been excommunicated for adultery, if not apostasy. Her husband and four children began to see the church in a different way. "It hurts so much," she recalled, knowing that even if she was no longer silenced, she was effectively blacklisted. However, when asked whether she would leave the church, she responded: "No, why would I leave? It's my church. I chose it."[54]

What had happened? In 1981, church apostle Boyd K. Packer delivered an address to church educators entitled "The Mantle Is Far, Far Greater." Perhaps the most conservative of the general authorities, Packer believed that certain intellectual activities threatened the faith of the Saints. The price of academic achievement, he stressed, was too often a loss of religious testimony. Packer did not challenge the historical accuracy of scholarship like Newell's; instead he questioned the very relevance of objective history for Latter-day Saints, especially when the outcome was not uplifting. Packer felt that average members could not understand the frailties of former church leaders and the complexities of the past. Secular history encouraged disbelief. "There is a war going on," he told the educators, "and we are engaged in it. It is the war between good and evil, and we are belligerents defending the good." To remain neutral or to attempt to engage many sides of a complicated story gave "equal time to the adversary." Consequently, church employees must "build faith, not destroy it." The church must join the struggle on the side of a carefully controlled, inspirational history.

Tensions rose. In 1980, Packer and other conservative leaders had managed to shrink the church's historical division and transfer it to BYU. Leonard Arrington was removed as head in 1982, and his proposed sixteen-volume church history was canceled (non-church presses published parts of the research). D. Michael Quinn, a young historian employed by BYU, disputed Packer's perspective on scholarship—and then found his scholarship blacklisted and his employment threatened.[55]

During the ten months that their bishops kept Newell and Avery from talking about their book at church, Spencer W. Kimball died. He had been in poor health since having brain surgery in 1981 and, at ninety, had withdrawn from actively shaping church policy. Mormons speculated that his absence provided an opportunity for conservative factions in the church to gain influence. When Ezra Taft Benson became president of the church in November 1985, those conservative voices became dominant. Gone were the overtures toward inclusiveness begun by Kimball. At eighty-six, Benson would be the last prophet born in the nineteenth century. He had been a church apostle since 1943 while simultaneously serving as Secretary of Agriculture during the Eisenhower administration. An anticommunist warrior, in the early sixties Benson had described the John Birch Society in glowing terms. Benson, like Packer, saw the church as engaged in a battle between good and evil. He warned that the world was increasing in wickedness and urged the Saints to store food to survive the "Days of Tribulation."[56]

The level of national wickedness was debatable. What was incontrovertible was that the United States was becoming more conservative. In 1980 Americans elected Ronald Reagan as president in a landslide, and Republicans won control of the Senate for the first time since the elections of 1954. Although Congress did extend the ERA ratification deadline to the end of June 1982, no other state legislature ratified the amendment and it failed to become a part of the Constitution. The debate over the ERA was over, and antifeminists claimed a victory. Grassroots conservative organizing, much of it conducted by the nation's women, ushered in a new era in American politics.

Conservative governing reinforced traditionalist impulses in religion and vice versa. The Iranian Revolution of 1979 had ousted a secular-oriented dictator and replaced him with a theocracy. In Rome, a Polish pope sought to temper what he understood to be the overly liberal tendencies of the "spirit of Vatican II" of the sixties. Even the Jesuits, known for their openness, rebuked Father William R. Callahan—who had testified on the same ERA subcommittee hearing panel as Sonia Johnson—for his agitation for women's ordination. In 1989 they expelled him from the order.[57] The Vatican stripped Hans Küng in Germany and Charles Curran in the United States of their authority to teach as Catholic theologians. Pope John Paul II banned even the *discussion* of women's ordination.[58] Evangelical Protestants organized groups like the Moral Majority and the Christian Coalition to pressure Republicans to move rightward on the political spectrum. Evangelicals believed that only through upholding the traditional family, fighting for prayer in schools, and asserting Christian beliefs could the nation be saved.

Although Latter-day Saints held many values in common with Protestant conservatives, the increasing influence of fundamentalism worked to limit mutual understanding. Many evangelicals saw Latter-day Saints not as fellow Christians but as members of a cult. The popular anti-Mormon film

The God Makers (1982) presented itself as a shocking exposé of the secret and subversive plot by Mormons to destroy the lives of misled Christians. In 1983 ex-Mormons Sandra and Jerald Tanner founded the Utah Lighthouse Ministry, which published historical materials that tried to prove the Mormon church false. Not since the antipolygamy tirades of the early twentieth century had Mormons experienced such vitriolic condemnation.

If such bullying were not enough to create an embattled feeling in church leaders, in 1985 disgruntled Latter-day Saint and master forger Mark Hofmann set off nail bombs that killed two Salt Lake City residents. Hoffman had been selling fake nineteenth-century documents that challenged the founding narratives of the church to private collectors and concerned church leaders. When it looked like his fraud had been revealed, Hoffman murdered in cold blood. Trusting the knowledge of historical experts, church authorities had purchased forty-eight worthless documents and then were ridiculed for being duped. It would not be hard to imagine that for conservatives like President Benson and Boyd Packer, their worst fears about secular history were materializing.

While never directly addressing the growing number of female historians and theologians who offered their perspectives on Mormon history and thought, Benson made it clear that the church did not appreciate their efforts. Two weeks prior to the 1987 BYU Women's Conference, Benson spoke via satellite specifically to Mormon parents. The church then published "To the Mothers in Zion" as a pamphlet and later distributed it as part of the book *Come, Listen to a Prophet's Voice* (1990). Ignoring two decades of rethinking of women's place in the modern world, Benson described a type of motherhood long praised by church leaders. "Contrary to conventional wisdom, a mother's calling is in the home, not in the marketplace," Benson insisted. "The counsel of the Church has always been for mothers to spend their full time in the home in rearing and caring for their children." The oldest of eleven, Benson urged young couples not to delay starting a family. "Have your children and have them early," he told parents. He urged them not to limit family size for "material possessions, social convenience, and so-called professional advantages." Men were to be the breadwinners, and women had every right to expect men to support them because that was the divine order. Women should only work outside the home if the situation demanded it.[59] The prophet called Mormons to be a countercultural force in American society and to reject the conventional.

When anonymous session evaluations were written for the 1987 BYU Women's Conference, attendees commented on the mixed messages coming from their church. The prophet asked women not to work outside the home, and yet the conference sessions prominently featured professional Latter-day Saint women: "It is totally frustrating to see and experience one thing but be told to do another." The conference panelists "didn't do what the prophet suggests. Why are they put up as our examples?" The Women's Conference left another attendee wondering, "should we stay home or go out and fulfill ourselves, getting advanced degrees or work?" Evaluations mentioned tensions in the sessions between working and nonworking mothers as well as between those who supported Benson's counsel and "some [who] actually thought it was wrong for him to say." One full-time homemaker commented that she was "not satisfied with the conference at all" because from her perspective all of the speakers tried to convince the audience that "it's okay to work and run a home." She speculated, "I really don't feel the prophet would be real pleased if he heard some of these classes." An exasperated conference-goer declared, "I'm tired of hearing about women and what they can accomplish outside of the home. Let's hear it for all the women that sacrifice to stay in the home! And stop glamorizing all the women who work!" Those conference-goers who worked or who were returning to school or the workplace were not sure what to think: "How do I follow the prophet," asked one woman, "and remain true to myself?"[60]

These frustrated Latter-day Saint women had a point. Who was the righteous Mormon woman? BYU was hiring young female faculty members who were upholding reproductive rights, conducting research in women's studies, and teaching about the psychology of gender from a scientific perspective. The discredited Leonard Arrington retired in 1987, and that same year his associate Maureen Ursenbach Beecher and her co-editor Lavina Fielding Anderson published *Sisters in Spirit*. Released by a secular university press, it had received funding from the National Endowment for the Humanities. *Sisters in Spirit* reprinted influential articles, including Linda Wilcox's essay on Heavenly Mother and Linda Newell's on women giving healings and blessings. It also added newly commissioned essays by historians Jill Mulvay Derr and Carol Cornwall Madsen, who had both worked in the Historical Department. Who was to be emulated, the scholars at BYU or the stay-at-home mothers praised by President Benson?

Conservatives could not tolerate a church divided. In 1989 church apostle Dallin Oaks rejected those "alternate voices" who spoke without divine authority. Like the critics of Sonia Johnson who believed she had been duped by Satan, Oaks held that alternate voices were "pursuing personal interests such as property, pride, prominence, or power." Their intent was not to deepen knowledge; rather, their "secret object" was to "deceive and devour the flock."[61] That same year, BYU declined to invite Margaret Toscano back to teach. The "Strengthening Church Members Committee," which kept files on individuals who publicly criticized the church, expanded its reach. To comply with President Benson's vision of Mormon womanhood and the concerns of some attendees, the BYU Women's Conference was redesigned to downplay scholarship by women.

Then, in 1990, without consulting either the organizers of the Women's Conference or the Relief Society, the First Presidency and Quorum of the Twelve Apostles decided that the Relief Society would cosponsor the Women's Conference. And they insisted that the tone, topics, and participants must reflect the concerns of "average" Latter-day Saint women and not academics. In 1993 the BYU Board of Trustees (while its two female members were absent) decided not to invite Laurel Thatcher Ulrich to that year's Women's Conference. Although Ulrich had won a Pulitzer Prize, Peggy Fletcher Stack, writing for the *Salt Lake Tribune*, speculated that Ulrich's role in founding the feminist magazine *Exponent II* had scuttled her chances to be invited to Provo.[62] Mormon women embraced the new orientation of the Women's Conference: attendance jumped from 6,500 in 1993 to over 20,000 in 2001.[63]

In 1991 church apostle Gordon B. Hinckley took on the question of the Heavenly Mother, citing multiple scriptural references that enjoined believers to pray to the Father in Heaven—with no mention of praying to the Mother. Indeed, Hinckley called any prayers to Heavenly Mother "misguided."[64] That same year, two weeks after the *Sunstone* symposium, the First Presidency and the Quorum of the Twelve Apostles issued a statement noting that they were "saddened" that members and individuals who held church positions participated in "recent symposia."[65] *Sunstone* was precisely the type of venue for "alternate voices" that Dallin Oaks hoped to stamp out.

"Alternate voices," however, persisted. The nineteen essays Maxine Hanks assembled in *Women and Authority* (1992) attempted to demonstrate that feminism was intrinsic to Mormonism. Janice Merrill Allred, Margaret Toscano's sister, further developed the meanings of the celestial feminine in "Toward a Mormon Theology of God the Mother," which she gave in 1992 at a *Sunstone* symposium. That same year, Jill Mulvay Derr, Janatha Russell Cannon, and Maureen Ursenbach Beecher published *Women of Covenant* with the church-owned Deseret Book Company. The volume introduced to the current generation of Latter-day Saint women the past accomplishments of the Relief Society. Here, too, were Latter-day Saint women who healed, blessed, and ran organizations—while fully supporting their church and often managing large families.

Assertions of Mormon feminism, which ranged from moderate to modest, triggered a pointed reaction. In the spring of 1993, during a talk about the benefits of correlation, Boyd K. Packer spoke of a "drift" taking place in the church. Influenced by social and political unrest, the Saints were being "caught up and led away." Three dangerous forces were to blame: the gay and lesbian rights movement, the feminist movement, and "the so-called scholars or intellectuals." Packer quoted extensively from the letters of three members who each asked for sympathy: a gay man, a scholar, and an abused woman. Packer declared no comfort be given to these members, because they rejected the plan of salvation and the commandments of God. "We face invasions of the intensity and seriousness that we have not faced before," Packer warned.[66]

A few months after Packer's talk, in September 1993, six Latter-day Saints were either excommunicated or disfellowshipped in court trials. Half of those disciplined were women: Maxine Hanks had edited *Women and Authority* and Lavina Fielding Anderson, *Sisters in Spirit.* Lynne Kanavel Whitesides had helped found the feminist-oriented Mormon Women's Forum. Of the three men whose cases were heard in church courts, one was an ultraconservative biblical scholar and one was D. Michael Quinn, the historian who had challenged Packer. The third male, Paul Toscano, was Margaret Toscano's husband. In 1995 Margaret's sister Janice was excommunicated and in 2000 so was Margaret.

Margaret Toscano remembered that she began the decade of the eighties thinking, "We can work this out. It's our church, we want it to be good and true." By the end of that decade, however, she realized that church leaders were intractably hostile to female intellectuals. What's more, even Latter-day Saint *women* had little patience for academic speculation.[67] The optimism of those who hoped to link modern scholarship to Latter-day Saint faith slowly vanished. A climate of fear prevailed among Mormon intellectuals. A chill descended on those working in Latter-day Saint institutions. The freewheeling exploration of Mormon thought and history of the past thirty years was over. Scholars had failed to bridge divisions among Latter-day Saint women or between feminists and church leaders.

Women teaching at BYU who showed any sympathy for feminism realized that they were working in a hostile environment. As with the Women's Conference, where inspirational talks replaced scholarship, during the nineties the message of the flagship Latter-day Saint university was realigned. Under pressure from conservative general authorities, voices were silenced. Some women saw their teaching contracts go unrenewed (Cecilia Konchar Farr, Gail Turley Houston). Others left BYU for more hospitable universities (Tomi-Ann Roberts, Martha S. Bradley, Martha Nibley Beck, Reba Keele). Women who continued to be employed by the church became exceedingly cautious about the areas they researched. They continued to employ scholarly methodologies, but not on Mormon topics. BYU encouraged its faculty to construct national academic profiles, and this, too, directed women to look beyond the borders of their state and religion. Scholars like Margaret Toscano and Martha Bradley moved to the University of Utah, where they worked safely on a variety of topics, including Mormonism. Signature Books, an independent press founded in 1980, published Mormon scholars and writers whose research cast them as "alternate voices."

Feminist Mormons succeeded in cultivating an enduring platform for their ideas. They had, in some ways, returned to the nineteenth century, when women's writings were published in the *Woman's Exponent*—a nationally distributed journal not funded by the church. However, the negative statements about "alternate voices" also made faithful women cautious about history and theology that did not come from church sources. Participating in the *Sunstone* symposium or reading books published by Signature Books marked one as a doubting Mormon. Likewise, a woman might pursue a professional career or work outside of the home, but it would be best not to celebrate those nonfamily achievements. In the secular world, Mormon women demanded equal pay for equal work and rejected any intimation that they were "toadies and bootlickers" in their church. But what contributions women would be encouraged to make was still an open question.

CHAPTER 8

———— • ◆ • ————

A Church of Converts

B y the early nineties, committed Latter-day Saint women had begun to seriously wonder what the church could offer them. Historians and feminist thinkers told a tale of loss: during the nineteenth century women performed powerful roles in the church, but over the twentieth century those roles were diminished. Mormon women were not taking advantage of expanding professional possibilities at the same rates as their non-Mormon counterparts. Public tensions between conservative and progressive women were tearing at the sisterhood of Saints. Even women who had little interest in feminism increasingly saw their religion as a se- ries of "don'ts." Especially in the tight Mormon communities of Utah, some women were disenchanted with the limits placed on them. The ward had become a place of unspoken hierarchies, inwardly focused and provincial. Each new excommunication or rumor about firings at BYU reminded many women of their own frustrations with the church. Gender divisions were challenging the church's ability to speak to modern Latter-day Saint women in its historical home.

But there was a countervailing force: a rededication to missions. Converts provided a counterpoint to the narrative of decline. In 1960, 90 percent of Mormons lived in the United States, mostly in the intermountain West.[1] In 1996 the church announced that more members lived outside of the United States than inside. That year 53,000 missionaries proselytized around the globe, with foreign membership growing at a rate of 6 percent versus 2 percent domestically.[2] What had happened was that in 1978, at approxi- mately the same time that Sonia Johnson was being excommunicated and the ERA was dividing Latter-day Saint women, Spencer W. Kimball lifted the ban against black men receiving the priesthood. Black couples could now secure an eternal marriage by being sealed in the temple. The church increased the number of missionaries sent to Africa and Latin America, and the Southern Hemisphere proved to be productive territory for Mormons, as it had for many other Christian denominations. In the years since 1960, the church grew from 1.7 million to 15.6 million members.[3] Of the 1.7 million individuals baptized during the first four years of the new millennium, 76 percent were adult converts.[4] Church growth primarily came not from fertile Mormon mothers but from youthful proselytizers. Even with low rates of retention, it made institutional sense to shift the focus from motherhood to missionaries.[5]

Ayanda Sidzatane's biography is not atypical. Sidzatane's grandmother raised nine children in a tiny house in a segregated township attached to Benoni, near Johannesburg, South Africa. Sidzatane's mother, the eldest daughter, became pregnant at sixteen and eventually brought two children into her mother's chaotic household. In the late eighties, when Sidzatane was four or five, two young men in white shirts and nametags began knocking on doors in the neighborhood, trying to get people to listen to their "discussions" about God's visit to an American prophet named Joseph Smith. Something about the Mormon concept of heaven appealed to the grandmother, and the elders baptized her in 1991. Sidzatane and her mother eventually followed, but her mother became inactive. Then, when Sidzatane was thirteen, her father informed her that God had called him to be a pastor of a church that required he cut off all communication with his family. Only then did Sidzatane's mother started regularly attending church with her teenage daughters.

Sidzatane's mother pulled her family out of poverty. She got an education and began working as a bank teller. Although apartheid limited her opportunities, her talent was recognized by a white supervisor and she advanced. The salary she earned enabled her to educate both her daughters and her younger siblings. She bought her own home and was strict with her children. Like many African women raised in complicated, female-dominated kin groups, Sidzatane remembers being frequently left alone. Her mother's job supported the extended family, but it also stressed and preoccupied her. Sidzatane's sister became "rebellious," spending her time partying and distracting her overworked mother even more. Sidzatane felt neglected and unloved. When her father left, she concluded that no one cared about her. As a teen she would hum a song: "Nobody likes me/ Everybody hates me/Guess I'll eat some worms."

Sidzatane was transformed by the spiritual life of Mormonism. Her developing relationship with God convinced her that someone always loved and cared about her. "Everything that I did was centered on making sure that I pleased God because I knew that he accepted me and loved me for who I was," she recalled. "He was willing to listen to me when no one else would listen to me." Sidzatane learned how to pray—to talk in an intimate way to God. "When I opened my Scriptures and read," she related, "he speaks to me and he guides me in everything that I do." For Sidzatane, at Mormonism's core was the experience of an intense and abiding relationship with God. "I knew that when I prayed," she noticed, "it felt good."

While her sister and all of her cousins fell away from ward life, Sidzatane participated in youth activities. She kept her distance from men, watching her sister and cousins have babies and then complain about their boyfriends. In 2008, at the age of twenty-one, Sidzatane went on a mission to Botswana, a neighboring African country. For eighteen months, she and a partner (a "companion") walked door to door, talking to people about God, religion, and life. All four of her companions were from the United States, and she learned much from them. She also changed her views about men. The male missionaries and the mission president who directed them all placed God first. "There are good men out there," she decided. "There are responsible men that love their families and give up two years of their lives to serve God, without deserting their family or using religion as an excuse." Marriage, as taught by the church, became a viable option for her. When she returned from her mission, she got a job working at the Missionary Training Center in Johannesburg. There, she fell in love with a returned missionary. They married in the temple, and when one of her twins died, she was cared for by the women of the Relief Society. By 2015 she would be president of the Relief Society in a racially mixed ward.[6]

Sidzatane's story resonates with others told in the Global South, what was once called the Third World. In the colonial and postcolonial worlds of Africa, Latin America, and Asia, social and religious patterns had been profoundly rearranged. Economic pressures divided communities as men moved to cities to find work, and women stayed in villages with extended kin. In South Africa, vicious racial segregation forced families apart, and poverty led to drinking, sexual abuse, and violence. Women in particular were vulnerable to the unraveling social order. They gravitated to Christian communities—Pentecostals, charismatic Catholics, Jehovah's Witnesses, Seventh-day Adventists, and indigenous churches—that fed their spiritual longings and supported their social needs. All of these communities offered intense experiences of God, often accompanied by miraculous healings. The men drawn to these churches were told to support their families, curtail their drinking, and respect their wives. Church communities in the sprawling cities of the Southern Hemisphere—and even in the urban centers of North America—offered the displaced city dweller a quasi-village setting of face-to-face relationships, mutual economic support, and opportunities for leadership.

Latter-day Saint missionaries competed for converts in the vibrant religious marketplace of the modern world. They offered much the same support as other Christian denominations. However, unlike congregations that flourished precisely because they were rooted in local customs and leadership, Latter-day Saints offered the appeal of something different. The church tied its members into a global network of Mormonism. Yes, Latter-day Saints cultivated prayer life and homegrown leadership, but in addition missionaries from many countries helped out in the ward and church leaders could distribute glossy magazines from the United States. Yes, there were women's groups that took care of the needy, but there were also satellite dishes that helped connect isolated villages to the rest of the world. The very lack of Mormon architectural or ritual diversity signaled that one belonged to an international organization, not simply a local one. The widespread reach of the church was seen as evidence of the truth of its message. A South African could go to church in Botswana with her American missionary companion and feel right at home.

Mormonism also differed from other Christian communities of the Global South in the importance it places on the leadership of a "living prophet" and the church apostles. Pentecostals have powerful pastors, but their authority typically does not extend beyond their congregations. Only the rare charismatic speaker could utilize modern media to get his message out to a wider audience. Fragmentation among Protestant churches was commonplace. While Catholics upheld the Magisterium of the pope and his bishops, the very vastness of Catholic history, bureaucracy, and culture limited the influence of the Magisterium. Latter-day Saints were much more inclined to "follow the prophet" than Catholics were the pope, and the highly centralized Mormon organization (unlike Pentecostalism) was much more responsive to the specific directions of the church president.

The impact of the living prophet on both global and domestic Mormonism cannot be underestimated. In 1995 Gordon B. Hinckley became president. Hinckley had worked in almost every media- and evangelizing-based office of the church.[7] He had been a missionary in London in the mid-thirties, developed the idea of using multilingual films for temple rituals in the early fifties, and oversaw church operations in Asia in the sixties. As church president, he promoted the building of smaller and more numerous temples around the world. Hinckley's international orientation differed from that of the inward-looking church built around apocalyptic binaries of good and evil. The defensiveness that marked the seventies and eighties was contrary to the personality of the new president. From the halls of the Church Office Building, Hinckley had experienced the unproductive divisiveness of *The God Makers*, the Mark Hoffman murders, and the excommunications of vocal Saints. Steering the church away from the Cold War conservatism of Ezra Taft Benson, Hinckley downplayed the elements of Mormonism that rooted it in the nineteenth-century past and accentuated its universal elements. He looked toward the future, and toward global Christianity.

President Hinckley wanted the Saints to be understood and liked. With little fanfare, he stopped most of the attacks on Mormon liberals (though he did permit the excommunication of Margaret Toscano). Shortly after becoming church president, he made candid comments on *60 Minutes* and *Larry King Live*, spurring media interest in this approachable, disarming, and open religious leader.[8] The 1997 Sesquicentennial festivities commemorating the first Saints to arrive in the Salt Lake Valley were highly publicized. Then in 2002 Salt Lake City hosted the Winter Olympics, and helpful Mormon volunteers personified Hinckley's friendly orientation by welcoming the world to Zion. Hinckley's administration also cultivated a new openness to academic history. A set of church employees wrote an honest depiction of the Mountain Meadows massacre, a new state-of-the-art archive/library was planned, and the church-owned Deseret Bookstore permitted the sale of an unflinching depiction of Joseph Smith. Rather than fuel controversies, Hinckley sought to defuse them. "The minute President Hinckley came in and got control over everything," BYU sociologist Marie Cornwall remembered, "everything died down."[9] Before his death in 2008 at the age of ninety-seven, Hinckley solidified Mormonism as an open, global religion.

Women in leadership also grew more attuned to the needs of an international church. In 1990 Elaine L. Jack became the first Relief Society president to be born outside of the United States. A Canadian American, she had previously served in the Young Women presidency. Jack chose Chieko N. Okazaki, a convert from Buddhism born in Hawaii to parents of Japanese descent, to be her counselor along with Aileen H. Clyde. The women traveled around the world setting up focus groups to ask women about their lives and their experiences with the Relief Society. Although they struggled to get male church leaders to listen to their findings, it was becoming increasingly clear that, if the church wanted to grow, it needed to recognize the diverse needs of women. "These weren't naysayers or complainers," recalled Clyde. "There were so many women out there who were not being addressed" and who were frustrated by being told, "you haven't got this figured out yet" or "you need to be told yet again." These women, Clyde insisted, desired to be the ideal Mormon woman but "that hadn't come about."[10] Adaptations needed to be made. In order to make—and keep—converts, church leaders needed to better understand the real lives of Latter-day Saint women.

Mormonism has always been a missionary religion. In 1837, only seven years after its establishment as a church, influential Mormons traveled to northern England to make converts among displaced textile workers. Four years before the Saints settled in Salt Lake City, missionaries traveled to French Polynesia. In 1851 more than 33,000 Saints lived in the British Isles, compared to only 12,000 living in Utah.[11] This ratio would soon change as an emigration fund brought converts to the land of Zion. Between 1852 and 1887, more than 73,000 Europeans left their homelands and settled in the American West.[12] Missionary efforts slowed in the late nineteenth century as attacks by the federal government caused financial and community instability. Then, in the early twentieth century, just as the church regained its economic footing, two global wars and the Great Depression limited the number of missionaries and religious immigrants. In 1950 the church supported barely three thousand full-time missionaries but was in the process of revitalizing domestic and foreign missionary activities. During the next two decades, church membership increased more by adult converts than by children being baptized.[13] By 1977, missionaries numbered 25,300, and they distributed materials written in twenty-three different languages.[14] Converts were told to build up Zion in their own countries, and by the late seventies global membership reached four million.[15]

Racism, however, limited Mormon proselytizing. In the nineteenth century, anti-Mormon Protestants accused the Latter-day Saints of being a mongrel race whose very beliefs physically imprinted onto their bodies the undesirable traits of "Indians," "Negroes," "Orientals," and other "heathens." One reason anti-Mormons thought this way was because early nineteenth-century Mormons were unusually receptive to African Americans, Native Americans, and Pacific Islanders. Joseph Smith—at the very least—approved of the ordination of black Saints Elijah Abel and Q. Walker Lewis.[16] This attitude did not last long. To fight the accusations against them, Latter-day Saints embraced the racial ideology of the day and declared the superiority of white men and women. Mormon leaders crafted theological explanations for why all blacks should be excluded from temple rituals and black men denied the powers of the priesthood. Members circulated the belief (not backed by the official church) that "the Negro Race has been cursed for taking a neutral position" in the great primordial battle against Lucifer.[17] In 1908 missionaries were explicitly told to avoid "proselyting among the Negro people."[18] Consequently, while Protestant and Catholic missionary work followed in the wake of colonial expansion, Latter-day Saints restricted their global outreach.

Black Saints challenged this discrimination. Jane Manning James, an African American Mormon who had traveled from Nauvoo with the Saints, persistently requested that she be accorded temple blessings as promised to her by Joseph Smith. Her requests were denied, but in 1894 church leaders allowed a special temple ceremony through which she was sealed to the Prophet as his eternal servant. Even this condescending act did not enable James to enter the temple; one of Joseph Smith's plural wives served as her proxy.[19] The idea that those of African descent were spiritually unequal to whites persisted in Mormonism and set a distinct limit to Latter-day Saint universalism.

While the church limited the religious activities of African American women, white women found a limited place in the proselytizing church. During the nineteenth and early twentieth centuries, a few women accompanied their missionary husbands to provide domestic support. However, unlike Protestants and Catholics, who permanently settled in the mission field and established institutions, Latter-day Saints expected converts to come to Utah rather than establish Mormon communities. Consequently, the church did not need women to staff foreign mission schools, orphanages, or hospitals as Protestants and Catholics did.

When Latter-day Saint women participated in mission work they did so in ways almost equal to men. In 1898 the first single women were "set apart" as missionaries, preaching but not baptizing. Up until the mid-twentieth century, missionary work was not standardized and included vigorous public proselyting. Preaching alone in parks and on the street, independent Latter-day Saint women drew attention to their message. They also demonstrated that they were not, as some Protestants portrayed them, the mindless white slaves of lecherous Mormon men. In 1919 Canadian Mildred Davies competed for the attention of bystanders with Pentecostals in California. At one point, the Pentecostals had started to play music and sing, but, Davis related, this "only seemed to spur me on. I spoke louder, and I felt, oh, so good. The crowd gathered in around me and for twenty minutes I stood before them. My prayers for help were answered; and it was only by the power of the Lord that I could say a word."[20] That year the total missionary force of almost one thousand included 136 women.[21] During the Progressive Era, women gravitated to missionary work not unlike the way they gravitated to civic service in their local communities.

Not surprisingly, the valorization of domesticity after World War II and the modernization of missionary work in the fifties and sixties caused a major shift: the mission field became an inappropriate place for women. David O. McKay, who had been in the First Presidency since 1937, was a firm believer in the global expansion of Mormonism but believed missionary work should be done by priesthood holders.[22] As the priesthood—the Lord's Army—gained more prominence in Mormon life, male missionaries embodied the heroic ideal of the righteous Saint. Men sacrificed their personal comfort and independence as they had in the military, to march with their fellow Saints toward conquering the world for Christ. Church leaders also took inspiration from American capitalism in a quest for Progressive Era efficiency that would facilitate growth. Tallying up baptisms, rather than the quality or duration of the conversion, became the goal. Standardized manuals and unified approaches were promoted.[23] Like efficient salesmen, missionaries memorized dialogues, collected statistics, taught using flannel discussion boards and flipcharts, and dressed in business attire. Rather than spontaneously preaching in the streets, they systematically knocked on doors and delivered standardized lessons. In 1974 President Spencer W. Kimball told members that just as every man was to tithe and marry in the temple, so too he expected every man to serve a two-year mission.[24] Male participation skyrocketed.

Women assumed an awkward place in this world of religious soldiers and salesmen. Since women could not baptize converts (because only men had the power of the priesthood) and accumulating baptisms was the goal, female missionaries were seen as liabilities. In 1951 the official age for a woman missionary was set at twenty-three to encourage women to concentrate on marriage, not mission. Women were to raise mission-bound sons and wait for mission-bound boyfriends, not dream of mission service for themselves. Although in 1964 the church lowered the age limit for women to twenty-one, most members still assumed that sister missionaries were women with spotty marriage prospects. As late as 1980, Amanda Holmes felt that she was rather brave to respond positively to a mission call asking her to leave South Africa and journey to England. She still remembers the joke going around at the time: "A cannibal says to his wife, 'What's for dinner tonight?' And she says, 'Sister Missionaries.' And he says, 'Oh, leftovers again!' "[25] Missionary work was a masculine activity and women were indulged but not encouraged.[26] Despite this, Latter-day Saint women felt called to serve, and in 1981 approximately 15 percent of the total missionary force was female.[27]

In 1978 Kimball surprised the Mormon community by announcing that God had revealed that there should be no more racial restrictions on full participation in the church. Latter-day Saints attributed the revelation to divine intervention, but it also was clear that the civil rights movement had shone a harsh light on Mormon racism. Ferreting out who—in the complicated racial world of countries like Brazil—was of African descent had become arduous. Anticolonial feelings in newly independent nations restricted Latter-day Saint missionary activities. For Mormonism to expand in the Southern Hemisphere the church would have to alter its racial policies. And women would become much more active in mission work.

Immediately after the revelation, missionaries were sent in larger numbers to Africa and South America. While in 1970 there were slightly over 14,000 missionaries, ten years later there were almost 30,000.[28] Proselytizing in America's urban centers also increased. African Americans joined the church, but they found that even though the priesthood ban had been lifted, racism and ignorance remained. Until recently, Saints discouraged intermarriage and stories still circulated about why blacks were inferior. In their wards, whites snubbed some black converts and made others feel uncomfortably the center of attention. Missionary work among people of color, at home and abroad, held great potential, but traditional methods of conversion were faltering.

Although the military/salesman missionary approach remains vivid in the Mormon cultural memory, by the mid-eighties social science research conducted by the church indicated that the model was inadequate. The number of converts had plateaued, with far too many of the recently baptized becoming inactive. Returned missionaries, who were supposed to take on ward leadership roles, were not doing so. To remedy this, the church began to experiment with alternatives to the memorized lessons, and in 1995 President Hinckley initiated a thorough review of the Missionary Department.[29] Leaders determined that there were too many complex programs and that "missionaries were more prone to rely on their memories than on the Spirit of the Lord."[30] Hinckley looked to his own mission experiences in the thirties for inspiration as well as to innovations in modern communications.

In 2004 a new manual, Preach My Gospel, and a revised missionary program significantly altered the style and content of proselytizing. The Missionary Department eliminated memorization and cut back on the number of lessons potential converts were taught. Teachers told missionaries to speak from their hearts. They were to internalize a set of principles, not to memorize lessons. Training instructors asked missionaries to start spontaneous conversations and conduct informal meetings in order to cultivate relationships—between themselves and others and between God and others. The needs of the potential convert, rather than the missionary, were to be placed in the forefront. "Talking, talking," summarized Ginevra Palumbo from Italy, "is what I do on mission."[31] The new model stressed mutual exchange, not conquering or selling.

Although there is no evidence that social science research on gender influenced church leaders, feminist theory helps explain why the new model played to the strengths of women. At the same time that the missionary program was being revamped, linguist Deborah Tannen published You Just Don't Understand: Men and Women in Conversation (1990). The book remained on the New York Times bestseller list for four years. The book's central insight is that men and women, because of their differing childhood experiences, use language in different ways; what sounds natural to one sex might seem awkward to the other.

Tannen's studies convinced her that through their conversations men attempted to establish competence and assert power. Men's talk was "report talk," centering on giving information and trying to fix problems. Men minimized uncertainty and overstated their abilities. The unified model of missionary work played to these strengths. Clear-cut, memorized dialogues gave the impression of certainty. Missionaries addressed vague or uncomfortable questions with prescribed responses or ignored the queries as irrelevant. The missionary knew the truth by heart, and he worked diligently to convince those who did not have the truth that he was right. With the non-Mormon in the subordinate position, the missionary was center stage. Flannel boards, flipcharts, and statistics gave the aura of science, and missionaries could compete with one another by tallying baptisms.

The style of missionary work that developed out of *Preach My Gospel* relied less on instilling religious knowledge and more on nurturing religious experience. Being open to the Spirit fostered what Deborah Tannen called "rapport talk," which seeks to make connections and establish intimacy. Women were more adept at this than men. Women maintained complex networks of friendships and kin, networks that demanded mastery of a language of closeness, support, and relationship. If making connections was the goal of conversation, differences were minimized, consensus was stressed, and humility was demonstrated. Missionaries trained using *Preach My Gospel* were asked to understand a few core principles and then to adapt the communication of those messages to the needs of the non-Mormon. Rather than stoically ringing doorbells, they were to engage in casual conversations on buses, train stations, or city parks. The new model privileged trust and closeness between missionary and investigator. Spirit-filled missionaries were empathetic, patient, selfless, and prayerful and could solve problems communally. Making a convert was not the result of the Lord speaking through one heroic missionary but of the sustained efforts of many.

With the decline of the military/salesman model, women's communication skills became more valued. Obviously not all women were masters of "rapport talk," just as there were men who were uncomfortable with being in the Army of the Lord. However, after 2005 it was clear that missionary training developed skills stereotypically associated with women: ease talking about feelings, group sharing of accomplishments, and acceptance of the relational elements of religious experiences. Then, in 2012, church leaders announced a drop in the age of missionaries—men could apply at eighteen and women at nineteen, allowing many women to take time for mission work before marriage. In 2013 half of the applications for missionary service came from women.[32] The Missionary Department also changed dress standards. The requirement that sister missionaries wear sedate business attire was eased and perky colors and knee-length dresses became acceptable.[33] The church also gave women influential roles in "Mission Leadership Councils."[34] By 2015 the missionary force grew to over 89,000.[35] A year later, when enthusiasm about the age change calmed, there were 20,000 sister missionaries among the 75,000-strong missionary force.[36] No other religion—Christian or not—comes even close to maintaining this number of full-time missionaries.[37]

The increase in the number of women spending eighteen months isolated from their families and concentrating on religious work meant a serious change in Mormon culture. Missionary work invigorated women's religious lives. Within Latter-day Saint communities, missionaries are accorded special respect because they have deepened their spirituality, broadened their knowledge, and sacrificed for a greater good. Returned sister missionaries had also made that first important convert—themselves. Increasingly, Mormon men would have to wait for their girlfriends to return from their missions, just as women waited for their boyfriends. Returned sister missionaries swapped stories of bravery and humility, just as men did. Women gained the same experience in public speaking, organization, self-confidence, and foreign languages that made Mormon men desirable in the business world. And, with the downplaying of individual achievement in "winning" converts and counting the numbers of baptisms, the fact that only the elders baptized became less significant to the mission experience. Thinking about her work in Sicily, Taylor Holiday reflected, "I feel like, at the end, it's not really us doing anything anyways . . . it's not our glory anyway. At the end of the day, it's that person's day."[38]

Contemporary missionaries are taught that, if they open themselves to the Spirit, they can teach anyone in the world to do the same. Rather than proving the truth of the faith through argument, missionaries urge the non-Mormon to feel and recognize the Spirit—to be open to the possibility of the supernatural. Reading the Scriptures, praying, and leading a virtuous life were just preparation. Potential converts would understand the truth of Mormonism only when they felt the emotional intensity of a personal revelation from God.

For many female converts, the skepticism they faced from family and friends challenged the authenticity of their religious experience. "When I started investigating the church as a teenager," recalled Belinda Moore of South Africa, "My uncle saw the Book of Mormon in our house, and he was livid with my mom for allowing the Book of Mormon and [then] me investigating this church, because of the things he had heard."[39] Vida Teye, an immigrant from Ghana living in Sicily, recalled friends telling her, "It's a cult. When you join the church, you become a rich person. They drink blood."[40] Michelle Klintworth became interested in the Latter-day Saints during a year traveling through the United States. Her concerned South African mother gave her anti-Mormon literature. "Looking back on it now," her mother reflected, "we were horrible. We didn't try to listen."[41] While men also faced hostility when they converted, friends and families feared that women were more vulnerable to being lured into a sexist religion that would rob them of their independence and intelligence.

In addition, parents often expected women to carry on the religious traditions—or lack thereof—of their families. A California convert faced censure from her Japanese American parents who "did not maintain a religious identity." "If you are going to join a church, why don't you join something normal?" they asked her.[42] As potential mothers and nurturers of communal values, daughters were believed to be more reliable cultural transmitters then sons. Families feared that if women converted to Mormonism it might break up families and communities. African American convert Mary Sturlaugson's own brother asked her if she wanted to be a "rotten traitor to my race."[43] It made little difference whether women came from families and communities that belonged to one religion, had experimented with many, or abjured them all: conversion caused ruptures in families.

Contending with these anti-Mormon attitudes helped steel some women for life in their wards. Detra Bennett was a Jew and a liberal—she worked in the Clinton administration—before she converted. While she was willing to change her religion, she did not want to change her politics. The climate of the ward, she told an interviewer, did not support either her political or religious sensibilities. "It's not fun going to church and not feeling the Spirit," she regretted. "The Spirit goes right out of the room. It's *sucked* out of the room." Still, she persisted in attending each Sunday. "I'm going to take the attitude that they're not going to hijack my religion," she asserted, "because it took a lot of work to become a member of this church and I just don't want to give up on it so easily. And I think maybe they don't have the *right* to hijack my religion."[44] Women who fought to become Mormons had to overlook the limitations of the ward in order for the deeper dimensions of their faith to flourish.

Convert women are well aware of Mormon feminine stereotypes. Amanda Holmes recounted how, as a young South African missionary, her American companion told her that those born in Utah were "chosen," most likely because their spirits had been more virtuous in preexistence. Africans, even white South Africans, were considered less "valiant." Holmes—now a professional marriage counselor who deals with Latter-day Saint women who had been raped or are victims of domestic abuse—drew a sharp division between South African Mormon women and the imaginary Utah ideal. African women have "centering principles" but otherwise cannot be easily pigeonholed. Holmes positively contrasted those Saints with the "Wasatch Front" Mormon who

> has a number of children, bakes her own bread, sews her own clothes, cleans her own house. She sells Avon makeup out the boot of her car, she goes to all of her meetings, her hair is always perfectly combed and brushed, her makeup is all on, and she has a wonderful meal all prepared, and if she is asked to bring a plate of treats [dessert], they are always home baked.[45]

Not raised with longstanding pioneer traditions or by model Mormon mothers, convert women celebrated their diverse lifestyles and poked fun at Mormon caricatures. They validated their righteousness not by their domesticity but by their steadfastness.

For women like Michele Stitt, an American who has lived in South Africa and Switzerland, being a Mormon abroad was both challenging and rewarding. "There [in an imagined Zion]," she explained, "it is not a problem because you don't stand out. But here [in South Africa] you stand out. You've got to fight for your beliefs, you've got to be committed to everything that you stand for."[46] Being different could be taxing, but Mormons who lived abroad gained from experiencing multiple cultures. The Mormon feminine stereotype had less power over women's lives.

Convert experiences highlight the perfectionism in which some Mormon women feel trapped. Jutta Baum Busche joined the church with her husband in 1958 and served as the first matron of the Frankfurt Temple in Germany. When church leaders appointed her husband to the First Quorum of the Seventy, the couple moved to Salt Lake City. In 1990 she gave a talk at the BYU Women's Conference about the difficulty of living in Utah. Intimidated by the perfection of the women around her, she felt guilty when "I didn't run every morning, bake all my own bread, sew my own clothes, or go to the university." Busche felt like a failure because she could not fit in and feared that others would not approve of her. What she passed on to women at the conference was not that she worked harder at excelling but rather that "I should be myself." Converts could critique Mormon culture because they came from outside it. "I had to learn not to worry about the behavior of others and their code of rules," Busche admitted. "I had to learn to overcome my anxious feeling," by setting aside ideas about conforming and measuring up.[47]

Converts do not compare themselves against a Mormon domestic ideal because they were not raised with that ideal. Rather, they looked at their lives—especially their religious lives—before and after their conversion. They positioned their new religion in contrast to their old. For instance, both Protestant and Catholic charismatic groups stress Bible reading, but convert women in South Africa argued that it was Mormonism that motivated them to cultivate an intimate relationship with God's word. Their new church not only brought them closer to the Scriptures but also enabled them to have their *own* Bibles. Aurah Agyare Dwomoh, who was raised in a Pentecostal church, recalled that "in the Full Gospel, only the preacher had the Bible and he would read it to them. At home growing up my mom had a Bible and all of us had to share it. My dad was the only one who read it [aloud]. But with the LDS you had access to your own set of Scriptures, you could read it on your own."[48] Mormon missionaries urged potential converts to open themselves to the Holy Ghost by reading the Scriptures. In addition, the sophisticated publishing operations and distribution networks of the Latter-day Saints enabled them to place books and magazines in the hands of every potential convert, even children. In developing countries, where not everyone is literate, owning books is often precious. Having and reading one's own Scriptures was a sign of spiritual maturity for the individual as well as of institutional strength. Women in particular benefited because a proliferation of reading materials ensured that they did not have to compete with men for ownership of books.

Irene Tschabala, who worked as a housekeeper in a Johannesburg home and also had experiences with many Protestant communities, believed that it was only the Mormons who really took the Bible seriously. Other groups merely had powerful preachers who told members what to do: "You don't need to read the Scriptures because there isn't anything you can do with the knowledge of those Scriptures. You can't preach." Tschabala stressed the Latter-day Saint connection between religious reading and personal revelation: "Here, you need to learn and grow spiritually. You need to search for yourself, what is it that Heavenly Father wants me to do. What has he given me to do what he wants me to do."[49] Converts were taught to look to the Scriptures for answers to their questions about life.

Comments about women "preaching" must be understood within the context of Mormon "intellectual rituals."[50] A Mormon religious service is called a "meeting," partially for historical reasons but also because much of what takes place is communal discussion about religious matters. Relief Society, Priesthood, and Sunday School meetings all entail a "teacher" facilitating a conversation about a weekly topic chosen from Salt Lake City. Even Sacrament Meetings, which have a more conventional worship structure, are dominated by unscripted prayers that members stand and deliver. During a monthly "testimony meeting," members attest to God's role in their lives and the truth of Mormonism. Women teach and speak at all of these meetings. They are expected to read from texts, formulate ideas, and vocalize their thoughts in a setting that looks like a classroom. The discussions can sound predictable and formulaic, but for many women the content of what is said is less important than the fact that they have said it. While men can dominate the conversations and more articulate women overshadow the less skilled, a good teacher will ensure that multiple voices are heard.

Irene Tschabala also thought of Latter-day Saint women as "preachers" because women are "set apart" for leadership positions within the ward. No convert is permitted to attend services for long without having a "calling" within the congregation. She does not volunteer—she is chosen. Winnie Sixishe, a black South African who currently attends a majority white ward, has held multiple callings since her conversion in 1991. She has been Relief Society president, a teacher in the adult Sunday School, president of the Young Women's organization, both a Seminary (high school level) and Institute (college level) instructor, a translator of Scriptures, and a ward missionary. Now that she and her husband are retired, they volunteer in the Johannesburg Temple.[51] Converts are frequently first in charge of children in Primary (Sunday School), but because of the needs of their branches and small wards they quickly move into other leadership positions. When Belinda Moore converted in 1992, her first calling was as an assistant secretary in the Relief Society; all she did was send out birthday cards. Raised in a white Afrikaans-speaking family, she took on increasingly more responsibility in her multiracial ward, going on a mission at the age of twenty-five and later becoming Relief Society president.[52] In newly established wards, where social structures are not entrenched, women have greater access to responsibility and eventually authority.

As a Relief Society president, Belinda Moore helped shy women to take on more visible roles. Callings are expected to push women beyond their "comfort zones" so that they can develop new skills. "All my life, since I've been at school, I've been a shy person and not been able to stand in front of people," disclosed Tessa Brown. A member of the South African "colored" community of mixed racial heritage, she believed her reticence "has changed since I've joined the church." She told me how Relief Society callings that required her to teach lessons helped her feel confident. The Latter-day Saint integration of religion with everyday life showed her how to set goals, manage time, and stick to a budget, "all the things you want to do but you never have the skills to do it."[53] In discussions during Sunday School, where adult men are present as well, women are expected to voice their thoughts. At first they might simply read printed materials aloud, but as they grow more secure, they express their own ideas. This becomes especially important in the racially mixed wards of South Africa, where nonwhite women learn to feel empowered enough to speak and white women secure enough to listen.

Mormon meetings, unlike the services of Pentecostal Protestants and charismatic Catholics, are restrained. Sociologists have documented that Christian growth in the Southern Hemisphere and in urban America often occurs in denominations where praying is enthusiastic, singing is vigorous, and miraculous healing is commonplace. Mormon worship, however, has no such theatrical elements. Speaking in tongues was an aspect of nineteenth-century worship, but contemporary Saints now understand that particular gift of the Holy Ghost as providing missionaries with their unusual ability to learn foreign languages. Revelatory experience comes not in "fire or wind" but in a "still small voice" (I Kings 19:11–12). Latter-day Saints tear up when they tell stories about the divine in their lives, but they do not shout and dance. Since the administration of David O. McKay, Mormon worship has stressed the serene and the tranquil. Emotion is present but controlled. Converts who embrace the quiet character of the Latter-day Saints, like South African Thandeka Diamini, have little patience with "happy clappy churches." "People are just going crazy, singing and praying at the top of their lungs," she reported. "You can't even hear the person next to you." Diamini came to appreciate the understated ways of Mormons, seeing other churches not as Spirit-filled but "just noisy."[54]

A bland worship style might be unattractive to those used to praising the Lord "with timbrel and dance" (Psalm 150:4), but its very nondescript character works well for a global church where converts come from a tangle of cultures. Wen Wu was born in mainland China to parents convinced of the truth of communist atheism. As a young woman, she went to France to study business and languages at the University of Aix-en-Provence. Drawn to a table stacked high with copies of the Book of Mormon, she learned that the missionaries offered free English courses. African and Chinese students joined the classes to improve their English. After several weeks of classes, she told one of the sister missionaries that "you must have magic power because after I met you, I felt so happy." Wu had also gone to Catholic and Jehovah's Witness services in France, but "I didn't feel anything." Eventually she and several other foreigners from her class ("one guy from Martinique, his friend, many Chinese people") were baptized.[55] Then, Wu fell in love with another foreign student studying at the university—a Latter-day Saint Italian. The couple married in the Swiss temple, moved to Sicily, had two children, and used English as their common, home language.

The worship style of Sacrament Meetings—which vacillate between silence, unscripted prayer, and a few rudimentary hymns—makes sense in a world where members negotiate multiple identities. In the modern world, where one person might participate in or appropriate many different cultures, the church's refutation of the local is not merely an outgrowth of American imperialism. Contemporary Mormonism is a transnational faith through which cultural markers are kept to a minimum and members are expected to embrace "Gospel Culture." Mormons argue that Gospel Culture is the essence of Christianity, but it also is a set of approved images, languages, gestures, and performances that make up transnational Mormon culture. Transnational Mormonism originates in the intermountain West but has evolved to the point that members see it as "Mormon," not "American." Common principles and specific cultural markers enable American missionaries to feel comfortable serving at the Johannesburg Missionary Training Center, a Swedish elder to function competently in his mission in Soweto, and a South African sister missionary to know how to behave on Temple Square in Salt Lake City.

Defining Gospel Culture, however, entails constant negotiation between church leaders and members. In South Africa, Latter-day Saints struggle to accept the pronouncements of authorities in Salt Lake concerning their complicated marriage customs. Women in particular are caught between their loyalty to inspired leadership and how their extended kin networks define what it means to be a legitimate "wife." In many African tribal communities, before marriage comes a complicated process of gift exchange between families called *lobola*. The payment of *lobola* is what accords a woman the powers and respect of being a wife. Without it, Thandeka Diamini explains, families "will not recognize you, period. You'll be, like, a girlfriend and they'll make you feel that way."[56] The exchange formalizes relationships between families, but it also symbolically reflects how well a husband will be able to support his wife. Many South African Latter-day Saints believe that for generations, this tradition promoted strong values, respect, and family unity. However, greed has corrupted those who practice the tradition. As industrial capitalism came to overshadow agricultural life, the focus was increasingly on the sum involved. A male-dominated cash economy replaced a female-dominated barter economy. Frequently it is the individual groom, not the family, who has to earn the money before the couple can marry. Delays can lead the couple to cohabitate and have children before marriage. Or, the newly married couple takes on debt or goes without funds for schooling.

In the fall of 2010, Apostle Dallin Oaks delivered a talk that was broadcast to all the Mormon churches in Africa. He commended Africans for their commitment to family and their upholding of high standards of modesty. He also told African men that the custom of letting their wives do all the work at home while the husband rested "is not pleasing to the Lord." However, it was his comments on what he called a "bride price" that ended any speculation about where it fit into Gospel Culture. "Priesthood leaders should teach parents to discontinue this practice," he taught, "and young people should follow the Lord's pattern of marriage in the holy temple without waiting for the payment of a bride price."[57] Oaks held a naïve colonial understanding of this tradition: he saw it as men buying women and ignored its larger, positive ramifications. As with other entrenched cultural practices, like wine drinking in Italy or smoking in China, *lobola* was condemned as going against Gospel Culture. Black South African Saints were disappointed that Oaks did not try to see the deeper meaning of their tradition.

On the face of it, ending *lobola* should have been easy: men would save money and wedding preparations would be less complicated. However, for many Latter-day Saint women, ending *lobola* placed them in the awkward position of not actually being married. Without *lobola*, the status of being a wife would not be recognized by non-Mormon family members. Ayanda Sidzatane married for time and eternity in the temple, without *lobola*. However, when the newlyweds went to visit Sidzatane's husband's family in another city, the female relatives refused to let her help in the kitchen. The relatives had been excluded from the marriage ceremony, and without *lobola* Sidzatane did not merit the respect of a wife. How could she perform her wifely duties? In the future, Sidzatane and her husband would have to carve out a new place for themselves within the complicated relationship network of their extended families.

Women understood the criticism of *lobola* within the wider context of Mormon family practices, practices of which they greatly approved. As hinted in Oaks's chiding of lazy men, Latter-day Saint leaders promoted Western ideas of romantic love and companionate marriage. A husband and wife who had open communication and who shared domestic responsibilities produced strong families. Men were to financially *and* emotionally support their wives. "Our men are held responsible for their activities," clarified Tessa Brown. "They are head of the house. They need to work. They need to be responsible. They need to be there for their families."[58] Since Latter-day Saint gender roles were not as sharply divided as in other African religions, Mormon wives could expect the help of husbands. "We'll clean together, we'll bathe the baby," recounted a Botswanan wife. "We do everything together. Even yesterday, he was busy with the car, and I just came and helped."[59] In many African churches, men and women sit in separate areas, but Aurah Dwomoh preferred the Mormon churches, where it was common for a man to sit next to his wife, "with his arm around [her shoulder]."[60] In a culture defined by apartheid, where households were broken up and men often went months without seeing their families, male involvement was cherished. Mormon women felt that their religion made their lives easier.

Even in more egalitarian Europe, Latter-day Saint women felt the same way. When she moved to Sicily, Wen Wu noticed that Italian men rarely helped around the house. She remembered, however, a talk given by a stake president encouraging men to help their wives at home. He told a story of how he himself would come home tired after work, plop down on the couch, and watch television. His wife could not stand this behavior, so she talked to him and "he started to change. He started to help his wife to do several things at home."[61] Ideas about healthy family relationships that originated in Salt Lake City challenged local standards of masculinity. Women felt supported by their church in their efforts to engage their husbands not only in childrearing but in housework.

For Italian Katia Coda, it was as a missionary that she learned how to successfully manage a marriage. After eighteen months of working with companions from different cultures, she felt well prepared for a husband. She believed missionary work, like marriage, required flexibility, orientation toward a common goal, patience, and good communication skills. Both a marriage and a mission are founded on love and spiritual principles, Coda decided. From her mission experience, she learned that "we have to change, not the world around us."[62] Erica Rossi, who saw the struggles her Italian parents faced, wanted to make sure she married a man who had served a mission with honor as she had. He would know how to strive effectively with his partner to secure the family's welfare. "So, I'm really selective in that," she insisted. "I want this and I will work for this, because I don't want the kind of life that [my parents] lived."[63] For many converts who struggled growing up, the Mormon emphasis on family provided useful strategies for improving home life.

When Rossi finishes her mission and eventually marries, she hopes, she will not have to work outside of her home. She aspires to a home unlike the one she grew up in, where her mother worked full time and was often exhausted. "I want to be the kind of mom that can help her children. I want to take care of them, because these days are really hard," she clarified. "So, I want to teach them and be their teacher, their first teacher. I just feel that so strongly."[64] Rossi did not embrace the Mormon cultural stereotype, but she did value the church's support of motherhood.

For most of the world's women, however, wage work is a necessity. Outside of the affluent West, women work at hard, boring, insecure, and often dangerous jobs. They might prefer to stay at home, but they cannot—they work not only for themselves and their children, but also for their extended families. With less education and fewer resources to call upon than men, women are more vulnerable to employment fluctuations, wage discrimination, and sexual harassment. Mormon converts are often young and bring children with them into the faith. While they, too, dream of being supported by a priesthood holder, the reality is that they often look to the church to help them provide for their families. Mariagrazia Zummo's ward in Palermo, Italy, has a self-reliance program, of which women take advantage. A female friend's calling is as an "employment specialist" who helps unemployed women network and those with modest jobs maintain a positive attitude toward working.[65] The goal is to see that all work—even if it is menial—has value. Given Italy's high unemployment rate, it is a challenge to find the sisters jobs. However, Latter-day Saint candidates can attest to potential employers that they do not drink, smoke, or take drugs. Those women who have positions in the ward can keep an eye out for openings for others. If anything, convert women see the ward as facilitating their ability to work rather than making them feel guilty for doing so.

As with many Christian communities, wards are like a village where people develop friendships and networks. This is especially important when migrants move from country to city and from country to country. For women, church life provides a safe and supportive environment. Latter-day Saint women connect with others through weekly church services, and women are expected to fulfill their callings, as well as participate in an array of youth conferences, charitable activities, and stake events. Wards tap into traditional notions—once common in Europe as well as in Africa—that the self is realized through connection with others. One knows who one is only in relationship with family, friends, and neighbors. It is that network of relationships that can be called upon to provide care and employment. Individual spirituality is undergirded by communal values.

Of course, the close-knit character of the ward has downsides. Tight communities can be sources of gossip, backbiting, and rigid social hierarchies. In Latter-day Saint wards in Europe and in American cities, converts often come from Africa, Asia, and Latin America. Their multiple languages and cultures provide challenges for the more established Saints, even if they want to welcome the new converts. Newcomers, who have not yet built up alternative social systems, can easily slip into old ways and inactivity. Especially in Europe and America, differences in race, class, language, and ethnicity strain wards. As a missionary in Sweden, American Sydney Dawson found much of her time was taken up trying to convince the more introverted native-born Swedes to socialize with the more extroverted foreign converts. She organized "fellowship activities," like talent shows and barbeques. "If they have one friend who's active in the ward," she observed, "they'll stay [in the ward] . . . if every person had one buddy, then they felt welcome."[66] Especially in small wards and branches, the constant influx of missionaries can positively disrupt entrenched ward habits and open members up to the wider world of Mormonism. The local is enriched by the global.

Sylvia Cabus emigrated from the Philippines to the United States with her family when she was two. She grew up in Southern California, attending all-girls Catholic schools but not feeling very religious. After college, she joined the Peace Corps and then developed a career that took her outside of the United States. By her mid-twenties, she surprised her family by converting to Mormonism and then marrying a Muslim. Cabus settled near Washington, DC, and in 2011 would proudly tell an interviewer that she thought it was a "mark of confidence that I am a Relief Society teacher because I wouldn't give myself that calling. I wouldn't give myself the platform one Sunday a month to espouse my feminist views, but somehow I still have that calling and people seem comfortable with where I'm coming from." She was on the editorial board of *Exponent II*, was a faithful reader of the blog *Feminist Mormon Housewives*, and always located people in her ward who "I could commiserate with or talk things through and be really honest about my feelings." She expects that continuing revelation, since it is a basic church principle, will enable the church to embrace a variety of different cultures.

For Cabus, a telling incident occurred in August 2010 when her ward experienced a sudden influx of new attendees at their Sunday Sacrament meeting. Mormons from around the country were joining with other conservatives to attend the "Restoring Honor" celebration hosted by leading right-wing talk-show host (and Mormon convert) Glenn Beck. "That Sunday," she related, "just like every Sunday, everyone who administered and passed the sacrament was African American, including the elders." Cabus felt that "that's the kind of subtle, yet effective statement that I think we could promote that shows people, this is the reality of the church now. What did you expect from fifty years of missionary work, quite frankly?" Cabus has no illusions about the problems of multiethnic and multiracial wards: women of color are less likely to marry other members, and the church's materials still celebrate the world of white, middle-class North Americans. However, she is convinced that Latter-day Saints who have lived in urban wards in the United States or served in Europe are already seeing a demographic shift that is coming. "I really think in ten years," she speculates, "the church in Europe is going to be a black church."[67]

In many ways, the transformation of the Church of Jesus Christ of Latter-day Saints since 1995 reflects trends in global Christianity. Churchgoing has declined in Western Europe and risen in the Southern Hemisphere. Even the United States, still the exception to secularizing trends in industrialized nations, is experiencing a rise in the number of individuals who choose "none" when asked about religious affiliation. Recent studies show that almost a quarter of the American population is religiously unaffiliated, up from 16 percent in 2007.[68] It is immigrants from Latin America, Africa, and Asia who are keeping church membership from declining further.

Women in Latter-day Saint communities, as in congregations of Pentecostals or charismatic Catholics, find that religious participation can open up lines of authority and support unavailable to them in the wider society. Latter-day Saint women, like other Christian women in the Global South, are drawn to religions that present clear moral boundaries and that value family stability. Many assent to patriarchy when it is tempered. They are willing to accord men headship of the family if men support and protect their children and privilege the emotional needs of wives over the sociability of friends. New Christian communities that value face-to-face encounters reproduce in urban settings the communal orientation of the village, and women play a critical role.

Where the Latter-day Saints depart from other Christian churches is in the benefits that a wealthy global church can provide its members. The peculiar character of Latter-day Saint history is diluted outside the United States, but a distinctive religious culture does remain. Women whose lives often revolve around their homes and neighborhoods find that Mormonism opens them up to a transnational and complicated world. From English lessons offered by visiting female missionaries, to pamphlets on family finances, to loans to support education and training, the centralized nature of the church provides distinct benefits.

Unlike the heritage Mormon, who remembers the past, the church of converts is a church of the present. The tensions between women, which structured Mormonism in the seventies and eighties, have little relevance to women who converted in the nineties. Missionaries are taught to approach women interested in their message "where they are at," and they secure the convert's loyalty by recognizing and valuing the complexity of her life. The intensity of the initial religious experience and the female convert's continual spiritual growth frequently counter the limits of ward life and male hierarchical leadership. Women's framework for evaluating Mormonism is their own past. It is the continual influx of new members, stimulated by the efforts of missionaries who are themselves newly "converted," that keeps a narrative of gain—rather than loss—at the forefront of the church.

CHAPTER 9

———•◆•———

Equal Partners

In 1993 the three leaders of the Relief Society, president Elaine L. Jack and her two counselors, Chieko Okazaki and Aileen H. Clyde, began an international study of Latter-day Saint women. Prior to arriving in various cities around the globe, they asked stake Relief Society presidents to organize focus groups made up of twelve women willing to answer the following question: "What has been your experience with the Relief Society and if you had power or responsibility, what would you do to change the organization?" When the Relief Society leaders looked at the responses, they were surprised to find that the women did not actually discuss the Relief Society; rather, they spoke about the gap that existed between the reality of their lives and the ideal that the church presented. "I don't go to church," one woman reported, "because what they tell me about myself, it's just too painful."[1]

Clyde knew that those reports dovetailed with the church's own in-house research "about the number of LDS women who are having to work outside the home." Clyde concluded that alterations needed to be made so that "when they came to Relief Society they were glad they came rather than feeling that they had been reminded once again that they weren't doing the right thing." In order to pass on to the full church what they had learned about the lives of Mormon women, the leaders intended to structure the fall 1995 Relief Society conference around the diverse variety of faithful families that "were thriving and surviving."[2] Some of those families had both parents living at home and others only one, but the Relief Society leaders wanted to demonstrate that religion was the anchor of each.

Then, two weeks before the October 1995 conference, the Relief Society leaders were called into the office of church president Gordon B. Hinckley.

After speaking at some length, the president told them, "We're going to have to have you change your general meeting. We would like you to address the traditional family. We do not want you to demonstrate the many kinds of families at this time." Clyde recollected that he spoke "lovingly and intelligently" but that it was "a bit of a shock to us."[3] He then went on to inform the women that he had decided to present a "proclamation on the family" at their coming Relief Society meeting. Okazaki remembered thinking, "How come we weren't consulted?"[4]

Years later, after "The Family: A Proclamation to the World" had achieved almost canonical standing in the Latter-day Saint community, Clyde and Okazaki voiced unusual candor in describing their feelings about their lack of participation in constructing the influential document. Frustrated, but recognizing the complicated lives of the First Presidency, Okazaki speculated that "sometimes I think they get so busy that they forget that we are there." Her explanation highlighted her commitment to the inspired leadership of church; the men simply had heavy responsibilities that distracted them from utilizing the talents of the Relief Society, Young Women, and Primary general boards. Still, Okazaki knew that female leaders had significant insights into the family—insights shared with them by a diverse group of Latter-day Saint women. "As I read it," she reflected, "I thought that we could have made a few changes in it."[5] Always careful to respect the prophetic voice, however, Okazaki refrained from pointing out what those changes might have been.

Clyde more pointedly summarized women's place within the Mormon leadership structure: "You know, they don't care what we do over here in our playpen as long as we stay in our playpen and are good to each other." Interviewed ten years after the Proclamation, her hurt was still palpable. She described how the Relief Society leaders had worked all year long "trying to find ways to strengthen [women] and help them in their daily struggles," but "the Brethren were doing that also and were writing a proclamation which they never counseled with us about at all." When church apostle Dallin Oaks intimated that the women should be excited about being privy to such an important upcoming announcement, Clyde recalled thinking, "Do you realize how we feel to have had this proclamation coming forward for a year and our not even having any idea about it?" Still, like Okazaki, Clyde did not confront male leadership or even politely articulate her feelings. "It was not my place as second counselor," she clarified, "and I knew it and I wouldn't do that."[6]

Because candid reflections of Mormon women in power are so rare (President Elaine Jack has never shared her perspective publicly), it is important to take Clyde and Okazaki's concerns seriously. Their most obvious disappointment was that the process of shaping a document on the family—an institution intimately shaped by women—excluded women's insights. That the lack of consultation surprised them suggests that their previous experience with the hierarchy had been more positive. If female church leaders had always been simply left "in our own playpen," then why the disenchantment and frustration? By 1995 enough had changed within American society and within the church to raise the expectations of the Relief Society general presidency. American women had moved into leadership positions in business, education, and even religion. By not being consulted, the *auxiliary* status of the Relief Society was not just reaffirmed but boldly underscored. It was something that had dogged Mormon women's organizations since the turn of the century.

Another concern of the Relief Society general presidency was less obvious and more complicated: how to articulate Mormon ideals so that they better aligned with Mormon behavior. While feminists have observed that "much of the 'residue' of sexism seems firmly in place" in the Proclamation, a more accurate appraisal is that it set a new and significant trajectory for official discourse.[7] In its ambiguity, restraint, and brevity—its "theology of silence"—the Proclamation joined other authoritative moves by church leaders in the nineties to adjust official doctrine and rituals to better match the behaviors of actual Mormons.

In the years since 1995, the Proclamation on the Family has assumed a dominant place in Mormonism.[8] Frequently quoted at general conferences, cited in Sacrament Meetings, and memorized by eager Saints, its definition of the family and its summary of the duties of mothers and fathers are well known. Every student who majors in "Family Life" at BYU takes a course based on it. It has been attached to legal briefs and cited as the justification for political activism. The norms stipulated in the Proclamation are not merely imposed from above. On the popular social media platform Pinterest, Latter-day Saints post pictures of it on display in their homes: framed and set between hall lamps, printed over a couple's wedding picture, made into bookmarks, transformed into a children's board game, or embossed on a wooden plank and tied with a burlap bow. Certainly, the ubiquity of the Proclamation within contemporary Mormonism gives it an authoritative character, but more importantly the text resonates with core Latter-day Saint values that most members revere.

Aileen Clyde acknowledged in a 2005 interview that the Proclamation was a doctrinal statement, but she also asserted that it legitimized particular church policies in order to get "ahead of some things that were going on in the society."[9] It is impossible to ascertain why the First Presidency issued a statement on the family at that particular time, as the relevant oral histories and institutional documentation are not open to scholars. There is evidence to suggest, however, that church leaders were addressing two contemporary social trends: the desire of gays and lesbians to marry and the desire of heterosexuals not to marry. In 1989 Denmark, a nation in which many Mormons had ethnic roots, became the first country in the world to legally recognize same-sex unions. A year later, three same-sex couples in Hawaii applied for marriage licenses. When they were refused, they sued, arguing that denying their right to marry violated their equal protection rights. The case caught the attention of church leaders. Latter-day Saints had a notable presence in Hawaii, having first come to the islands in 1850. Mormons built a temple there in 1916 (the first outside of the contiguous United States), a university in 1955, and a Polynesian-themed cultural center in 1963. In 1991, out of a total state population of 1.1 million, there were 51,000 Saints.[10] Church leaders felt a moral and political duty to become involved in the Hawaii marriage cases.

Until the fifties, Latter-day Saint church leaders paid little attention to homosexual relations. After World War II, as in most of American society, Mormon antagonism toward gays and lesbians intensified. In 1968 "homosexual acts" were added to the list of excommunicable sins in the church handbook. During the seventies, the church both condemned homosexuality and declared that it could be cured.[11] Mormons, who participated in many sex-segregated activities and who valorized the heterosexual couple, were particularly alarmed by the gay rights movement. Unlike those Protestants and Catholics who cite biblical texts as proof of the sinfulness of homosexuality, Latter-day Saints have wider theological reasons for rejecting it. For Mormons, exaltation entails eternal reproduction. The celestial couple populates and nurtures worlds. Both the highest aspiration a Mormon can have and the loftiest goal he or she can reach has to do with reproducing—either children or spirits.

Prompted by the court cases in Hawaii, in November 1991 the First Presidency sent a letter ("Standards of Morality and Fidelity") to all church members repeating its earlier condemnation of homosexual acts. "Sexual relations are proper only between husband and wife appropriately expressed within the bonds of marriage," the letter emphasized. "Any other sexual contact, including fornication, adultery, and homosexual and lesbian behavior, is sinful. Those who persist in such practices or who influence others to do so are subject to Church discipline." In a shift in tone from previous condemnations, the letter told struggling members to seek counsel from church leaders and expected those leaders to respond with "love and understanding."[12] The First Presidency broke new ground by distinguishing two distinct dimensions of sexual immorality: immoral thoughts and immoral behavior. As Catholics had been doing since 1976, Mormons separated orientation from activity.[13] Thoughts "should be overcome" but only acting on feelings constituted "sinful behavior."[14] This left open the possibility that one could have same-sex attraction and still be a righteous Saint.

In 1994 another church statement specifically addressed the issue of same-sex marriage (what the statement called "same-gender marriage"). The short text not only opposed the practice but called on members "to appeal to legislators, judges, and other government officials" to reject efforts to legalize or give official approval to same-sex marriage.[15] When considered together with the 1991 letter, it seemed that church leaders sought to distinguish among those with same-sex attraction (who should be met with love and counseling), those who sinfully acted on their desires (who should be disciplined), and those political movements that sought to legitimize same-sex marriage. Within individual congregations the ward bishop was charged with addressing same-sex attraction and homosexual activities. Political movements, if they challenged the moral order, necessitated a wider response. As with the ERA, church leaders determined that reconfiguring who could marry was serious enough to merit institutional involvement.

The 1991 and 1994 statements made the church's position on sexual conduct clear, but a definitive doctrinal text was missing. If church leaders were going to call on members to lobby for a particular type of marriage, then members needed to know what that would be, what *did* constitute a divinely ordained family. Moreover, a statement that laid out the Latter-day Saint position on gender, marriage, and families needed to make sense to non-Mormons as well as Mormons or it could not be used in legal or political contexts. Consequently, when Gordon B. Hinckley delivered "The Family: A Proclamation to the World," he had both members and nonmembers in mind. The text's first sentence solemnly proclaims that "marriage between a man and a woman is ordained of God."[16] Human beings who marry—male and female individuals—are the beloved spirit sons or daughters of heavenly parents. Each person has a divine nature and destiny. The Proclamation does not specifically mention homosexuality nor does it set homosexual relations into a moral framework. Instead it warns obliquely that "individuals who violate covenants of chastity" will "one day stand accountable before God." Taking a positive stance, the Proclamation presents what Latter-day Saints are *for* rather than *against*. And, by speaking broadly, its message resembled that preached by other conservative Christians.

The Proclamation served as a moral guideline for Latter-day Saints opposing same-sex marriage and was added as an amicus brief in the Hawaii cases.[17] When a similar move to expand marriage rights occurred in California, Latter-day Saints pointed to the Proclamation as doctrinal justification for giving heterosexuals the exclusive privilege to marry. Church leaders encouraged members to actively work to pass Proposition 22 (2000) and then Proposition 8 (2008), amendments designed to restrict marriage to opposite-sex couples. On June 29, 2008, a letter was read in all California Sacrament Meetings asking Latter-day Saints to "do all [they] can to support the proposed constitutional amendment by donating of [their] means and time to assure that marriage in California is legally defined as being between a man and a woman."[18] Mormon women responded to their leaders' call and became the backbone of grassroots organizing. As they had done during the ERA battle, women assembled volunteers, canvassed door to door, created phone banks, and stuck signs on lawns—all to persuade voters to approve Proposition 8. Donations poured into California from across the nation. Other Christian groups were also active in the campaign, but their efforts were dwarfed by those of the Mormons. One scholar estimated that Latter-day Saints, who made up about 2 percent of the population of California, contributed $20 million—or about half of all individual contributions—to the Proposition 8 efforts.[19] A thousand individual donations, as well as a million-dollar one, came from Utah.[20]

Just as with the ERA, the battle over Proposition 8 caused ruptures among the Saints. Women who believed that Prop 8 only supported marriage and was not an antigay amendment discovered their gay and lesbian friends thought differently. Friendships frayed. "We are collegial now," a California Mormon insisted, "but we're not friends anymore. That was very painful for both of us. She just can't understand how I could belong to a church that hates her. That's how she sees it."[21] Many Mormons believed that they were strengthening marriage, not spreading hate. Other women argued that the pressures of church leaders unduly entangled religion with political matters. Young Mormons, who tended to be more open to LGBTQ issues, felt that the church's decision to make Prop 8 a moral cause created unnecessary friction within the Latter-day Saint community. Critics of the church's position held that unity, cohesiveness, and the Christ-like values of love, service, and humility were diminished in pursuit of "yes" votes.

It was not only the gay rights movement that challenged definitions of what constituted a "normal" family: Latter-day Saint leaders, like many Christian leaders in the nineties, were worried about how heterosexual families were changing. More Americans were choosing not to marry or marrying late, or divorcing and remarrying or cohabitating. In 1960, 72 percent of all adults ages eighteen and older were married, and the median age at first marriage was twenty for women and twenty-three for men.[22] In 1990 the percentage of married adults had declined to 58 percent, and by 2014 it had fallen to 50 percent.[23] Couples were also marrying later: in 1990 the median age for women at first marriage had risen to twenty-four, and in 2016 it stood at twenty-seven; for men the figures were twenty-six and thirty, respectively.[24] Researchers who recognized the sharp rise in the number of people living together without marrying dubbed America the "cohabitation nation."[25] By 2012 media outlets were regularly summarizing the impact these changes had wrought on the American class structure. Newspaper articles quoted social scientists who argued that economic inequality was widening because the poor and the wealthy behaved differently regarding marriage. People with more education were more likely to marry, to marry one another, and to have more stable family structures, whereas the less educated had complex, less stable partnerships that did not support economic advancement.[26]

On one level, Latter-day Saints in Utah countered the prevailing national trends. The Pew Research Center's "Religious Landscape Study" found in 2007 that 71 percent of Mormon adults across the country were married. However, Latter-day Saints were not immune to national trends. When the Pew Research Center conducted the study again in 2014, the number of married Mormon adults had declined to 66 percent. Although this percentage was the highest of all the communities they surveyed, it did show a decline.[27]

In 1995 the Proclamation on the Family firmly asserted a rationale for heterosexual marriage and family. On the most basic level, the text stipulates that marriage is ordained of God and is not merely a social or legal contract. The family, not the individual soul, forms the foundational unit of celestial exaltation and the human social order. Therefore "marriage between man and woman is essential to His eternal plan." In modern America, where autonomy and independence are signs of adulthood, the Proclamation insists that God's order is made up of intertwined and mutually dependent men and women. Whether or not to have children is not a personal decision but rather the first command that God gave to humanity—having children is a "sacred responsibility." "The sacred powers of procreation," the Proclamation asserts, are only to be between a "lawfully" married man and woman. Children are entitled to be born within "the bonds of matrimony" as well as to a mother and father who "honor marital vows with complete fidelity." Parents are obligated to love, guide, and support their children. The family is eternal, existing before individuals are born on earth and—with the proper temple rites—continuing after death. For Latter-day Saints, families rest on a foundation of divine principles as well as *enact* those principles.

The Proclamation presents gender as an essential characteristic that exists prior to our birth and that will continue after we die. And it is binary. While many contemporary Americans embrace multiple gender identities—or support those who do—the Proclamation adheres to a strictly dualistic understanding of humanity: male and female. Earthly families ideally should reflect that binary. By "divine design" fathers are

to "preside over their families in love and righteousness." They are to provide the "necessities of life" and "protection for their families." Mothers
are "primarily responsible for the nurture of their children." One sex (or
gender as Latter-day Saints consistently put it) cannot fully exist without
the other.

From the Mormon perspective, mothers and fathers have complementary responsibilities within the family. That two sexes (and only two
sexes) complement each other is an idea common to Christians, Jews, and
Muslims. The Proclamation on the Family departs from more theologically
conservative Christian communities, however, by insisting that within the
family men and women share authority as equal partners. With this statement church authorities turned away from both the historical patriarchy of
Mormonism and evangelical Protestantism's renewed effort to place men as
the head of Christian families.

To highlight the significance of the church's emphasis on "equal partners," it is useful to compare the Proclamation on the Family with a
statement written at approximately the same time by Southern Baptist
leaders. In 1925, in order to address theological controversies arising in its
congregations, the Southern Baptists had issued a creedal statement called
"The Baptist Faith and Message." In 1997 the Southern Baptist convention agreed to add to the statement a section on the family. The following
year, "Article XVIII: The Family" was approved by the assembled Baptists
at their annual convention (held that year in Salt Lake City). Like the
Proclamation on the Family, Article XVIII stated that God ordained the
family as the "foundational institution of human society." Marriage was between one man and one woman. It provided companionship and sexual
expression ("according to biblical standards") while serving as the means
"for procreation of the human race." A husband's duty was to "provide for,
to protect, and to lead his family." Mothers were to manage the household,
"nurturing the next generation."[28] In all of this, Mormons and Southern
Baptists agreed.

Nevertheless, Article XVIII departs from the Proclamation in its account of the domestic relationship between men and women. For both
Baptists and Mormons, the husband and the wife who stand before God
are of equal worth. However, Article XVIII states that the marriage relationship models "the way that God relates to his people." Following the biblical
allegory of Christ loving (yet ruling) the church, "a wife is to submit herself
graciously to the servant leadership of her husband even as the church willingly submits to the headship of Christ." Consequently, the wife "has the
God-given responsibility to respect her husband and to serve as his helper"
in the family.[29] Southern Baptists, in other words, assume an asymmetry in
power relationships within the home.

By contrast, the Proclamation bases its understanding of the husband/
wife relationship on the model of heavenly parents. Human beings are the
literal sons and daughters of heavenly parents. While only God "as their
Eternal Father" is worshipped, the Heavenly Mother shares parenthood
with the Father. The model Latter-day Saint leaders chose was not the inequality between Christ and humanity but rather the equality of two divine
figures. By replacing the Christ/church allegory with a married couple god-
head, Latter-day Saints circumvent the domestic hierarchy that Southern
Baptists see working in the ideal family. For Mormons, the ideal parents—
though a dim reflection of the celestial family—must be equal partners.
Wives do not submit to husbands, even husbands schooled in the practice
of "servant leadership."[30]

One reason the Proclamation never asks wives to "submit" is because
by the nineties, Latter-day Saints had developed a new understanding of
Adam and Eve. The Proclamation on the Family was written in the context of liberalizing trends in Mormonism to reinterpret what happened the
Garden of Eden by making Eve a more active agent and by rethinking her
role in the primeval drama.

As early as the nineteenth century, "Nauvoo theology" provided a radically optimistic vision of human potential and destiny. This philosophy
contrasted with the Calvinistic orientation, which fixed individuals in a particular spiritual order. The Book of Abraham (a text Joseph Smith worked
on that entered the Mormon scriptural canon in 1880) explains how God
offered humans the opportunity to be embodied on earth and how their
freedom to choose good or evil was essential to achieving eternal progress. More explicitly, the Book of Moses (a translation of parts of the Bible
that Mormons believe was revealed to Joseph Smith in the early eighteen-
thirties) illustrates how Adam and Eve made important decisions that
enabled their eternal progress.

Much of the story of the Garden of Eden is the same in the Bible and
in the Book of Moses.[31] Both describe what many non-Mormons see as a
punishment (a curse) that God pronounces on Eve after she is "beguiled"
by Satan, eats of the fruit, and gives it to Adam: "I will greatly multiply
thy sorrow and thy conception. In sorrow thou shalt bring forth children,
and thy desire shall be to thy husband, and he shall rule over thee" (Moses
4:22 = King James Version Genesis 3:16). The notion of wifely submission
is thus introduced in the Scriptures.

However, the Book of Moses provides additional texts that move away
from the curse imagery. After eating, Adam speaks first: "Blessed be the
name of God, for because of my transgression my eyes are opened, and
in this life I shall have joy, and again in the flesh I shall see God" (Moses

5:10). Eve then speaks, elaborating: "Were it not for our transgression we never should have had seed, and never should have known good and evil, and the joy of our redemption, and the eternal life which God giveth unto all the obedient" (Moses 5:11). In 1893 Latter-day Saint theologian James Talmage interpreted these passages to mean that once Eve ate, she became mortal but Adam remained immortal. Adam then faced a dilemma: how not to transgress the law given by God not to eat of the fruit but still to fulfill God's first commandment, to "multiply and replenish the earth" (Genesis 1:28 = Moses 2:28). According to Talmage, because they were "in such dissimilar conditions the two could not remain together," Adam abided by the greater commandment and ate of the fruit in order to reproduce.[32] Adam's decisions allowed the progress of humanity because now free will had been exercised. A problem had been presented and a decision was made. Such proper choices would enable human beings to grow and develop.

When Talmage interpreted the Garden of Eden story, he presented Adam as the active thinker and Eve as the slightly dimwitted one who was seduced by Satan, reflecting Victorian gender norms. Adam, Talmage writes, ate the fruit from the Tree of Knowledge "with a full comprehension of the nature of his act." Talmage underscored his point by quoting the New Testament: "Adam was not deceived; but the woman, being deceived, was in the transgression" (1 Timothy 2:14).[33] Near the end of his discussion of the Garden of Eden, Talmage turns to the Book of Mormon and Lehi's telling of the Eden story. In this narrative, Adam is the sole actor because transgression actually has positive ramifications. If Adam had not transgressed, he would have remained in Eden in a state of innocence with no children and no ability to choose good over evil or to experience joy and misery. Only through such choices and experiences could progress occur. Eve then drops out of the drama. Talmage ended his exegesis by citing Lehi's well-known summary of the events (which ignores Eve altogether): "Adam fell that man might be, and men are that they might have joy" (2 Nephi 2:25).[34] For Talmage, rooted in a patriarchal culture, Adam—not Eve—is the one who figures out that he must become mortal. Eve was deceived and therefore "she was made subject to her husband."[35] With the exception of some nineteenth-century female writers for the *Woman's Exponent*, Talmage's interpretation set the standard for Mormon thought until quite recently.

Talmage's perspective echoed in the Latter-day Saint temple endowment ceremony until the liturgy was changed in 1990. In the temple, Mormons receive the instructions and covenants of the Holy Priesthood that they need for exaltation and salvation. After members are washed and anointed, they don special clothing and participate in a "recital of the most prominent events of the Creation," including the Garden of Eden drama.[36] Prior to the alteration of the ritual, Eve is told that because she "hearkened to the voice of Satan and hast partaken of the forbidden fruit," her sorrows will be "multiplied."[37] She will bring forth children in sorrow, but that pain will not destroy her as she "mayest be preserved in child-bearing." As in the Bible, Eve's "desire shall be to thy husband" and he "shall rule over thee."[38] However, the endowment liturgy adds the nonbiblical modifier "in righteousness." Eve covenants to obey Adam's law "as you obey our Father."

In 1990 church authorities removed, without explanation, the whole passage regarding Eve's "curse." The current temple instruction does not mention Adam ruling over Eve with the implication of Eve's submission. There is no more mention of the pangs of childbirth or of being "preserved" because of her childbearing. Pregnancy is disconnected from cosmic disobedience. Rather than promising to obey Adam's law, Eve directly covenants "to obey the law of the Lord, and to hearken to your [Adam's] counsel as you hearken unto the Father." While church leaders markedly altered Eve's punishment, Adam's changes little. Only one deletion was made: no longer is Adam exiled from paradise because he listened "unto the voice of thy wife" but simply because he has "partaken of the forbidden fruit." As in the pre-1990 version, Adam has to "by the sweat of thy face" eat "thy bread all of the days of thy life." It is the earth—not woman—that is "cursed for thy sake," now bringing forth "thorns, thistles, briars, and noxious weeds to afflict and torment man."[39] The elimination of "he shall rule over thee in righteousness" from the temple ritual profoundly transformed the understanding of where women fit into the cosmological ordering of male/female relations.

This reimagining of the Garden of Eden drama was further developed by two scholars, Valerie Hudson Cassler and Alma Don Sorensen, colleagues then in BYU's department of political science (Cassler had also studied with Sorensen as a student). In 1994 they were asked to present a talk at the BYU Women's Conference about equality and gender issues, which they then expanded into a book called *Women in Eternity, Women of Zion* (2004). While Latter-day Saints experience Eve's relationship to God, Adam, and Satan ritualistically in the temple, Cassler and Sorensen explored the interactions more philosophically.

For Cassler and Sorensen, Eve has an active, informed, and positive role to play in bringing humanity into existence. Sorensen addressed the moral instructions that God gave the first woman. "He told her she should turn to Adam," Sorensen wrote in his chapter, "so they might form a union like unto the unions found in the highest heaven and He indicated what the nature of that union should be." Sorensen then quoted the biblical text that Adam "shall rule over thee." He explained:

We are convinced that "rule over" is an unfortunate translation here, and for two related reasons. First, the Hebrew term rendered here as "rule over" can also mean "rule with."

In fact, we understand that when the Hebrew word "*msh'l*" (usually translated as "rule")
is used in conjunction with "*bet'*" (in most cases translated as "with," "in," "by," or "at"),
the better translation is "rule with" rather than "rule over."

In addition, Sorensen explained, such a rule is in accordance with the celestial order, which "is one of equal power."[40]

Sorensen and Cassler's elimination of "rule over" might have languished in obscurity if the translation change had not been reproduced in 2007 in an article in the church's magazine *Ensign*. "Equal Partners," by Bruce C. Hafen and his wife Marie K. Hafen, included this new understanding of the biblical text. Bruce Hafen at the time was a member of the Quorum of the Seventy, and he had been dean of the BYU Law School. The article repeated that "*over* [as] in 'rule over' uses the Hebrew *bet*, which means ruling *with*, not ruling *over*."[41] The new translation gained authority because of Bruce Hafen's leadership position within the church. In their essay, the Hafens also cited President Spencer W. Kimball as not liking the English translation "rule" and preferring the word "preside."[42] They might have quoted (but did not) church apostle L. Tom Perry, who at the spring 2004 conference told members "there is not a president or a vice president in a family." Somewhat inconsistently, the apostle explained that the father is the head in his family but that the couple are united and are on equal footing.[43]

Valerie Hudson (dropping her married name Cassler) promoted this new understanding of the biblical text. In 2013 she published an online essay for the church entitled "Equal Partnership in Marriage" and quoted the Hafens' article—not her own book—as the source for translating "ruling over" as "ruling with." She also quoted the Hafens as explaining that the original Hebrew for *meet* (as in "helpmeet") "means that Eve was adequate for, or equal to, Adam." Although Hudson did not mention it, church president Howard W. Hunter in 1994 also believed that "*meet* means equal," using this as his basis for asserting, "For a man to operate independent of or without regard to the feelings and counsel of his wife in governing the family is to exercise unrighteous dominion."[44]

While the church hierarchy and influential Latter-day Saint writers were trying to establish equal leadership in the family, conservative Protestants were doing the opposite. In 1990 an evangelical football coach, Bill McCartney, founded the Promise Keepers with the goal of bringing men back into the family and to Christ. By 1997 the organization succeeded in motivating and organizing between 600,000 and 800,000 men from across the country to gather at the National Mall in Washington, DC. There the men offered prayers and manly embraces with the hopes of reawakening Christian manliness and domestic empowerment. Although Promise Keepers would fade within the decade, during the nineties the renewed focus on masculinity contrasted with Mormon efforts to downplay male authority—but not involvement— in the home.

Not unlike the temple ceremony, where parts of the liturgy were quietly removed, the Proclamation of the Family speaks louder in what it does *not* say than what it does. The Proclamation avoids the rhetorical flourishes that typically surround Latter-day Saint mentions of motherhood. There is only one short sentence in the text that describes the responsibilities of a mother and nothing about general gender characteristics of females. How a father presides and a mother nurtures is not laid out. In particular, the Proclamation is silent on how much time women should devote to activities beyond nurturing—like careers.

When compared with the sentiments expressed by Latter-day Saint leaders at the same time, the Proclamation's "silent theology" is particularly notable. The brevity of the Proclamation contrasts with the elaborate, and typically conservative, reflections of prominent church leaders. In 1993, two years before the Proclamation on the Family, Apostle Boyd K. Packer published his reflections on motherhood in the *Ensign*. The first couple, and by implication all couples, he argued, are different from one another and "some roles are best suited to the masculine nature and others to the feminine natures." Man is "the protector, the provider." Woman, through childbirth is "also co-creator with God and the primary nurturer of her children."[45]

Packer fleshed out that phrase by looking to Mormon history—not to the eighteen-forties of Joseph Smith but to the nineteen-forties. Packer asserted that "the most devastating effect" of World War II was on the family because women entered the workforce. This effect (which he does not describe) "lingers to this generation." For Packer, the ideal Mormon mother was the housewife of the fifties who left the factory for the kitchen. He then quoted extensively from a 1942 First Presidency message read by J. Reuben Clark (discussed in chapter four). Clark recounted how "legions of choice spirits [are] waiting for their tabernacles of flesh" with the goals of becoming "perfect souls." Parents are to accept the sacred obligation to train and care for their children. Mothers, however, have a holy calling, a "consecration of devotion" for the divine service of motherhood that cannot be passed to others. If a mother does so, "for gold, for fame, or for civic service," as the Bible says: "a child left to himself bringeth his mother to shame."[46] Packer, who had married in 1947, longed for the days of his midcentury youth. Neither the hardworking pioneer mother whose babies were cared for by their siblings nor the civically engaged Progressive Era woman who employed a hired girl, held allure for the apostle.

Two years later, the Proclamation turned away from this idealized motherhood. Nowhere does the document intimate that working mothers could not also be the primary nurturers of their children. Nor does it present the wage labor of women as the enemy of the family. It does not note, praise, or condemn women's civic responsibilities, volunteer work, or humanitarian efforts. The Proclamation offers a theology of silence regarding women's activities outside of "nurturing." It also calls on a theology of forgetting. Ezra Taft Benson in 1980 had stressed that a living prophet is more important to the community than a dead prophet.[47] This instruction persevered, while his plea in "To the Mothers of Zion" (1987) that mothers "spend their full time in the home rearing and caring for their children" was absent.[48] Earlier warnings about wage labor could easily be overlooked, if one so chose. The past did not need to be dealt with; it could be ignored.

Indeed, according to the Proclamation what brings about the "calamities foretold by ancient and modern prophets" are activities stereotypically associated with men: violations of chastity, child and spousal abuse, and the failure to fulfill family responsibilities.[49] Rather than elaborate on what it means for women to be "primarily responsible for the nurture of their children," the Proclamation takes pains to pull away from that ideal. The "divine design" may at times need adjustment: "Death, disability, or other circumstances," the Proclamation observes, "may necessitate individual adaptation." And the text is silent on what might entail "other circumstances" or how the decision to adapt to those circumstances is made.

The gendered world that Packer longed for is absent from the Proclamation. It is marked instead by Hinckley's positive attitude, optimism, and trust of the basic goodness of the Saints. Legal marriages—still between one man and one woman who produce and nurture children—are critical to the earthly and divine order. Men and women naturally have different functions, but the "silent theology" of the Proclamation allows individuals to determine what those differences are. Certainly the Proclamation was limited by pragmatic concerns and defined by current needs, but its brevity worked for the expansion of women's roles.

By rendering the portrait of the ideal family in a few brushstrokes, Mormon leaders brought doctrine closer in line with the behavior of the Saints. There is no better example of this alteration of official thought than the reworking of church guidelines on birth control. Although the Proclamation on the Family was publicly announced at a Relief Society general meeting and enshrined in Latter-day Saint homes, instructions on birth control appeared only in the far more bureaucratic *General Handbook of Instructions*. The Proclamation is an expression of church doctrine and the *Handbook* of policy and practice, yet both lay out a set of principles that reflect a willingness to accommodate shifting norms.

In the early twentieth century, church authorities, like most Christian leaders, confronted the possibility that their members were using artificial means to limit childbearing. In 1916 the Relief Society presidency asked for guidance on the sensitive matter of family planning, and the response was unequivocal: there would be eternal consequences for those who used contraception. "Those who attempt to prevent their offspring from coming into the world in obedience to this great command [Genesis 1:28, 'be fruitful and multiply']," thundered Apostle Joseph Fielding Smith, "are guilty of one of the most heinous crimes in the category. There is no promise of eternal salvation and exaltation for such as they."[50] Sixty years later, the rhetoric was less fiery but the point was the same: it "is contrary to the teachings of the Church to artificially curtail or prevent the birth of children," stipulated the 1976 Handbook. "Those who practice birth control," it predicted, "will reap disappointment by and by."[51]

In spite of such prophetic instructions and the Mormon affection for large families, birthrates had sharply declined between the mid-fifties and the mid-sixties, slightly increased the next decade, and then continually declined after the early eighties.[52] Rather than intensifying its prohibition of contraceptives, however, the Handbooks reveal a gradual softening. The 1983 and 1985 editions included the biblical command to "multiply and replenish" but dropped the specific prohibition against artificial birth control found in the 1976 edition. Handbooks from the eighties also added a statement that husbands should be considerate of their wives and that the couple should exercise self-control "in all of their relationships."[53] The 1989 Handbook continued this trend toward accepting contraceptives by leaving out the command to "multiply and replenish" while repeating the injunction for wifely consideration.[54]

Then in 1998, three years after the Proclamation on the Family, the Handbook carried a statement that would have been inconceivable two decades earlier: "The decision as to how many children to have and when to have them is extremely intimate and private," it maintained, "and should be left between the couple and the Lord." While not mentioning contraceptives, the Handbook made it clear that family size was not the business of church leaders, relatives, or neighbors. To underscore that point, the Handbook plainly stated that "Church members should not judge one another in this matter." Evaluating righteousness based on how many children a woman had was wrong. And, in a gesture toward bringing Mormon attitudes on sexuality into line with modern notions of marital pleasure, the Handbook added a new concept: sex was not just for procreation but was a "means of expressing love and strengthening emotional and spiritual bonds between husband and wife."[55] Church guidelines, especially once Gordon B. Hinckley became president, were adjusted to adapt to real-world Latter-day Saint practices.

Latter-day Saint birthrates provide an example of how members uphold principles (e.g., to "multiply and replenish") on their own terms. In comparison with other faiths, Mormons have larger families. In 2014 the Pew Research Center surveyed religious communities throughout the country and placed the Mormons at the top of the fertility scale, with an average of 3.4 children. The next in line were members of historically black Protestant denominations at 2.5, slightly more than the national average of 2.1.[56] In 2014 Utah had the highest birthrate in the nation, at 17.4 births per 1,000 people (the national average was 12.5).[57]

But Utah's birthrate was actually at a historical *low* in 2014. Mormons were having children, but fewer of them. In 1960 the number of children born to an average Utah woman was 4.3, and by 1990 that number had declined to 2.6.[58] By 2014 the fertility rate in Utah was 2.3 while the national fertility rate hovered around 1.8.[59] Utah, of course, only has a majority of Mormons, so the numbers understate those for the Latter-day Saint population. However, even Utah County, which is 82 percent Mormon, showed a decreasing birthrate in 2016.[60] The US Census Bureau frequently cites Utah as the "fastest-growing state," but this belies the fact that, like elsewhere in the Western world, Latter-day Saint family size is contracting.[61] Mormons have more children, but they have long followed national demographic trends toward raising smaller families.

The change in attitude toward contraceptives in the 1998 *Handbook* neither departed from the core concept of the divine nature of families nor placed the regulation of birth entirely in the hands of women. Rather, it eliminated stipulations on family size that Mormons had been ignoring anyway and accentuated the idea that important decisions should be made jointly by women, men, and God. Mormon women had been reducing their family size since the sixties, but after 1998 they could use birth control without guilt. They did not have to wonder if their desire not to get pregnant was a sign of worldliness or the tempting of the Adversary. They did not have to question that the "promptings" they received to delay childbearing were truly from God. Even church leaders no longer seemed to model the large Mormon family. In 2017 the members of the three-person First Presidency had an average of 2.3 children, and members of the General Relief Society Presidency 1.7. Of the apostles, the three most senior in line to become church president (all born in the twenties and thirties) had an average of 7.7 children. The remaining nine apostles (all but one born in 1940 or later) had a mean number of 3.3 children.[62]

By modifying their stance on birth control, Mormons avoided the erosion of institutional leadership over sexual ethics that had occurred in other Christian communities. Altering the policy on family planning not only reduced tensions within the community of Saints but also strengthened the position of the Mormon hierarchy among members. Catholics also acknowledge a centralized and sacred authority but responded quite differently to papal leadership. In his 1968 encyclical *Humanae Vitae*, Pope Paul VI, against the recommendation of his own commission, reiterated the Catholic prohibition on artificial birth control. Catholics were only to use natural methods to prevent unwanted pregnancies, methods that were complicated and far from foolproof. Catholic laypeople in the United States simply ignored these admonitions: a 2011 study showed that 98 percent of Catholic women of reproductive age had used some form of artificial birth control during their lives.[63] Upholding the church's stance on contraceptives no longer marked one as a "good" Catholic but rather as a counterculture conservative.

Shortly after *Humanae Vitae* was promulgated, sociologists noticed that the church's ability to teach authoritatively about sexual ethics was weakening.[64] In 1993 American bishop Kenneth Untener wrote that laypeople were increasingly ignoring the hierarchy's counsel on important matters, and he compared the church's refusal to realistically discuss contraceptives to "a dysfunctional family that is unable to talk openly about a problem that everyone knows is there."[65] By not addressing the gap between the behavior of Catholics and Catholic sexual ethics, church leaders lost their ability to influence the lives of their flock. Institutional authority eroded as Catholics became more and more convinced of the primacy of their own individual consciences.

After the Proclamation on the Family, Mormons felt more comfortable with their domestic decisions. Kristina Tinney, for example, fully agreed with her chosen religion's position that the family was ordained of God and essential to the plan of salvation. In her home country of Sweden, where most couples have small families (although slightly more than the European Union average of 1.55), she had four children.[66] However, she and her husband consciously decided when to have those children, partially so that Tinney could maintain a full-time job since in Sweden, "that's what you did." Her commitment to the values of Mormonism inspired her larger-than-normal family, but neither her faith nor her family size stopped her from developing a career. When she translated Relief Society president Julie B. Beck's 2007 conference address for her Swedish ward, she felt a mismatch between Swedish and American Mormonism. Beck's talk, "Mothers Who Know," focused exclusively on the home: "I remember thinking, oh, that's how they do it in the States, it doesn't really apply to us." Tinney assumed that "they don't understand how things work in the rest of the world." When her daughter in Norway gave birth, her son-in-law (who was the ward's bishop), took parental leave to watch their baby so his wife could go back to work.[67]

By quietly adjusting their attitude toward contraceptives, removing Eve's punishment from the temple endowment ceremony, avoiding the rhetorical condemnation of women's labor outside of the home, and opting not to define male or female "gender" in explicit terms, Latter-day Saint church leaders reframed the institutional understanding of Mormon womanhood. Because the Proclamation text is literally enshrined in the households of many conservative Latter-day Saints and cited incessantly by church leaders, its liberalizing themes have been under-acknowledged. Families continue to be central, but Latter-day Saints increasingly understand that when a church leader describes a family it was only *one* possible type of family. When leaders become too explicit in their depictions of motherhood or their stories of family life, members feel comfortable ignoring them. The Proclamation on the Family—with its terse descriptions, its caveats, and its modifiers—provided a doctrinal explanation for the expanding multiplicity of Latter-day Saint lives. It did not encourage that multiplicity, but it did recognize—via its theology of silence—the complexity of Mormon lives. Presented by powerful and respected authorities, the Proclamation paved the way for other institutional efforts like the "I'm a Mormon" campaign (2010–) and the *Meet the Mormons* (2014) movie, which *did* celebrate Mormon diversity.

The Proclamation on the Family also turned attention away from women, who had traditionally been the focus of much of church leaders' writings on the family, and toward men. Rather than stress the importance of women making a proper Mormon home where men ruled as patriarchal authorities, it employed the more nebulous and softer word "preside." This transformation of patriarchal power, dramatically demonstrated in the revised temple ritual, was set forth as an institutional norm in the Proclamation. However, as Caroline Kline has pointed out, feminist Mormons have wondered: How, if men always preside, can women truly be their equals?[68] Even ceremonial presiding negates equality if it is permanent. The Proclamation ignored the feminist move to replace the dualistic model with a unified one. Gender roles may be blurred, but men and women remain essentially separate.

The Proclamation on the Family reinforced the metaphysical binary that serves as the basis for the essential structure of both heaven and earth. "For it must needs be, that there is an opposition in all things," explains the Book of Mormon; if this were not so, "righteousness could not be brought to pass, neither wickedness, neither holiness nor misery, neither good nor bad" (2 Nephi 2:11–12). As there is a Heavenly Father and a Heavenly Mother, there are earthly fathers and mothers who correspond to that divine dualism. As much as the limited gender description in the Proclamation opened up Mormonism to diversity, this essential binary limits Mormon acceptance of the multiple ways that people experience sexual identity. The Proclamation on the Family avoided the antigay rhetoric of earlier official church publications, but it celebrated the heterosexual couple. The contentious debate over Prop 8 shook the Latter-day Saint community, which values consensus and harmony, and in its aftermath Mormons worked hard to be more compassionate toward those who felt attacked by Prop 8. Yet the Proclamation remains a deeply painful document for many Latter-day Saints who embrace sexualities different from the heterosexual binary.

Moreover, what the Proclamation on the Family left unresolved was the asymmetrical leadership that so infuriated the normally composed Chieko Okazaki and Aileen Clyde. Male church leaders laid out a doctrinal foundation for diversity within the home and society, but they did not alter the dynamics of church authority. A mother could justly insist that she was not the "vice president" of the family, but the Relief Society was still an *auxiliary* under the authority of the priesthood. The problems raised by Okazaki and Clyde—the lack of consultation, the disregard for the unique insights of women, the absence of collaborative planning, even the bureaucratic preoccupations of inspired leaders—remained. In the home, Latter-day Saints had in theory replaced "rule over" with "rule with," but the same could not be said for male and female relationships within the church hierarchy.

CHAPTER 10

———•◆•———

Internet Mormons

In 1989, the year that Apostle Dallin H. Oaks warned about "alternate voices" and counseled the Saints to "listen to the voice of the Church," a British computer scientist was working in a physics lab in Geneva, Switzerland.[1] The Latter-day Saint apostle wanted to limit the types of information church members considered reliable and truthful. Tim Berners-Lee struggled to find a way that scientists in his lab could widely distribute and share information. He wrote up a document on "information management" that took advantage of the newly invented system of connected computers called the "internet."[2] Berners-Lee envisioned a system of interlinked documents made up of texts and images that could be stored, consulted, and used in a variety of locations. After a few years of development, the system became known as the World Wide Web.

The *New York Times* first mentioned the commercial implications of the internet in 1993, the year that six Latter-day Saints were famously excommunicated for apostasy. The article described how a new software program would facilitate web browsing and provide a "map to the buried treasure of the Information Age."[3] Echoing the revolutionary potential of unlimited information moving seamlessly and swiftly, *Time* magazine sported a cover where the "Info Highway" zoomed right into a close-up of an eye.[4] At the very point in time when Latter-day Saints were frightened about sharing ideas, a powerful new form of mass communication was being born.

When Gordon B. Hinckley became church president in 1995 only eighteen million homes had modem-equipped computers that could access the internet, and only 3 percent of Americans had ever signed on to the two-year-old World Wide Web.[5] That same year, however, online retailing began with the founding of Amazon, eBay, and Craigslist.[6] Utah itself was already a part of the digital revolution: in 1969 computer scientists at the University of Utah built one of the original four nodes of the network that would grow into the internet. During the nineties, the state became a top location for tech startups as well as established computer companies. Novell, Intel, the maker of WordPerfect, and Micron all opened plants and offices not far from Salt Lake City. The climate for tech companies was excellent: an educated, hardworking workforce; ample land; an international airport; a business-friendly local government; alluring outdoor recreation; and reportedly the highest percentage of foreign-language speakers in the country.[7] Mormons and tech worked well together. Having accepted the media's importance to religious evangelization, President Hinckley must have realized the potential for change the new information age would bring.

By 2000 more than half of all Americans were using the internet.[8] With the new millennium came even more innovations in online technology: Facebook (2004), YouTube (2005), Etsy (2005), Twitter (2006), the iPhone (2007), Instagram (2010), Pinterest (2010) as well as growth in the Utah e-economy: Ancestry (1996), Overstock (1999), Adobe (2009), Domo (2010), Qualtrics (2013). In 2012 Utah promoters christened the area south of Salt Lake City "Silicon Slopes" and bragged about its 6,600 tech companies.[9] Even the federal government opened a $1.5 billion cybersecurity center for storing surveillance data in Utah.[10] Four years later, Utah had the fastest-growing personal income in the nation, and Salt Lake City tied with Denver for the city with the lowest unemployment rate.[11]

The rise of the internet, the expansion of the World Wide Web, the development of digital commerce, and the growth of the tech industry in Mormon-dominated Utah all facilitated the increasing openness of the church after a period of mistrust.[12] Church members marginalized in the eighties and nineties—intellectuals, feminists, gays—gravitated to social media as a safe place to express their ideas. Mormon women across the political and cultural spectrum formed "e-sisterhoods" and used the web to "theologize," inspire, and mobilize. Blogging reinvigorated Mormon domesticity, giving the stay-at-home mom not only a platform to assert the spiritual significance of nurturing children but also a place in the commercial economy. Church leaders embraced the web as a tool to "inoculate" members with accurate and thoughtful interpretations of historical topics that "are sometimes misunderstood."[13] At the same time, they stifled dissent when it moved from online discussions to in-person protesting.

On the one hand, the internet intensified the trajectory to simplify and condense that had begun in the sixties. In order to speak to an increasingly diverse global community, the male hierarchy cultivated a small set of core principles that were expressed over and over in church talks and publications. Social media amplified that well-defined message. If those principles were challenged, the response from both local and international leaders would be direct and uncompromising.

Women, on the other hand, employed social media in a distinctly different way. Rather than use the web to consolidate the religion, women exploited the technology in order to expand the number of voices heard throughout Zion. In the first decades of the new millennium, women created tightly knit e-sisterhoods where they "conversed" with people who understood their words, problems, and ideas. The internet facilitated the telling of much more complicated stories about lives and faith, stories that would not be understood (or accepted) in the wider, more diverse global church. While the hierarchy was bound by a commitment to uniformity, Latter-day Saint women demonstrated the myriad ways that Mormonism could be experienced in the modern world. Technology provided women a means to supplement both the standardization of official discourse and the formulaic inclinations of meetinghouse rituals. Sharing stories that were specific, rather than universal, enlivened women's faith but could also lead to disenchantment if the gap between individual and institutional Mormonism turned out to be too wide. From their homes, Mormon women fully embraced this new social media to engage with ideas, articulate beliefs, organize resistance, raise money, celebrate families, and display creativity—all efforts that had been receding from the institutional church.

During the summer of 2004, Lisa Butterworth felt like she was the "only liberal Mormon in the universe."[14] Democrat John Kerry was attempting to unseat the incumbent president, George W. Bush, and the chatter in the ward hallways frequently turned to politics. After college, Butterworth had moved to Boise, Idaho, for her husband's job. While she hoped to talk about politics, church doctrine, and intellectual matters with her husband and neighbors, they were interested in other things. Butterworth remembers feeling isolated. She struggled with her faith but eventually came to believe, in an intense and intimate way, that Mormonism was true. Butterworth, however, never forgot how jealous she felt when the boys passed the sacrament at church while the girls watched. She knew there was something wrong with her high school seminary teacher who told her that nothing good came out of the feminist movement.[15]

At church Butterworth usually kept her progressive political and theological opinions to herself, but one Sunday she spoke up. The lesson that week explored the trials of marriage, and the woman teaching the class considered Mormonism's first prophet: "What challenges," she queried, "did Joseph and Emma face?" The responses came quickly: they lost children, they frequently had to move. Butterworth remembered that seemingly a million things were proposed, "but never the most obvious difficulty they faced, polygamy. Not a single person brings it up." Summoning up her courage, Butterworth offered plural marriage as a cause of marital strife. "The teacher completely shut me down," Butterworth told an interviewer, "She did everything but jump over the chairs and stuff socks in my mouth." Once the subject was changed, the woman went on with her lesson. Butterworth knew that Joseph Smith's polygamy was a historical fact, but she opted to go back to her policy of silence because she did not "want to be the troublemaker."[16]

During previous decades, Lisa Butterworth might have written a letter about her situation to "Mary Marker," the advice columnist at the *Deseret News*, or she might have submitted an article about her experiences to *Exponent II*. But Lisa Butterworth was a "Gen Xer," a member of the first internet generation. A new search engine, the product of a company called "Google," had made finding things on the World Wide Web quick and efficient. Butterworth typed in "Mormon feminist," but all that came up was a newspaper article asking, "where have all the Mormon feminists gone?"[17] Butterworth then discovered the online publications called "blogs" written by a community of faithful—and intellectually oriented—Latter-day Saints. Liberal Mormons dominated the "Bloggernacle," a term that combined "blog" with "tabernacle," the building where Latter-day Saints assembled for their twice-yearly conference. "I became a blog addict," Butterfield recalled. She was not alone: by 2005 an estimated eight million Americans maintained blogs, thirty-two million people read them, and $100 million worth of advertising appeared on them.[18]

Butterworth's initial enthusiasm for the Bloggernacle soon waned. Only Mormon men blogged, and, while their articles were compelling, their issues were not her issues. In August 2004, Butterworth contacted a few other women, and they agreed to found a blog for women. "I went into 'Blogger,' which makes it very easy [to design]," explained Butterworth, "and I chose pink because I wanted to embrace my femininity and it was a trendy color at the time. Then I wrote down 'feminist' and 'Mormon.' And thought, 'hmm,' it was an obvious kind of title. I wanted something a little catchier; what else describes me? And I thought, 'housewife'! That sounds so 'oxymoronish.' That's great, that will really pique people's interests." To give the blog an ironic punch, the *Feminist Mormon Housewives* tagline was "Angry activists with diapers to change."

Feminist Mormon Housewives was the first blog on which Latter-day Saint women explored topics of interest to Latter-day Saint women. It created a new avenue for women to participate in Mormon culture using language rooted in their experience. The content the women produced ranged widely, from political commentaries to details of the minutiae of home life. Within six months the *Feminist Mormon Housewives* blog had been mentioned in the *New York Times* and *Newsweek* and on NPR.[19] Thousands of people were reading the writings of women living around Boise, Idaho. *Feminist Mormon Housewives* became the central blog for the Latter-day Saint feminist community; by 2015 it averaged more than 47,000 unique visitors per month.[20]

Many of the elements in Butterworth's story have long been part of Mormon history: faithful women, longing to move beyond the confines of home and ward, use the written word to communicate their unique experiences. Pioneer memoirs, missionary diaries, and church magazine stories all speak to the Latter-day Saint passion for recording and sharing. *Feminist Mormon Housewives* was just the latest in a long line of publications that helped form a community of like-minded women.

Butterworth's blog, however, reached a wider audience and it did so with more spontaneity and informality than was found in print. Feminists who felt silenced in their wards found consolation and self-expression in *Feminist Mormon Housewives*. Reading and commenting on blog posts facilitated social connection, which diminished women's sense of isolation. The blandness of church materials was supplemented by relevant reflections by average women. In their early history, Mormon women's blogs created a safe environment where people listened and avoided contention, but the landscape soon shifted: commenters on blogs became aggressive, challenging writers and not seriously grappling with their ideas. In response, in 2011 Facebook developed closed groups. As a result, *Feminist Mormon Housewives* maintained a private page of over 3,700 members who were approved by a moderator and who agreed to a code of confidentiality.[21] Thus, despite a harsher online world, in either public or semiprivate online forums, women could focus their questions and delve deeper than they felt they could in their wards. Creative women, who had college degrees but no full-time employment, found that blogging enabled them to explore ideas and foster meaningful relationships. Children could be put down to nap, and then the computer put to work.

As with all new media technology, church leaders initially expressed a "wait and see" attitude. Then in 2008, Apostle Russell Ballard encouraged members to embrace the internet in order to further the work of the church. Ballard also asked members to respond to online articles to ensure accuracy in reporting about Mormons.[22] With the apostle's statement, any concern about the internet vanished: a private activity could be transformed into a public religious witness. Feminists did not have a monopoly on social media. In blogs like *The Small Seed* (2012), *Segullah* (2007), and *A Well-Behaved Mormon Woman* (2008), women directly addressed their own spiritual concerns in a literary manner, seeking to both support the church hierarchy and to articulate their own faithful insights.

Russell Ballard's encouragement provoked a flurry of responses, including ones from women who—like Lisa Butterworth—understood themselves primarily as wives and mothers. Changing national cultural and social trends regarding domesticity increasingly placed housewives at the center of a lucrative industry of lifestyle blogs. This latest repositioning of house-wifery began in the nineties, when businesswoman Martha Stewart dis-covered that American women would buy imaginative homemaking ideas. Stewart developed a media empire that included a magazine with a cir-culation of 1.5 million readers, a cable television show, and a mail-order company.[23] Despite her conviction for insider trading in 2004, Stewart's businesses continue to provide complicated recipes, intricate craft projects, and perfect party-planning ideas. While critics attacked her for her phony WASP elitism, Stewart tapped into the longstanding desire of women to listen to (if not follow) expert domestic advice and to embrace (if not make) the beautiful.

Stewart's good taste and high-gloss domesticity gave way in the new mil-lennium to an earthy, "do-it-yourself" mentality. Young women with en-vironmental concerns wanted slower, more self-fulfilling lives. Retreating from the corporate and the consumerist, the "maker community" revived the practical domestic arts of canning, bread baking, knitting, and chicken raising. Women created a hipster version of what many of their mothers believed to be the drudgery of homemaking. In the hands of Gen X, some aspects of domesticity had become cool. More women were opting to be stay-at-home moms or work part time. The female workforce peaked in 1999 at 74 percent of adult American women and by 2014 had fallen to 69 percent.[24]

In the new millennium, more women saw domesticity not as a problem but as chic self-expression. They looked to the internet for decorating tips, childrearing advice, yummy recipes, and help looking fresh and modern. Young Latter-day Saint women tapped into, and indeed became the pri-mary drivers of, this larger trend toward a "new" domesticity. Not only did their church literature valorize home and family, but their own mothers and grandmothers had developed symbolic and practical systems of suc-cessful homemaking. Lifestyle bloggers (nicknamed "Mormon mommy bloggers") found the web an effective medium through which to celebrate their lives as wives and mothers. Countering what they believed were neg-ative portrayals of women at home, they modeled healthy, confident, and fashionable motherhood. Mommy blogging followed the well-trodden path of Latter-day Saint women who described motherhood as demanding, fulfilling, and as attractive as any profession. In 2011 a non-church writer who was working on a book about the new domesticity published an article about Latter-day Saint women that went viral. "I'm a young, feminist atheist who can't bake a cupcake," Emily Matchar wrote. "Why am I addicted to the shiny, happy lives of these women?"[25] Although its data source is sketchy, the *Deseret News* asserted that 35 percent of blog-reading or -writing moms lived in Utah.[26]

A few bloggers directly combined religion with stories of children and cooking. Stephanie Nielson of *Nie Nie Dialogues* included quotations from church leaders and links to the Book of Mormon. After Nielson had established her blog, she and her husband were in a horrible airplane accident that left her with serious burn injuries. Her writing took on a new direction, reflecting the struggles of a mother trying to reclaim her life after a tragedy. Nielson became an inspirational speaker. So did Al Fox Carraway, whose blog explored her outsider status as a convert with tattoos.[27]

More typically, Mormon bloggers avoided religious messaging. Nodding to Russell Ballard's desire that members use the internet to further the work of the church, *Love Taza*'s Naomi Davis included a link on her site labeled "We Believe," which brought the reader to www.mormon.org. Yet, it is the family itself and not devotional musings that most bloggers offered as witness to the blessings of living the gospel. Lifestyle bloggers presented the home as a wholesome place of deep meaning and loveliness. Caroline Armelle Drake wrote that her mission was "to inspire families and individuals to create and build lasting memories through well thought out meals, traveling and exploring new places together, and creating beautiful surroundings to have a special place to enjoy a happy and fulfilled life."[28] Mormon mommy blogs ranged widely, from the elegant and fashion oriented (*Lyndi in the City*) to the cleverly crafty (*Crafting Chicks*) to recipes for families on budgets (*Deals to Meals*). Women updated traditional Mormon values of industry and thriftiness while proudly claiming a well-organized (and well-appointed) home as the center of their lives. Free of indecision about childrearing practices or resentment of home-making demands, bloggers represented domesticity as inspirational and fashionable.

Blogs often echo—most likely unconsciously—Latter-day Saint visual culture. In 2017 Leigh Anne Wilkes appeared on the front page of *Your Homebased Mom* stirring a white crockery bowl, in a white kitchen, wearing white pants and a light cream sweater.[29] When Melissa from *320 Sycamore* renovated her bathroom and kitchen, she replaced the oaken cabinets with white ones, and added white towels and white basins.[30] Video-blogger Hailey Haugen Devine wore brightly colored Piper & Scoot clothes as she was driven through the snowy mountains in a white vintage Bentley.[31] True, the color white is trendy, but the blond children, platinum-dyed hair, white rooms, and pastel clothing of Mormon mommy blogs also has a religious dimension. The whiteness of fashion blogging mirrored the white environment of the Saints: white stone temples, prints of a white-robed Jesus and white angels, white men's Sunday shirts, and white temple clothing. Both in church and on blogs, the color white signified purity, cleanliness, innocence, virginity, dignity, and holiness. On a less obvious level, white clothing and rooms also spoke to a world without labor, a paradise freed from sweat and dirt.[32]

Mormons place a high value on expressing sexual intimacy only within heterosexual marriage, and Latter-day Saint visual culture tightly connects the color white with spiritual purity. These are core Mormon principles. Around the world, church architecture and art reproduces the association between white and holiness. In their blogs and on Instagram women update modesty and chastity stipulations so they make sense in a modern, elite-oriented, consumer culture. Without mentioning their Latter-day Saint commitments, bloggers presented a modernized version of Spencer W. Kimball's 1954 admonition, "Be Ye Clean."

And yet, this focus on the "white" household only makes sense within the world of affluent North Americans. Bloggers speak a "language" that makes sense in the fantasy life of a particular type of woman but not to women living in most of the world. In addition to the cultural gap, there is a "digital divide" that limits the ability of Latter-day Saint women to even access such mommy blogs. In 2016 more than 88 percent of Americans used the internet compared with 52 percent of South Africans and 28 percent of Ghanaians.[33] Although smartphones have enabled a dramatic rise in web access in developing countries, the electronic infrastructure that makes for easy digital communication in North America is often unavailable in countries where Mormonism is growing. Consequently, women outside of the affluent West are not yet able to use the internet to enrich and complicate core Latter-day Saint principles.

The effortless perfection that Mormon mommy blogs display is also a result of the commercialization of domesticity in North America. Advertising has always presented the home as a site of desire, display, and consumption. By 2003 technical innovations made it possible to automatically place advertisements on blog content: when a reader clicked on the ad, it generated income for the blogger. Companies also gave women goods or services and asked them to review them on their blogs or merely to use the product in "sponsored posts." As blogging became commercialized, homes increasingly looked more elegant and crafts became more complicated. Social media itself became a part-time job, and for some women a family business. Behind the white, labor-free images of wholesomeness and festivity were women at work.

Mormon women also discovered that they could sell their own domestic products online. Rather than explain how to make a wall ornament and then supply a link to purchase the materials, Mormon women joined Etsy and sold their own art. A peer-to-peer e-commerce site, Etsy connects handmade products with buyers.[34] The decorations Brandy Reed sold in her Etsy shop, "The Polka Dotted Girl," were made in her Gilbert, Arizona, house. "I love that I can make an income and be home," she told a reporter. "I think that is why so many LDS women learn to be independent and make an income in that way."[35] Reed did not blog but only posted pictures of her home décor goods. As the image-sharing applications Instagram and Pinterest became more popular, younger users turned away from blogging. The production of stories or even recipes gave way to the production of images.

Women commercializing domesticity and religion followed a well-established Mormon tradition of kitchen-table publishing. In the nineteenth century, Emmeline Wells supported herself with the *Woman's Exponent*. Helen Andelin in 1963 self-published *Fascinating Womanhood*, and then went on to sell workshop materials so women could continue to teach her techniques. In 1992 Betty Eadie and a friend founded Gold Leaf Press in order to distribute *Embraced by the Light*. Eadie's story of life after death sold one million copies within the year and ended up #1 on the *New York Times* bestseller list for an astonishing seventy-eight weeks.[36] Both Andelin and Eadie believed that they were on a mission to present their insights to a wider, non-Mormon audience. Their publications, not unlike mommy blogs, resonated with many American women—Latter-day Saint or otherwise. Just as the internet makes it difficult to distinguish between private and public, commercialized domesticity conflated the roles of "nurturer" and "provider" as well as "reality" and "fantasy."

The lifestyle blogs of Latter-day Saint women express the central Mormon principle that gender is God-given and that women have irreplaceable roles in the family. Through blogging Latter-day Saint women live out that theology via their focus on fashionable appearance. Although absent the cloying preference for feminine childishness relished by Helen Andelin, Mormon mommy blogs resonate with Fascinating Womanhood themes: through makeup, fashion, recipes, crafts, and home decoration, women can assert a manifestly feminine identity. The popularity of cosmetic surgery among intermountain West Mormon women is just the most extreme sign of this.[37] Motherhood need not wear down the body or the household. Both women and their homes need to be desirable and "put together." The higher the production value, the more idealized the home, the more "followers" or clicks, and the more advertising revenue. The perfect

Mormon family, which real Latter-day Saints and even church leaders attest does not exist, is vividly alive on the internet.

At the same time, church leaders continually stress—in their publications if not in appointments to the highest ranks of male leadership—Latter-day Saint internationalism. The multimillion-dollar "I'm a Mormon" advertising campaign foregrounded the many different kind of people who embraced the global faith. To reinforce and expand that message, *The Mormon Women Project* produces podcasts, interviews, and church lessons that highlight the many different experiences of Latter-day Saint women.[38] *Aspiring Mormon Women*, which seeks to support women in their educational and career goals, posts stories of women who struggle to balance work, education, home, and spirituality. Women featured on the site urge other women to reject "either/or" Mormonism.[39] Just as lifestyle bloggers stress the Latter-day Saint family, other women use social media to make real the church's commitment to supporting the diversity of its members.

The World Wide Web enabled Latter-day Saint women to commercialize the perfect Mormon family, but it also facilitated the construction of safe spaces for women to gather when the ideal family dissolves. A mother of five children, Wendy Montgomery supported her church's understanding of marriage and the family. Montgomery lived near Bakersfield, California, and like other Latter-day Saints she went door to door reminding her neighbors to vote on Proposition 8. Then in 2012, her teenage son's grades began to falter and he retreated into his bedroom. After some careful questioning by Montgomery, Jordan came out as gay. He told close family and friends and then posted a letter on Facebook about his sexual orientation.

What made Wendy Montgomery an activist was her ward's response to Jordan. At first everyone said "we still love you," but then even her long-time friends stopped speaking to her. At church people refused to pass the sacrament plate Jordan handed them. Ward members told the bishop that they did not want Montgomery to teach their young women. Although the family had been in the congregation for ten years, the tensions became so high that they transferred to another ward.[40]

About that same time, Gina Crivello began to blog about her efforts to set up a gay/straight alliance group at the Utah high school where she taught. Through a private Facebook message thread, Crivello linked up with other women, including Wendy Montgomery. The women talked about their families and their struggles at church with honesty and laughter. "We all had LGBT children," related Yvette Zobell, "and we had that one thing in common . . . it was so important to have someone we could relate to."[41] The women soon decided to go beyond their Facebook conversations and formed a support group for LGBTQ children called "Mama Dragons."[42]

By 2016 the group had a thousand members.[43] Yet another sisterhood was created.

The Mama Dragons came into being because too many Latter-day Saints were judging and discarding their LGBTQ children. Following Jesus' call to love all, the women saw themselves as listening to the commands of the gospel to attend to the outcasts of their own communities. They continued the longstanding focus of Latter-day Saint women on compassionate service, but their loving and caring was necessitated by the behavior of other Mormons. Using the skills and charitable values cultivated in the Relief Society, they met struggling Saints as they came home from psychiatric hospitals, offered shelter to gay kids living on the streets, talked with skeptical parents and church authorities, and raised funds for pro-LGBTQ organizations.[44] Although men formed a Dragon Dads auxiliary, most of the activities were run by women.

Erika Munson, who started another pro-LGBTQ organization, "Mormons Building Bridges," also looked to motherhood as a model for improving gay/straight relations. Adopting the theme "all families matter," supporters marched in Pride parades and staffed "hugging booths" at Pride festivals. [45] Their Facebook group required all to adhere to polite conversation, avoiding contentious debates and mean-spirited language. Mormons Building Bridges and the Mama Dragons addressed controversial issues like sexual identity from within the safe confines of Mormon-style maternal behavior. With decorum and unconditional love, they called the Saints to show tenderness to all their children and provide care for those in need.

Mama Dragons and Mormons Building Bridges found a secure place within the Latter-day Saint community because the institutional church had become more accepting of faithful LGBTQ members. In 2010 BYU permitted students to organize a gay/straight alliance club, and two years later they posted on YouTube a nine-minute video as a part of the "It Gets Better" movement.[46] Explaining that there were over 1,800 LGBTQ undergraduates on campus, the video showed students giving their names and majors and saying, "I'm Mormon, and I'm a lesbian" (or gay, or bisexual). In 2016 the church launched its official website *Mormon and Gay*, replacing the 2012 *Mormons and Gays* website. The elimination of the plural "s" marked a significant shift in how the official church understood queer Latter-day Saints. Members could have what the church called "same-sex attraction" and still be faithful. On *Mormon and Gay*, church leaders explain that those who live the laws of chastity may fully participate in church callings and temple rituals. One could be both Mormon *and* gay—within distinct limits.

Alongside church leaders' openness to celibate gay Latter-day Saints came an assertion of restrictions directed at those who engaged in homosexual *practices*. In 2015 the *Handbook of Instructions* was updated to say that members who entered same-sex marriages would be regarded as in apostasy and subject to a disciplinary council for possible excommunication. Engaging in homosexual relations, especially cohabitation, was a "serious transgression" at the same level as spouse abuse and adultery and could merit a disciplinary council. Children of those living in "same-gender relationships" could not be baptized or receive other ordinances until they were eighteen years old and no longer living with their parents, and they would have to disavow the "same-gender cohabitation and marriage" of their parents.[47] In a 2017 *Ensign* article on the war between good and evil, General Authority Larry R. Lawrence rejected any possibility of authentic love in gay marriage. "Marriage between a man and a woman is ordained of God," he declared, repeating what his readers knew already, "but same-sex marriage is only a counterfeit. It brings neither posterity nor exaltation. Although his [Satan's] imitations deceive many people, they are not the real thing. They cannot bring lasting happiness."[48] Church leaders recognized that faithful families had LGBTQ children who needed understanding and that Utah's unusually high youth suicide rate was disturbing, but they would not countenance any diminishing of the divine character of heterosexual marriage.[49]

Mama Dragons and Mormons Building Bridges defended and cared for people ostracized in the Latter-day Saint community, but they did so in acceptable Mormon ways as mothers and community caregivers. On websites, LGBTQ supporters refrained from criticizing church leaders or challenging church policy on same-sex marriage. They did not demand theological reworking of doctrines regarding gender or develop their own interpretations of sexual ethics. Even private Facebook forums monitored language and content. Protection from official disapproval could only be ensured in e-sisterhoods if women stayed within acceptable religious norms.

If women challenged church authorities, or demanded the right to *paternal* practices, then neither digital nor physical sisterhoods could protect them. It seemed inevitable that Latter-day Saint feminists would use the web to demand fundamental changes in the leadership structure of Mormonism. The Proclamation on the Family may have promoted equality between marital partners, but no similar text had altered church organizational structures. In 2007 Kynthia Taylor used her blog *Zelophehad's Daughters* to challenge the Proclamation's ambiguous definition of male leadership, accusing it of being too "chicken to stand up for what it believes."[50] The informality of online communications enabled feminists to be more sharply critical of the church. By 2012 Stephanie Lauritzen, the blogger behind *Mormon Child Bride*, became fed up with the continual (but insular) web chatter about women's issues. She argued that such conversations were rarely noticed outside of feminist circles and never changed anything. Lauritzen decided to organize a direct action that would highlight what she believed to be the rigid gender roles that reinforced inequality in the church.[51] She started a Facebook group called "All Enlisted."

All Enlisted invited Latter-day Saint women to perform a simple symbolic gesture: on December 16, 2012, they were to wear pants to church. Although the church has no official dress code for churchgoing, on Sundays Mormon women traditionally wear dresses or skirts while men put on white shirts, dark pants, and ties. All Enlisted wanted Mormons to become more aware of their conventional gender patterns by disrupting social norms.[52] As a protest, "Wear Pants to Church Day" was a flop: only a few women actually wore pants that Sunday.[53] But as a move from digital criticism to "analog," in-person protest, "Wear Pants to Church Day" was a success. Mormon feminists demonstrated that they could move from reading blogs to organizing. The web could mobilize as well as support and comfort. Feminists of the eighties and nineties, who had published in print media and founded feminist organizations, now joined with younger feminists who understood the potential of social media. Using both Facebook and conventional news channels, Mormon women spread their message across the country.

Until "Wear Pants to Church Day" garnered media coverage, most Latter-day Saints had no idea what was going on in the feminist Bloggernacle. It was the national media, not All Enlisted, that caught the significance of the gesture. Wearing pants obviously was about authority—women wanted to "wear the pants" in the church "family." Non-Mormons were interested in the action because the country was experiencing what *Newsweek* called the "Mormon Moment."[54] Television channels broadcast shows about polygamy, and an irreverent musical about Mormon missionaries in Africa had Broadway audiences in stitches. Latter-day Saint Stephenie Meyer's bestselling books about vampires were being made into movies. Mormon Mitt Romney, the former governor of Massachusetts, had recently lost an election against the incumbent president, Barack Obama. The nation was primed for stories about the peculiar Mormons. "Wear Pants to Church Day" received news coverage because Mormons were important. Feminists realized that they, too, could have a Mormon Moment.

The organizers of "Wear Pants to Church Day" were unsure how to proceed after their action, but other feminists had more well-defined ambitions. Kate Kelly, a recent law school graduate working as a lawyer for a human rights center in Washington, DC, felt that while the secular world would not tolerate gender inequality, her religious world did. In January 2013, Kelly contacted other Mormon feminists and discussed organizing both a direct action and a website. Three months later, on the anniversary of the founding of the Relief Society, "Ordain Women" was launched. Borrowing a technique from the church's "I'm a Mormon" campaign, supporters posted their pictures and autobiographical statements on the website. With their spouses and children surrounding them, these average Mormons told stories of continuing inequality, sexism, and the desertion of women from the church. They detailed how struggling congregations filled with converts could not take full advantage of the skills of female leadership and how the Heavenly Parents meant for all of their children to have priesthood powers. Word that Ordain Women had been launched spread across the Bloggernacle and within twenty-four hours it had 10,000 discrete hits.[55]

From the beginning Ordain Women was more than a website; Kate Kelly wanted a direct action that called attention to women's desire for priesthood ordination. Previous generations of feminists had already laid out the theological and historical case for expanded female leadership. Now it was time for "thoughtful, faith-affirming strategic action."[56] The Ordain Women community brought together veteran feminists like Lorie Winder Stromberg and Margaret Toscano with younger feminists like April Young Bennett, Hannah Wheelwright, and Chelsea Shields Strayer. Through on-line discussions and conference calls, the women organized a direct action to occur at the October 2013 general conference. Ordain Women requested 150 tickets to the priesthood meetings—gatherings restricted to men. The request was denied. Instead, the church announced that for the first time, the priesthood session would be broadcast live on television and over the internet.[57]

Knowing church authorities would not honor their appeal for tickets, the women planned to respectfully wait in the standby ticket line at the Conference Center. Kate Kelly and the other supporters of Ordain Women stressed that they were faithful Latter-day Saints, not radicals. Kelly frequently referred to her mission to Spain, her encouraging husband and parents, and how important her religion was to her identity. She was a proud BYU graduate. The profiles on the Ordain Women site detailed women's church callings and overflowed with family pictures. Kelly and her organizing board were well aware that demonstrations in favor of the Equal Rights Amendment were too bold and brazen for most Mormons and that, in the words of Chelsea Strayer, Ordain Women needed to "strategically control their message."[58] During a training session, Ordain Women organizers told protesters to wear their Sunday best dresses and never to shout or raise their voices. The women did not carry signs or banners. By being sensitive to the Mormon style of womanhood, Ordain Women leaders believed they would have a better chance of reaching a wider audience of

Latter-day Saints. "This was not a protest," summarized Lorie Stromberg, "it was a plea. 'The 'ask' was priesthood."[59]

The national media covered the dispute, motivating Mormons and non-Mormons alike to reflect on the status of women in religious leadership. Believing in the justness of their cause, Ordain Women began organizing an action for the next conference, to be held in April 2014. Shortly before the spring meetings, Jessica Moody from the church's Public Affairs office wrote to the Ordain Women organizers asking them to cease their protests. Moody's comments indicate that, despite their declared intentions, Ordain Women had transgressed established Latter-day Saint boundaries. She emphasized the seriousness of the protestors' actions, insisting that "ordination of women to the priesthood is a matter of doctrine that is contrary to the Lord's revealed organization for His Church." Moody's letter positioned the protestors as standing outside of the legitimate world of Mormon women, writing that the "women in the Church, by a very large majority, do not share your advocacy for priesthood ordination for women and consider that position to be extreme." Moody finished by explaining that since the group had declared the ordination of women to be "non-negotiable," they actually detracted "from the helpful discussions that Church leaders have held as they seek to listen to the thoughts, concerns, and hopes of women inside and outside the Church leadership."[60] Perhaps unintentionally, Moody's letter was dated March 17, the anniversary of the founding of the Relief Society.

The letter deftly positioned proponents of women's ordination outside of mainstream Mormonism. Here was a public relations spokes*woman* reiterating the gender binary where men were presiders who defined church doctrine, interpreted the will of Heavenly Father, and organized "His Church." By demanding priesthood, women like Kate Kelly obfuscated the inspired changes already taking place within the church that were bringing women (like Moody herself) into church leadership. By asking the women not to detract from the sacred environment of the temple, Moody implied that their past efforts *had* desecrated holy space. She also told them that news media cameras would not be permitted on Temple Square, suggesting that publicity was what the women truly desired. The meaning of Moody's letter was indisputable: women *did* speak with authority in the church in appropriate places (she was a female professional writing on behalf of the institution), but female ordination was against church doctrine established not by mere men but by the Lord. Ordain Women was attempting to erase foundational Latter-day Saint beliefs.

The March letter was the first salvo in a harsh response to Ordain Women. The April protest proceeded as planned, with the women standing outside the priesthood session and being denied entry yet again. Social media volunteers had posted photos, videos, and commentaries on multiple platforms encouraging supporters to participate in the action virtually. They used Facebook and Twitter announcements to raise funds. Then, two months later, a disciplinary council excommunicated Kate Kelly. Kelly's bishop stated that "You are entitled to your views but you are not entitled to promote them and proselyte others."[61] In other words, the direct action on Temple Square and the spreading of Ordain Women's message on the internet were Kelly's main offenses. Six months later, April Young Bennett's stake president refused to give her a temple recommend unless she resigned from Ordain Women's board of directors. Temple recommends attest to a member's worthiness to enter the sacred area of the temple. The upcoming temple wedding of her brother convinced her to resign her position.[62] Other feminists feared that they, too, would face disciplinary action. The internet had made organizing social movements easier, but church leaders would not tolerate public demonstrations that contradicted their authority.

Although Ordain Women sought to learn from the history of Sonia Johnson and the protests over the Equal Rights Amendment, history did repeat itself. The web provided a safe place for minority perspectives, but the space around Temple Square was certainly not neutral. A group of women speaking online was difficult to discipline, but Kate Kelly visibly presented herself as the founder, chief organizer, and energizing force behind Ordain Women. In addition, the national media found it convenient to select one person (whose quirky haircut and eyeglasses marked her as a "personality") as the head of a burgeoning social movement. Multiple sources presented Kate Kelly as "presiding," ignoring the collaborative efforts of Ordain Women organizers. Despite the demure "pleas" by women wearing Sunday dresses, church leaders determined that Ordain Women offered a serious challenge to the faith.

After Kelly's excommunication, Mormon women who did not support female ordination depicted Kelly (like Sonia Johnson) as an agent of evil who promoted rebellion against God and his prophets. "Today's Mormon Feminists are bolder than ever," wrote Kathryn Skaggs in *A Well-Behaved Mormon Woman*, "likely due to the support of liberal media outlets."[63] On conservative blogs and websites, women asserted their commitment to obedience, their feelings of equality, and their belief that women have power. Skaggs and Angela Fallentine, an American living in New Zealand at the time, established the Facebook group *Mormon Women Stand*. Its goal was to create a "social media haven" for women "who, without hesitation, sustain the Lord's prophet." By fall 2017 it had 52,700 followers.[64] As with Sonia Johnson's excommunication a generation earlier, some Mormons wondered why dissenters did not just leave the church. And, as in the eighties, women did leave.[65]

The excommunication of Kate Kelly clearly demonstrated the continued willingness of male church leaders to assert their right to define orthodox religious thought and behavior. However, since the birth of the internet, asserting religious authority has become more complicated. Not only do blogs and Facebook pages present various theological perspectives, but Latter-day Saints can read online accounts of Mormon history that differ from what they learn at church. As one Utah woman acknowledged, "You can just type your question in [to a search engine], you don't have to be afraid to ask your bishop. We grew up being afraid to ask questions. People were afraid of being judged. You can ask your question in the privacy of your own home."[66] The internet would supply an array of answers. Which one was true?

By the first decade of the new millennium, the information revolution had convinced influential church leaders that publishing only sanitized versions of its history was dangerous. Members needed to be able to trust the accuracy of materials presented by their church if they were going to resist falsehoods, develop their faith, and trust their leaders.[67] In order to clarify their authoritative teachings, church departments posted key historical documents and short essays on controversial topics. In 2008 the church digitally published the 1842 Nauvoo Relief Society minutes. Now readers could decide for themselves what Joseph Smith said about women and "priesthood keys." In 2013 short "Gospel Topics Essays" were placed on the church's website (www.lds.org). The articles ranged from exploration of race to DNA studies to Joseph Smith's First Vision. Between December 2013 and October 2014 (at the same time that All Enlisted and Ordain Women were organizing protests), three Gospel Topics essays summarized the history of plural marriage.[68] The complicated past of early Latter-day Saint women was straightforwardly acknowledged. Although the essays were unattributed so they could carry the weight of the church itself, they benefited from the scholarship of professional historians, including four specialists in Latter-day Saint women's history.[69] The Gospel Topics essays also contributed updated and approved history for church curricula.

This is not to say that the Gospel Topics essays or the documentary collections altered Latter-day Saint practices. For example, the Gospel Topic essay "Joseph Smith's Teaching About Priesthood, Temple, and Women" (2015) taught that "like most other Christians in their day, Latter-day Saints in the early years of the Church reserved public preaching and leadership for men." The essay did not contradict the established church position, concluding that Joseph Smith used terms broadly and never *acted* to confer priesthood offices on women. That the Nauvoo minutes indicated that Joseph Smith approved of women performing healings did not motivate new policies on who could and could not heal. Indeed, it was

Ordain Women that posted staged photographs illustrating what blessing and healing by women *might* look like.[70] Yes, women did bless and heal in the past, but the Gospel Topic essay reminded readers that by 1926 church president Heber J. Grant had told members to call the elders and not the sisters "to administer to the sick." Women received priesthood ordinances in the temple but not "ecclesiastical office."[71]

Church historians hoped the Gospel Topics essays would reassure members about controversial hot-button topics such as race or polygamy, but some Latter-day Saint women were not reassured. Although the details of Joseph Smith's polygamy were familiar to scholars, many members were surprised to learn of his multiple marriages or the fact that in 1857 probably half of the Mormons in Utah Territory had experienced life in a polygamous family.[72] Moreover, by excommunicating historians like D. Michael Quinn, many Mormons cast a wary eye on scholarship that was not necessarily "faith promoting." Throughout the dark days of the eighties and nineties, Latter-day Saints had bravely defended their church's position against doubters and anti-Mormons. They shunned "alternate voices." Now, however, the church was saying it was true that Joseph Smith had married a fourteen-year-old-girl and that longstanding racial policies did not date to the earliest church. Women had trusted the church, but now it was posting seemingly different messages. What else, some wondered, would be "reinterpreted"?

The new historical honesty unsettled many Mormon women and some even felt deceived. "I got married and had children, but I lived someone else's life," reflected Amy Manly. "Even though I love my children, have a wonderful husband, and a wonderful life that is not the life I would have chosen for myself [. . .]. I did everything I was asked to do [. . .]. I gave it myself completely. And they betrayed me."[73] From Manly's perspective, the past defensiveness of church leaders was wrong. Often the online essays sided with the history told by the dissenters. In a religious community in which history merges with theology, altering history had serious ramifications. "I got more information than I probably wanted to know," Linda Sego concluded, "and I feel so betrayed. I never will be able to trust the church again."[74] For women who had followed President Ezra Taft Benson's advice to concentrate exclusively on the home and who remembered how earlier historical controversies ended, the new Gospel Topic essays were not simply an effort to finally present accurate history. The alteration of the church's attitude threw into question other principles by which women had lived their lives. The more the church opened up its history as evidence of the diverse and expanded world of women, the more some women wondered why they had been so obedient in the past.

Other women felt encouraged and inspired—rather than betrayed—by modifications in the church. In 2012, Neylan McBaine, who at that time was working for church-owned Bonneville Communications, gave a lecture on gender and participation in the church's organizational structure. McBaine first told stories of smart and capable women who had left the church, citing their inability to reconcile their restricted roles in the church with their expanding roles in American society. McBaine told her own story, describing how even though she was a well-paid professional who had authority over men in the workplace, as a "member of my ward's primary [children's group] presidency, I have to get approval from my bishop to join Junior and Senior primary opening exercises. Am I on the path to apostasy because I wonder why this is so?"[75] McBaine wanted to make it clear that the pain that women felt about their exclusion from church governance was real.

Two years later, McBaine published *Women at Church: Magnifying LDS Women's Local Impact*, a practical guide to the problem of exclusion along with possible solutions. To bring women into the church authority structure, McBaine stressed the importance of reinvigorating Latter-day Saints' commitment to cooperative leadership. She also emphasized the importance of making the existing female leaders in the church more visible. McBaine joined with Fiona Givens, Margaret Young, Maxine Hanks (who had been baptized back into the church), and Melissa Wei-Tsing Inouye as Latter-day Saint women who sought to craft a "middle way" between the status quo and the push for women's ordination.[76]

McBaine acknowledged that men can be condescending and patronizing to women, but she also pointed out that women fail to speak up. Generational, educational, and cultural differences limit how women express themselves. Some are timid and afraid of overstepping boundaries. Others will offer opinions informally but are unwilling to do the hard work to alter ward or stake life. Still other women undermine those who are trying to be creative or innovative. Rather than engage in a direct way, women assert their influence behind the scenes, sometimes in manipulative ways. To improve exchanges between men and women, both sexes would have to learn new ways of communicating. McBaine did not advocate for women's ordination, but she did argue for women having more confidence in asserting power throughout the church (not just in the ward) and for the church hierarchy to cultivate women's unique contributions.

Political scientist Valerie Hudson [Cassler] aimed to enlarge the understanding of priesthood, which she developed in the online journal *Square Two*. Hudson argued that Latter-day Saint men had access to "priesthood" power and women to "priestesshood" power.[77] Together the powers combined to create "Priesthood" (with a capital "P"), the powers of heaven.

Such authority mirrored the "diarchy of celestial heaven"—neither a patriarchy nor a matriarchy but a combination of male and female powers. In the summer of 2015, Hudson elaborated on this concept as she celebrated the new policy of placing female church leaders on the highest-level executive councils of the church:

> If God is our Heavenly Mother and our Heavenly Father, united in the new and everlasting covenant of marriage, then together their powers constitute the Priesthood of God. Understood in this way, priestesshood is the power of God the Mother, and priesthood is the power of God the Father. When married, those powers are infinite in scope and make divinity possible.

The closer the earthly order mirrored the patterns established by the Heavenly Parents, the sooner "new and wonderful blessings" would arrive.[78] Hudson's theology buttressed the metaphysical binary of Mormonism that celebrated heterosexuality as divinely ordained.

That "our Parents rule together in Heaven," Hudson argued, was a foundational belief, not a peripheral one. Heavenly Mother "is the absolute equal partner of Heavenly Father."[79] Hudson was not alone in this impression: after the Proclamation on the Family's reference to "heavenly parents," mention of Heavenly Mother became more acceptable. A 2011 scholarly article published in *BYU Studies* counted over six hundred mentions of Heavenly Mother or Heavenly Parents (mostly the latter) in past Latter-day Saint publications—convincing the authors that there has never been a "sacred silence" surrounding this celestial figure.[80] The Gospel Topics online essay "Mother in Heaven" reiterated that "the doctrine of Heavenly Mother is a cherished and distinctive belief among Latter-day Saints," but the essay also repeated President Gordon B. Hinckley's comment that since Jesus prayed only "unto the Father," the Saints should do likewise.[81] Although no worshiping of Heavenly Mother would be permitted, the Saints wrote theological reflections and poetry about her, and blogged about her place in their lives.

Then, in 2016, Deseret Book Company published a children's book, *Our Heavenly Family, Our Earthly Families*, which dramatically brought Valerie Hudson's diarchy into mainstream Mormonism. The book's front cover reproduced a painting by Provo artist Caitlin Connolly of Heavenly Father and a distinctly pregnant Heavenly Mother. The Divine Couple lean into one another, with the Mother's head slightly lower than the Father's. Their bodies merge into one. Departing from traditional Mormon artistic style, both parents have halos. They also both have platinum-tinted white hair, a symbolically pure counterpart to their ocher robes. Spilling from the Heavenly Parent's unified body/dress are a series of circles that transform into faces and then into heads on bodies. The resulting spirit children are of various shapes and colors, but they all wear white robes.

For a church-owned publishing house to approve of a cover depicting a deity with a rounded belly and breasts is a remarkable assertion of theological self-confidence. From its very inception, Mormonism set itself apart from other Christian traditions by defining God as embodied, modern-day miracles as real, and the Book of Mormon as a literal description of an ancient past. In the twentieth century, however, Latter-day Saints came under the influence of Progressive Era Protestantism, which preferred a controlled and rational faith. By the end of the century, Mormons found ethical and political allies among conservative Protestants who insisted that true Christianity must be centered on the Bible. The contemporary Mormon attitude toward Heavenly Mother, however, departs from these Protestant cousins on the left and right. From Valerie Hudson's theological deliberations, to Caitlin Connolly's paintings, to Rachel Hunt Steenblik's poetry, Mormon women offer speculations about the female nature of deity.[82] The internet has provided a readily available outlet for such thoughts.

Not all Latter-day Saints are active online, but the internet has provided an efficient and effective way of linking the like-minded. Women in particular use the web to enrich, deepen, push, and challenge the limits set by male church leaders. From designing religious goods for the home, to writing theological reflections, to organizing social action, women go online to circumvent the structures of a highly centralized church. Even the most orthodox of women, who understand themselves only as spreading the inspiration of the prophets, pick and choose what they will publish. As global Mormonism grows more diverse and digital, international Saints will claim identities separate from the Latter-day Saints of the intermountain West. New Zealander Gina Colvin started the blog *Kiwi Mormon* and the podcast *A Thoughtful Faith* in order to tilt the e-conversation away from the United States by raising critical questions about the impact of American culture on an international church. Likewise, African American Latter-day Saints are increasingly becoming more active on social media. In 2009, Tamu Smith and Zandra Vranes founded the blog *Sistas in Zion*, which uses humor to refute racial and religious stereotypes.

Almost by definition, social media works against the universalizing character of a global religion. Lifestyle blogging presents a perfect home life that excludes almost everyone—single women as well as queer women, but also non-American members, Mormons of color, poor women, and almost every married woman who has an ordinary, disorganized household. One male blogger despairingly dubbed Mormon mommy blogging "lifestyle porn" because it offers an unrealistic picture of home life that is addictive, and that can lead to disappointment and inadequacy.[83] Such criticism again puts Latter-day Saint women in a double bind—they are asked to celebrate motherhood, but not too much, and certainly not to make money off it. They are expected to look good, to be organized, to be educated—but not too much.

Other critics see social media as directing the attention of women away from their ward and the church hierarchy, where it rightly belongs. In a moment of exasperation about women who sit silently during Sunday gospel doctrine lessons, Mary Ellen Elggren asked, "Why aren't they participating?" The flight from interpersonal exchange made no sense to this outspoken senior Mormon. For Elggren, women "need to participate, and if they have something on their mind, they ought to bring it up. And it ought to be discussed. And for them to just sit there with something bugging them and then come home and broadcast their griefs over Facebook, I think that is the dumbest thing they could do. What is that all about?"[84] Elggren resented the turn toward a privatized religion that favors the computer over the congregation. While blogs and Facebook do provide space for marginalized Mormon women to say, "I belong, too," this is a fragile group. Feminists, Mormons of color, international members, and working women will need to "see" themselves in the real, "analog" world of Mormonism if they are to become vital contributors to the sisterhood of Saints. A "filter bubble" might make one feel comfortable in the virtual ward of social media, but it is just that—a bubble.

In general, however, Mormon women use social media as an organizational tool in order to accomplish things in the real world. This could be as straightforward as arranging dates for a book club meeting or as complex as addressing thorny social problems. Shortly after Donald Trump's 2016 inauguration, Sharlee Mullins Glenn, a children's book author, started a private Facebook group to vent her political frustrations. Five months later she was standing outside of a Homeland Security office in West Valley City, Utah, shouting in a bullhorn surrounded by friends who held signs protesting the deportation of Silvia Avelar-Flores.[85] Like the Mama Dragons, Mormon Women for Ethical Government moves back and forth between online discussions, web articles, and daily calls for action. They both quote from church prophets and demand civil discourse of their members. At its core, Mormonism is a communal religion that relies on the commitments of its members not only to pray together but to do service projects, teach the church's youth, maintain standards of dress and comportment, and support its missionary outreach. While the digital world of Mormonism is alluring, women will not exchange the intensity of face-to-face interactions for the comfort of the computer.

Epilogue

Women have been a powerful force in shaping Mormonism since its earliest days, but that power has taken different forms at different times. How will the next generation of Mormon women influence the church? Women—whether through their blog posts, influence on the family, social activism, formal theology, or economic pursuits—will be key drivers of change. And that will be true even if, from the Latter-day Saint perspective, God directs the decisions of church prophets.

Since the nineties, feminist values have shaped Latter-day Saint ritual and social life. The 1990 temple alterations brought Eve more positively into the drama of the Garden of Eden story and associated her with visionary wisdom rather than personal weakness. The 1995 Proclamation on the Family pulled away from past descriptions about *how* women should nurture and encouraged more gender equality within families. Using the imprecise word "nurture" meant that conservative women could point out that females are still divinely ordained to be caregivers while liberals could stress that nurturing did not exclude professional or civic pursuits. Given the broadness of the term, even single, divorced, widowed, and queer celibate Mormon women can nurture without hewing to conventional motherhood. By cultivating a theology of silence and forgetting, Latter-day Saint leaders carved out space for diversity and choice within their communities.

Motherhood itself has increasingly become a choice and not a mandate for Mormon women. Beginning in the eighties, *Church Handbooks* softened the longstanding understanding that bringing numerous spirit children into the world marked a woman as righteous. Family size, church leaders eventually explained, was a decision to be made "between the couple and the Lord." Education, wage labor, and civic volunteering are all more attainable when women have some control over when and how often they give birth. Certainly parenting becomes more manageable. At the same time, by stipulating that the decision was the couple's and not only the woman's, the policy reinforced the communal nature of Mormonism. In marriage, both the husband and wife have claims upon each other. Reproduction on earth rests on a spiritual foundation because it mirrors celestial expansion. The importance of the autonomous individual, which feminists and other thinkers take as indicative of a modern society, is moderated by such policies. Mormons instead stress community—on earth and in heaven—and that emphasis will continue to shape the future of Latter-day Saint women.

Latter-day Saint women are free to fill in the details regarding femininity and motherhood, and their perspectives range widely. The "style of our own" Mormonism of the intermountain West still echoes within the male leadership structure, but Latter-day Saint women freely adapt that culture to their own lives. Whether one lives in Boston or Botswana, being a Mormon woman no longer automatically means belonging to a specific class, political party, or racial group. Church leaders celebrate such diversity, but women also bring with them complicated family structures and social traditions that challenge naïve notions about religious unity. Convert women in particular will continue to expand the cultural expressions of Mormonism, urging members to reject enduring feminine stereotypes. They will seek to create places of comfort rather than of judgment in their wards.

Constructing a ward life that uplifts all women must include placing women in leadership positions. Since the nineties, church leaders have sought to encourage mutual decision-making by insisting that women be included in councils—in the family, ward, and church hierarchy.[1] Latter-day Saints note that even the heavens are run by councils, but this recent inclusion of women in community leadership works against traditional practices of patriarchal authority.[2] And there's a similar shift in family life—men have been told to be partners with their wives, not autocrats.

Whether or not men will listen to women as they speak at home and in councils is another question altogether. Women are not permitted on all councils, and they typically are in the minority, often watching rather than directing. Priesthood ordination gives men the authority to "preside," but when and how they must preside is not well defined. Clearly, men have no experience being under the authority of women at church. Church apostles may assert the importance of mutual consultation, but unless someone teaches men how to successfully run meetings and listen to women, members will struggle to form effective councils. Likewise, women will need to learn to communicate more forcefully. It has been almost fifty years since Latter-day Saint women had control over their wards' money or their agendas. If women in councils—in wards or at higher administrative levels—are patronized or if the majority of women prefer to be passive, greater visibility in leadership circles will only lead to frustration.

The rising numbers of sister missionaries should also be predictive of women's expanding voice within the church. Modifications to the missionary program signaled a willingness to make the mission field more hospitable and to provide young women with spiritual knowledge and pragmatic leadership training. Returning sister missionaries will likely feel more secure in robustly voicing their ideas in councils and other settings. Men who have worked with women on their missions should be more comfortable with female leadership. Lowering the missionary age also underscored an acceptance of women marrying later, facilitating their authority at home as well as at church. Especially for women outside of the affluent West, the missionary experience may be the only chance women have to move outside their local environments.

By encouraging younger—and senior—women to be missionaries, the church highlighted its willingness to cultivate women's leadership potential. However, as the church opens up opportunities for women and calls them to take on a fuller palette of responsibilities, it expects them to be supportive of its authority. Obedience remains a foundational value. Missionary life is the training ground for learning how to follow as well as how to lead. Women who serve as missionaries will not necessarily be the agents of change. The sacrifices they make may easily function to uphold the status quo, placing a brake on liberalizing trends.

Consequently, whether Latter-day Saint women will "lean into" executive roles in the church as they become available is not clear. Many women already struggle to manage two shifts—as mothers and workers. If official discourse also encourages them to be "aspiring women"—to be achievers in school, career, and community—then women will have much on their plates, and a third shift as "minister" might simply be too much. Latter-day Saint women will not turn away from intense involvement with their families, and so it is possible that they will find it more useful to support efforts to bring men more fully into the home rather than themselves trying to move more fully into the church. The problem of the future might be less a feminist one of expanding official roles for women and more a pragmatic one of women choosing not to put their energy into church life.

Women may be also less eager to take on ward leadership roles if they continue to be excluded from certain ritual activities. Latter-day Saint women publicly offer prayers, teach, and bear their testimonies. As presidents of Young Women, Primary, and Relief Society, they choose their counselors and direct their teachers. Women play critical ritual roles in the temple. Still, each Sunday, only boys pass the Sacrament. Mothers are not brought into the sacred circle of Melchizedek priesthood holders when new babies are blessed. Latter-day Saints have not altered the language of common hymns or scriptural translations to make them more gender-inclusive, as some other Christian denominations have. Mormon reverence for the King James Version of the Bible and belief that gender is an irreplaceable category works against any such change. Sister missionaries teach potential converts, but only the elders may baptize. The fact that women ritually healed in the past has not altered who may administer to the sick in the present.[3] In 2018 teens were given new roles in the temple. Boys could perform proxy baptisms and girls could assist or be "helpers."[4] Changes to temple work, however, also call attention to the ritual difference between male and female members. In a world where girls are encouraged to accomplish as much as their brothers, will assisting be adequate to keep young women committed?

It will take high-level change to bring women into ritual activities, perhaps even a theological rethinking of the nature of Latter-day Saint ordinances. On a pragmatic level, many Mormons seem to accept Helen Andelin's conclusion about what happens when women become active: "as you lift, he sets the bucket down."[5] In mixed situations, some women themselves prefer men to preside. However, for women who are inclined to assert spiritual power there are evolving opportunities in the ward and temple. Unlike in other faith communities, in which organizational activities are not seen as having religious dimensions, Latter-day Saints have a long tradition of seeing the sacred within the profane. It is in the multiple ways of service, Latter-day Saints explain, that they follow in Jesus' footsteps. Women who constantly look for power and recognition contravene this core Mormon value.

The speed at which women's place in leadership and liturgical structure changes will be a carefully choreographed dance between cautious church authorities, persistent female members, and the general pressures of national cultures. It is certainly possible that church leaders dealt harshly and swiftly with Kate Kelly in order to demonstrate their authority. Periodically, the hierarchy asserts control both by publicly declaring who has committed apostasy and by discreetly adjusting to changing social mores. Male power will maintain its central place in Mormonism by occasionally flexing its muscles.

While most Mormon women uphold feminist values—gender equality in the workplace, respect for women's voices, the right to birth control—only a minority consider themselves "feminists." The Ordain Women protests generated considerable conversation among Latter-day Saint women in the United States but not in other parts of the world. "Feminism" is still a dirty word for many Mormon women, one they associate with agitating for women's ordination or denying the importance of the family. Mormon women insist that their religion empowers them and that God has made men and women different but not unequal. For them, radical change that includes women's ordination, is unnecessary.

However, a minority of Latter-day Saint women claim the label "feminist." They assert their right—as Mormons—to balance a career with motherhood, to question church policies, and to expand their leadership roles within the church. Just as conservative women see antifeminism as Mormon, liberals see feminism as a legacy of their unique history and beliefs. But unlike in other religious communities where believers form congregations of the like-minded, Mormon wards are geographically based. Especially outside of Utah, wards are made up of women who hold a variety of opinions on feminism. As they interact with each other in Relief Society meetings or on service projects, polarization is modified and a more moderate perspective on feminism cultivated.

In a world in which images and objects are central to religion—as in every other aspect of life—Mormon women have tremendous influence over how their religion is lived. Mormon women are masters of the internet. Through social media, women decide which elements in a religion to "pin" or "post," and which to ignore. They decide which church leader's comments should be made into decorative plaques and which should be forgotten. Women make and market the goods they believe will make the home virtuous and, in the process, the home takes on a Mormon feel. For some women, that effort offers employment possibilities that merge the domestic, the economic, and the religious. It will be women, and not simply the official publications of the church, who will either celebrate the diversity of their religious community or retreat to a comfortable tribalism that merely updates midcentury Mormonism.

Women who are not satisfied with such pragmatic influences or who are frustrated by a perceived lack of real change will leave the church—as they did over polygamy, the ERA, Proposition 8, and the 2015 policy on same-sex marriage and apostasy. If history is any guide, women who turn their backs on the church will see their act as an awakening and not as a retreat. Disenchanted women will take their talents, creativity, courage, and spiritual enthusiasm to other religious traditions or social and political causes. Most critically, if the gap between generations of women widens—between orthodox, domestically oriented mothers and heterodox, career-oriented daughters—the church will have a difficult time maintaining women's commitments among communities of well-to-do Mormons. Children who see their mothers leave the church often go along with them.

The high value that Latter-day Saints place on marriage and family means that questions of sexuality will always linger in the background. After World

War II, Mormons created a profoundly resilient culture that endured the challenges of the feminist movement until almost the end of the century. That style, however, was particularly problematic when it came to sexuality. Doctrinally, men and women are held to the same high standards of premarital chastity. However, Latter-day Saints, like other conservative religious communities, direct their worries about modesty and virginity toward girls and women. In the past, revered leaders such as Spencer W. Kimball and Boyd K. Packer dramatically and memorably expressed their teachings on sexuality. Mothers passed on their concerns to their children not to "pull off their fragrant petals."[6] While official discourse might reflect a theology of forgetting and not repeat past condemnations, the very intensity of the sexual language makes it difficult to relegate such judgments to history. The revelation by kidnap and sexual abuse victim Elizabeth Smart that she felt that no one would ever want to marry her because she had been raped numerous times underscored the enduring power of the "chewed gum" imagery of Mormon purity culture.[7]

In 2016 BYU came under international scrutiny when female students who reported sexual assaults were brought up for honor code violations. While the college eventually adopted an amnesty policy that generally shields students who reported sexual assaults, the wider problem remained: How does a religion instill the value of chastity while still recognizing the positive nature of female sexuality and the all-too-real presence of male aggression? In a religion organized and staffed by "average" people, what images *should* be used if the past imagery of plucked flowers and licked cupcakes are deemed detrimental? Latter-day Saints will have to develop a more sophisticated understanding of sexuality and its relationship to the sacred character of the body in order to confront the negative effects of "style of our own" sexuality.

As with the stress on purity, however, the very significance of the heterosexual couple in the theology and sociology of Mormonism generates its own challenges. In the intermountain West, there are more single Latter-day Saint women than men.[8] Although the evidence is thin, there is a general sense that Utah men leave the religion at higher rates than women.[9] The older women get, the more difficult it becomes to find appropriate marriage partners. While many see Mormon attitudes toward homosexuality as detrimental, far more pressing is the "singles problem." Singles are less active, more apathetic, and more apt to leave the religion entirely.[10] To address this challenge, the church establishes wards made up of the unmarried and organizes social events. It pays particular attention to securing the commitments of young men, who are the only holders of the priesthood. Members develop dating apps and matchmaking services. With Americans (including Latter-day Saints) marrying later and converts often arriving wedded to non-Mormons, the "singles problem" will continue to weigh heavily on the Saints.

How does a religious community that vigorously promotes marriage and the family not exclude the many single, divorced, widowed, and queer women who make up their congregations? Although global Mormonism is diverse, some Latter-day Saint women reinforce a constricted perspective on womanhood—often as a business endeavor. The asymmetry of the "singles problem" then motivates women to concentrate on physical appearance and, in turn, deliver a steady stream of readers to lifestyle fashion bloggers. As makers of social media, Latter-day Saint women have greatly contributed to the revalorization of homemaking. However, in doing so they create images of wives and mothers who look remarkably similar to each other. It is not simply men who delay marriage while searching for the perfect woman; Mormon women, too, set unrealistic expectations for themselves. Women who want to combat such stereotypes do not have an easy way to resist such images in our media-saturated society.

The success of the Mormon mommy blogs speaks to the continual importance of a gender divide not only in Latter-day Saint theology but in the American imagination. That it seems almost impossible to eradicate the stereotype of "the" Mormon woman speaks more to the endurance and prevalence of unrealistic gender standards that many Western women and men hold (and that spreads globally) than to a theologically based "eternal sex." There never has been a singular "Mormon woman." Despite this reality, Americans continue to elevate a minority of Latter-day Saints into a fantastical majority. American women, who find themselves rattled by the myriad choices available to them, and overworked in the "second shift," find something reassuringly optimistic about Mormons. There is a vicarious pleasure in watching the confident Mormon mommy who is as clever as a pioneer and as pretty as young Marie Osmond. While this might actually pull some women toward conversion, more often it is a "virtual" conversion. Who does not want to be a part of a big, beautiful, happy, and tension-free Mormon family?[11]

Real Latter-day Saint women build and sustain their religion. In recent years, church leaders have addressed places where women can be brought more fully into leadership, but at a cautious pace. It remains to be seen whether this rate will be sufficient to keep women vitally committed to their faith or what further changes will be brought about. Latter-day Saints take pride in prophetic insight that permits adjustments to their religion. The context in which women live their religion will increasingly be relevant as Mormonism becomes fully global. Women from wealthy nations, where they work alongside of and in front of men, will be the most sensitive to the places where their church limits their activities. They also will be the most reluctant to contribute their energies to a community that contravenes deeply held values, the very values cultivated in the Latter-day Saint family and ward. It will be women who determine whether the next generation remains committed to their faith—and precisely what shape that faith will take.

ACKNOWLEDGMENTS

There are many people to thank for their care and support during the writing of *Sister Saints*. Paul Reeve, in the Department of History at the University of Utah, patiently read each chapter. He kept me from making egregious errors, but all others I claim as my own. Likewise, Derek Hoff, whose knowledge of modern American history is boundless and who excels at careful reading, took time out to help a colleague. In the Department of World Languages and Cultures, Margaret Toscano, who has been my friend since my arrival in Utah, always provided insight. The University of Utah supported my research through a sabbatical and Research Committee Grant that enabled me to use the talents of our amazing graduate student, Charlotte Hansen Terry. Now working on her doctorate, Charlotte carries on the important work of historical scholarship—as do Constance Lewis, Justin Bray, and Joseph Stuart, all graduate students who helped me with their conversations and correctives. I also took full advantage of the University of Utah's Undergraduate Research Opportunities Program, which funded Tiffany Law, Lynley Hogan, and Kristen Beck. Without their eye for current Latter-day Saint culture, *Sister Saints* would be far less rich.

Working in Mormon Studies brings one into contact with many bright and gracious individuals. Jonathan Stapley shared hard-to-locate materials with me, while Patrick and Melissa Mason facilitated my research travels. I particularly want to thank Kate Holbrook, specialist in women's history at the Church History Department, for her perceptive comments. Ken Cannon and Dave Hall were invaluable for sorting out pre–World War II Mormonism. Brian Birch, Kristine Haglund, Tona Hangen, Amy Hoyt, Caroline Kline, Julie Neuffer, Quincy Newell, Carol Madsen, Marie-Therese Maeder, Andrea Radke-Moss, Jana Reiss, and Heather Stone set aside time from their own scholarship to talk with me about mine.

Latter-day Saints in many parts of the world trusted me with their stories. They took time out from busy days to help a stranger better understand their faith. While the perspective of an outsider can never match those of the insiders, I do hope that they recognize their lives in this history. I specifically want to thank Linda and Michael Dunn for their care while I was in

South Africa as well as Cristian Mannino in Italy. In Utah, Hollie Fluhman checked to see that women's voices did not get lost in any scholarly ob-fuscation. The many interviews that I conducted were expertly transcribed by Chris Dunsmore. Those interviews supplemented the rich collection of women's writings and oral histories preserved in the archives of the University of Utah, Brigham Young University, Claremont University, the Huntington Library, and the Church History Library. Thank you to the archivists who watch over these valuable texts. At Oxford University Press, Theo Calderara kept me from getting lost in all those stories. My agent, Michelle Tessler, weathered the transition from Catholics to Mormons with characteristic encouragement.

Every scholar needs a friend who will read a "zero" draft even before it goes off to the experts. I am blessed with having two such friends. John Hurdle—who has husbanded me through all my book writing—lent his scientist's eye for precision to my prose. Linda Jansen, my friend since junior high, helped me make the text understandable to the curious reader. There is nothing so precious in life than to have a husband and a friend who can challenge your mind as well as soothe your soul. I dedicate this book to Ann Braude, who has always inspired me with her commitment to women's history and her all-encompassing friendship. Latter-day Saints place a high value on family, and contact with them has made me even more apprecia-tive of my own. My father Ken, at age ninety-two, and my daughter Brigit, at twenty-two, each provided their love in their own ways. Thank you all.

NOTES

ABBREVIATIONS

BYU   L. Tom Perry Special Collections, Harold B. Lee Library, Brigham Young University

CHL   Church History Library, The Church of Jesus Christ of Latter-day Saints

Claremont   Claremont Mormon Women Oral History Collection, Library of the Claremont Colleges, Claremont, California

D&C   Doctrine and Covenants

HL   Huntington Library, San Marino, California

JD   *Journal of Discourses*

UU   Special Collections, Marriott Library, University of Utah

ONLINE RESOURCES
[SPECIFIC ARTICLES CAN ALSO BE RETRIEVED BY SEARCHING FOR TITLE OF ARTICLE]

Conference Reports (1880–2011):

     https://archive.org/details/conferencereport?&sort=date&page=1

General Conference (1971–present):

     https://www.lds.org/general-conference/conferences?lang=eng

Encyclopedia of Mormonism:

     http://eom.byu.edu/index.php/Encyclopedia_of_Mormonism

Ensign:

     https://www.lds.org/ensign/2017?lang=eng

Improvement Era:

     https://archive.org/details/improvementera?&sort=date

Journal of Discourses:

     http://jod.mrm.org/1

Liahona: https://www.lds.org/liahona/2017?lang=eng

Relief Society Magazine:

     http://lib.byu.edu/collections/relief-society-magazine-index/

Relief Society Memories of Rexburg and North Rexburg States, 1883–1945:

     https://archive.org/stream/reliefsocietymem00reli#page/n3/mode/2up

Susa Young Gates, diary:

     https://dcms.lds.org/delivery/DeliveryManagerServlet?dps_pid=IE1883501

Newspaper articles available online: *New York Times, Salt Lake City Tribune, Deseret News*

PREFACE

1. T. J. Jackson Lears, *No Place of Grace: Antimodernism and the Transformation of American Culture, 1880–1920* (New York: Pantheon Books, 1981), 12.

CHAPTER 1

1. "Editorial Notes," *Woman's Exponent* (February 1, 1884): 132.
2. Emmeline Whitney to Newel K. Whitney, October 10, 1847, Newel K. Whitney Collection, BYU. Partially reproduced in Carol Cornwall Madsen, "A Mormon Woman in Victorian America" (PhD dissertation, University of Utah, 1985), 45.
3. Emily Faithfull, *Three Visits to America* (Edinburgh: David Douglas, 1884), 151; 152.
4. "Emily Faithfull's Book," *Woman's Exponent* (November 15, 1884): 92. All quotes in this paragraph come from this article.
5. Jan Shipps, *Mormonism: The Story of a New Religious Tradition* (Urbana: University of Illinois Press, 1985), 110.
6. Emmeline B. Wells, diary, January 26, 1890, BYU.
7. The History of Helena Erickson Rosbery (1883), HL. The date of her conversion is not mentioned, but she was born in 1828. For ease of reading, spelling and punctuation have been modified.
8. Mary Nixon Bulkley, autobiographical sketch, CHL.
9. Richard K. Jensen, "Perpetual Emigrating Fund Company," in Allan Kent Powell, ed., *Utah History Encyclopedia* (Salt Lake City: University of Utah Press, 1994), 419–20.
10. "Homespun" (Susa Young Gates), *Lydia Knight's History: The First Book of the Noble Women's Lives Series* (Salt Lake City: Juvenile Instructor Office, 1883), 22, discussing Joseph Smith's visit to the Canadian borderlands on October 24, 1833 (21). The visit is also mentioned in Smith's journal, October 27–28, 1833: "had a good meeting one of the sisters got the gift of toungues (sic) which made the saints rejoice may God increase (sic) the gifts among them for his sons sake," 16–17 (http://josephsmithpapers.org/paperSummary/journal-1832-1834#!/paperSummary/journal-1832-1834&p=17) [JS Journal].
11. Ruth May Fox, diary, February 8, 1895, CHL.
12. Wells, diary, March 15 and April 11, 1890, BYU.
13. Emmeline B. Wells, "A Venerable Woman, Presendia Lathrop Kimball," *Woman's Exponent* (June 1, 1883): 2.
14. Donald G. Godfrey and Brigham Young Card, *Diaries of Charles Ora Card: The Canadian Years* (Salt Lake City: University of Utah Press, 1993), 269, for December 23, 1894, as quoted in Martha Sonntag Bradley and Mary Brown Firmage Woodward, *4 Zinas: A Story of Mothers and Daughters on the Mormon Frontier* (Salt Lake City: Signature Books, 2000), 298.
15. Eliza Maria Partridge Lyman, diary, March 19, 1880, HL.
16. Susanna Morrill, "Relief Society Birth and Death Rituals: Women at the Gates of Mortality," *Journal of Mormon History* 36 (Spring 2010): 129.
17. Gregory A. Prince, *Power from on High: The Development of Mormon Priesthood* (Salt Lake City: Signature Books, 1995), 202, quoting a patriarchal blessing located in the Irene Bates Collection, UU.
18. Minutes of the Sixth Meeting of the Society, April 28, 1842, in "A Book of Records, Containing the proceedings of The Female Relief Society of Nauvoo," March 17, 1842–March 16, 1844; handwriting of Eliza R. Snow, Phoebe M. Wheeler, Hannah M. Ells, and an unidentified scribe. Digitized at: http://josephsmithpapers.org/paperSummary/nauvoo-relief-society-minute-book and reproduced in Jill Mulvay Derr et al., eds., *The First Fifty Years of Relief Society: Key Documents in Latter-day Saint Women's History* (Salt Lake City: The Church Historian's Press, 2016), 55.
19. Ibid.
20. Margaret McNeil Ballard, autobiography (1917), BYU.

21. Martha Cragun Cox, autobiography (1928–30), CHL.
22. Emmeline B. Wells, "Pen Sketch of an Illustrious Woman," *Woman's Exponent* (October 15, 1880): 74.
23. Ballard, BYU.
24. Nauvoo Relief Society, Minutes, March 17, 1842, in Derr, *The First Fifty Years*, 31.
25. Nauvoo Relief Society, Minutes, April 28, 1842, in Derr, *The First Fifty Years*, 56; March 30 [31st], 1842, in Derr, *The First Fifty Years*, 43.
26. Brigham Young, Discourse to High Priests Quorum, March 9, 1845. Nauvoo High Priests Quorum Record, 1841–45 CHL. Excerpted in Derr, *The First Fifty Years*, 171.
27. Brigham Young, Discourse to Seventies Quorums, March 9, 1845, Record of Seventies, Book B, 1844–48, pp. 77–78, First Council of Seventies Records, CHL. Excerpted in Derr, *The First Fifty Years*, 171.
28. "History of Joseph Smith," *Deseret News*, September 5 and 19, 1855.
29. Historian's Office, Journal, August 8, 1855, CHL. As cited in Derr, *The First Fifty Years*, 199.
30. Historian's Office, Journal, March 29–30, 1855, CHL. As cited in Derr, *The First Fifty Years*, 199.
31. "The Women of Utah Represented at the International Council of Women, Washington, D. C.," *Woman's Exponent* (April 1, 1888): 164.
32. Ibid.
33. "R. Society Reports," *Woman's Exponent* (June 15, 1872): 18.
34. Comment made regarding raising worms in spring of 1900. Matilda S. Andrus, oral history [c. 1960s], CHL.
35. "General Relief Society Conference," *Woman's Exponent* (November 15, 1899): 78.
36. Spawn fish: *Journal of Discourses* (April 8, 1868): 203; telegraph, schoolbooks, men's tailoring: *Journal of Discourses* (April 7, 1873): 20, 16, 16; obstetrics: Derr, *The First Fifty Years*, 530.
37. Brigham Young, "Obeying the Gospel," *Journal of Discourses* (July 18, 1869).
38. Brigham Young, "The Order of Enoch," *Journal of Discourses* (October 9, 1872).
39. Eliza Maria Partridge Lyman, diary, November 25, 1878, HL.
40. Dean May, "A Demographic Portrait of the Mormons, 1830–1980," in D. Michael Quinn, *The New Mormon History: Revisionist Essays on the Past* (Salt Lake City: Signature Books, 1992): 125.
41. Salt Lake City population from Thomas G. Alexander and James B. Allen, *Mormons and Gentiles: A History of Salt Lake City* (Boulder, CO: Pruett Publishing, 1984), 87–89.
42. Jane H. Blood, diary, December 25, 1880, CHL.

CHAPTER 2

1. Jill Mulvay Derr and Karen Lynn, Davidson, eds., *Eliza R. Snow: The Complete Poetry* (Provo, UT: BYU Press, 2009), 312–14.
2. Eliza R. Snow, *Poems, Religious, Historical, and Political*, vol. 1 (Liverpool: F. D. Richards, 1856), 1f.
3. Michael Hicks, " 'O My Father': The Musical Settings," *BYU Studies Quarterly* 36 (January 1996): 35.
4. Samuel Morris Brown, *Heaven as It Is on Earth: Joseph Smith and the Early Mormon Conquest of Death* (New York: Oxford University Press, 2012), 222.
5. Orson Pratt, "Celestial Marriage," *Journal of Discourses* (August 29, 1852).
6. Joseph F. Smith, "Discourse," Oneida Stake Conference, Franklin, ID, January 20, 1895, published in *The Latter-day Saints' Millennial Star* 58/12 (March 19, 1896): 180.
7. *Encyclopedia of Mormonism*, s. v. "Mother in Heaven."
8. Helen Mar Whitney, *Why We Practice Plural Marriage* (Salt Lake City: Juvenile Instructor Office, 1884), 7.

9. Diary and Autobiography of Eliza Maria Partridge Lyman (1846–85), speech inserted into diary at entry January 17, 1879, HL.

10. Emmeline B. Wells, "Women Talkers and Women Writers," *Woman's Exponent* (August 15, 1876): 44.

11. Rose Budge Shepard, interview by James E. Hulett, March 23, 1937, HL.

12. Mrs. Orson Smith, interview by James E. Hulett, March 18, 1937, HL.

13. Esther Anderson Huntsman, interview by James E. Hulett, April 9, 1937, HL.

14. "Statement of Mrs L[ucy]. W[alker]. Kimball" copied for the Federal Writers Project by Elvera Manful, Ogden, Utah, Weber County, January 1940, from a copy borrowed from Mrs. Kimball's niece, Mrs. Lydia Rogerson, HL. Also in the Kimball Young Collection, BYU.

15. L. Oliver Skanchy, interview by James E. Hulett, March 15, 1937, HL. Oliver Skanchy said the family had nine children, but Anthon Skanchy says he has four in his autobiographical sketch. John A. Widtsoe, trans. and edited, *Anthon L. Skanchy: A Brief Autobiographical Sketch of the Missionary Labors of a Valiant Soldier for Christ* (np: np, 1915): 34. https://archive.org/stream/anthonlskanchybr00skan#page/n3/mode/2up

16. Kathryn M. Daynes, *More Wives than One: Transformation of the Mormon Marriage System, 1840–1910* (Carbondale: University of Illinois Press, 2001), 99–103.

17. Republican Party Platform of 1856, June 18, 1856 (http://www.presidency.ucsb.edu/ws/?pid=29619).

18. *Reynolds v. United States* as cited in Sarah Barringer Gordon, *The Mormon Question: Polygamy and Constitutional Conflict in Nineteenth-Century America* (Chapel Hill: University of North Carolina Press, 2002), 133.

19. D. Michael Quinn, "LDS Church Authority and New Plural Marriages, 1890–1904," *Dialogue* 18 (Spring 1985): 27. Quinn references several diaries noting this meeting but the original notes are not available.

20. Annie Clark Tanner, *A Mormon Mother: An Autobiography* ([1941]; Salt Lake City: University of Utah Press, 1969), 56.

21. Andrew Jenson, ed., "A Chronology of Important Events of the Year, 1885," in *The Historical Record*, vol. 6 (Salt Lake City: n.p., 1887), 1–23 and notes 5, 16, 17, and 23, unattributed explanatory endnotes for "Mormon Women's Protest, An Appeal for Freedom, Justice and Equal Rights" (1886) (http://www.fairmormon.org/Misc/MormonWomenProtest.pdf).

22. Ken Driggs, "The Prosecutions Begin: Defining Cohabitation in 1885," *Dialogue* 21 (Spring 1988): 120, citing 970 convictions and 106 acquittals, with the church claiming that 1,300 Mormons had been imprisoned.

23. Carol Cornwall Madsen, "A Mormon Woman in Victorian America" (PhD dissertation, University of Utah, 1985), 86–88.

24. Emmeline Wells diary, January 27, 1890, and April 9, 1890, BYU.

25. The following information is based on the excellent article by Kenneth L. Cannon II, "The Tragic Matter of Louie Wells and John Q. Cannon," *Journal of Mormon History* 35 (Spring 2009): 126–90.

26. Emmeline Wells diary, May 14, 1887, BYU.

27. A March 5, 1869, *New York Times* article claims that the newspaper hatched upon the idea of Utah female suffrage idea "a year or two ago" and quotes from the published article. I have not been able to locate the original article. B. H. Roberts in his *Comprehensive History of the Church* said that Hamilton Wilcox, New York member of the Universal Franchise Association, appeared before the House Committee on Territories on February 27, 1869, to ask for Utah female suffrage (vol. 5:323f).

28. *Deseret News*, March 31, 1869.

29. *Deseret News*, March 24, 1869.

30. Laurel Thatcher Ulrich, *A House Full of Females: Plural Marriage and Women's Rights in Early Mormonism, 1835–1870* (New York: Alfred A. Knopf, 2017), 378, citing Minutes of a Ladies Mass meeting, January 6, 1870, in Relief Society Minutes and Records, 1868–1873, Fifteenth Ward, CHL.

31. Beverly Beeton, "Woman Suffrage in Territorial Utah," *Utah Historical Quarterly* 46 (Spring 1978): 102.

32. Elizabeth Cady Stanton, "On Marriage and Divorce," 1871 (http://gos.sbc.edu/s/stantoncady3.html).

33. Carol Cornwall Madsen, *An Advocate for Women: The Public Life of Emmeline B. Wells, 1870–1920* (Provo, UT: BYU Press, 2006), 134.

34. Ibid., 154.

35. Ibid., 168.

36. Eliza R. Snow, "Discourse," July 24, 1871, reprinted in Jill Derr et al., *The First Fifty Years of Relief Society: Key Documents in Latter-day Saint Women's History* (Salt Lake City: Church Historian's Press, 2016), 365–72.

37. Carol Cornwall Madsen, "Creating Female Community: Relief Society in Cache Valley, Utah, 1868–1900," *Journal of Mormon History* 21 (1995): 142, citing "Utah Woman Suffrage Association," *Women's Exponent* 19 (April 1, 1891): 147.

38. Lisa Bryner Bohman, "A Fresh Perspective: The Women Suffrage Associations of Beaver and Farmington, Utah," *Utah Historical Quarterly* 59 (Winter 1991): 14.

39. Ibid., 10.

40. D&C, Official Declaration 1.

41. "The Manifesto and the End of Plural Marriage" (https://www.lds.org/topics/the-manifesto-and-the-end-of-plural-marriage?lang=eng&old=true#32), citing Kenneth L. Cannon II, "Beyond the Manifesto: Polygamous Cohabitation Among LDS General Authorities After 1890," *Utah Historical Quarterly* 46, no. 1 (Winter 1978): 24–36.

42. Kenneth L. Cannon II, "After the Manifesto, Mormon Polygamy 1890–1906," *Sunstone* 8 (January/March 1983): 28.

43. Sigrid Hockenson Skanchy, interview by James E. Hulett, May 20, 1938, HL.

44. For instance, see E. M. Wright interview by James E. Hulett, March 10, 1937, HL.

45. Josephine Spillsbury Vance, interview by Fay Ollerton, October 27, 1935, HL.

46. Ken Driggs, "Twentieth-Century Polygamy and Fundamentalist Mormons in Southern Utah," *Dialogue* 24 (Winter 1991): 46.

47. B. Carmon Hardy, *Solemn Covenant: The Mormon Polygamous Passage* (Carbondale: University of Illinois Press, 1992), 342.

48. Emmeline B. Wells, diary, September 29, 1890, BYU.

CHAPTER 3

1. Thomas G. Alexander, *Mormonism in Transition: A History of the Latter-day Saints, 1890–1930* (Urbana: University of Illinois, 1996), 5.

2. Ann Cook, diary, August 2, 1894, CHL.

3. *Improvement Era* (September 1915): 1024.

4. Data gathered from looking at the Relief Society minute books of the First through Tenth Wards in Salt Lake City, housed in CHL. Statistics gathered from the minute books were total membership, total meetings, average attendance, and percentage attendance. Continued concern about low attendance led to a membership campaign in 1937; see *Relief Society Magazine* (November 1937): 728.

5. Jonathan A. Stapley and Kristine Wright, "Female Ritual Healing in Mormonism," *Journal of Mormon History* 37 (Winter 2011): 78.

6. Alexander, *Mormonism in Transition*, 101.

7. Jill Mulvay Derr, Janath Russell Cannon, and Maureen Ursenbach Beecher, *Women of Covenant: The Story of the Relief Society* (Salt Lake City: Deseret Book Company, 1992), 174, citing Relief Society General Board Minutes, 1892–1911, October 3, 1896.

8. Ibid., 174, citing Relief Society General Board Minutes, 1892–1911, March 26, 1901.

9. Ibid., 175. It is unclear what primary source was used to obtain this amount.

10. Ibid., 175. It is unclear what primary source was used to obtain this quote.

11. Circular of Instructions no. 12 issued in 1913 as described in "Real Estate and Buildings," *Relief Society Magazine* (March 1915): 131.

12. "Real Estate and Building Fund," *Relief Society Magazine* (March 1915): 130.

13. Emmeline B. Wells, diary typescripts, August 28, 1904, BYU.

14. Annie Wells Cannon, diary, May 24, 1880, BYU.

15. Emmeline Wells, diary transcripts, June 16, 1900, BYU.

16. For a biography of Annie Cannon see "Our Mother," Margaret Cannon Clayton, UU.

17. Annie Clark Tanner, *A Mormon Mother: An Autobiography* (Salt Lake City: University of Utah Press, 1969), 207.

18. Mary Susannah Sumner Fackrell Fowler, diary typescript, April 3, 1900, CHL.

19. Fowler diary: Teasdale visit, April 18, 1900; letter read at meeting, April 22, 1900; $10 donation to ward, April 26, 1900; purchase of Bible, May 2, 1900, CHL.

20. George F. Richards, *Seventy-Seventh Semi-Annual Conference* (October, 1906): 69.

21. "Straightforward," David Roy Hall, "In the Utah Vanguard: Amy Brown Lyman as Progressive Mormon Activist, Welfare State Builder, and Modern Woman in a Dual Career Family" (PhD dissertation, University of California, Santa Barbara, 2004), 19. The descriptions come from interviews from the following colleagues (all at CHL): Fayne R. Perkins Lohmoelder: "precise, cut and dry. It was either right or it was wrong"; Vervene H. Pingree: "outspoken; if she didn't like anybody, you would know about it"; Helen M. Ross: quick-paced, moved and spoke quickly, had sharp brown eyes, was very determined, and "a perfectionist who knew social work."

22. Emmeline B. Wells to Amy Brown Lyman, letter, October 6, 1909, CHL.

23. Tanner, *A Mormon Mother*, 283–85.

24. Emmeline B. Wells, diary transcript, January 9, 1904, BYU.

25. Ending female healing was uneven. A mid-twenties description of a pair of Latter-day Saint women healing, one who was called "Grandma Eardley," is found in Anna Fullmer Griffiths, diary, March 20, 1926, and another by Sisters Smith and Miller, July 9, 1931, CHL. A clear statement that women should not wash, anoint, or administer to the sick was made in 1946 by Joseph Fielding Smith in response to a Relief Society query; letter, Relief Society Washing and Anointing File, CHL.

26. Cynthia Sturgis, " 'How're You Gonna Keep 'Em down on the Farm?': Rural Women and the Urban Model in Utah," *Agricultural History* 60 (Spring 1986): 197.

27. Dave Hall, *A Faded Legacy: Amy Brown Lyman and Mormon Women's Activism, 1872–1959* (Salt Lake City: University of Utah Press, 2015), 71f.

28. Hilda E. Miller Harvey, interview by Loretta L. Hefner, 1979, CHL.

29. Helen M. Ross, interview by Loretta L. Hefner, 1979, CHL.

30. Genevieve Thornton, "The Relief Society Social Service Department," *Relief Society Magazine* (January 1931): 15.

31. Bruce D. Blumell, "Welfare Before Welfare: Twentieth-Century LDS Church Charity Before the Great Depression," *Journal of Mormon History* 6 (1979): 89–106 at 102, citing Amy Lyman Brown, "Social Service Work in the Relief Society, 1917–1928" [an unavailable, restricted text. The Church History title is slightly different: *A Brief History of Social Service Work in Relief Society, 1917–1927*] and *Handbook of the Relief Society* (1931), 54.

32. Jill Derr, "A History of Social Services in the Church of Jesus Christ of Latter-day Saints, 1916–1984," unpublished study, 45, CHL. Author's possession.

33. Ibid., 36.

34. Lydia D. Alder Bearn, interview by Loretta L. Hefner, 1979, CHL. See also Derr et al., *Women of Covenant*, 237.

35. Evelyn H. Lewis, interview by Loretta L. Hefner, 1979, CHL.

36. Helen M. Ross, interview by Loretta L. Hefner, 1979, CHL.

37. Annie Wells Cannon, diary, October 19, 1921, BYU.

38. Cannon made this reflection in her diary after she had an "interview" with Gates following her mother's death. Annie Wells Cannon, diary, May 21, 1921, BYU.

39. Susa Young Gates, diary, May, [no date], 1922, CHL; also available online.

40. According to Cannon, Clarissa Williams, who was on the General Board and would become Relief Society president after Wells, made the statement. Annie Wells Cannon, diary, April 1, 1921, BYU.

41. Ibid., March 19, 1921, BYU.

42. Ibid., April 2, 1921, BYU.

43. Ibid., April 19, 1921, BYU.

44. Ibid., 1921, end page, BYU.

45. Ibid., February 4, 1921, BYU.

46. Jeannette A. Hyde, "Responsibility of Woman as a Citizen," *Relief Society Magazine* (June 1923): 309f.

47. Derr et al., *Women of Covenant*, 210, citing Emmeline B. Wells and Olive D. Christensen to President of Relief Society, November 20, 1911, Relief Society Circular Letters, 1914–1922, CHL. See also "Circular of Instructions," *Relief Society Magazine* (March 1915): 129.

48. Ibid., 210, quoting Relief Society General Board Minutes, February 4, 1915.

49. Ibid., 213, quoting Relief Society General Board Minutes, May 23, 1918.

50. Ibid., 231, quoting Relief Society General Board Minutes, April 4, 1922.

51. Loretta L. Hefner, "The National Women's Relief Society and the U. S. Sheppard-Towner Act," *Utah Historical Quarterly* 50 (Summer 1982): 260.

52. *Relief Society Memories of Rexburg and North Rexburg States, 1883–1945*, "History of Burton Ward Relief Society, 1943–1945," 42, CHL. Also online.

53. Amy Lyman Brown, "Historical Events in the Relief Society," *Relief Society Magazine* (August 1927): 395.

CHAPTER 4

1. Markku Ruotsila, "Senator William H. King of Utah and His Campaigns Against Russian Communism, 1917–1933," *Utah Historical Quarterly* 74 (Spring 2006): 148, quoting 66th Cong., 1st Sess., *Congressional Record* 58 (November 18, 1919): 8706–08.

2. Ibid., 149.

3. William H. King, 69th Cong., 2nd Sess., *Congressional Record* 68 (January 13, 1927): 1577.

4. Ibid., 1576.

5. Ibid., 1578.

6. Ibid., 1581.

7. Ibid., 1583.

8. Dave Hall, *A Faded Legacy: Amy Brown Lyman and Mormon Women's Activism, 1872–1959* (Salt Lake City: University of Utah Press, 2015), 101. By this date, King's first wife and Lyman's sister-in-law had died, and he had remarried.

9. Carolyn M. Moehling and Melissa A. Thomasson, "The Political Economy of Saving Mothers and Babies: The Politics of State Participation in the Sheppard-Towner Program," *Journal of Economic History* 72 (March 2012): 99.

10. Quote is the subheading. The headline read: "Be Guided by the Facts: Don't Be Deceived by False Promises. Senator King's Record at Washington is one of OPPOSITION to Utah's Welfare," *Salt Lake Tribune* (November 2, 1928).

11. On pure milk and vitamins, see *Relief Society Magazine* (August 1925): 423. For an example of technical advertisements, see *Relief Society Magazine* (September 1926): ad pages, and for the Report, see *Relief Society Magazine* (October 1927): 482.

12. Joseph F. Darowski, "Utah's Plight: A Passage Through the Great Depression" (master's thesis, BYU, 2004), 56f.

13. Evelyn Hodges Lewis, interview by Loretta L. Hefner, 1979, CHL.

14. Hilda E. Miller Harvey, interview by Loretta L. Hefner, 1979, CHL.

15. Annie D. Palmer, "The Social Worker in the Unemployment Emergency," *Relief Society Magazine* (January 1932): 17.

16. John F. Bluth and Wayne K. Hinton, "The Great Depression," in Richard Poll, ed., *Utah's History* (Provo, UT: BYU Press, 1978), 485.

17. Helen M. Ross, interview by Loretta L. Hefner, 1979, CHL.

18. Evelyn Hodges Lewis, interview by Loretta L. Hefner, 1979, CHL.

19. *One Hundred Third Annual Conference* (April 1933): 103.

20. Garth L. Mangum and Bruce D. Blumell, *The Mormons' War on Poverty: A History of LDS Welfare, 1830–1990* (Salt Lake City: University of Utah Press, 1993), 126.

21. Ibid., 133. This reflection is probably from Harold B. Lee's diary, but it is restricted. A fuller description, supposedly quoting from the diary, is in L. Brent Goates, *Harold B. Lee: Prophet & Seer* (Salt Lake City: Bookcraft, 1985), 142–43. The earliest published statement by Lee is Harold B. Lee, "Admonitions for the Priesthood of God," *Ensign* (January 1973): 104.

22. Vera W. Pohlman, interview by Loretta L. Hefner, 1980–81, CHL.

23. Ann Amelia Chamberlin Esplin, interview by Ronald Esplin, 1973, CHL.

24. "Notes from the Field," *Relief Society Magazine* (December 1936): 775.

25. Hilda E. Miller Harvey, interview by Loretta L. Hefner, 1979, CHL.

26. Ann Amelia Chamberlin Esplin, interview by Ronald Esplin, 1973, CHL.

27. Evelyn Hodges Lewis, interview by Loretta L. Hefner, 1979, CHL.

28. Leonard Arrington, "The New Deal in the West: A Preliminary Statistical Inquiry," *Pacific Historical Review* 38 (1969): 315.

29. John F. Bluth and Wayne K. Hinton, "The Great Depression," in Richard Poll, ed., *Utah's History* (Provo, UT: BYU Press, 1978), 488f. See also Joseph F. Darowski, "The WPA Versus the Utah Church," in Brian Q. Cannon and Jessie L. Embry, eds., *Utah in the Twentieth Century* (Logan: Utah State University Press, 2009), 167–85.

30. Vera W. Pohlman, interview by Loretta L. Hefner, 1980–981, CHL.

31. Amy Lyman Brown, "Some Challenges to Women," address delivered at Utah State Agricultural College, July 1940. Amy Lyman Brown Papers, BYU.

32. Derr et al., *Women of Covenant*, 297ff., citing "Memo of Suggestions," 1–6, Church Union Board Executive Committee Minutes, CHL.

33. J. Reuben Clark, Jr., "Our Homes," *Relief Society Magazine* (December 1940): 802.

34. J. Reuben Clark, Jr., *One Hundred Tenth Annual Conference* (April 1940), 21.

35. Dorothy M. Brown and Elizabeth McKeown, *The Poor Belong to Us: Catholic Charities and American Welfare* (Cambridge, MA: Harvard University Press, 1997), 194.

36. "Wheat to Be Stored," *One Hundred Tenth Annual Conference* (April 1940), 16.

37. Derr et al., *Women of Covenant*, 288, citing Relief Society General Board minutes of April 19, May 24, and June 7, 1944.

38. Annie Wells Cannon, diary, January 7, 1940.

39. Ibid., April 19, 1940.

40. Ibid., August 27, 1940.

41. *Deseret News* (November 13, 1943).
42. Belle S. Spafford, interview by Jill Mulvay Derr, 1976, CHL.
43. "Messages of the First Presidency," *113th Semi-annual Conference* (October 1942), 12f.

CHAPTER 5

1. Belle S. Spafford, interview by Jill Mulvay [Derr], November 1975–March 1976, 65.
2. Susan M. Hartmann, "Women's Employment and the Domestic Ideal in the Early Cold War Years," in Joanne Meyerowitz, ed., *Not June Cleaver: Women and Gender in Postwar America, 1945–1960* (Philadelphia: Temple University Press, 1994), 86.
3. John E. Christensen, "The Impact of World War II," in Richard Poll, ed., *Utah's History* (Provo, UT: BYU Press), 510.
4. Ibid., 505.
5. Miriam B. Murphy, "Gainfully Employed Women, 1896–1950," in Patricia Lyn Scott and Linda Thatcher, eds., *Women in Utah History: Paradigm or Paradox?* (Logan: Utah State University Press, 2005), 210.
6. Ibid., 212; 211.
7. Maureen Ursenbach Beecher and Kathryn L. MacKay, "Women in Twentieth-Century Utah," in Richard Poll, ed., *Utah's History* (Provo, UT: BYU Press, 1978), 577. It is impossible to determine what percentage of those women were Latter-day Saints, but the overall Mormon population of the state consistently hovers around 60 to 70 percent.
8. Seven Year Report of the President (1950–51 to 1956–57) of BYU, 167; Ernest L. Wilkinson Papers, Box 171, folder 7, BYU. Student body statistics from BYU (http://yfacts.byu.edu/Article?id=104).
9. Lillie Buhler Day, typescript autobiography, 38, BYU.
10. Belle S. Spafford, "If You Live Up to Your Privileges," *Relief Society Magazine* (November 1951): 725. Spafford laid out a similar summary of social forces with the conclusion that woman's greatest mission was that of wife and mother. "The Place of Latter-day Saint Woman [*sic*]," *The Improvement Era* (May 1958): 335; 354. Spencer W. Kimball in 1963 wondered if the destructive actions of the nation's teens were due to fathers "furnishing cars and money" and "mothers making money" who abandon their homes. After acknowledging that some mothers must work, he suggested, "let every working mother honestly weigh the matter and be sure the Lord approves before she rushes her babies off to the nursery, her children off to school, her husband off to work, and herself off to her employment" ("Keep Mothers in the Home" [December 1963]: 1071f.). Similar concerns were voiced frequently in *The Improvement Era*—by Thomas S. Monson, "What Is Man, that Thou Art Mindful of Him" (September 1964): 762; David O. McKay, "The Realm of Women" (August 1965): 676f.; A. Theodore Tuttle, "On Being a Father" (June 1967): 87; and John H. Vandenberg, "Keepers at Home" (December 1967): 79f. and "Choosing a Career" (November 1969): 90.
11. James E. Talmage, "The Eternity of Sex," *Young Woman's Journal* (October 1914): 600–04.
12. Spafford, "The Place of Latter-day Saint Woman," 354.
13. Vesta P. Crawford, "Household of Faith," *Relief Society Magazine* (May 1950): 295–98.
14. David O. McKay, "A Woman's Influence," *Relief Society Magazine* (December 1950): 800.
15. https://www.plannedparenthood.org/files/1514/3518/7100/Pill_History_FactSheet.pdf, citing Bernard Ashbell, *The Pill: A Biography of the Drug that Changed the World* (New York: Random House, 1995).
16. Ezra Taft Benson, *One Hundred Thirty Ninth Annual Conference* (April 1969), 12. Reprinted in *Improvement Era* (June 1969): 44.
17. Sylvia Probst Young, "The Lasting Joys," *Relief Society Magazine* (April 1953): 249–53; Blanche Sutherland, "Second Best," *Relief Society Magazine* (April 1954): 229–35.

18. Rodello Hunter, *A Daughter of Zion* (New York: Alfred A. Knopf, 1972; reprint Salt Lake City: Signature Books, 1999), 114; "Did you Know that . . ." *The Improvement Era* (January 1965): 78.

19. Levi S. Peterson, *Juanita Brooks: Mormon Woman Historian* (Salt Lake City: University of Utah Press, 1988), 185.

20. Andrew Hamilton, "Florence Smith Jacobsen: Saving Our Material Heritage" (http:// www.keepapitchinin.org/2013/04/02/guest-post-florence-smith-jacobsen-saving-our-material-heritage/#footnote_1_21537).

21. Lael J. Littke, "Mama Lives in the Kitchen," *Relief Society Magazine* (February 1964): 97. In a 1977 interview, Camilla Kimball (Spencer W. Kimball's wife) also echoed this sentiment. She preferred being called a homemaker, not a housewife, because "a homemaker needs to have all the skills in the world. She needs to be an accountant, an economist, a dietician, a psychologist and a sociologist. She needs to know something about everything. Everything. Everything that she can learn will make her a more efficient homemaker." Camilla Kimball, interview by Jessie Embry, 1977, CHL. Reciting the variety of tasks that mothers accomplish was common in both church and nonreligious literatures. See, for instance, William J. Critchlow, "Women and the Priesthood," *Improvement Era* (December 1965): 1120ff.

22. Number of members in 1940: W. Paul Reeve and Ardis E. Parshall, *Mormonism: A Historical Encyclopedia* (Santa Barbara, CA: ABC-Clio), 57; population increase: Terryl L. Givens, *People of Paradox: A History of Mormon Culture* (New York: Oxford University Press, 2007), 231.

23. Jay M. Price, *Temples for a Modern God: Religious Architecture in Postwar America* (New York: Oxford University Press, 2013), 98.

24. Givens, *People of Paradox*, 245.

25. #054 born 1923, interview by Jacqueline Mayer, February 8, 2010, Claremont Mormon Women Oral History Project, Honnold Library, Claremont Graduate University, Claremont.

26. Hunter, *A Daughter of Zion*, 90.

27. Zina Pearl Heninger Burr, diary, November 15, 1953, CHL.

28. Veronica Dalhender, interview by Colleen McDannell, February 11, 2015.

29. Spafford interview, 209; also *Relief Society Magazine* (December, 1950): 825.

30. #0084 (born 1938), interview by Annette Billings on November 23, 2009, Claremont.

31. Hazel Lamoreau to Mary Marker [no date], ACCN 1862, Box 36, Folder 2, Ramona W. Cannon Letters, UU.

32. *Relief Society Magazine* 1963 (January): 66; (February): 147; and (June): 475.

33. Hunter, *A Daughter of Zion*, 91. The Annual Report of 1952 noted that "theology and testimony meetings continued to have the largest attendance, followed in order by social science, literature, and work meetings." *Relief Society Magazine* (September 1953): 612.

34. #025 born 1917, interviewed December 26, 2009, Claremont.

35. "New Titles for Lesson Courses," *Relief Society Magazine* (June 1966): 460.

36. Spafford interview, 101.

37. [No name] to Mary Marker, [circa 1948–49]. ACCN 1862, Box 34, Folder 3, Ramona W. Cannon Letters, UU.

38. "Mary Marker" was Romana Wilcox Cannon, who epitomized the outward-looking Mormon women of the Progressive Era. She graduated from the University of Utah in 1908 with a bachelor's degree, studied languages in Berlin and Paris, traveled to Rome, Athens, Constantinople, and Cairo, and completed a master's degree in 1913 in English and philosophy—the third woman in the state to earn such a degree. A year later she married a widower with three children. Her marriage brought her into one branch of the vast and well-respected Cannon family. After her marriage, she moved

to Colombia, had four children (for a total of seven), and began submitting articles to the *Relief Society Magazine*. Joseph J. Cannon was also president of the Latter-day Saint British mission and the family lived there from 1934 to 1937. After her husband's death and stints of teaching, she was approached by the *Deseret News* to write a "Dear Abby"–like column, which she began when she was sixty. Over 1,400 "Dear Mary Marker" letters sent to her are preserved at the University of Utah. At the time of her death in 1978 at the age of ninety-one, she was pursuing a doctorate in sociology at the University of Utah.

39. [No name] to Mary Marker, [circa 1948–49]. ACCN 1862, Box 36, Folder 2, Ramona W. Cannon Letters, UU.

40. Madelene C. Scott to Mary Marker, November 2, 1951. ACCN 1862, Box 34, Folder 7, Ramona W. Cannon Letters, UU.

41. [Ely, Nevada] to Mary Marker, [circa 1948–49]. ACCN 1862, Box 36, Folder 2, Ramona W. Cannon Letters, UU.

42. "Lazy Susan" to Mary Marker, March 9, 1955. ACCN 1862, Box 35, Folder 4, Ramona W. Cannon Letters, UU.

43. David O. McKay, *The Latter-day Saint Millennial Star* (May 8, 1924): 296.

44. Alberta Banks to Mary Marker, March 2, 1948. ACCN 1862, Box 34, Folder 3, Ramona W. Cannon Letters, UU.

45. Mrs. O. H. Lamoreaux to Mary Marker, March 16, 1955. ACCN 1862, Box 35, Folder 6, Ramona W. Cannon Letters, UU.

46. Elise E. Hart to Mary Marker, March 18, 1955. ACCN 1862, Box 35, Folder 6, Ramona W. Cannon Letters, UU.

47. Mrs. E. F. Kehl to Mary Marker, [no date]. ACCN 1862, Box 36, Folder 3, Ramona W. Cannon Letters, UU.

48. "A Tired but Happy Mother" to Mary Marker, September 5, 1953. ACCN 1862, Box 34, Folder 6, Ramona W. Cannon Letters, UU.

49. [Salt Lake City] to Mary Marker, April 15, 1955. ACCN 1862, Box 35, Folder 1, Ramona W. Cannon Letters, UU.

50. "Self-Improved Mama" to Mary Marker, June 26, 1952. ACCN 1862, Box 35, Folder 2, Ramona W. Cannon Letters, UU.

51. B. B. Kinder to Mary Marker, April 14, 1960, and "One Who Has Learned Much," December 1, 1960. ACCN 1862, Box 36, Folder 1, Ramona W. Cannon Letters, UU.

52. Mrs. Floyd I. Galway to Mary Marker, March 17, 1955. ACCN 1862, Box 35, Folder 6, Ramona W. Cannon Letters, UU.

53. Ruth Chapman to Mary Marker, 1955. ACCN 1862, Box 35, Folder 4, Ramona W. Cannon Letters, UU.

54. "Fed Up With Smoking" to Mary Marker, October 5, 1955. ACCN 1862, Box 35, Folder 4, Ramona W. Cannon Letters, UU.

55. See also Isaiah 52:11 and 3 Nephi 20:41. "Clean" used to mean generalized righteousness also occurs in D&C 88:74, 90:36, 110:5; and 133:5; Alma 5:19; Ether 4:6; and 2 Nephi 25:16.

56. Joseph F. Smith, Conference Address, 1913.

57. Spencer W. Kimball, "A Style of Our Own," BYU Devotional, February 13, 1951. Available only in audio (https://speeches.byu.edu/talks/spencer-w-kimball_style/).

58. Katie Clark Blakesley, "'A Style of Our Own': Modesty and Mormon Women, 1951–2008," *Dialogue* 42 (Summer 2009): 22. See also Frances L. Carr Longden, interview by Jill Mulvay Derr, 1974, CHL.

59. Spencer W. Kimball, "Be Ye Clean," BYU Devotional, May 4, 1954.

60. For example, see Spencer W. Kimball, "Save the Youth of Zion," *Improvement Era* (September 1965): 760–63; Boyd K. Packer, "Why Stay Morally Clean," conference

address, April 9, 1972; Dr. Bruce B. Clark, "Virtue Nourishes the Soul," *Relief Society Magazine* (January 1967): 74.

61. Mary Marker column, published but no date, ACCN 1862, Box 34, Folder 2, Ramona W. Cannon Letters, UU.

62. Ramona Canon probably was well aware of the Victorian association of virtuous women with flowers. The Latter-day Saint publication developed for girls, the *Young Women's Journal* (1889–1929), spread ideas of proper female behavior based on general middle-class standards. For an example of such female virtues see vol. 26 (1915): 197–99. The earliest source I have found that connected a woman's purity with a plucked rose was Elise C. Carroll's "Ladder of Graces," vol. 38 (1927): 710. Mary Marker column, September 8, 1952, ACCN 1862, Box 33a, Folder 4, Ramona W. Cannon Letters, UU.

63. Kenneth Roman, *The Kings of Madison Avenue: David Ogilvy and the Making of Modern Advertising* (New York: Palgrave Macmillan, 2009), 120.

64. Joseph L. Wirthlin, "A Mother's Influence," *Relief Society Magazine* (May 1950): 294. Wirthlin was continuing a thought developed by J. Reuben Clark and published in *One Hundred Ninth Semi-Annual Conference* (October 1938): "Please believe me when I say that chastity is worth more than life itself. This is the doctrine my parents taught me; it is truth. Better die chaste than live unchaste. The salvation of your very souls is concerned in this" (138). Spencer W. Kimball in 1969 reiterated "the doctrine" but in this version, he extended its meaning to involuntarily losing one's chastity and referred specifically to women: "Also far-reaching is the effect of loss of chastity. Once given or taken or stolen it can never be regained. Even in forced contact such as rape or incest, the injured one is greatly outraged. If she has not cooperated and contributed to the foul deed, she is of course in a more favorable position. There is no condemnation where there is absolutely no voluntary participation. It is better to die in defending one's virtue than to live having lost it without a struggle." *The Miracle of Forgiveness* (Salt Lake City: Bookcraft, 1969), Chapter 14 under "Restitution" and under section "Restitution for Loss of Chastity."

65. David O. McKay, *One Hundred Fifth Annual Conference* (April 1935): 116 quoting J. E. McCulloch, *Home: The Savior of Civilization* (Washington, DC: The Southern Co-operative League, 1924), 42. Many repeated this phrase, often attributing it solely to McKay. See Richard L. Evans, "No Other Success Can Compensate for Failure in the Home," *Improvement Era* (December 1964): 1100–02 and N. Eldon Tanner, "The Wonderful Work of Women," *Relief Society Magazine* (December 1967): 889.

66. David O. McKay, *One Hundred Thirty-Third Annual Conference* (April 1963): 130.

67. "One Who Tried" to Mary Marker (with response), January 28, 1963, ACCN 1862, Box 38, Folder 1, Ramona W. Cannon Letters, UU.

68. Wanda Lifferth to Mary Marker, June 26, 1963, ACCN 1862, Box 38, Folder 1, Ramona W. Cannon Letters, UU.

69. For instance, see "A Wife" to Mary Marker [and response], January 17, 1961, ACCN 1862, Box 38, Folder 1, Ramona W. Cannon Letters, UU.

70. [No Name] to Mary Marker, December 7, 1951, ACCN 1862, Box 34, Folder 5, Ramona W. Cannon Letters, UU.

71. "Words of Wise Advice" to Mary Marker December 6, 1952, ACCN 1862, Box 34, Folder 2, Ramona W. Cannon Letters, UU.

72. Lauramay Nebeker Baxter, interview by Loretta L. Hefner, 1979, CHL. See also the following interviews by Loretta L. Hefner conducted in 1979: Mary L. Dillman Eldredge; Bonnie M. Wilson Gustafson; Hilda E. Miller Harvery; Rayne R. Perkins Lohmoelder; Ione J. Simpson.

73. Bonnie L. Berrett Dalton, interview by Jessie Embry, 1977, CHL.

74. Ibid.

CHAPTER 6

1. [No name] to Mary Marker, January 23, 1970. ACCN 1862, Box 38, Folder 2, Ramona W. Cannon Letters, UU.
2. Thomas S. Monson, "The Women's Movement: Liberation or Deception?" *Ensign* (January 1971).
3. [No name] to Mary Marker, January 23, 1970.
4. Oral history, Bonnie L. Berret Dalton, interview by Jessie Embry, May 1977, CHL.
5. Devery S. Anderson, "A History of Dialogue, Part One: The Early Years, 1965–1971," *Dialogue* 32 (1999): 44.
6. Interview #007 [b. 1935, Los Angeles], interviewed September 15, 2009. Mormon Women's Oral History Project, Honnold Library, Claremont Graduate University [Claremont].
7. Devery S. Anderson, "A History of Dialogue, Part Two: Struggle to Maturity, 1971–1982," *Dialogue* 33 (2000): 14.
8. Laurel Thatcher Ulrich, "Mormon Women in the History of Second Wave Feminism," *Dialogue* 43 (2010): 49.
9. Claudia Lauper Bushman, "Women in Dialogue: An Introduction," *Dialogue* 6 (Summer 1971): 5.
10. Ibid., 8.
11. Belle S. Spafford oral history, interview by Jill Mulvey Derr, November 1975–March 1976: 203, CHL.
12. Dalton interview, 1977. CHL.
13. Belle S. Spafford oral history, 29 and 41, CHL.
14. Interview #004 [b. 1935, Oakland], July 14, 2009, Claremont.
15. Interview #028 [b. 1920, Oakland], interview by Rita Bosely, December 23, 2009, Claremont.
16. Belle S. Spafford oral history, 210, CHL.
17. Claudia Bushman interview by Colleen McDannell, June 18, 2016. Notes in author's possession.
18. Belle S. Spafford oral history, 170, CHL.
19. Interview #003 ["J" b. 1926], interview by Claudia Bushman, June 17, 2009, Claremont.
20. Interview #003 ["A" b. 1927], interview by Claudia Bushman, June 17, 2009, Claremont.
21. Julie Debra Neuffer, *Helen Andelin and the Fascinating Womanhood Movement* (Salt Lake City: University of Utah Press, 2014), 20f.
22. Julie Debra Neuffer, "Fascinating Womanhood: Helen Andelin and the Politics of Religion in the 'Other' Women's Movement, 1963–2006" (PhD dissertation, Washington State University, 2007), 67f.
23. Neuffer, *Helen Andelin*, 45.
24. Helen B. Adelin, *Fascinating Womanhood* ([1965]; updated edition, New York: Bantam Dell, 2007), 317.
25. Helen B. Adelin, *Fascinating Womanhood* (Santa Barbara, CA: Pacific Press, 1963), 223.
26. Susan Kohler, "*Woman's Exponent* Revisited," *Exponent II* 1 (July 1974): 1.
27. Claudia Bushman, "*Exponent II* Is Born," *Exponent II* 1 (July 1974): 2.
28. Carrel Hilton Sheldon, "Launching *Exponent II*," *Exponent II* 22 (Summer 1999) as cited in http://www.exponentii.org/history.
29. Kristine Haglund, interview by Colleen McDannell, April 30, 2014. Author's possession.
30. Kate Gardner, "What the ERA Will Mean to You," *Exponent II* 1 (July 1974): 2.
31. Louise Durham, "Jaroldeen Edwards Speaks in Boston," *Exponent II* 1 (July 1974): 2.
32. Belle S. Spafford, "The American Woman's Movement," an address delivered July 12, 1974, at the Lochinvar Club, New York City, New York, as reprinted in Gayle Morby Chandler,

"Belle S. Spafford: Leader of Women" (master's thesis, BYU, 1983), 129–40. An excerpt of the address, which included the statement on the ERA, was published in *Exponent II* 2 (October 1974): 1.

33. Barbara B. Smith, interview by Jessie L. Embry, June–July 1977: 65–68, CHL.
34. Ibid.
35. Ibid.
36. "Church News," *Deseret News* (January 11, 1975).
37. First Presidency Statement on ERA, October 22, 1976, as reprinted in "The Church and the Proposed Equal Rights Amendment: A Moral Issue," March 1980 (https://www.lds .org/ensign/1980/03/the-church-and-the-proposed-equal-rights-amendment-a-moral-issue?lang=eng).
38. Dianne Fife Kay, interview by Robin Kay [daughter c. 1982], Oral History, BYU.
39. Dianne F[ife] Kay, "Forces Affecting the Family." Panel discussion cosponsored by the Junior League of Honolulu and the University of Hawaii, March 29, 1978. Conservative Women Opposed to the Equal Rights Amendment, BYU.
40. Dianne F[ife] Kay, "Testimony by Dianne F. Kay Before House Judiciary Committee Pertaining to Spousal Liabilities [c. 1978]." Conservative Women Opposed to the Equal Rights Amendment, BYU.
41. Barbara B. Smith interview, 69.
42. Rebecca Cornwall, "Mormons and the IWY," *Exponent II* 4 (Fall 1977): 4.
43. Mormons for ERA was officially organized during the winter of 1978. The cofounders of the organization were Hazel Davis Rigby, Maida Rust Withers, Teddie Wood, and Sonia Johnson. The organization was officially incorporated April 11, 1980 (http:// socialarchive.iath.virginia.edu/ark:/99166/w6h45zbt).
44. Helen Candland Stark to Spencer W. Kimball, March 10, 1979. Algie Ballif Forum Records, 1976–1990, box 21, folder 21, UU.
45. Eleanor Ricks Colton, "My Personal Rubicon," *Dialogue* 14 (Fall 1981): 101–04.
46. Elaine Cannon, "If We Want to Go Up, We Have to Get On," *Ensign* (November 1978). [October 1978]

CHAPTER 7

1. Sonia Johnson, "Patriarchal Panic: Sexual Politics in the Mormon Church," address delivered to the American Psychological Association Meetings, New York City, September 1, 1979. Reprinted in Joanna Brooks, Rachel Hunt Steenblick, and Hannah Wheelwright, eds., *Mormon Feminism: Essential Writings* (New York: Oxford University Press, 2016), 74; 75. Brooks et al. omitted the paragraph about "Black people," which is in the copy preserved in Sonia Johnson Papers [SJP] and online at https://diogenesii.files.wordpress .com/2010/08/patriarchal-panic_sexual-politics-in-the-mormon-church.pdf.
2. Johnson, "Patriarchal Panic," 76–78.
3. Sonia Johnson, "Equal Rights and the Church of Jesus Christ of Latter-day Saints (Mormon)," Testimony before the US Senate Constitutional Rights Subcommittee, August 4, 1978, SJP, UU 4. Citing Discourse by Brigham Young, July 18, 1869, in JD.
4. Latter-day Saint regulations require church leaders to keep court proceedings strictly private, so this court summary is based on the reports of the accused and their supporters; see Sonia Johnson, *From Housewife to Heretic* (Garden City, NY: Doubleday, 1981), 227–353.
5. Jeffrey H. Willis to Sonia Johnson, November 27, 1979, SJP, UU.
6. Jeffrey H. Willis to Sonia Johnson, December 5, 1979, SJP, UU.
7. Johnson, *From Housewife to Heretic*, 373.
8. Ibid., 253; 389.
9. According to Barbara B. Smith's autobiography, *A Fruitful Season* (Salt Lake City: Bookcraft, 1988), 163, she declined because she felt she would not get the proper attention

since the media was presenting Johnson as a "martyr for women's rights." She suggested that Campbell appear when Johnson decided she would not debate with any woman. See also Johnson, *From Housewife to Heretic*, 360–63.

10. *Phil Donahue Show* transcript, December 12, 1979, SJP, UU. All of the quotes in the proceeding paragraphs are from this transcript.

11. Robert L. Simpson, "Courts of Love," *Ensign* (July 1972): 48. Johnson, *From Housewife to Heretic*, 391; 394.

12. The total number of letters sent to Sonia Johnson is not known, although in *From Housewife to Heretic* she states "that over 5,000 letters, cards, and telegrams" arrived and "at least 85 percent are supportive of both the Equal Rights Amendment and of me, and more than half of the Mormon mail is positive" (355). In SJP, there are three boxes (11, 12, 13) of pro-ERA correspondence designated as LDS, ex-LDS, or alienated-LDS. Accepting some error given the difficulty of determining names by gender, there were 407 pro-ERA letters by women out of a total of 473. Anti-ERA letters by LDS are in box 15; of those 254 letters, 200 were by women.

13. Janie Budd [Huntsville, AL] to Sonia Johnson, no date, SJP, UU.

14. Organizational conformity: Don W. Allen and Martha Williams [New York, NY] to Sonia Johnson, December 6, 1979; Hypocrisy: Darlene Anderson [Murray, UT] to Sonia Johnson, February 8, 1980; chauvinistic policies: Imogene Anderson [Fresno, CA] to Sonia Johnson, November 17, 1979, SJP, UU.

15. Janie Budd [Huntsville, AL] to Sonia Johnson, no date, SJP, UU.

16. The 1983 and 1985 editions of the *General Handbook of Instructions* state that inactivity did not merit a church court unless the individual was influencing others toward apostasy or made a written request to remove his [or her] name from the records of the church. Only then would a church court for excommunication be held (1983:51; 1985:55). In 1989 a new section was added, "Removing Names from Church Records," which outlined an administrative procedure that required sending a letter to one's bishop requesting removal (p. 58). *General Handbook of Instructions* is not publicly available. I consulted the copies in the Lester E. Bush papers, UU.

17. Viann Anello [San Jose, CA] to Sonia Johnson, December 6, 1979, SJP, UU.

18. Catherine Foster [Visalia, CA] to Sonia Johnson, January 4, 1979 [1980?], SJP, UU.

19. Bettie Eardley [Kaysville, UT] to Sonia Johnson, February 24, 1980, SJP, UU.

20. Leda Farley [Salem, UT] to Sonia Johnson, n.d., SJP, UU.

21. Eleanor Leonard [Chattanooga, TN] to Sonia Johnson, n.d., SJP, UU.

22. Norma Geiger [Upland, CA] to Sonia Johnson, January 22, [1980?], SJP, UU.

23. Bonnie Carter [Edmonds, WA] to Sonia Johnson, January 8, 1980, SJP, UU.

24. Ethel Atkins [Chico, CA] to Sonia Johnson, n.d., SJP, UU.

25. Xana Hansen [Brewer, ME] to Sonia Johnson, February 27, 1979, SJP, UU.

26. Sixty-First Semi-annual General Conference of the Church, Monday, October 6, 1890. Reported in *Deseret Evening News* (October 11, 1890), 2.

27. Ezra Taft Benson, "Fourteen Fundamentals in Following the Prophet," address given February 26, 1980, at BYU and published in the *Liahona Magazine* (June 1981).

28. Maribeth Forrey [Salem, OR] to Sonia Johnson, n.d., SJP, UU.

29. Antoinette Bush [Montgomery, AL] to Sonia Johnson, January 16, 1980, SJP, UU.

30. Sherrie Brook [West Jordan, UT] to Sonia Johnson, January 16, 1980, SJP, UU.

31. Spencer W. Kimball, "Privileges and Responsibilities of Sisters," Women's Fireside (September 16, 1978). This address was given at a special general meeting of women held prior to the October 1978 General Conference. It was broadcast by closed-circuit communication to 1,400 locations. According to Kimball's biographer, poet and essayist Emma Lou Thayne was asked by the president to review a draft and to offer suggestions, some of which were taken. Edward L. Kimball, *Lengthen Your Stride: The Presidency of Spencer W. Kimball* (Salt Lake City: Benchmark Books, 2009), 254.

32. Karen Leeper [Aurora, MO] to Sonia Johnson, January 9, 1980, SJP, UU.

33. Janine Johnson [Blackfoot, ID] to Sonia Johnson, n.d., SJP, UU.

34. LaRayne Day [Draper, UT] to Sonia Johnson, January 16, 1980, SJP, UU.

35. Nancy Graham [Albuquerque, NM] to Sonia Johnson, January 14, 1981 [1980?], SJP, UU.

36. On the restriction, see *General Handbook of Instructions*, 1968: 44. On its removal, see Marvin K. Gardner, "Report of the Seminar for Regional Representatives," *Ensign* (November 1978): 100–01.

37. Spencer W. Kimball, "The Role of Righteous Women," *Ensign* (November 1979): 102, quoting John Widtsoe, "Evidences and Reconciliations," *Improvement Era* (March 1942): 188. See Chapter 8, note 66, for the possible origin of this phrase.

38. Carrie Taylor Anguiano, "The Relief Society and President Spencer W. Kimball's Administration" (master's thesis, BYU, 2013), 39–42.

39. Mary Jane Woodger, "Elaine Anderson Cannon, Young Women General President: Innovations, Inspiration, and Implementations," *Journal of Mormon History* 40, no. 4 (Fall 2014): 198 and Jennifer Reeder and Kate Holbrook, eds., *At the Pulpit: Latter-day Saint Women Speak* (Salt Lake City: Church Historians Press, 2017), 345.

40. Holly C. Metcalf, *Love's Banner: Memories of the Life of Elaine Cannon* (Kenmore, WA: Lamb and Lion, 2011), 204. I would like to thank Kate Holbrook for this reference.

41. Woodger, "Elaine Anderson Cannon," 194, citing Elaine A. Cannon interview by Gordon Irving, December 28, 1984; April 30, 1979, CHL.

42. "Church Consolidates Meeting Schedules," *Ensign* 10 (March 1980): 73 and Hal Knight, "Meeting Schedule Approved," *Church News* (February 2, 1980).

43. When the three-hour schedule was introduced, homemaking was taught as part of the second meeting of the month in Relief Society. In 1984 the homemaking lesson was moved to a monthly meeting on a weekday evening. In 1987 the "cultural refinement" lesson, which had evolved out of the earlier social science lessons, was eliminated. The decision to bring together the lessons of the Relief Society and the Melchizedek Priesthood was made in 1996, but the first shared lesson, on Brigham Young, was not distributed until January 1998. Tina Hatch, " 'Changing Times Bring Changing Conditions': Relief Society, 1960 to the Present," *Dialogue* 37 (2004): 92–95.

44. Linda Wilcox, "The Mormon Concept of a Mother in Heaven" was first published in *Sunstone* 5 (September/October 1980): 9–17. All quotes are from this issue. The article was reprinted in *Sunstone*'s 1999 silver anniversary issue (78–87). An expanded version was published in Lavina Fielding Anderson and Maureen Ursenbach Beecher, eds., *Sisters in Spirit: Mormon Women in Historical and Cultural Perspective* (Urbana: University of Illinois Press, 1987), 64–77, and then reprinted in Joanna Brooks et al., eds., *Mormon Feminism: Essential Writings* (New York: Oxford University Press, 2016), 78–85.

45. Linda Sillitoe, "New Voices, New Songs: Contemporary Poems by Mormon Women," *Dialogue* 13 (Winter 1980): 58.

46. In 1980 the Religious Studies Center at BYU published *The Words of Joseph Smith* as the first full collection of Joseph Smith's Nauvoo discourses. The texts were strictly faithful to the original sources. Margaret Merrill Toscano, "The Missing Rib: The Forgotten Place of Queens and Priestesses in the Establishment of Zion," *Sunstone* 10 July 1985): 16–22. All quotes are from this issue. The essay was reprinted in Brooks et al., *Mormon Feminism*, 134–44.

47. Toscano, "The Missing Rib," 19.

48. Ibid., 19.

49. Ibid., 18.

50. Ibid., 22.

51. Margaret and Paul Toscano, *Strangers in Paradox: Explorations in Mormon Theology* (Salt Lake City: Signature Press, 1990), 147.
52. Linda King Newell and Valeen Tippetts Avery, *Mormon Enigma: Emma Hale Smith* ([1984]; 2nd ed., Urbana: University of Illinois Press, 1994), xii.
53. Linda Newell thought this at the University of Utah "Panel on Women's History," October 27, 2016, but in a 1987 interview she disagreed that the ban had anything to do with her co-editorship of *Dialogue*. Lavina Anderson," Reflections from Within: A Conversation with Linda King Newell and L. Jackson Newell, "Dialogue" 20 (Winter 1987): 27.
54. Lavina Fielding Anderson, "The LDS Intellectual Community and Church Leadership: A Contemporary Chronology," *"Dialogue"* 26 (Spring 1993): 48.
55. Michael Quinn's response was first given in November 1981 in a lecture to a BYU student history association. Quinn intended to publish the talk in *Sunstone* magazine but after talking with church leaders decided to withdraw the essay. The lecture was then printed and distributed in 1982 (without Quinn's permission from an illicit tape recording) by the anti-Mormons, Jerald and Sandra A. Tanner. Eventually the essay was expanded and published as "On Being a Mormon Historian (and Its Aftermath)," in George D. Smith, ed., *Faithful History: Essays on Writing Mormon History* (Salt Lake City: Signature Books, 1992), 69–96.
56. Ezra Taft Benson, Conference address, "Prepare for the Days of Tribulation" (October 1980) and "Honored Place of Woman," *Ensign* (November 1981).
57. Douglas Martin, "Rev. William R. Callahan Dies at 78: Dissident Who Challenged Vatican," *New York Times* (July 10, 2010).
58. *Ordinatio sacerdotalis* (1994).
59. Ezra Taft Benson, "To the Mothers in Zion," Fireside for Parents, February 22, 1987 (http://emp.byui.edu/jexj/new/talks/talks/ETB%20To%20the%20Mothers%20 in%20Zion.pdf).
60. In 1986 and 1987 conference organizers typed up comments given on evaluation forms by those who attended the Women's Conference. Comments ranged from the logistics of the conference (e.g., the room was too hot) to philosophical reflections on women in the modern world. In 1986 comments were drawn from 325 evaluation sheets, with 500 evaluations given in 1987. These quotations come from the "Other Comments" section (pp. 51–59) of the "Selected Comments from Participants' Evaluation Sheets, 1987 BYU Women's Conference," where organizers assembled "the attitudes and feelings" on President Benson's recent "To the Mothers in Zion" talk. BYU Women's Conference, box 1, folder 9, BYU.
61. Dallin H. Oaks, "Alternate Voices" (General Conference, April 1989).
62. Peggy Fletcher Stack, "LDS Pulitzer Prize Winner Puzzled by Rejection as Speaker at BYU," *Salt Lake Tribune* (February 6, 1993) and Jan Shipps, "Dangerous History: Laurel Ulrich and Her Mormon Sisters," *Christian Century* 110 (October 20, 1993): 1012–15.
63. Lewis, "From Womanhood to Sisterhood," 103.
64. Gordon B. Hinckley, *Daughters of God*, Conference Address, October 1991.
65. Statement on Symposia, August 23, 1991 (https://www.lds.org/ensign/1991/11/news-of-the-church/statement-on-symposia?lang=eng). Peggy Fletcher Stack, "LDS Church Decries Sunstone Sessions, Calls Content Insensitive, Offensive," *Salt Lake Tribune* (August 24, 1991) and Martha Sonntag Bradley, "Theological Discussion or Support Group," *Sunstone* (July 2002): 38f.
66. Boyd K. Packer, "Talk to the All-Church Coordinating Council," May 18, 1993 (http:// emp.byui.edu/HUFFR/All%20Church%20Coordinating%20Council--Boyd%20K.%20 Packer.htm).
67. Margaret Toscano, interview with author, September 15, 2016.

CHAPTER 8

1. Gary Shepherd and Gordon Shepherd, *Mormon Passage: A Missionary Chronicle* (Carbondale: University of Illinois Press, 1998), 11.

2. Jay M. Tod, "More Members Outside the US than in US," March 1996 (https://www .lds.org/ensign/1996/03/news-of-the-church/more-members-now-outside-us-than-in-us?lang=eng). The number of missionaries cited in "Statistical Report 1996" was 52,938 (https://www.lds.org/general-conference/1997/04/statistical-report-1996?lang=eng), with a membership population of 9,694,549.

3. "The Annual Report of the Church, 1971" cites a 1960 membership of 1,693,180 (https://www.lds.org/ensign/1972/07/the-annual-report-of-the-church?lang=eng) and a 2015 membership of 15,634,199 (http://www.mormonnewsroom.org/article/2015-statistical-report-april-2016-general-conference).

4. "Mormon Missionary Work: A Brief History and Introduction" (https://lib.byu.edu/collections/mormon-missionary-diaries/about/mormon-missionary-work/).

5. Accurate retention rates are impossible to determine because the church does not make public its statistics. A frequent number given, without source acknowledgment, is that "half or more of all converts stop attending church within a year of their baptism." Brady McCombs, "Number of LDS Converts, Missionaries Increasing; Conversion Rate Declines," *Deseret News*, April 17, 2015 (http://www.deseretnews .com/article/865626695/Number-of-LDS-converts-missionaries-increasing-conversion-rate-declines.html). Groups like Cumorah.com who attempt to track such statistics give more nuanced numbers (http://www.cumorah.com/index.php?target=church_growth_articles&story_id=13 or http://www.cumorah.com/index.php?target=law_harvest&chapter_id=7).

6. Ayanda Sidzatane, interview by Colleen McDannell, February 3, 2015.

7. Hugo N. Olaiz, "Gordon B. Hinckley and the Ritualization of Mormon History," *Sunstone* 149 (April 2008): 25.

8. J. B. Haws, *The Mormon Image in the American Mind: Fifty Years of Public Perception* (New York: Oxford University Press, 2013), 166f.

9. Ibid., 191, and Marie Cornwall, interview by Greg Prince, March 8, 2012, Mormon Women's Voices Oral History Project, 2005–13, UU.

10. Aileen Hales Clyde, interview by Kathleen Flake, October 7 and 8, 2005, Mormon Women's Voices, UU.

11. *Encyclopedia of Mormonism*, "British Isles, Church in."

12. Richard L. Jensen, "Perpetual Emigrating Fund Company," *Utah History Encyclopedia* (http://historytogo.utah.gov/utah_chapters/pioneers_and_cowboys/perpetualemigratingfundcompany.html).

13. Shepherd and Shepherd, *Mormon Passage*, 4.

14. "Statistical Report 1977," May 1978 (https://www.lds.org/ensign/1978/05/statistical-report-1977?lang=eng) and "Status Report on Missionary Work," October 1977 (https://www.lds.org/ensign/1977/10/status-report-on-missionary-work-a-conversation-with-elder-thomas-s-monson-chairman-of-the-missionary-committee-of-the-council-of-the-twelve?lang=eng).

15. Francis M. Gibbons, "Statistical Report 1977" (https://www.lds.org/ensign/1978/05/statistical-report-1977?lang=eng).

16. "Race and the Priesthood" (https://www.lds.org/topics/race-and-the-priesthood?lang=eng&old=true).

17. "Race and the Priesthood," citing Joseph Fielding Smith to Alfred M. Nelson (January 31, 1907), CHL.

18. Matthew L. Harris and Newell G. Bringhurst, eds., *The Mormon Church and Blacks: A Documentary History* (Urbana: University of Illinois Press), 55, quoting "The Negro and the Priesthood," *Liahona: The Elder's Journal* 5 (April 18, 1908): 1164–67.

19. W. Paul Reeve, *Religion of a Different Color: Race and the Mormon Struggle for Whiteness* (New York: Oxford University Press, 2015), 202. Reeve documented that Diantha Huntington Jacobs Smith Young stood in as proxy for James.

20. Mildred Jennie Harvey Davies, autobiography, 1975: 26, CHL.

21. Per statistics compiled by Mathew McBride (2017), there were 136 women and 999 men.

22. Vella Evans, "Women's Image in Authoritative Mormon Discourse: A Rhetorical Analysis" (PhD dissertation, University of Utah, 1985), 153.

23. In 1952 the Missionary Committee published *A Systematic Program for Teaching the Gospel*. In 1961, the Church Missionary Department (successor to the Committee) released *A Uniform System for Teaching Investigators*. The system was revised and updated in 1973. The 1952, 1961, and 1973 approaches all entailed lengthy memorized discussions.

24. Spencer W. Kimball, "When the World Will Be Converted," *Ensign* (October 1974).

25. Amanda Holmes, interview by Colleen McDannell, February 4, 2015.

26. Alice Buehner, "The Communicational Function of Wearing Apparel for Lady Missionaries for the LDS Church" (master's thesis, BYU, 1982), 2.

27. Tally S. Payne, "'Our Wise and Prudent Women': Twentieth-Century Trends in Female Missionary Service," Carol Cornwall Madsen, ed., *New Scholarship on Latter-day Saint Women in the Twentieth-Century* (Provo, UT: BYU Press), 127 [Table 1].

28. Shepherd and Shepherd, *A Mormon Passage*, 10.

29. In response to a perceived decline, in 1986 the church released new missionary discussions, and in 1988 a manual entitled the *Missionary Guide* that was a training manual for teaching. The 1986/1988 revision was intended to move away from memorized lessons but did not fully succeed. *Preach My Gospel* was released in November 2004. Benjamin Hyrum White, "The History of *Preach My Gospel*," *Religious Educator* 14, no. 1 (2013): 129–58 (https://rsc.byu.edu/archived/volume-14-number-1-2013/history-preach-my-gospel).

30. Gordon B. Hinckley quoted in Adam C. Olson, "New *Preach My Gospel* Program Being Launched in Missions Worldwide," *News of the Church*, January 2005 (https://www.lds.org/ensign/2005/01/news-of-the-church?lang=eng).

31. Ginevra Palumbo, interview by Colleen McDannell, March 4, 2016.

32. Annie Knoz, "College Time for Younger Mormon Women," *Salt Lake Tribune*, October 4, 2014 (http://www.sltrib.com/info/staff/1661180-155/women-mission-utah-college-age-enrollment).

33. Joseph Walker, "LDS Church Tweaks Dress and Grooming Requirements for Missionaries," *Deseret News*, July 12, 2013 (http://www.deseretnews.com/article/865583066/LDS-Church-tweaks-dress-and-grooming-requirements-for-missionaries.html).

34. "Church Adjusts Mission Organization to Implement 'Mission Leadership Council'" (http://www.mormonnewsroom.org/article/church-adjusts-mission-organization-implement-mission-leadership-council).

35. "2015 Statistical Report" (http://www.mormonnewsroom.org/article/2015-statistical-report- april-2016-general-conference).

36. Peggy Fletcher Stack, "And It Came to Pass that the Mormon Missionary Surge Did Cease—Tally Now at 75K," *Salt Lake Tribune*, April 4, 2016 (http://www.sltrib.com/home/3730604-155/and-it-came-to-pass-that).

37. Shepherd and Shepherd, *Mormon Passage*, 9.

38. Taylor Holiday, interview by Colleen McDannell, March 5, 2016.

39. Belinda Moore, interview by Colleen McDannell, February 10, 2015.

40. Vida Teye, interview by Colleen McDannell, March 5, 2015.

41. Michelle Klintworth and Val Caldwell, interview by Colleen McDannell, February 5, 2015.

42. #031 (born August 13, 1956), interview by Claudia Bushman, February 15, 2010, Claremont.

43. Mary Frances Sturlaugson, *A Soul So Rebellious* (Salt Lake City: Deseret Book Company, 1980), 44.

44. Detra Bennett, interview by Alicia Kimball, March 7, 2011, Mormon Women's Voices, UU.

45. Amanda Holmes, interview by Colleen McDannell, February 4, 2015.

46. Michele Stitt, interview by Colleen McDannell, February 12, 2015.

47. Jutta Baum Busche, "The Unknown Treasure," in Jennifer Reeder and Kate Holbrook, eds., *At the Pulpit: 185 Years of Discourses by Latter-day Saint Women* (Salt Lake City: Church Historian's Press, 2017), 233–39.

48. Aurah Agyare Dwomoh, interview by Colleen McDannell, February 10, 2015.

49. Irene Tschabala, interview by Colleen McDannell, February 6, 2015.

50. Bernhard Lang, "On Intellectual Ritual," in *Sacred Games: A History of Christian Worship* (New Haven, CT: Yale University Press, 1997), 139.

51. Winnie Sixishe, interview by Colleen McDannell, February 8, 2015.

52. Belinda Moore, interview by Colleen McDannell, February 10, 2015.

53. Tessa Brown, interview by Colleen McDannell, February 11, 2015.

54. Thandeka Diamini [pseudonym], interview by Colleen McDannell, February 10, 2015.

55. Wen Wu [Mannino], interview by Colleen McDannell, March 4, 2016.

56. Thandeka Diamini interview.

57. The November 20, 2010, address was reproduced as "The Gospel Culture" (March 2012) and reinforced by member of the First Presidency Dieter F. Uchtdorf and Apostle David A. Bednar in November 2014 (http://www.mormonnewsroom.co.za/article/church-members-throughout-southeast-africa-gather-for-broadcast).

58. Tessa Brown interview.

59. Anonymous, interview by Caroline Kline, June 14, 2015, interview 32, pp. 10–11, transcript, Gender Narrative and Religious Practice in Southern Africa Oral History Collection, Special Collections, Claremont Colleges Library, Claremont, California.

60. Aurah Agyare Dwomoh in small-group interview by Colleen McDannell, February 2, 2015.

61. Wen Wu Mannino interview.

62. Katia Coda, interview by Colleen McDannell, March 7, 2016.

63. Erica Rossi, interview by Colleen McDannell, March 5, 2016.

64. Ibid.

65. Mariagrazia Zummo [Mannino], interview by Colleen McDannell, March 5, 2016.

66. Sydney Dawson, interview by Colleen McDannell, April 21, 2016.

67. Sylvia Cabus, interview by Alicia Kimball, April 5, 2011, Mormon Women's Voices, UU.

68. "U.S. Public Becoming Less Religious," Pew Research Center, November 3, 2015 (http://www.pewforum.org/2015/11/03/u-s-public-becoming-less-religious/).

CHAPTER 9

1. Aileen H. Clyde, interview by Kathleen Flake, October 7, 2005, Mormon Women's Voices, UU.

2. Ibid.

3. All of the previous quotes are from Aileen Clyde, "Women's Lives, Women's Voices" conference held at Scripps College, Claremont, California, February 2011 (video at https://www.youtube.com/watch?v=HFCWUoXr1Dg&feature=youtu.be&t=1m4s).

4. Greg Prince, "'There Is Always a Struggle': An Interview with Chieko N. Okazaki," *Dialogue* 45 (Spring 2012): 136.

5. Ibid.

6. Aileen H. Clyde, interview with Kathleen Flake, October 5, 2005, UU.

7. Holly Theresa Bignall, "Hope Deferred: Mormon Feminism and Prospects for Change in the LDS Church" (PhD dissertation, Iowa State University, 2010), 147.

8. There were three other proclamations given by the First Presidency and the Quorum of the Twelve Apostles. They are considered "solemn and sacred in nature" but are not currently a part of the Latter-day Saint canon, the "Standard Works." *Encyclopedia of Mormonism*, s. v. "Proclamations of the First Presidency and the Quorum of the Twelve Apostles."

9. Aileen H. Clyde, interview by Kathleen Flake, October 5, 2005.

10. *Encyclopedia of Mormonism*, s. v. "Hawaii, the Church in" and "State of Hawaii, General Population and Housing Characteristics" (http://census.hawaii.gov/census90/1990rep6/).

11. In 1971 the church published a thirty-three-page pamphlet, *New Horizons for Homosexuals*, where it declared "sex perversion is a hidden menace" (4) but that "it is curable" (10) (http://www.connellodonovan.com/horizons7.html).

12. The First Presidency to All Members of the Church of Jesus Christ of Latter-day Saints, "Standards of Morality and Fidelity," November 14, 1991 (for a scan of the letter see http://www.ldspapers.faithweb.com/cgi-bin/i/standards.jpg).

13. National Council of Catholic Bishops, "To Live in Christ Jesus" (pastoral letter), November 11, 1976 (https://archive.org/stream/toliveinchristjecath/toliveinchristjecath_djvu.txt). Upheld in "Address of His Holiness John Paul II to the Bishops of the United States," October 5, 1979 (http://w2.vatican.va/content/john-paulii/en/speeches/1979/october/documents/hf_jp-ii_spe_19791005_chicago-usa-bishops.html).

14. "Standards of Morality and Fidelity."

15. "First Presidency Statement Opposing Same-Gender Marriages," February 1, 1994 (https://www.lds.org/ensign/1994/04/news-of-the-church/first-presidency-statement-opposing-same-gender-marriages?lang=eng).

16. "The Family: A Proclamation to the World."

17. *Baehr v. Miike*, Amicus Curiae Brief of the Church of Jesus Christ of Latter-day Saints (http://www.qrd.org/qrd/usa/legal/hawaii/baehr/1997/brief.mormons-04.14.97). Utah Congressman Jim Hansen read the Proclamation into the *Congressional Record* on November 17, 1995.

18. Monica Youn, "Proposition 8 and the Mormon Church: A Case Study in Donor Disclosure," *George Washington Law Review* 81 (November 2013): 2115, citing the June 29, 2008, letter (http://www.mormonnewsroom.org/article/california-and-same-sex-marriage). See also other statements on same-sex marriage collected in http://www.mormonnewsroom.org/article/same-sex-marriage-and-proposition-8.

19. Youn, "Proposition 8," 2126.

20. Tony Semerad, "Utahns, LDS Church Spent More on Prop. 8 than Previously Known," *Salt Lake Tribune* (February 9, 2009).

21. Claremont Oral History Collection #017 (2009), 28, as quoted in Anna Terry Rolapp, "Proposition 8," Claudia L. Bushman and Caroline Kline, eds., *Mormon Women Have Their Say* (Salt Lake City: Greg Kofford Books), 291.

22. Cited numbers: women 20.3 and men 22.8. D'Vera Cohn et al., "Barely Half of U. S. Adults Are Married—A Record Low," Pew Research Center, December 14, 2011 (http://www.pewsocialtrends.org/2011/12/14/barely-half-of-u-s-adults-are-married-a-record-low/).

23. "Marriage" (Data), Pew Research Center (http://www.pewresearch.org/data-trend/society-and-demographics/marriage/).

24. Historical Marital Status Tables, US Census Bureau (https://www.census.gov/data/tables/time-series/demo/families/marital.html).

25. Sharon Sassler and Amanda Smith, *Cohabitation Nation: Gender, Class, and the Remaking of Relationships* (Berkeley: University of California Press, 2017).

26. Jason DeParle, "Two Classes, Divided by 'I Do,'" *New York Times*, July 14, 2012 (http://www.nytimes.com/2012/07/15/us/two-classes-in-america-divided-by-i-do.html). For a more developed reflection see W. Bradford Wilcox and Wendy Wang, "The Marriage Divide: How and Why Working-Class Families Are More Fragile Today," Research Brief for Opportunity America-AEI-Brookings Working Class Group, September 2017 (http://www.aei.org/wp-content/uploads/2017/09/The-Marriage-Divide.pdf).

27. *America's Changing Religious Landscape*, Pew Research Center, released May 12, 2015, 62 (http://www.pewforum.org/files/2015/05/RLS-08-26-full-report.pdf).

28. Southern Baptist Convention, *The Baptist Faith and Message*, 1998 (http://www.utm.edu/staff/caldwell/bfm/versions.html).

29. Ibid.

30. The concept of "servant leadership" has been used in Christian circles to integrate power and authority into a Christological understanding of humility. The term originated with the eclectic thinker Robert K. Greenleaf (1904–90). Men as "servant leaders" in the home take on domestic activities and in business world assume service roles; see Bethany Moreton, *To Serve God and Wal-Mart: The Making of Christian Free Enterprise* (Cambridge, MA: Harvard University Press, 2009), 107–24.

31. In the Creation story God creates the heavens and the earth (Moses 2 = Gen. 1). The Tree of Life and the Tree of the Knowledge of Good and Evil were planted (Moses 3:9 = Gen. 2:9). God makes Adam and tells him not to eat of the Tree of the Knowledge of Good and Evil (Moses 3:17 = Gen. 2:17). Woman is made (Moses 3:23 = Gen. 2:23). Eve was "beguiled" by Satan (Moses 4:6; 19 = Gen. 3:13), leading her to eat the fruit and give it to Adam (Moses 4:12 = Gen. 3:6).

32. The first lectures that make up the book were given in 1893. James E. Tamage, *The Articles of Faith* (Salt Lake City: The Deseret News, 1899), 68 (https://archive.org/details/articlesfaithas00talmgoog).

33. Tamage, *Articles of Faith*, 68.

34. Ibid., 68.

35. Ibid., *Articles of Faith*, 70.

36. *Encyclopedia of Mormonism*, s. v. "Endowment."

37. The Mormon church does not reproduce various temple liturgies or provide histories of their development, explaining that such matters are too sacred to be discussed outside of the temple precincts. Other Latter-day Saints, often after they have left the institutional religion, have posted the liturgical changes online. I have used *The LDS Endowment, The Garden* (http://www.ldsendowment.org/parallelgarden.html). See also "The Mormon Temple Endowment Ceremony" (http://mit.irr.org/mormon-temple-endowment-ceremony) and "The Mormon Temple Endowment Ceremony" (http://lds-mormon.com/compare.shtml).

38. See I Timothy 2:15–16 (King James Version): "And Adam was not deceived but the woman being deceived was in the transgression. Notwithstanding she shall be saved in childbearing, if they continue in faith and charity and holiness with sobriety" and Genesis 3:16: "Unto the woman he said, I will greatly multiply thy sorrow and thy conception; in sorrow thou shalt bring forth children; and thy desire shall be to thy husband, and he shall rule over thee."

39. *The LDS Endowment*.

40. Alma Don Sorensen and Valerie Hudson Cassler, *Women in Eternity, Women of Zion* (Springfield, UT: Bonneville Books, 2004), 92. In his note to this retranslation, Sorensen thanked Donald Parry, a professor of Hebrew Bible and Dead Sea Scrolls at BYU.

41. Bruce C. Hafen and Marie K. Hafen, "Crossing Thresholds and Becoming Equal Partners," *Ensign* (August 2007).

42. Spenser W. Kimball, "The Blessings and Responsibilities of Womanhood," *Ensign* (March 1976) (https://www.lds.org/ensign/1976/03/the-blessings-and-responsibilities-of-womanhood?lang=eng).

43. L. Tom Perry, "Fatherhood, an Eternal Calling," April 2004 General Conference. (https://www.lds.org/general-conference/2004/04/fatherhood-an-eternal-calling?lang=eng.)

44. Howard W. Hunter, "Being a Righteous Husband and Father," General Conference, October 1994.

45. Boyd K. Packer, "For Time and All Eternity," General Conference, October 1993.

46. Ibid.

47. Ezra Taft Benson, "Fourteen Fundamentals in Following the Prophet," address given February 26, 1980, at BYU and published in the *Liahona Magazine* (June 1981).

48. Ezra Taft Benson, "To the Mothers in Zion," Fireside for Parents, February 22, 1987 (http://emp.byui.edu/jexj/new/talks/talks/ETB%20To%20the%20Mothers%20in%20Zion.pdf).

49. The quotes in this paragraph are all from "The Family: A Proclamation to the World."

50. [Joseph Fielding Smith], "Birth Control," *Relief Society Magazine* 3 (July 1916): 367f.

51. *General Handbook of Instructions*, no. 21 (n.p., 1976), 105.

52. Figure 4.6, Birthrates, in Tim B. Heaton, "Vital Statistics," in *Latter-day Saint Social Life: Social Research on the LDS Church and Its Members* (Provo, UT: Religious Studies Center, BYU, 1998), 105–32 (https://rsc.byu.edu/archived/latter-day-saint-social-life-social-research-lds-church-and-its-members/4-vital-statistics).

53. *General Handbook of Instructions* (Salt Lake City: The Church of Jesus Christ of Latter-day Saints, 1983), 77, and *General Handbook of Instructions* (Salt Lake City: The Church of Jesus Christ of Latter-day Saints, 1985), 11–13.

54. *General Handbook of Instructions* (Salt Lake City: The Church of Jesus Christ of Latter-day Saints, 1989), 11–14.

55. *General Handbook of Instructions: Book 1, Stake Presidencies and Bishoprics* (Salt Lake City: The Church of Jesus Christ of Latter-day Saints, 1998), 158.

56. *America's Changing Religious Landscape*, 64.

57. Brady McCombs, "Utah Birthrate Reaches Historic Low," *Salt Lake Tribune*, December 30, 2015 (http://www.sltrib.com/home/3362824-155/utah-birthrate-reaches-historic-low-).

58. Utah Department of Health, *Sociodemographics of Utah Women* (http://health.utah.gov/opha/publications/other/wmnhlth/section1.pdf).

59. Pamela S. Perlich, *Utah's Fertility Rate Is at Historic Low*, Kem C. Gardner, Policy Institute, University of Utah (http://gardner.utah.edu/utahs-fertility-rate-is-at-historic-low/).

60. "Utah County Birthrate Down," *Salt Lake Tribune*, January 6, 2017 (http://www.sltrib.com/home/4790339-155/story.html).

61. US Census, *Utah Is Nation's Fastest-Growing State*, December 20, 2016 (https://www.census.gov/newsroom/press-releases/2016/cb16-214.html).

62. I'd like to thank Kristen Beck for assembling the data on church authorities in office in May 2017. She used these sites: (https://www.lds.org/church/leaders/quorum-of-the-twelve-apostles?lang=eng); (https://www.lds.org/church/leaders/general-auxiliaries?lang=eng); (http://bystudyandfaith.net/2015/10/children-of-the-apostles-updated-analysis); and (http://www.mormonnewsroom.org/topic/quorum-of-the-twelve-apostles).

63. Guttmacher Institute, *Guttmacher Statistic on Catholic Women's Contraceptive Use*, February 15, 2012 (https://www.guttmacher.org/article/2012/02/guttmacher-statistic-catholic-womens-contraceptive-use).

64. Michael Hout and Andrew Greeley, "The Center Doesn't Hold: Church Attendance in the United States, 1940–1984," *American Sociological Review* 52 (June 1987): 332f.

65. Kenneth Utener, "*Humanae Vitae*: What Has It Done to Us and What Is to Be Done Now?" *Commonweal* 120 (June 1993): 14, as discussed in Peter Steinfels, "Vatican Watershed— A Special Report, Papal Birth Control Letter Retains Its Grip," *New York Times*, August 1, 1993 (http://www.nytimes.com/1993/08/01/us/vatican-watershed-a-special-report-papal-birth-control-letter-retains-its-grip.html?pagewanted=all).
66. *Marriages and Births in Sweden* (http://ec.europa.eu/eurostat/statisticsexplained/index .php/Marriages_and_births_in_Sweden).
67. Kristina Olergard Tenney, interview by Colleen McDannell, September 14, 2015.
68. Caroline Kline, "Saying Goodbye to the Final Say, The Softening and Reimagining of Mormon Male Headship Ideologies," in Patrick Q. Mason and John G. Turner, eds., *Out of Obscurity: Mormonism Since 1945* (New York: Oxford University Press, 2016), 230.

CHAPTER 10

1. Dallin H. Oaks, "Alternate Voices," April 1989 (https://www.lds.org/general-conference/ 1989/04/alternate-voices?lang=eng).
2. "Tim Berners-Lee's Proposal," *CERN* (http://info.cern.ch/Proposal.html).
3. Martin Kenney, "The Growth and Development of the Internet in the United States," in Bruce Kogut, ed., *The Global Internet Economy* (Cambridge, MA: MIT Press, 2003), 84, citing John Markoff, "A Free and Simple Computer Link," *New York Times* (December 8, 1993).
4. I'd like to thank Derek Hoff for this reference. *Time* magazine cover, April 12, 1993.
5. Pew Research Center, "Americans Going Online . . . Explosive Growth, Uncertain Destinations," October 16, 1995 (http://www.people-press.org/1995/10/16/ americans-going-online-explosive-growth-uncertain-destinations/).
6. Pew Research Center, "World Wide Web Timeline," March 11, 2014 (http://www .pewinternet.org/2014/03/11/world-wide-web-timeline/).
7. "On Utah's 'Silicon Slopes,' Tech Jobs Get a Lift," NPR (http://www.npr.org/2012/03/ 12/148252561/on-utahs-silicon-slopes-tech-jobs-get-a-lift).
8. The exact number is 52 percent according to Pew Research Center, "Internet/Broadband Fact Sheet," January 12, 2017 (http://www.pewinternet.org/fact-sheet/internet-broadband/).
9. "On Utah's 'Silicon Slopes.'"
10. Domestic Surveillance Directorate, Utah Data Center (https://nsa.gov1.info/utah-data-center/).
11. Lee Davidson, "Utah Leads Nation in Personal Income Growth," *Salt Lake Tribune* (September 28, 2016).
12. In its article "Best States for Business," *Forbes* explains that "Utah occupies the top spot [in 2016] for the sixth time in seven years," and then goes on to mention the state is two-thirds Latter-day Saints and is "the most religiously homogeneous state in the U.S." (https://www.forbes.com/places/ut/#). For the statement that 88 percent of Utah state legislators are Mormons, see Lee Davidson, "With Utah Legislature's Mormon Supermajority, Is It Representative of the People," *Salt Lake Tribune* (December 12, 2016).
13. M. Russell Ballard, "The Opportunities and Responsibilities of CES Techers in the 21st Century," given on February 26, 2016, and reproduced in *Liahona* as "By Study and By Faith," December 2016.
14. Emily W. Jensen, "Mormon Women Speak Online," *Deseret News*, November 13, 2010 (http://www.deseretnews.com/article/705362483/Mormon-women-speak-online .html).
15. Biographical information comes from an almost three-hour-long interview by Jon Dehlin at Mormon Stories Podcast posted on March 2, 2010 (http://www.mormonstories.org/ 129-131-feminist-mormon-housewives-founder-lisa-butterworth/).

16. Butterfield interview by Jon Dehlin, March 2, 2010.

17. Peggy Fletcher Stack, "Where Have All the Mormon Feminists Gone," *Salt Lake Tribune*, October 3, 2003.

18. "History of Mommy Blogging" (https://fialakerns.com/research/momblogstudy/history-of-mommy-blogging/) and Debra Nussbaum Cohen, "Faithful Track Questions, Answers and Minutia on Blogs," *New York Times*, March 5, 2005 (http://www.nytimes.com/2005/03/05/us/faithful-track-questions-answers-and-minutiae-on-blogs.html?_r=0).

19. Mormon Stories interview. Peggy Fletcher Stack, "LDS Web Site Offers 'A Safe Place to Be Feminist and Faithful," *Salt Lake Tribune*, October 5, 2007 (http://archive.sltrib.com/story.php?ref=/lds/ci_7098023).

20. Jessica Finnigan and Nancy Ross, "Mormon Feminists and Social Media: A Story of Community and Education," in Gordon Shepherd et al., eds., *Voices for Equality: Ordain Women and Resurgent Mormon Feminism* (Salt Lake City: Greg Kofford Books, 2015), 341.

21. Rosemary Avance, "Constructing Religion in the Digital Age: The Internet and Modern Mormon Identities" (dissertation, University of Pennsylvania, 2015), 140 (note 2).

22. M. Russell Ballard, "Sharing the Gospel Using the Internet," July 2008, based on a commencement address given at BYU-Hawaii on December 15, 2007 (https://www.lds.org/ensign/2008/07/sharing-the-gospel-using-the-internet?lang=eng) and speech given at BYU Management Society, Washington, DC April 19, 2008 (http://www.mormonnewsroom.org/additional-resource/transcript-of-elder-m-russell-ballard-s-speech-given-at-brigham-young-university-management-society).

23. (https://newrepublic.com/article/119140/martha-stewart-profile).

24. (https://www.nytimes.com/2014/12/14/upshot/us-employment-women-not-working.html) and slightly different statistics at (http://equitablegrowth.org/research-analysis/declining-labor-force-participation-rate-causes-consequences-path-forward/).

25. Emily Matchar, "Why I Can't Stop Reading Mormon Housewife Blogs," January 15, 2011. *Salon* (http://www.salon.com/2011/01/15/feminist_obsessed_with_mormon_blogs/), which was reposted in the on-line magazine *LDS Living* and *Homeward Bound: Why Women Are Embracing the New Domesticity* (New York: Simon & Schuster, 2013).

26. Alicia Purdy, "Utah Women Bloggers Are Top in the Nation," *Deseret News*, May 14, 2012.

27. Theresa Davis, "Al Fox Carraway Tells Conversion Story at BYU," *Daily Universe*, November, 17, 2015 (http://universe.byu.edu/2015/11/17/al-fox-carraway-tells-conversion-story-at-byu1/).

28. *Armelle* (http://www.armelleblog.com/about).

29. Leigh Anne Wilkes, "About" (http://www.yourhomebasedmom.com/about/).

30. "Master Bathroom After," *320 Sycamore* (http://www.320sycamoreblog.com/2012/02/master-bathroom-after.html) and "Kitchen After" (http://www.320sycamoreblog.com/2011/12/kitchen-after.html).

31. Videographer Hailey Haugen Divine blogs at "Somewhere Devine" (https://www.somewheredevine.com/). See "Piper and Scout" (https://vimeo.com/116015420) and "Little Toy Car" (https://www.somewheredevine.com/2015/02/little-toy-car.html).

32. I would like to thank Noel Voltz for her insight into the symbolic nature of white.

33. Internet Users by Country (http://www.internetlivestats.com/internet-users-by-country/).

34. Alex Moazed, "4 Steps for Etsy"(http://www.huffingtonpost.com/alex-moazed/4-steps-for-etsy-to-keep-_1_b_6956480.html). Matt Egan, "Etsy Now Worth Over $3 Billion," *CNN Money* (http://money.cnn.com/2015/04/15/investing/etsy-ipo-16-a-share-wall-street/).

35. (http://www.azcentral.com/story/news/local/scottsdale-contributor/2016/10/20/lds-meets-diy-how-faith-builds-crafts-businesses-arizona-mormons/92479288/).

36. Betty J. Eadie on her official web page cites the seventy-eight weeks on the bestseller list (https://www.embracedbythelight.com/leftside/embraced/ebtlindex.htm) and Massimo Introvigne cites "more than seventy weeks" in his "Embraced by the Church? Betty Eadie, Near-Death Experiences, and Mormonism," *Dialogue* 29 (Fall 1996): 106.

37. Susan R. Madsen, Janika Dillon, and Robbyn T. Scribner, "Cosmetic Surgery and Body Image Among Utah Women," *Utah Women Stats*, April 10, 2017 (http://www.uvu.edu/ uwlp/docs/uwscosmeticsurgery.pdf) and Joylin Namie, " 'In the World, but Not of the World': The Paradox of Plastic Surgery Among Latter-day Saint Women in Utah," *Journal of the Utah Academy of Sciences, Arts, and Letters* 90 (2013): 225–48.

38. The Mormon Women Project (https://www.mormonwomen.com/).

39. Aspiring Mormon Women (http://aspiringmormonwomen.org/).

40. Rich Valenza interview with Wendy Williams Montgomery, "Wendy Williams Montgomery, Mormon Mother, Shares Story About Gay Son," *Huffpost*, March 28, 2014 (http://www.huffingtonpost.com/2014/03/28/wendy-gay-family_n_5042297.html).

41. The previous quotes all come from "Allies Dinner 2016: Mama Dragons Allies Award Video," published November 7, 2016 (https://www.youtube.com/watch?v=UShqoVtuBEw).

42. Mama Dragons, Allies Award Video.

43. "Allies Dinner 2016: Mama Dragons Allies Award Speech," published November 4, 2016 (https://www.youtube.com/watch?v=E_omqLzxyOI).

44. Mama Dragons, Allies Award video.

45. Erika Munson, "Balancing Personal Conviction and Compassion for Same-Sex Couples," *Deseret News*, July 27, 2014.

46. Jack Healy, "Gentle Dissent in Mormon Church on Gay Marriages," *New York Times*, June 11, 2012. "Gets Better at Brigham Young University" (https://www.youtube.com/ watch?v=Ym0jXg-hKCI).

47. *General Handbook of Instructions* 1 (2015), 16.13; 6.7.2; 6.7.3 (https://www.scribd.com/ doc/288685756/Changes-to-LDS-Handbook-1-Document-2-Revised-11-3-15-28003- 29).

48. Larry R. Lawrence, "The War Goes On," *Ensign* (April 2017).

49. Michael L. Price, "Utah Officials Unsure Why Youth Suicide Rate Has Nearly Tripled Since 2007," *Salt Lake Tribune*, July 2, 2016 (http://www.sltrib.com/news/4075258- 155/story.html).

50. "The Trouble with Chicken Patriarchy," Joanna Brooks et al., eds., *Mormon Feminism* (New York: Oxford University Press, 2016), 237–39.

51. Rosemary Avance, "Constructing Religion in the Digital Age: The Internet and Modern Mormon Identities" (dissertation, University of Pennsylvania, 2015), 140.

52. Timothy Pratt, "Mormon Women Set Out to Take a Stand, in Pants," *New York Times*, December 19, 2012 (http://www.nytimes.com/2012/12/20/us/19mormon.html).

53. Avance, "Constructing Religion," 146.

54. Walter Kirn, "The Mormon Moment," *Newsweek*, June 5, 2011.

55. Lorie Winder Stromberg, "The Birth of Ordain Women: The Personal Becomes Political," in Gordon Shepherd et al., *Voices for Equality*, 16.

56. "Mission Statement," *Ordain Women* (http://ordainwomen.org/mission/).

57. Stromberg, "The Birth of Ordain Women," 17; 22.

58. Counterpoint Conference, University of Utah, November 9, 2013.

59. Stromberg, "The Birth of Ordain Women," 23.

60. To April Young Bennett, Debra Jenson, Kate Kelly, and Hannah Wheelwright from Jessica Moody, March 17, 2014 (http://www.deseretnews.com/media/pdf/1317612.pdf).

61. "Ordain Women Releases LDS Bishops Letter Giving Reasons for Kelly's Excommunication," *Deseret News* June 23, 2014 (http://www.deseretnews.com/media/ pdf/1365030.pdf).

62. "An Announcement of April Young Bennett," *Exponent II* (January 15, 2015) (http://www.the-exponent.com/an-announcement-from-april-young-bennett/).

63. "Ordain Women Founder Kate Kelly Charged with Apostasy," *A Well-Behaved Mormon Woman* (c. June 12, 2014) (http://wellbehavedmormonwoman.blogspot.com/2014/06/ordain-women-founder-kate-kelly-apostasy.html), repeating blog post "Mormon Feminists Openly Seek Priesthood Ordination" (c. March 22, 2013) (http://wellbehavedmormonwoman.blogspot.com/2013/03/mormon-feminists-openly-seek-priesthood.html).

64. Tad Walch, "New LDS Women's Group Quickly Gains Steam on Facebook," *Deseret News*, April 3, 2014.

65. While there is anecdotal evidence of Kate Kelly and John Delin's excommunication as "the straw that broke the camel's back" there also was an organized mass resignation; see Benjamin Wood, "Kate Kelly Joins Latter-day Saints Gathered Outside of Mormon Headquarters for Mass Resignation Event," *Washington Post*, July 27, 2015.

66. Linda Sego, interview by Colleen McDannell, September 14, 2015.

67. Laurie Goodstein, "It's Official: Mormon Founder Had Up to Forty Wives," *New York Times*, November 10, 2014.

68. See "Gospel Topics" (https://www.lds.org/topics?lang=eng). "Plural Marriage and Families in Early Utah" (December 16, 2013); "Plural Marriage in Kirtland and Nauvoo" (October 22, 2014); "The Manifesto and the End of Plural Marriage" (October 22, 2014).

69. Tad Walch, "Women Hired by LDS Church History Department Making Huge Strides in Mormon Women's History," *Deseret News*, February 7, 2016.

70. Peggy Fletcher Stack, "Picture This," *Salt Lake Tribune*, January 5, 2015.

71. Joseph Smith's Teachings about Priesthood, Temple, Women," October 2015 (https://www.lds.org/topics/joseph-smiths-teachings-about-priesthood-temple-and-women?lang=eng).

72. "Plural Marriage in Kirtland and Nauvoo" and "Plural Marriage and Families in Early Utah."

73. Pseudonym, interview by Colleen McDannell, 2015.

74. Linda Sego, interview by Colleen McDannell, September 14, 2015.

75. Neylan McBaine, "To Do the Business of the Church: A Cooperative Paradigm for Examining Gendered Participation Within Church Organizational Structure," FAIRMormon (2012) (https://www.fairmormon.org/conference/august-2012/to-do-the-business-of-the-church-a-cooperative-paradigm).

76. Peggy Fletcher Stack, "Forget Priesthood," *Salt Lake Tribune*, August 29, 2014.

77. V.[alerie] H.[udson] Cassler, "Zion in Her Beauty Rises: Current Discourse on Women and the Priesthood by Ballard, Dew, and Oaks," *SquareTwo* (Spring 2014) (http://squaretwo.org/Sq2ArticleCasslerOaksBallardDew.html).

78. V.[alerie] H.[udson] Cassler, "A Day to Be Remembered: New Stirrings Towards Diarchy in LDS Church Government," *SquareTwo* (Summer 2015) (http://squaretwo.org/Sq2ArticleCassler18August.html).

79. Cassler, "Zion in Her Beauty Rises."

80. David L. Paulsen and Martin Pulido, "A Mother There: A Survey of Historical Teachings About Mother in Heaven," *BYU Studies* 50 (2011): 7.

81. "Mother in Heaven" (https://www.lds.org/topics/mother-in-heaven?lang=eng).

82. Jana Riess, "Writer Seeks Mormonism's Heavenly Mother—Through Poetry," *Salt Lake Tribune*, September 6, 2017, discussing Rachel Hunt Steenblick, *Mother's Milk: Poems in Search of Heavenly Mother* (n.p.: By Common Consent, 2017). See also the 2014 poetry and art contest, "A Mother Here" (http://www.amotherhere.com/index.php#sthash.UY5fKLGa.dpbs).

83. Mike Thayer, "Utah: Lifestyle Porn Capital of the World," *Mike Thayer*, c. January 2017 (http://mike-thayer.com/lifestyle-porn/).

84. Mary Ellen Elggren, interview by Colleen McDannell, May 31, 2016.

85. Andrea Smardon, "Trump's Policies Have Turned Some Mormon Women in Utah into Political Activists," *PRI The World*, June 7, 2017; Ben Lockhart, " 'She Doesn't Deserve This': Family Laments Mother's Arrest, Pending Deportation," *Deseret News*, May 3, 2017; Courtney Tanner, "Trump's Election Triggered an 'Unabashedly Faithful' Group of Activists: Mormon Women," *Salt Lake Tribune*, September 27, 2017; Mormon Women for Ethical Government (https://www.mormonwomenforethicalgovernment .org/faqs/).

EPILOGUE

1. M. Russell Ballard, "Counseling with Our Councils," General Conference, April 1994.

2. "Councils Follow Heavenly Pattern, Say Leaders in Roundtable Discussion" (https:// www.lds.org/church/news/councils-follow-heavenly-pattern-say-leaders-in-roundtable-discussion?lang=eng) and *Encyclopedia of Mormonism*, s. v. "Council in Heaven."

3. Kate Holbrook and two former church historians, Jill Mulvay Derr and Carol Cornwall Madsen (along with Mathew J. Grow), published *The First Fifty Years of the Relief Society* (Salt Lake City: Church Historians Press, 2016), a hefty documentary collection that illustrated women's involvement in medicine and ritual healing, evidence of their ownership of church buildings, and their protests of antipolygamy legislation, in addition to the original Nauvoo minutes and their 1855 alteration. Soon after its publication, the text was digitized and placed online for global access. In 2017 historian Jennifer Reeder along with Kate Holbrook brought out *At the Pulpit: 185 Years of Discourses by Latter-day Saint Women*, also with the Church Historians Press.

4. Tad Walch, "Mormon Teens to Have Greater Opportunities for Temple Service in 2018," *Deseret News*, December 14, 2017.

5. Helen B. Andelin, *Fascinating Womanhood* ([1965]; updated edition, New York: Bantam Dell, 2007), 317.

6. See the plucked rose reference in Elise C. Carroll, "Ladder of Graces," vol. 38 (1927): 710. September Mary Marker column, September 8, 1952, ACCN 1862, Box 33a, Folder 4, Ramona W. Cannon Letters, UU.

7. Alex Dominguez, "Elizabeth Smart Speaks About Abstinence Education," *Salt Lake Tribune*, May 6, 2013; Molly Oswaks, "Elizabeth Smart Is Standing Up for Rape Victims—and Tearing Down Purity Culture," *Broadly*, September 1, 2016 (https:// broadly.vice.com/en_us/article/mbqjka/elizabeth-smart-is-standing-up-for-rape-victimsand-tearing-down-purity-culture).

8. Rick Phillips and Ryan T. Cragun cite a ratio in Utah of three females for every two males in "Mormons in the United States 1990–2008: Socio-demographic Trends and Regional Differences: A Report Based on the American Religious Identification Survey 2008" (Program on Public Values, Trinity College, 2011), 5 (http://commons.trincoll.edu/aris/ files/2011/12/Mormons2008.pdf). In 2017 Carole M. Stephens, First Counselor in the Relief Society presidency, stated that "more than half of our women [over 18] are single," and Liz Hale, a clinical psychologist being interviewed with her, set the number at 51 percent. See "When Life Is Less than Ideal," Gospel Solutions for Families, Mormon Channel, published March 9, 2017 (https://www.youtube.com/watch?v=xORaJNv6swI).

9. Phillips and Cragun, "Mormons in the United States," 4. Popularized in Jon Birger, "What 2 Religions Tell Us About the Modern Dating Crisis," *Time*, August 24, 2015; Peggy Fletcher Stack, "Mormonism's Dating Dilemma Is a Guy Thing—There Aren't Enough of Them," *Salt Lake Tribune*, August 26, 2015, and Jana Riess, "More Mormon Men

Are Leaving the LDS Church, Say Researchers—But Especially in Utah," *Religion News Service*, September 16, 2015.

10. While the church does not make official documentation of the problem available, a leaked presentation recorded in 2008 provides some background. See YouTube video, "In Which They Fret Over the Young Single Adults" (https://www.youtube.com/watch?v=FBH04SooaY0) and Jana Riess's reflection, "Worldwide, only 25 percent of young single Mormons are active in the LDS Church," *Religion News Service*, October 5, 2016 (http://religionnews.com/2016/10/05/leaked-worldwide-only-25-of-young-single-mormons-are-active-in-the-lds-church/).

11. In the souvenir book for the *Book of Mormon* musical, Steven Suskin writes on the dedication page, "We all did this because we secretly wanted to have a big happy Mormon family and now we do. So this is dedicated to our big happy Mormon family to everyone who helped make this show what it is—you guys are amazing." *The Book of Mormon, The Testament of a Broadway Musical* (New York: Newmarket Press, 2012), n.p.

BIBLIOGRAPHIC ESSAY

CHAPTER 1

This description of the early life of Emmeline B. Wells is based on Carol Cornwall Madsen's 1985 University of Utah dissertation, "A Mormon Woman in Victorian America," parts of which have been published in *Emmeline B. Wells: The Public Years 1870–1920* (Salt Lake City: Deseret Book, 2005) and the article, "Emmeline B. Wells, 'Am I Not a Woman and a Sister,'" *BYU Studies* 22 (Spring 1982): 161–78. While I worked with her dissertation, more accessible is *Emmeline B. Wells: An Intimate History* (Salt Lake City: University of Utah Press, 2016).

On the *Woman's Exponent*, see Sherri Cox Bennion, "The *Woman's Exponent*: Forty-Two Years of Speaking for Women," *Utah Historical Quarterly* 44 (Summer 1976): 222–39. Emmeline Wells kept diaries during much of her life. L. Tom Perry Special Collections of the Harold B. Lee Library at Brigham Young University [BYU] has the original diaries from 1844 to 1920. These have been digitized and can be viewed online; see https://sites.lib.byu.edu/muw/2016/03/17/emmeline-b-wells-diaries/. BYU has a typescript available to researchers since the original diaries are not open for public research. Copies of the original diaries are also held in Special Collections at the J. Willard Marriott Library of the University of Utah [UU].

On Emily Faithfull's career, see James S. Stone, *Emily Faithfull: Victorian Champion of Women's Rights* (Toronto: P. D. Meany, 1994) and for her personal life, Martha Vicinus, "Lesbian Perversity and Victorian Marriage: The 1864 Codrington Divorce Trial," *Journal of British Studies* 36 (1997): 70–98. Contemporary accounts of her lectures appeared in the *New York Times* on October 25, 1872; January 26, 1873; February 12, 1873; February 16, 1873; December 2, 1882; November 10, 1883; and November 26, 1893; and on June 4, 1895, her obituary contained biographical information. Faithfull's antipathy toward Mormonism was typical of the British literature of the time, see Karen M. Morin and Jeanne Kay Guelke, "Strategies of Representation, Relationship, and Resistance: British Women Travelers and Mormon Plural Wives, ca. 1870–1890," *Annals of the Association of American*

Geographers 88 (September 1998): 436–462. Morin and Guelke, following Emmeline Wells's lead, consistently misspell Emily Faithfull's name.

Overviews of Mormon history are numerous. Of particular use have been Matthew Bowman, *The Mormon People: The Making of an American Faith* (New York: Random House, 2012); Thomas F. O'Dea, *The Mormons* (Chicago: University of Chicago Press, 1957); and Claudia Lauper Bushman and Richard Lyman Bushman, *Building the Kingdom: A History of Mormons in America* (New York: Oxford University Press, 1999). The definitive biography of Joseph Smith is Richard Bushman, *Joseph Smith: Rough Stone Rolling* (New York: Alfred A. Knopf, 2005), but Fawn M. Brodie's classic *No Man Knows My History: The Life of Joseph Smith* (New York: Alfred A. Knopf, 1945) has a literary insightfulness that makes it indispensable.

Linda Wilcox DeSimone's introduction to a reprint of Fanny Stenhouse's *Exposé of Polygamy: A Lady's Life Among the Mormons* (Logan: Utah State University Press, 2008) provides a strong portrayal of this complicated woman. See also Ronald W. Walker, "The Stenhouses and the Making of a Mormon Image," *Journal of Mormon History* 1 (1973): 51–72. Ann Eliza Young was on the antipolygamy circuit and wrote *Wife No. 19; or, The Story of a Life in Bondage, Being a Complete Exposé of Mormonism, and Revealing the Sorrows, Sacrifices and Sufferings of Women in Polygamy* (Hartford, CT: Dustin, Gilman & Co., 1875). Latter-day Saint female apostates have received little scholarly attention; however, two bestselling fictional pieces have been written about Ann Eliza Young: David Ebershoff, *The 19th Wife: A Novel* (New York: Random House, 2008) and Irving Wallace, *The Twenty-Seventh Wife* (New York: Signet Books, 1962). The divorce papers of Maria Bidgood Jarman include her story of her husband and are located at the Huntington Library. On the wives of dissenters, see Beverly Beeton, "A Feminist Among the Mormons: Charlotte Ives Cobb Godbe Kirby," *Utah Historical Quarterly* 59 (Winter 1991): 23–31 and the discussion of Augusta Adams Cobb Young in John G. Turner, *Brigham Young: Pioneer Prophet* (Cambridge, MA: Harvard University Press, 2012), 101.

End Times mentality is outlined in Grant Underwood, *The Millenarian World of Early Mormonism* (Urbana: University of Illinois Press, 1993). Several nineteenth-century Christian communities promised intense spiritual experiences for their followers. See Ann Taves, *Fits, Trances, and Visions: Experiencing Religion and Explaining Experience from Wesley to James* (Princeton, NJ: Princeton University Press, 1999). There was considerable overlap with supernaturalism of Methodism; see Christopher Jones, "We Latter-day Saints Are Methodists: The Influence of Methodism on Early Mormon Religiosity," master's thesis, BYU, 2006, and his article "Mormonism in the Methodist Marketplace: James Covel and the Historical Background of Doctrine and Covenants 39–40," *BYU Studies*

Quarterly 51, no. 1 (2012): 67–98; Kathleen Flake, "From Conferences to Councils: The Development of LDS Church Organization, 1830–1835," in *Archive of Restoration Culture Summer Fellows' Papers, 1997–1999* (Provo, UT: Joseph Fielding Smith Institute for LDS History, 2000); and John H. Wigger, *Taking Heaven By Storm: Methodism and the Rise of Popular Christianity in America* (New York: Oxford University Press, 1998).

On early Mormonism's charismatic character, see Linda King Newell, "Gifts of the Spirit: Women's Share," in Maureen Ursenbach Beecher and Lavina Fielding Anderson, eds., *Sisters in Spirit* (Carbondale: University of Illinois Press, 1987), 111–50; and Lee Copland, "Speaking in Tongues in the Restored Churches," *Dialogue* 24 (1991): 13–33. For early examples, see Dan Vogel and Scott C. Dunn, " 'The Tongue of Angels': Glossolalia Among Mormonism's Founders," *Journal of Mormon History* 19 (Fall 1993): 1–34 and Martha Sontag Bradley, "Spiritual Riches," 4 *Zinas: A Story of Mothers and Daughters on the Mormon Frontier* (Salt Lake City: Signature Press, 2000), 51–76. Samuel Morris Brown discusses the importance of Adam's language in "Seerhood, Pure Language, and the Silence of the Grave," in *In Heaven as It Is on Earth: Joseph Smith and the Early Mormon Conquest of Death* (New York: Oxford University Press, 2012), 115–41.

The definitive statements on healing are two essays by Jonathan A. Stapley and Kristine Wright: "The Forms and the Power: The Development of Mormon Ritual Healing to 1847," *Journal of Mormon History* 35 (Summer 2009): 42–87 and "Female Ritual Healing in Mormonism," *Journal of Mormon History* 37 (Winter 2011): 1–85. Susanna Morrill provides an exceedingly sensitive analysis of the spiritual nature of women's healing in "Relief Society Birth and Death Rituals: Women at the Gates of Mortality," *Journal of Mormon History* 36 (Spring 2010): 129. For a general overview see Lester E. Bush, Jr., *Healing and Medicine Among the Latter-day Saints* (New York: Crossroad, 1993), 85–89.

The temple is considered to be too sacred to discuss in detail, so scholarship in its ritual evolution is rare. See David John Buerger, *The Mysteries of Godliness: A History of Mormon Temple Worship* (San Francisco: Smith Research Associates, 1994), 11–68. On developing concepts of priesthood see Gregory A. Prince, *Power from on High: The Development of Mormon Priesthood* (Salt Lake City: Signature Books, 1995), 115–48.

The best history of the Relief Society was published by a church-owned press, so while the scholarship is strong the tone at times is celebratory. See Jill Mulvay Derr, Janath Russell Cannon, and Maureen Ursenbach Beecher, *Women of Covenant: The Story of Relief Society* (Salt Lake City: Deseret Book Company, 1992). There are excellent introductions and documents included in Jill Mulvay Derr, Carol Cornwall Madsen, Kate Holbrook, and Matthew J. Grow, *The First Fifty Years of the Relief Society: Key Documents in*

Latter-day Saint Women's History (Salt Lake City: Church Historian's Press, 2016). The hefty work is all online (and thus word searchable) at https://www.churchhistorianspress.org/the-first-fifty-years-of-relief-society.   On the Nauvoo minutes, see Derr et al., *First Fifty Years,* 3–149; Derr et al., *Women of Covenant,* 23–50; and Jill Mulvay Derr and Carol Cornwall Madsen, "Preserving the Record and Memory of the Female Relief Society of Nauvoo, 1842–92," *Journal of Mormon History* 35 (Summer 2009): 88–117.

Early Mormonism through the eyes of Joseph Smith's wife is carefully told in Linda King Newell and Valeen Tippetts Avery, *Mormon Enigma: Emma Hale Smith* (Garden City, NY: Doubleday and Co., 1994), and for an analysis of how Emma Smith has been represented, see Max Perry Mueller, "Changing Portraits of the Elect Lady: Emma Smith in Mormon, RLDS, and LDS Historiography, 1933–2005," *Journal of Mormon History* 37, no. 2 (Spring 2011), 183–214. On the period before the Relief Society was reestablished, see Richard L. Jensen, "Forgotten Relief Societies, 1844–67," *Dialogue* 16 (Spring 1983), 105–25, and for an excellent social history see Carol Cornwall Madsen, "Women and Community: Relief Society in Cache Valley, 1868–1900," *Journal of Mormon History* 21 (Spring 1995): 126–54. Jessie L. Embry wrote "Relief Society Grain Storage Program, 1876–1940," as her 1974 master's thesis at BYU; it was published as "Grain Storage: The Balance of Power Between Priesthood Authority and Relief Society Autonomy," *Dialogue* 15 (Winter 1982): 59–66.

The classic study of Mormon economics is Leonard J. Arrington, *Great Basin Kingdom: An Economic History of the Latter-day Saints, 1830–1900* ([1958] 3rd ed., Urbana: University of Illinois Press, 2005). On home industry, see Leonard J. Arrington, "The Economic Role of Pioneer Mormon Women," *Western Humanities Review* 9 (Spring 1955): 145–64; Maureen Ursenbach Beecher, "Women's Work on the Mormon Frontier," *Utah Historical Quarterly* 49 (Summer 1981): 284; Linda Thatcher, "Women Alone: The Economic and Emotional Plight of Early LDS Women," *Dialogue* 25 (1992): 45–55; E. V. Wallis, "The Women's Cooperative Movement in Utah, 1869–1915," *Utah Historical Quarterly* 71 (2003): 315–31; and Claudia L. Bushman, "Mormon Domestic Life in the 1870s: Pandemonium or Arcadia?" *Arrington Annual Lecture,* Paper 4, 1999. For specific discussion of sericulture, see Chris Rigby Arrington, "The Finest of Fabrics: Mormon Women and the Silk Industry in Early Utah," *Utah Historical Quarterly* 46 (Fall 1978): 376–96 and Bradley, *4 Zinas,* 237–241. On women's key role in rising consumerism, see Russell Belk, "Battling Worldliness in the New Zion: Mercantilism Versus Homespun in 19th Century Utah," *Journal of Micromarketing* 14 (Spring 1994): 9–22 and Greg Umbach, "Learning to Shop in Zion: The Consumer Revolution in Great Basin Mormon Culture,

1847–1910," *Journal of Social History* 38 (2004): 29–161. Jennifer Reeder uses material culture to provide an innovative entry into Mormon women's lives in her 2013 George Mason University dissertation, " 'To Do Something Extraordinary': Mormon Women and the Creation of a Usable Past."

Demographic change is best documented in Dean May, "A Demographic Portrait of the Mormons, 1830–1980," in D. Michael Quinn, *The New Mormon History* (Salt Lake City: Signature Books, 1992), 121–33. On social change, see Ethan R. Yorgason, *Transformation of the Mormon Culture Region* (Urbana: University of Illinois Press, 2003); Thomas A. Alexander, *Mormonism in Transition: A History of the Latter-day Saints, 1890–1930* (Urbana: University of Illinois Press, 1996); and Thomas G. Alexander and James B. Allen, *Mormons and Gentiles: A History of Salt Lake City* (Boulder, CO: Pruett Publishing, 1984). For the implication of this transformation on class, see Marilyn Reed Travis, "Social Stratification and the Dissolution of the City of Zion in Salt Lake City, 1847–1880," PhD dissertation, University of Utah, 1995. For the impact of the railroad, the rising number of Gentiles in Zion, and generational attitudes, see Lisa Olsen Tait, "The *Young Woman's Journal* and Its Stories: Gender and Generations in 1890s Mormondom," 2010 dissertation, University of Houston.

CHAPTER 2

The notion that because Latter-day Saint women lived in polygamy they were exotic, "orientals" whose makeup was fundamentally other than American citizens, is developed in Paul Reeve, *Religion of a Different Color: Race and the Mormon Struggle for Whiteness* (New York: Oxford University Press, 2015); J. Spencer Fluhman, *"A Peculiar People": Anti-Mormonism and the Making of Religion in Nineteenth-Century America* (Chapel Hill: University of North Carolina Press, 2002), 103–25; and Christine Talbot, *A Foreign Kingdom: Mormons and Polygamy in American Political Culture, 1852–1890* (Carbondale: University of Illinois Press, 2013), 63–104. For an analysis of how anti-Mormonism worked out historically see Patrick Q. Mason, *The Mormon Menace: Violence and Anti-Mormonism in the Postbellum South* (New York: Oxford University Press, 2011). The classic study of anti-Mormon fiction is Terryl L. Givens, *The Viper on the Hearth: Mormons, Myths, and the Construction of Heresy* ([1997] New York: Oxford University Press, 2013) and for a comparative perspective, see David B. Davis, "Some Themes of Counter-Subversion: An Analysis of Anti-Masonic, Anti-Catholic, and Anti-Mormon Literature," *Mississippi Valley Historical Review* 47 (September 1960): 205–24.

For a discussion of the various ways Christians have understood eternal life, see Colleen McDannell and Bernhard Lang, *Heaven: A History* (New Haven, CT: Yale University Press, 1988), and for the nineteenth century see pp. 228–306. For the extended kinship that extends into the past and into the future as well from the celestial to the earthly spheres, see Samuel Morris Brown, *In Heaven as It Is on Earth: Joseph Smith and the Early Mormon Conquest of Death* (New York: Oxford University Press, 2012), 145–278; Carmon Hardy, "Lords of Creation: Polygamy, the Abrahamic Household, and Mormon Patriarchy," *Journal of Mormon History* 20 (Spring 1994): 119–52; Jonathan A. Stapley, *The Power of Godliness: Mormon Liturgy and Cosmology* (New York: Oxford University Press, 2018); and Kathleen Flake, "The Emotional and Priestly Logic of Plural Marriage," *Leonard J. Arrington Mormon History Lecture Series* (no. 15, October 1, 2009), 1–16.

The Jewish understanding of the *Shekinah* comes from the Talmud and was developed by medieval kabbalists. See Gershom Gerhard Scholem, *Origins of the Kabbalah* ([1962]; Princeton, NJ: Princeton University Press, 1990), 167–77. The classic exploration of maternal imagery in medieval devotionalism is Carolyn Walker Bynum, *Jesus as Mother: Studies in the Spirituality of the High Middle Ages* (Berkeley: University of California Press, 1982), 110–66. For other places where a divine feminine appears in Judaism and Christianity, see the bibliographical essay for Chapter 7.

On early concepts of Heavenly Mother, see Jill Mulvay Derr, "The Significance of 'O My Father' in the Personal Journey of Eliza R. Snow," *BYU Studies* 36, no. 1 (1996–97): 84–126; Susanna Morrill, "Mormon Women's Agency and Changing Conceptions of the Mother in Heaven," in Kate Holbrook and Matthew Bowman, *Women and Mormonism: Historical and Contemporary Perspectives* (Salt Lake City: University of Utah Press, 2016), 121–35; and Linda P. Wilcox, "The Mormon Concept of Mother in Heaven," in Maureen Ursenbach Beecher and Lavina Fielding Anderson, *Sisters in Spirit: Mormon Women in Historical and Cultural Perspective* (Urbana: University of Illinois Press, 1987), 64–77.

The literature on polygamy dwarfs all other scholarship on Latter-day Saint women. Most diaries, autobiographical sketches, and letters of women available at the Church History Library and BYU date from the nineteenth century and so many deal with polygamy. Special Collections at BYU has 231 oral histories of people reared in Mormon polygamist families. During the 1930s sociologist Kimball Young (grandson of Brigham Young and ex-Mormon) oversaw the collection of oral histories of those who had lived or were living in polygamy. Those materials are housed at the Huntington Library.

Some writings of plural wives have been published, such as Lu Ann Faylor Snyder and Phillip A. Snyder, *Post-Manifesto Polygamy: The 1899–1904 Correspondence of Helen, Owen, and Avery Woodruff* (Logan: Utah State University Press, 2009); Melissa Lambert Milewski, ed., *Before the*

Manifesto: The Life Writings of Mary Lois Walker Morris (Logan: Utah State University Press, 2007); Guenavere Allen Sandberg, *One Wife Too Many: The Whispers of Margaret McConnell, 1841–1898* (Utah: Agreka Books, 2000); Constance L. Lieber and John Sillito, eds., *Letters from Exile: The Correspondence of Martha Hughes Cannon and Angus M. Cannon, 1886–1888* (Salt Lake City: Signature Books, Inc., 1993); Jennifer Moulton Hansen, ed., *Letters of Catharine Cottam Romney, Plural Wife* (Urbana: University of Illinois Press, 1992); and the literary classic, Annie Clark Tanner, *A Mormon Mother: An Autobiography* ([1941]; Salt Lake City: University of Utah Press, 1969).

A dated but helpful bibliography is Davis Bitton, "Mormon Polygamy: A Review Article," *Journal of Mormon History* 4 (1977): 101–18. For a nineteenth-century theological justification, see David J. Whittaker, "The Bone in the Throat: Orson Pratt and the Public Announcement of Plural Marriage," *Western Historical Quarterly* 18 (July 1987): 293–314. On polygamy prior to Utah settlement, see Brian Hale, *Joseph Smith's Polygamy* (3 vols., Salt Lake City: Greg Kofford Books, 2013); Merina Smith, *Revelation, Resistance, and Mormon Polygamy: The Introduction and Implementation of the Principle, 1830–1853* (Logan: Utah State University Press, 2013); George Smith, *Nauvoo Polygamy: ". . . But We Called It Celestial Marriage"* (Salt Lake City: Signature Press, 2011); Todd Compton, *In Sacred Loneliness: The Plural Wives of Joseph Smith* (Salt Lake City: Signature Books, 1997); Martha Sonntag Bradley and Mary Brown Firmage Woodward, "Plurality, Patriarchy, and the Priestess: Zina D. H. Young's Nauvoo Marriages," *Journal of Mormon History* 20 (Spring 1994): 84–118.

By far the most compelling history of the lived experiences of polygamist women is Laurel Thatcher Ulrich, *A House Full of Females: Plural Marriage and Women's Rights in Early Mormonism, 1835–1970* (New York: Alfred K. Knopf, 2017). She builds on the work of: Paula Kelly Harline, *The Polygamous Wives Writing Club: From the Diaries of Mormon Pioneer Women* (New York: Oxford University Press, 2014); Jeffery Nichols, *Prostitution, Polygamy and Power in Salt Lake City, 1847–1918* (Carbondale: University of Illinois Press, 2008); Kathryn M. Daynes, *More Wives Than One: Transformation of the Mormon Marriage System, 1840–1910* (Urbana and Chicago: University of Illinois Press, 2001); Karen M. Morin and Jeanne Kay Guelke, "Strategies of Representation, Relationship, and Resistance: British Women Travelers and Mormon Plural Wives, ca. 1870–1890," *Annals of the Association of American Geographers* 88 (September 1998): 436–62; B. Carmon Hardy, *Solemn Covenant: The Mormon Polygamous Passage* (Urbana and Chicago: University of Illinois Press, 1992); LaMond Tullis, *Mormons in Mexico: The Dynamics of Faith and*

Culture (Logan, UT: Utah State University Press, 1987); Jessie L. Embry, *Mormon Polygamous Families: Life in the Principle* (Salt Lake City: University of Utah Press, 1987); Richard S. Van Wagoner, *Mormon Polygamy: A History* (Salt Lake City: Signature Books, 1986); Jesse L. Embry and Martha S. Bradley, "Mothers and Daughters in Polygamy," *Dialogue* 18 (Fall 1985): 99–107; Kahlile Mehr, "Women's Response to Plural Marriage," *Dialogue* 18 (Fall 1985): 84–97; Joan Iversen, "Feminist Implications of Mormon Polygyny," *Feminist Studies* 10 (Fall 1984), 505–21; Julie Dumfey, "Living the Principle of Plural Marriage: Mormon Women, Utopia, and Female Sexuality in the Nineteenth Century," *Feminist Studies* 10 (Fall 1984): 523–36; Eugene E. Campbell and Bruce L. Campbell, "Divorce Among Mormon Polygamists: Extent and Explanations," *Utah Historical Quarterly* 46 (Winter 1978): 4–20; Kimball Young, *Isn't One Wife Enough?* (New York: Henry Holt & Co., 1954).

For the legal implications of polygamy and antipolygamy legislation, see Nathan B. Oman, "Natural Law and the Rhetoric of Empire: *Reynolds v. United States,* Polygamy, and Imperialism," *Washington University Law Review* 88, no. 3 (2011): 661–706 and Sarah Barringer Gordon, *The Mormon Question: Polygamy and Constitutional Conflict in Nineteenth-Century America* (Chapel Hill: University of North Carolina Press, 2002). Polygamy did not end with the Manifesto and efforts by the Senate to uncover its continuance are documented by Kathleen Flake in *The Politics of American Religious Identity: The Seating of Senator Reed Smoot, Mormon Apostle* (Chapel Hill: University of North Carolina Press, 2004).

The lives of women and children under antipolygamy laws are documented in Lorie Winder Stromberg, "Prisoners for 'The Principle': The Incarceration of Mormon Plural Wives, 1882–1890" in Newel G. Bringhurst et al., eds., *The Persistence of Polygamy* (Independence, MO: John Whitmer Books, 2013) 298–325; Martha Sonntag Bradley, "Hide and Seek: Children on the Underground," *Utah Historical Quarterly* 5 (Spring 1983): 133–53; and Kimberly Jensen James, "'Between Two Fires': Women on the 'Underground' of Mormon Polygamy," *Journal of Mormon History* 8 (1981): 49–61.

For plural marriages experienced after the Manifesto, see Kenneth L. Cannon II, "Beyond the Manifesto: Polygamous Cohabitation among LDS General Authorities After 1890," *Utah Historical Quarterly* 46, no. 1 (Winter 1978): 24–36; Ken Driggs, "Twentieth-Century Polygamy and Fundamentalist Mormons in Southern Utah," *Dialogue* 24 (Winter 1991): 46; John Bennion, "Mary Bennion Powell: Polygamy and Silence," *Journal of Mormon History* 24 (Fall 1998): 85–128; and D. Michael Quinn, "LDS Church Authority and New Plural Marriages, 1890–1904," *Dialogue* 18 (Spring 1985): 8–105.

On Emmeline Wells and polygamy, see Kenneth L. Cannon II, "The Tragic Matter of Louie Wells and John Q. Cannon," *Journal of Mormon History* 35 (Spring 2009), 126–90 and Carol Cornwall Madsen, *Emmeline B. Wells: An Intimate History* (Salt Lake City: University of Utah Press, 2017), 233–58.

On Protestant women mobilizing against polygamy, see Jana Reiss, "'Heathen in Our Fair Land:' Presbyterian Women Missionaries in Utah, 1870–1890," *Journal of Mormon History* 26 (2000): 165–95; Joan Smyth Iversen, *The Anti-Polygamy Controversy in the U.S. Women's Movement, 1880–1925: A Debate on the American Home* (New York and London: Garland Publishing, Inc., 1997); Peggy Pascoe, *Relations of Rescue: The Search for Female Moral Authority in the American West, 1874–1939* (New York: Oxford University Press, 1990), 20–30.

For a collection of the key essays and primary documentation on Latter-day Saints and suffrage, see Carol Cornwall Madsen, *Battle for the Ballot: Essays on Woman Suffrage in Utah* (Logan: Utah State University Press, 1987), and for the Western context, see Rebecca J. Mead, *How the Vote Was Won: Woman Suffrage in the Western United States, 1868–1914* (New York: New York University Press, 2004). Historians dispute the reasons why suffrage was passed in 1870. An excellent summary of the debate is Andrea G. Radke-Moss, "Polygamy and Women's Rights: Nineteenth-Century Mormon Female Activism," in Newell G. Bringhurst and Craig L Foster, eds., *The Persistence of Polygamy: From Joseph Smith's Martyrdom to the First Manifesto, 1844–1890* (Independence, MO: John Whitmer Books, 2013), 262–97. Thomas G. Alexander argues that male church leaders supported women's rights for religious reasons, see "An Experiment in Progressive Legislation: The Granting of Woman Suffrage in Utah in 1870," *Utah Historical Quarterly* 38 (1970): 20–30. Without denying the influence of religion, Carol Cornwall Madsen argues that Latter-day Saint women were the primary agent of promoting their own rights Madsen, in *An Advocate for Women: The Public Life of Emmeline B. Wells, 1870–1920* (Provo, UT: BYU Press, 2006), 237–319. Laurel Thatcher Ulrich upholds this conclusion in *A House Full of Females*. Jill Mulvay (Derr) describes how conservative Eliza R. Snow dealt with the issue in "Eliza R. Snow and the Woman Question," *BYU Studies* 16 (Winter 1976): 250–64.

Other historians see suffrage as a political move by men to increase Mormon influence. See Beverly Beeton, "Woman Suffrage in Territorial Utah," *Utah Historical Quarterly* 46 (Spring 1978): 100–20, and its expansion in *Women Vote in the West: The Woman Suffrage Movement, 1869–1896* (New York: Garland Publishing, 1986). Lola Van Wagenen argues women had more agency; see *Sister-Wives and Suffragists: Polygamy and the Politics of Woman Suffrage, 1870–1896* (PhD dissertation, New York University,

1994) and its summary in "In Their Own Behalf: The Politicization of Mormon Women and the 1870 Franchise," *Dialogue* 24 (Winter 1991): 31–43.

For grassroots activity, see Lisa Bryner Bohman, "A Fresh Perspective: The Woman Suffrage Associations of Beaver and Farmington, Utah," *Utah Historical Quarterly* 59 (Winter 1991): 4–21; Linda Thatcher, "'I Care Nothing for Politics': Ruth May Fox, Forgotten Suffragist," *Utah Historical Quarterly* 49, no. 3 (Summer 1981): 239–35; Rebekah Ryan Clark, "An Uncovered History: Mormons in the Woman Suffrage Movement, 1896–1920" in Carol Cornwall Madsen and Cherry B. Silver, *New Scholarship on Latter-day Saint Women in the Twentieth Century: Selections from the Women's History Initiative Seminars, 2003–2004* (Provo, UT: Joseph Fielding Smith Institute for Latter-day Saint History): 19–38; Jean Bickmore White, "Woman's Place Is in the Constitution: The Struggle for Equal Rights in Utah in 1895," *Utah Historical Quarterly* 42 (Fall 1974), 344–69.

CHAPTER 3

The variety of responses to the 1890 Manifesto are laid out in Kathryn M. Daynes, *More Wives Than One: Transformation of the Mormon Marriage System, 1840–1910* (Urbana: University of Illinois Press, 2001), 184–87, and are fully described in the second half of B. Cannon Hardy, *Solemn Covenant: The Mormon Polygamous Passage* (Urbana: University of Illinois Press, 1992). That the Manifesto was widely understood to be a temporary, pragmatic measure and not a revelation is argued by Edward Leo Lyman in *Political Deliverance: The Mormon Quest for Utah Statehood* (Carbondale: University of Illinois Press, 1986), 126–36. The foundational examination of the continuation of polygamy among church leaders is D. Michael Quinn, "LDS Church Authority and New Plural Marriages, 1890–1904," *Dialogue* 18 (Spring 1985): 8–105.

For the first three decades of twentieth-century Mormonism, see Thomas G. Alexander, *Mormonism in Transition: A History of the Latter-day Saints, 1890–1930* (Urbana: University of Illinois, 1996); Matthew Bowman, "Eternal Progression, 1890–1945," *The Mormon People: The Making of an American Faith* (New York: Random House, 2012), 152–83; and his "Eternal Progression: Mormonism and American Progressivism," in Randall Balmer and Jana Riess, *Mormonism and American Politics* (New York: Columbia University Press, 2016), 52–70. The impact of non-church exploration on intellectually oriented Saints is evaluated in Thomas W. Simpson, *American Universities and the Birth of Modern Mormonism, 1867–1940* (Chapel Hill: University of North Carolina Press, 2016). Scholarship on the "lived religion" of Latter-day Saint congregational practices is rare and insubstantial; see William G. Hartley, "Mormon Sundays," in his *My Fellow Servants: Essays on the History of the Priesthood* (Provo, UT: BYU Studies, 2010), 343–54, with a more rigorous article on administrative reforms, "The Priesthood Reform Movement, 1908–1922," 301–20. Although less recent, a more thorough exploration is Ronald W. Walker, "'Going to Meeting' in Salt Lake City's Thirteenth Ward, 1849–1888: A Microanalysis," in Davis Bitton and Maureen Ursenbach Beecher, eds., *New Views of Mormon History: A Collection of Essays in Honor of Leonard J. Arrington* (Salt Lake City: University of Utah Press, 1987), 138–61. The best history of Latter-day Saint women during these years is Jill Mulvay Derr, Janath Russell Cannon, and Maureen Ursenbach Beecher, *Women of Covenant: The Story of Relief Society* (Salt Lake City: Deseret Book Company, 1992), 151–303.

In contrast, scholarship on the modernization of American society and culture in the first decades of the twentieth century is vast. For overviews see Jackson Lears, *Rebirth of a Nation: The Making of Modern America, 1877–1920* (New York: HarperCollins, 2009); Robert H. Weibe, *The Search for Order, 1877–1920* (New York: Hill and Wang, 1966); Cecilia Tichi, *Shifting Gears: Technology, Literature, and Culture in Modernist America* (Chapel Hill: University of North Carolina Press, 1987); and Lynn Dumenil, *The Modern Temper: American Culture and Society in the 1920s* (New York: Hill and Wang, 1995). For specific discussions of progressivism, see Ronald J. Pestritto and William J. Atto, eds., *American Progressivism: A Reader* (Lanham, MD: Rowman and Littlefield, 2008); Maureen A. Flanagan, *America Reformed: Progressives and Progressivisms, 1890–1920s* (New York: Oxford University Press, 2006); and Michael McGerr, *A Fierce Discontent: The Rise and Fall of the Progressive Movement in America, 1870–1920* (New York: Oxford University Press, 2005).

Scholarship on women's role in modernization has been particularly rich. On the development of the "science" of the home, see Helen Zoe Veit, *Modern Food, Moral Food: Self-Control, Science, and the Rise of Modern American Eating in the Early Twentieth Century* (Chapel Hill: University of North Carolina, 2013); Carolyn M. Goldstein, *Creating Consumers: Home Economics in Twentieth-Century America* (Chapel Hill: University of North Carolina Press, 2012); Megan J. Elias, *Stir It Up: Home Economics in American Culture* (Philadelphia: University of Pennsylvania Press, 2008); Rima D. Apple, *Perfect Motherhood: Science and Childrearing in America* (New Brunswick, NJ: Rutgers University Press, 2006); and Sarah Stage and Virginia B. Vincenti, eds., *Rethinking Home Economics: Women and the History of a Profession* (Ithaca, NY: Cornell University Press, 1997).

On reform via the women's club movement, see Ann Ruggles Gere, *Intimate Practices: Literacy and Cultural Work in US Women's Clubs,*

1880–1920 (Urbana: University of Illinois Press, 1997); Anne Firor Scott, *Natural Allies: Women's Associations in American History* (Urbana: University of Illinois Press, 1991); Theodora Penny Martin, *The Sound of Our Own Voices: Women's Study Clubs, 1860–1910* (Boston: Beacon Press, 1987); and Karen J. Blair, *The Clubwoman as Feminist: True Womanhood Redefined, 1868–1914* (New York: Holmes and Meier Publishers, Inc., 1980). On black and white women's differing response, see Linda Gordon, "Black and White Visions of Welfare: Women's Welfare Activism, 1890–1945," *Journal of American History* 78 (1991): 559–90. For white women using racist ideology to promote their own rights, see Louise Michele Newman, *White Women's Rights: The Racial Origins of Feminism in the United States* (New York: Oxford University Press, 1999). For Utah's unique religious situation, see Suzanne M. Stauffer, "A Good Social Work, Women's Clubs, Libraries, and the Construction of a Secular Society in Utah, 1890–1920," *Libraries and the Cultural Record* 46 (2011): 135–55.

Jonathan A. Stapley and Kristine Wright document the loss of women's role in healing in "Female Ritual Healing in Mormonism," *Journal of Mormon History* 37 (2011): 1–85.

Dave Hall has written extensively on Amy Brown Lyman, and my discussion relies on his research. See *A Faded Legacy: Amy Brown Lyman and Mormon Women's Activism, 1872–1959* (Salt Lake City: University of Utah Press, 2015), based on "In the Utah Vanguard: Amy Brown Lyman as Progressive Mormon Activist, Welfare State Builder, and Modern Woman in a Dual Career Family" (PhD dissertation, University of California, Santa Barbara, 2004); "A Crossroads for Mormon Women: Amy Brown Lyman, J. Reuben Clark and the Decline of Organized Women's Activism in the Relief Society," *Journal of Mormon History* 36 (2010): 205–49; "From Home Service to Social Service: Amy Brown Lyman and the Development of Social Work in the LDS Church," *Mormon Historical Studies* 9 (2008): 67–88; and "Anxiously Engaged: Amy Brown Lyman and Relief Society Charity Work, 1917–1945," *Dialogue* 27 (1994): 73–92. Matthew Bowman places Amy Brown Lyman within larger circles of Progressive Era reform in " 'The Best Social Practice': Mormon Women and the Professionalization of Reform," in Kate Holbrook and Matthew Bowman, *Women and Mormonism: Historical and Contemporary Perspectives* (Salt Lake City: University of Utah Press, 2016): 183–95.

Amy Brown Lyman's work makes more sense when seen within the wider push by women toward reform. See the classic statement on "maternalism" by Estelle Freedman, "Separatism as Strategy: Female Institution Building and American Feminism, 1870–1930," *Feminist Studies* 5 (1979): 512–29. The impact and decline of women's activism is documented in Robyn Muncy, *Creating a Female Dominion in American Reform, 1890–1935*

(New York: Oxford University Press, 1991); Molly Ladd-Taylor, *Mother-Work: Women, Child Welfare, and the State, 1890–1930* (Urbana: University of Illinois Press, 1995); and Theda Skocpol, *Protecting Soldiers and Mothers: The Political Origin of Social Policy in the United States* (Cambridge, MA: Harvard University Press, 1992). For how this played out in the West, including Utah, see Peggy Pascoe, *Relations of Rescue: The Search for Female Moral Authority in the American West, 1874–1939* (New York: Oxford University Press, 1993). The classic study of the relationship between early twentieth-century reform and feminism is Nancy F. Cott, *The Grounding of Modern Feminism* (New Haven, CT: Yale University Press, 1987), 85–114.

There is no scholarly literature on the role women played in Utah's political environment after statehood. A few pages on the state's first senator are found in Mari Graña, *Pioneer, Polygamist, Politician: The Life of Dr. Martha Hughes Cannon* (Guilford, CT: Twodot Press, 2009), 85–114.

CHAPTER 4

The Sheppard-Towner Act is often used as a gauge of the rise and fall of women's activism. The foundational article is J. Stanley Lemons, "The Sheppard-Towner Act: Progressivism in the 1920s," *Journal of American History* 55 (1969): 776–86, with elaboration in *The Woman Citizen: Social Feminism in the 1920s* (Urbana: University of Illinois Press, 1973), 153–248. A more recent examination is Carolyn M. Moehling and Melissa A. Thomasson, "The Political Economy of Saving Mothers and Babies: The Politics of State Participation in the Sheppard-Towner Program," *Journal of Economic History* 72 (2012): 75–103. For the Utah situation, see Loretta L. Hefner, "The National Women's Relief Society and the U. S. Sheppard-Towner Act," *Utah Historical Quarterly* 50 (1982): 255–67.

On William H. King, see Markku Ruotsila, "Senator William H. King of Utah and His Campaigns Against Russian Communism, 1917–1933," *Utah Historical Quarterly* 74 (2006): 147–63 and Laurence M. Hauptman, "Utah Anti-Imperialist: Senator William H. King and Haiti, 1921–1934," *Utah Historical Quarterly* 41 (Spring 1973): 116–27.

An influential group of women did not support progressive causes and eventually organized to support a conservative political agenda. An excellent study of that history is Kirsten Marie Delegard, *Battling Miss Bolsheviki: The Origins of Female Conservatism in the United States* (Philadelphia: University of Pennsylvania Press, 2011).

The story of how Latter-day Saints moved from being communitarian to capitalist is complicated. Matthew Bowman roots it in the 1860s controversies with William Godbe and his followers; see his "Approaching Zion: Mormon Ambivalence About Capitalism," in Amanda Porterfield,

Darren Grem, and John Corrigan, eds., *The Business Turn in American Religious History* (New York: Oxford University Press, 2017), 108–30. On the Mormons, the Depression era, and the Welfare Plan, see Bruce D. Blumell, "Welfare Before Welfare: Twentieth-Century LDS Church Charity Before the Great Depression," *Journal of Mormon History* 6 (1979): 89–106; Garth L. Mangum and Bruce D. Blumell, *The Mormons' War on Poverty: A History of LDS Welfare 1830–1990* (Salt Lake City: University of Utah Press, 1993); Leonard J. Arrington, *Utah, the New Deal and the Depression of the 1930s* (Ogden, UT: Weber State College Press, 1983); Joseph F. Darowski, "The WPA Versus the Utah Church," in Brian Q. Cannon and Jessie L. Embry, eds., *Utah in the Twentieth Century* (Logan: Utah State University Press, 2009); and Leonard J. Arrington and Wayne K. Hinton, "The Origin of the Welfare Plan of the Church of Jesus Christ of Latter-day Saints," *BYU Studies* 5 (1964): 67–85. For Clark's involvement, see D. Michael Quinn, *Elder Statesman: A Biography of J. Reuben Clark* (Salt Lake City: Signature Press, 2002). Women's place in this history may be found in Hall's writings on Amy Brown Lyman as well as Jill Mulvay Derr, "Changing Relief Society Charity to Make Way for Welfare," in Davis Bitton and Maureen Ursenbach Beecher, eds., *New Views of Mormon History: A Collection of Essays in Honor of Leonard J. Arrington* (Salt Lake City: University of Utah Press, 1987), 242–72.

Two articles examine how women negotiated power with the male church authorities: Jessie L. Embry, "Grain Storage: The Balance of Power Between Priesthood Authority and Relief Society Autonomy," *Dialogue* 15 (1982): 60–63 and Jill Mulvey Derr and C. Brooklyn Derr, "Outside the Mormon Hierarchy: Alternative Aspects of Institutional Power," *Dialogue* 15 (1982): 21–43.

Good surveys on the transformation of charity are Olivier Zunz, *Philanthropy in America: A History* (Princeton, NJ: Princeton University Press, 2012), 44–103 and Andrew Morris, *The Limits of Voluntarism: Charity and Welfare from the New Deal to the Great Society* (Cambridge, UK: Cambridge University Press, 2009), 1–110. On the trajectory toward efficiency and bureaucratization in Catholic charity, see Dorothy M. Brown and Elizabeth McKeown, *The Poor Belong to Us: Catholic Charities and American Welfare* (Cambridge, MA: Harvard University Press, 1997), 51–85, 193–95; M. Christine Anderson, "Catholic Nuns and the Invention of Social Work: The Sisters of the Santa Maria Institute of Cincinnati, Ohio, 1897 through 1920s," *Journal of Women's History* 12 (2000): 60–80; and Marian J. Morton, "The Transformation of Catholic Orphanages: Cleveland, 1851–1996," *Catholic Historical Review* 88 (2002): 65–89.

A thorough investigation of the events surrounding the excommunication is Gary James Bergera, "Transgression in the Latter-day Saint

Community: The Cases of Albert Carrington, Richard R. Lyman, and Joseph F. Smith. Part 2: Richard R. Lyman," *Journal of Mormon History* 37 (2011): 173–207.

CHAPTER 5

On postwar women who dissented from established Mormonism, see the chapters by Roger Launius and Linda Thatcher, "Maureen Wimple: Quiet Dissenter" and "Fawn Brodie" in *Differing Visions: Dissenters in Mormon History* (Carbondale: University of Illinois Press, 1998); Shirley E. Stephenson, "Fawn McKay Brodie: An Oral History Interview," *Dialogue* 14 (Summer 1981): 99–116; and the writings of Newell G. Bringhurst: "Fawn Brodie and Her Quest for Independence," *Dialogue* 22 (1989): 79–95; "Juanita Brooks and Fawn Brodie—Sisters in Mormon Dissent," *Dialogue* 27 (1994): 105–27; "Fawn M. Brodie and Deborah Laake: Two Perspectives on Mormon Feminist Dissent," *John Whitmer Historical Association Journal* 17 (1997): 95–113; and *Fawn McKay Brodie: A Biographer's Life* (Norman: University of Oklahoma Press, 1999). For a critical perspective on both Brooks and her biographer Bringhurst, see Louis Midgley, "The Legend and Legacy of Fawn Brodie," *FARMS Review of Books* 13 (2001): 21–71.

The literature on postwar American women is voluminous. The 1950s brought the first English translation of Simone de Beauvoir's *The Second Sex* (New York: Bantam Books, 1952; original French 1949) and Mirra Komarovsky's *Women in the Modern World* (Boston: Little, Brown and Company, 1953) both of which served as the unacknowledged scholarly foundation of Betty Friedan's more popular *The Feminist Mystique* (New York: W. W. Norton, 1963). Particularly insightful social/cultural histories are Elaine Tyler May, *Homeward Bound: American Families in the Cold War Era* (New York: Basic Books, 1988); Stephanie Coontz, *The Way We Never Were: American Families and the Nostalgia Trap* (New York: Basic Books, 1992), 23–41; and Wendy Kozol, *Life's America: Family and Nation in Postwar Photojournalism* (Philadelphia: Temple University Press, 1994). For surveys of the eras, see Eugenia Kaledin, *Mothers and More: American Women in the 1950s* (New York: Twayne, 1993) and Blanche Linden-Ward and Carol Hurd Green, *American Women in the 1960s: Changing the Future* (New York: Twayne, 1993). For the persistence of feminism in the postwar years, see L. Rupp and V. Taylor, *Survival in the Doldrums: The American Women's Rights Movement, 1945 to the 1960s* (Columbus: Ohio State University Press, 1990); Sylvie Murray, *The Progressive Housewife: Community Activism in Suburban Queens, 1945–1965* (Philadelphia: University of Pennsylvania Press, 2003); and Susan Lynn,

Progressive Women in Conservative Times: Racial Justice, Peace, and Feminism, 1945 to the 1960s (New Brunswick, NJ: Rutgers University Press, 1992). Recent scholarship on Betty Friedan and the writing of *Feminine Mystique* stresses that her ideas were nurtured *before* the sixties in a context of progressive politics and the labor movement; see Daniel Horowitz, *Betty Friedan and the Making of the* Feminine Mystique (Amherst: University of Massachusetts Press, 1998) and Stephanie Coontz, *A Strange Stirring:* The Feminine Mystique *and American Women at the Dawn of the 1960s* (New York: Basic Books, 2011).

On religious women's activism for cultural change during the postwar years, see the edited collection by Catherine A. Brekus, *The Religious History of American Women: Reimagining the Past* (Chapel Hill: University of North Carolina Press, 2007), especially Ann Braude, "Faith, Feminism, and History" (232–52); Amy Koehlinger, "'Are You the White Sisters or the Black Sisters?' Women Confounding Categories of Race and Gender" (253–78); and Pamela Susan Nadell, "Engendering Dissent: Women and American Judaism" (279–93). These three authors have edited or written studies that elaborate on postwar change: Ann Braude, ed., *Transforming the Faiths of Our Fathers: Women Who Changed American Religion* (New York: St. Martin's Press, 2004); Amy L. Koehlinger, *The New Nuns: Racial Justice and Religious Reform in the 1960s* (Cambridge, MA: Harvard University Press, 2007); Pamela Susan Nadell, *Women Who Would Be Rabbis: A History of Women's Ordination, 1889–1985* (Boston: Beacon Press, 1998). On Protestant ordination, see Mark Chaves, *Ordaining Women: Culture and Conflict in Religious Organizations* (Cambridge, MA: Harvard University Press, 1997). On the role of African American women in the civil rights movement, see Bruce A. Glasrud, ed., *Southern Black Women in the Modern Civil Rights Movement* (College Station: Texas A&M, 2013). The change in Catholic laywomen's lives is explored in Colleen McDannell, *The Spirit of Vatican II: A History of Catholic Reform in America* (New York: Basic Books, 2011), 29–54, 177–206. The rise of religious women in conservative movements is documented in the next chapter.

My conclusions on the postwar expansion of women's labor come from William Henry Chafe, *The American Woman: Her Changing Social, Economic, and Political Roles, 1920–1970* (New York: Oxford University Press, 1972), 218–25, and are reaffirmed by Claudia Goldin, *Understanding the Gender Gap: An Economic History of American Women* (New York: Oxford University Press, 1990) and Susan M. Hartmann, "Women's Employment and the Domestic Ideal in the Early Cold War Years," in Joanne Meyerowitz, ed., *Not June Cleaver: Women and Gender in Postwar America, 1945–1960* (Philadelphia: Temple University Press, 1994), 84–100. On working married women, see Kristin Celello, *Making Marriage Work: A History of Marriage and Divorce in the Twentieth-Century United States* (Chapel Hill: University of North Carolina Press, 2009), 72–102. The argument that women were returning to work not to disrupt gender power relations but to bolster the family budget was first made by sociologist Mirra Komarovsky in *Blue Collar Marriage* (New York: Random House, 1964) and was restated in Rosalind Rosenberg in *Divided Lives: American Women in the Twentieth Century* (New York: Hall and Wang, 1992), 158. On the impact of World War II on labor, see Maureen Honey, *Creating Rosie the Riveter: Class, Gender, and Propaganda During World War II* (Amherst: University of Massachusetts Press, 1984), 20–24.

On general attitudes about housewifery, domesticity, and the culture of consumption, see Glenna Matthews, *Just a Housewife: The Rise and Fall of Domesticity in America* (New York: Oxford University Press, 1987), 172–96; Annegret S. Ogden, *The Great American Housewife: From Helpmate to Wage Earner, 1776–1986* (Westport, CT: Greenwood Press, 1986), 171–92; and Ruth Schwartz Cowan, *More Work for Mother* (New York: Basic Books, 1983). For church attitudes toward housework and the homey architecture of the Relief Society building, see Kate Holbrook, "Mormons and Housework During Second Wave Feminism," in Patrick Mason and John G. Turner, eds., *Out of Obscurity: Mormonism Since 1945* (New York: Oxford University Press, 2016), 198–213.

Although we think of the postwar era as promoting motherhood, there also were significant forces that argued that "momism" was ruining the nation. This antimotherhood movement began with Philip Wylie's *Generation of Vipers* (New York: Rinehart, 1942), and Rebecca Jo Plant traces its multiple expressions in *Mom: The Transformation of Motherhood in Modern America* (Chicago: University Chicago Press, 2010). While Mormonism shared the antifeminism of those like Wylie who derided Progressive Era female activism, Latter-day Saints always upheld sentimental motherhood in this period. Jodi Vandenberg-Daves situates "momism" within a broader historical context in *Modern Motherhood: An American History* (Camden, NJ: Rutgers University Press, 2014), 173–209.

For histories of American population control, see Derek S. Hoff, *The State and the Stork: The Population Debate and Policy Making in US History* (Chicago: University of Chicago Press, 2012) and Elaine Tyler May, *America and the Pill: A History of Promise, Peril, and Liberation* (New York: Basic Books, 2010). The topic of Latter-day Saints and birth control is explored by Melissa Proctor, "Bodies, Babies, and Birth Control," *Dialogue* 36 (Fall 2003): 159–75.

Postwar church growth is documented in Jan Shipps, "The Scattering of the Gathered and the Gathering of the Scattered: The Mid-Twentieth-Century Mormon Diaspora," in her *Sojourner in the Promised Land: Forty*

Years Among the Mormons (Urbana: University of Illinois Press, 2000) and D. Michael Quinn, "I-Thou vs. I-It Conversions: The Mormon 'Baseball Baptism' Era," *Sunstone* (December 1993): 30–44. For the impact of growth, see Rodney Stark and Reid L. Neilson, *The Rise of Mormonism* (New York: Columbia, 2005), 95–113. Women's ward culture before correlation is summarized in Jill Mulvay Derr et al., *Woman of Covenant: The Story of Relief Society* (Salt Lake City: Deseret Book, 1992), 304–39.

"Mary Marker" was one of many female advice columnists in postwar America, although her presence in a church-owned newspaper is unique. For the history of such writing, see David Gudelunas, *Confidential to America: Newspaper Advice Columns and Sexual Education* (New Brunswick, NJ: Transaction Publishers, 2008). Newspaper advice columns must be situated within the broader category of advice directed toward women; see Sarah A. Leavitt, *From Catherine Beecher to Martha Stewart: A Cultural History of Domestic Advice* (Chapel Hill: University of North Carolina Press, 2002), 171–94; Nancy A. Walker, *Women's Magazines 1940–1960: Gender Roles and the Popular Press* (Boston: Bedford/St. Martin's, 1998), 1–20; and Barbara Ehrenreich and Deirdre English, *For Her Own Good: Two Centuries of Experts' Advice to Women* ([1978]; New York: Anchor Books, 2005), especially "Motherhood as Pathology," 231–91. For Protestant ministerial advice to couples, see Rebecca L. Davis, "Sacred Partnerships," in *More Perfect Unions: The American Search for Marital Bliss* (Cambridge, MA: Harvard University Press, 2010), 136–75.

The history of the Word of Wisdom was explored in the Autumn 1981 issue of *Dialogue*. Of note are Thomas G. Alexander, "The Word of Wisdom: From Principle to Requirement," 78–88, and Lester E. Bush, "The Word of Wisdom in Early Nineteenth-Century Perspective," 46–65. The classic statement calling on the Progressive Era notion of health is John A. Widtsoe and Leah D. Widtsoe, *The Word of Wisdom: A Modern Interpretation* (Salt Lake City: Deseret Book Company, 1937).

Historians influenced by second wave feminism documented the confluence of purity, domesticity, and piety in the women's culture of the nineteenth century. While their findings have been criticized for being limited by race, class, and region, their insights into sexuality, gender, and religion are invaluable. See Barbara Welter's 1966 classic article, "The Cult of True Womanhood," and "The Feminization of American Religion: 1800–1860," both reprinted in Welter, *Dimity Convictions: The American Woman in the 19th Century* (Athens: Ohio University Press, 1976); Ann Douglas, *The Feminization of American Culture* (New York: Knopf, 1977); Kathryn Kish Sklar, *Catherine Beecher: A Study in American Domesticity* (New Haven, CT: Yale University Press, 1973); Nancy F. Cott, *The Bonds of Womanhood: 'Women's Sphere' in New England, 1780–1835* (New Haven,

CT: Yale University Press, 1977); and Carroll Smith-Rosenberg, *Disorderly Conduct: Visions of Gender in Victorian America* (New York: Oxford University Press, 1985). Although modesty and chastity are important aspects of church culture, the scholarly literature on this area is limited. See Marvin and Ann Rytting, "Exhortations for Chastity: A Content Analysis of Church Literature," *Sunstone* (March–April 1982): 15–21 and Katie Clark Blakesley, "'A Style of Our Own': Modesty and Mormon Women, 1951–2008," *Dialogue* 42 (Summer 2009): 22.

On gender during the Cold War era, see Elaine Tyler May, *Homeward Bound: American Families in the Cold War Era* (New York: Basic Books, 2008), 91, and Wini Breines, *Young, White and Miserable* (Chicago: University of Chicago Press, 1992). Breines details in "Sexual Puzzles" and "The Other Fifties" the conflicting messages in the world of the "bad girl" (84–166). That the era saw an increase of nonmarital sexual activity, prior to more public sexual freedom in the sixties, is the argument of Alan Petigny in *The Permissive Society: America, 1941–1965* (New York: Cambridge University Press, 2009). On postwar masculinity, see K. A. Cuordileone, "'Politics in an Age of Anxiety': Cold War Political Culture and the Crisis in American Masculinity, 1949–1960," *Journal of American History* 87 (September 2000): 515–45. Michael S. Kimmel, in *Manhood in America: A Cultural History* (New York: Free Press, 1996), summarizes the era's men as "white-collar conformists" and "suburban playboys," 161–86. As of this publication there has been practically no scholarship on postwar Mormon masculinity. For a general view, see David Knowlton, "On Mormon Masculinity," *Sunstone* (August 1992): 19–31 and for a microanalysis of a church-produced film, David H. Newman, "It'll Be Zion to Me: Ideal Mormon Masculinity in *Legacy*" (master's thesis, Syracuse University, 2013).

For the importance of turn-of-the-century masculinity for American culture and especially for Protestantism, see Gail Bederman, "'The Women Have Had Charge of the Church Work Long Enough': The Men and Religion Forward Movement of 1911–1912 and the Masculinization of Middle-Class Protestantism," *American Quarterly* 41 (September 1989): 432–65, which is more fully developed in *Manliness and Civilization: A Cultural History of Gender and Race in the United States, 1880–1917* (Chicago: University of Chicago Press, 1995). For a comparative study see L. Dean Allen, *Rise Up, O Men of God: The Men and Religion Forward Movement and Promise Keepers* (Macon, GA: Mercer University Press, 2002). For Mormon masculinity, see Amy Hoyt and Sara M. Patterson, "Mormon Masculinity: Changing Gender Expectations in the Era of Transition from Polygamy to Monogamy, 1890–1920," *Gender & History* 23 (2011): 72–91. Although he shows no interest in gender constructions, Greg Prince provides the standard biography of the influential postwar Latter-day Saint president in *David O. McKay and the Rise of Modern Mormonism* (Salt Lake: University of Utah Press, 2005).

The classic study of gender asymmetry begins not with the valuation of male behavior but on the universal devaluation of women; see Sherry B. Ortner, "Is Female to Male as Nature Is to Culture," in Michelle Z. Rosaldo and Louise Lamphere, eds., *Women, Culture, and Society* (Stanford, CA: Stanford University Press, 1974), 68–87. Rosaldo in her introduction to the volume gives the example of New Guinea, where "women grow sweet potatoes and men grow yams, and yams are the prestige food, the food one distributes at feasts," or the group she studied in the Philippines whose main dietary staple is the rice that women grow, but the meat that men hunt is the most highly valued food (19). Ortner takes a structural approach, which I follow in my analysis. For a more recent rethinking of her argument see Alejandro Lugo, "Destabilizing the Masculine, Refocusing 'Gender': Men and the Aura of Authority in Michelle Z. Rosaldo's Work," in Alejandro Lugo and Bill Mauerer, eds., *Gender Matters: Re-Reading Michelle Z. Rosaldo* (Ann Arbor: University of Michigan Press, 2000), 54–89.

CHAPTER 6

The literature on the feminist movement of the sixties and seventies is expansive, but these books help contextualize Latter-day Saint activities. For primary documents, see Rosalyn Baxandall and Linda Gordon, *Dear Sisters: Dispatches from the Women's Liberation Movement* (New York: Basic Books, 2000) and Rachel Blau DuPlessis and Ann Snitow, *The Feminist Memoir Project* ([1998]; New Brunswick, NJ: Rutgers University Press, 2007). General surveys include Sara Evans, *Tidal Wave: How Women Changed America at the Century's End* (New York: The Free Press, 2003); Estelle B. Freedman, *No Turning Back: The History of Feminism and the Future of Women* (New York: Ballantine Books, 2002); Ruth Rosen, *The World Split Open: How the Modern Women's Movement Changed America* (New York: Viking, 2000); Cassandra Langer, *A Feminist Critique: How Feminism Has Changed American Society, Culture, and How We Live From the 1940s to the Present* (New York: Icon Editions, 1996); and Flora Davis, *Moving Mountains: The Women's Movement in America Since 1960* (New York: Simon & Schuster, 1991). More recent writings consider how ethnic and racial minorities understood women's liberation, see Maylei Blackwell, *¡Chicana Power! Contested Histories of Feminism in the Chicano Movement* (Austin: University of Texas Press, 2011), Anne M. Valk, *Radical Sisters: Second-Wave Feminism and Black Liberation in Washington, D. C.* (Urbana: University of Illinois Press, 2010); and Benita Roth, *Separate Roads* *to Feminism: Black, Chicana, and White Feminist Movements in America's Second Wave* (Cambridge, UK: Cambridge University Press, 2004).

On the prohibition of African American males from holding the priesthood, see the bibliography in Chapter 7.

On the influence of Latter-day Saints outside of Utah, see Jan Shipps, "The Scattering of the Gathered and the Gathering of the Scattered: The Mid-Twentieth Century Mormon Diaspora," in *Sojourner in the Promised Land: Forty Years Among the Mormons* (Urbana: University of Illinois Press, 2000), 258–77. The importance of the magazine *Dialogue* in the evolution of liberal Latter-day Saint thinking is narrated in two essays by Devery S. Anderson, "A History of *Dialogue*, Part One: The Early Years, 1965–1971," *Dialogue* 32 (1999): 15–67 and "A History of *Dialogue*, Part Two: Struggle to Maturity, 1971–1982," *Dialogue* 33 (2000): 1–96. Claudia Bushman's problems with church leaders is summarized in Claudia L. Bushman, "My Short Happy Life with Exponent II," *Dialogue* 36 (Fall 2003): 186. On Juanita Brooks, see Levi S. Peterson, *Juanita Brooks: Mormon Woman Historian* (Salt Lake City: University of Utah, 1988).

Unfortunately, because the archival materials on the church hierarchy are not open to researchers, there is no scholarly history of correlation. For an excellent summary, see Matthew Bowman, *The Mormon People* (New York: Random House, 2012), 184–215. On the Relief Society during these years, see Carrie L. Taylor, "The Relief Society and President Spencer W. Kimball's Administration," (master's thesis, BYU, 2013), and Tina Hatch, " 'Changing Times Bring Changing Conditions': Relief Society, 1960 to the Present," *Dialogue* 37 (2004): 65–98.

For general decentralizing trends in US religions since World War II, see Robert Wuthnow, *The Restructuring of American Religion* (Princeton, NJ: Princeton University Press, 1988). For autobiographical reflections on feminism's impact on religion, see Ann Braude, *Transforming the Faiths of Our Fathers: The Women Who Changed American Religion* (New York: St. Martin's Press, 2004). For women's increasing role in leadership, see Carl and Dorothy Schneider, *In Their Own Right: The History of American Clergy Women* (New York: Crossroads, 1997). I documented the changes in Catholicism during this period in *The Spirit of Vatican II: Catholic Reform in America* (New York: Basic Books, 2011). For a close look at Catholicism and feminism, see Mary J. Henold, *Catholic and Feminist: The Surprising History of the American Catholic Feminist Movement* (Chapel Hill: University of North Carolina Press, 2008). For an overview of changes in conservative Protestantism since the sixties, see Steven P. Miller, *The Age of Evangelicalism: America's Born-Again Years* (New York: Oxford University Press, 2014). Julie Ingersoll explores tensions within Protestantism regarding women in *Evangelical Christian Women: War Stories in the Gender*

Battles (New York: NYU Press, 2003). See Janet Stocks, "To Stay or to Leave? Organizational Legitimacy in the Struggle for Change Among Evangelical Feminists," in Penny Edgell Becker and Nancy L. Eiesland, eds., *Contemporary American Religion: An Ethnographic Reader* (Walnut Creek, CA: AltaMira Press, 1997), 99–120. Although much of the article is not on women, David R. Swartz argues that identity politics—of which feminism played an important role—split the rising evangelical left, enabling the right to become politically more powerful among conservative Protestants. See "Identity Politics and the Fragmenting of the 1970s Evangelical Left," *Religion and American Culture: A Journal of Interpretation* 21 (Winter 2011): 81–120.

My discussion of Helen Andelin is based on the work of Julie Neuffer, *Helen Andelin and the Fascinating Womanhood Movement* (Salt Lake City: University of Utah Press, 2014), which is based on her 2007 Washington State University dissertation.

Helen Andelin was a part of a wider reaction against the social changes of the sixties, and while she remained out of politics, other religious women did not. See Lisa McGirr, *Suburban Warriors: The Origins of the New American Right* ([2001], Princeton, NJ: Princeton University Press, 2015) and Michelle Nickerson, *Mothers of Conservatism: Women and the Post-War Right* (Princeton, NJ: Princeton University Press, 2012). Sara Diamond takes into account the rise of evangelical Protestantism but does not connect it to women's grassroots activism in *Roads to Dominion: Right-Wing Movements and Political Power in the United States* (New York: Guilford Press, 1995), 66–137. This blindness toward gender is typical of most of the scholarship on religion and the rise of the New Right. Likewise, scholarship on the involvement of conservative women in politics does not take religion seriously. For example, see Catherine E. Rymph, *Republican Women: Feminism and Conservatism from Suffrage Through the Rise of the New Right* (Chapel Hill: University of North Carolina Press, 2006), 160–238, and Donald T. Critchlow, *Phyllis Schlafly and Grassroots Conservatism* (Princeton, NJ: Princeton University Press, 2008). A wider analysis on how the perceived rearrangement of gender structures altered future politics is Robert O. Self, *All in the Family: The Realignment of American Democracy Since the 1960s* (New York: Hill and Wang, 2012). For more theoretical reflections on antifeminism, see Jerome L. Himmelstein, "The Social Basis of Antifeminism: Religious Networks and Culture," *Journal for the Scientific Study of Religion* 25 (1986): 1–15 and Susan E. Marshall, "Who Speaks for American Women? The Future of Antifeminism," *Annals of the American Academy of Political and Social Science* 515 (May 1991): 50–62.

Interviews with the Utah participants in the IWY are available in the JoAnn Freed Collection of Oral Histories, 1975–1977, Utah State

Historical Society, Salt Lake City. Although they are not Latter-day Saint women, "Women in Utah Politics Oral History Project, 1976–1994" in the University of Utah, Marriott Library, Special Collections, contains helpful perspectives about the ERA-IWY controversies. Martha Sonntag Bradley thoroughly and with a literary heart documents the interaction between Latter-day Saints, the ERA, and the IWY in *Pedestals and Podiums: Utah Women, Religious Authority, and Equal Rights* (Salt Lake City: Signature Books, 2005) as well as her earlier "The Mormon Relief Society and the International Women's Year," *Journal of Mormon History* 21 (Spring 1995). Unfortunately, because the Church History Library archives on the modern Relief Society as well as the General Authorities are closed to researchers, we are missing the leadership's point of view. For an overview, see Joan Hoff-Wilson, *Rights of Passage: The Past and Future of the ERA* (Bloomington: University of Indiana Press, 1986). Neil J. Young justly argues that the impact of the church on the defeat has been underestimated; see " 'The ERA Is a Moral Issue': The Mormon Church, LDS Women, and the Defeat of the Equal Rights Amendment," *American Quarterly* 59 (2007): 623–44. Much of the involvement was sketched out early by D. Michael Quinn, "The LDS Church's Campaign Against the Equal Rights Amendment," *Journal of Mormon History* 20 (Fall 1994): 85–155. O. Kendall White, Jr., writes about the ERA fight outside of Utah in "Overt and Covert Policies: The Mormon Church's Anti-ERA Campaign in Virginia," *Virginia Social Science Journal* 19 (Winter 1984): 14–16 and "Mormonism and the Equal Rights Amendment," *Journal of Church and State* 31 (Spring 1989): 249–67. James T. Richardson provides a religious comparison in "The 'Old Right' in Action: Mormon and Catholic Involvement in an Equal Rights Amendment Referendum," in David G. Bromley and Anson Shupe, eds., *New Christian Politics* (Macon, GA: Mercer University Press, 1984), 213–33. For a brief sense of how church leaders felt about the controversy, see "A Conversation with Beverly Campbell," *Dialogue* 14 (Spring 1981): 45–57.

CHAPTER 7

The Special Collections at the University of Utah, Marriott Library has the papers of Sonia Johnson, which include transcripts of her Senate subcommittee testimony, her controversial addresses, and the almost five hundred letters that were sent to her regarding her interview with Phil Donahue and her excommunication. Essays about and interviews with Johnson by women who knew her include Alice Allred Pottmyer, "Sonia Johnson Mormonism's Feminist Heretic," in Roger D. Launius and Linda Thatcher, eds., *Differing Vision Dissenters in Mormon History* (Urbana: University of

Illinois Press, 1994), 366–38; Linda Sillitoe, "Church Politics and Sonia Johnson: The Central Conundrum," *Sunstone* 5 (January–February 1980): 35; Mary L. Bradford, "The Odyssey of Sonia Johnson," *Dialogue* 14 (Summer 1981): 14–26 and in the same issue "All on Fire: An Interview with Sonia Johnson," 27–47; and Karen S. Langlois, "An Interview with Sonia Johnson," *Feminist Studies* 8 (Spring 1982): 6–17. For a literary analysis, see Heather M. Kellogg, "Shades of Gray: Sonia Johnson's Life Through Letters and Autobiography," *Dialogue* 29 (Summer 1996): 77–86. On the impact of her travels in Africa, see Russel W. Stevenson, "Sonia's Awakening: White Mormon Expatriates in Africa and the Dismantling of Mormon Racial Consensus, 1852–1978," *Journal of Mormon History* 40 (Fall 2014): 208–47.

Following Johnson's excommunication there was an effort by historians to better understand the history of Latter-day Saint ecclesiastical and disciplinary courts. Lester E. Bush wrote "Excommunication and Church Courts: A Note from the General Handbook of Instructions," *Dialogue* 14 (Summer 1981): 74–98 and "Excommunication: Church Courts in Mormon History," *Sunstone* (July–August 1983): 24–30. See also Collin Mangrum, "Furthering the Cause of Zion: An Overview of the Mormon Ecclesiastical Court System in Early Utah," *Journal of Mormon History* 10 (1983): 79–90 and Edwin Brown Firmage and R. Collin Mangrum, *Zion in the Courts: A Legal History of the Church of Jesus Christ of Latter-day Saints* (Urbana: University of Illinois Press, 1988).

Religious discipline through excommunication has biblical roots, see "'Cast out the Evil Man from Your Midst' (1 Cor 5:5:13b)," *Journal of Biblical Literature* 103 (1984): 259–61. It is practiced by many Christian communities, see Elizabeth Vodola, *Excommunication in the Middle Age* (Berkeley: University of California Press, 1986); David C. Brown, "The Keys of the Kingdom: Excommunication in Colonial Massachusetts," *New England Quarterly* 67 (1994): 531–66; and Justin K. Miller, "Damned If You Do, Damned If You Don't: Religious Shunning and the Free Exercise Clause," *University of Pennsylvania Law Review* 137 (1988): 271–302. Disciplining members via church trials or courts is also widespread; for instance, see L. R. Poos, "Sex, Lies, and the Church Courts of Pre-Reformation England," *Journal of Interdisciplinary History* 25 (1995): 585–607; Derek R. Peterson, "Morality Plays: Marriage, Church Courts, and Colonial Agency in Central Tanganyika, ca. 1876–1928," *American Historical Review* 111 (2006): 983–1010; Robert Elwood, "The Lord's Messenger: Racial Lynching and the Church Trial of Robert Elwood," *Journal of Presbyterian History* 79 (Summer 2001): 135–49.

The popularity of Johnson's memoir encouraged other presses to publish the stories of Mormon women. Carol Lynn Pearson, who prior to the 1980s had self-published her historical writing on Mormon women and her more inspirational books with church publishers, found that Random House was interested in her story of marriage to a gay man who died of AIDS. She published *Good-bye, I Love You* in 1986 and produced a one-act play on women's lives, *Mother Wove the Morning* (1989).

Because church leaders directed much of their attention at dissenters who had intellectual interests, the reflections by and about "apostates" are considerable. At the publishers when the "September Six" were on trial, a book edited by Roger D. Launius and Linda Thatcher, *Differing Visions: Dissenters in Mormon History* (Urbana: University of Illinois Press, 1994) focuses on historical cases and ends with Johnson. The other women who are examined are Maureen Whipple and Fawn Brodie. Sociologist Armand L. Mauss has made major contributions to this literature, see "Authority, Agency, and Ambiguity: The Elusive Boundaries of Required Obedience to Priesthood Leaders," *Sunstone* (March 1996): 20–31; "Rethinking Retrenchment: Course Corrections in the Ongoing Campaign for Respectability," *Dialogue* 44 (Winter 2011): 1–42; and "Authority and Dissent in Mormonism," in Philip Barlow and Terryl Givens, eds., *Oxford Handbook of Mormonism* (New York: Oxford University Press, 2015): 386–407. Mauss's own struggles are documented in *Shifting Borders and a Tattered Passport: Intellectual Journeys of a Mormon Academic* (Salt Lake City: University of Utah Press, 2012). For a more theoretical and comparative approach see David Bromley, ed., *The Politics of Religious Apostasy: The Role of Apostates in the Transformation of Religious Movements* (Westport, CT: Praeger, 1998).

On the Mormon concept of the devil and evil see Douglas J. Davies, *Joseph Smith, Jesus, and Satanic Opposition: Atonement, Evil and the Mormon Vision* (Farnham, UK: Ashgate, 2010) and his "Father, Jesus and Lucifer in Pre-Mortal Council," *International Journal of Mormon Studies* 3 (Spring 2010): 1–16. Terryl Givens also lays out the conflict in *Wrestling the Angel: The Foundations of Mormon Thought* (New York: Oxford University Press, 2014), 130–46. Kathleen Flake provides a subtle interpretation of Joseph Smith's understanding of evil in "Translating Time: The Nature and Function of Joseph Smith's Narrative Canon," *Journal of Religion* 87 (2007): 497–527, especially 515–20.

There is no concise history on the changing nature of the Mormon prophet/president. On rival claims to leadership, see D. Michael Quinn, "The Mormon Succession Crisis of 1844," *BYU Studies* 16 (Winter 1976): 187–233 and *The Mormon Hierarchy: Origins of Power* (Salt Lake City: Signature Press), 143–243. For a history of the increasing focus on obedience and church leaders, see Armand L. Mauss, *The Angel and the Beehive: The Mormon Struggle with Assimilation* (Urbana: University of

Illinois Press, 1994), 85–88, 126–30, and Gordon Shepherd and Gary Shepherd, *A Kingdom Transformed: Early Mormonism and the Modern LDS Church* (Salt Lake City: University of Utah, 2016), 73, 97, 213, 297. A theoretical perspective developed from comparative Mormon and Catholic history is Walter E. A. Van Beek, "The Infallibility Trap: The Sacralisation of Religious Authority," *International Journal of Mormon Studies* 4 (2011): 14–44.

Although the period from 1980 to 1995 is critical in church history, like most of the twentieth century it is under-researched. One approach to the period is the sprawling account of the presidency of Spencer W. Kimball (1973–85) written by his son, Edward. I have used Kimball's "unabridged original manuscript," *Lengthen Your Stride: The Presidency of W. Kimball* (Salt Lake City: Benchmark Books, 2009). For a general overview of BYU at the time, see Bryan Waterman and Brian Kagel, *The Lord's University: Freedom and Authority at BYU* (Salt Lake City: Signature Books, 2002), especially Chapter 2, "Women and Feminism at BYU," 20–70. On BYU's Women's Conference, see Velda Gale Davis Lewis, "From Womanhood to Sisterhood: The Evolution of the Brigham Young University Women's Conference" (dissertation, BYU, 2006); Mary E. Stovall and Carol Cornwall Madsen, eds., *As Women of Faith: Talks Selected from the BYU Women's Conferences* (Salt Lake City: Deseret Book Company, 1989); and the interview of Marie Cornwall by Gregory A. Prince (2012) in "Mormon Women's Voices," Special Collections, University of Utah.

During the mid-1980s Richard Bushman and his wife, Claudia, both professional historians, were members of a church ward in Elkton, Maryland. With the permission of church authorities, they organized a meticulous recording of ward rituals and events as well as conducting member interviews for a one-year period (September 1, 1984–August 31, 1985). While the primary materials were deposited at BYU (and are currently restricted), the book based on the collection provides a rare glimpse into ward life shortly after the block plan was established. See Susan Buhler Taber, *Mormon Lives: A Year in the Elkton Ward* (Urbana: University of Chicago Press, 1993). As a doctoral student in sociology at Harvard, Martha Nibley Beck (daughter of the influential Hugh Nibley) did fieldwork from 1985 to 1991 on Mormon women and role conflict. Her conclusions on traditionalists, feminists, and "internally defined" women (which she argues are the under-researched majority) are contained in her Harvard University dissertation, "Flight from the Iron Cage: LDS Women's Responses to the Paradox of Modernization" (1994).

Neither Elaine A. Cannon's personal or official papers are open to scholars. The only published account of her impact is Mary Jane Woodger, "Elaine Anderson Cannon, Young Women General President: Innovations,

Inspiration, and Implementations," *Journal of Mormon History* 40, no. 4 (Fall 2014): 171–207.

Leonard J. Arrington's team of women in the Historical Department set a standard for Mormon women's history that has not been exceeded. For the general reader, he published *Sunbonnet Sisters: True Stories of Mormon Women and Frontier Life* (Salt Lake City: Bookcraft, 1984). Senior researcher Maureen Ursenbach Beecher published "Three Women and the Life of the Mind," *Utah Historical Quarterly* 43, no. 1 (1975): 26–40; "Under the Sunbonnets: Mormon Women with Faces," *Task Papers in LDS History*, no. 4 (Salt Lake City: Historical Department, Church of Jesus Christ of Latter-day Saints, 1975); "The Eliza Enigma," *Dialogue* 11 (Spring 1978): 30–41; "'All Things Move in Order in the City': The Nauvoo Diary of Zina Diantha Huntington Jacobs," *BYU Studies* 19 (Spring 1979): 285–320; along with Carol Cornwall Madsen and Jill Mulvay Derr, Beecher wrote "The Latter-day Saints and Women's Rights, 1870–1920: A Brief Survey," *Task Papers in LDS History*; no. 29 (Salt Lake City: Historical Department, Church of Jesus Christ of Latter-day Saints, 1979); "Women's Work on the Mormon Frontier," *Utah Historical Quarterly* 49 (Summer 1981): 276–90; "The 'Leading Sisters': A Female Hierarchy in Nineteenth-Century Mormon Society," *Journal of Mormon History* 9 (1982): 25–39; "Women in Winter Quarters," *Sunstone* (July/August 1983): 11–19; and co-authored with Patricia Lynn Scott, "Mormon Women: A Bibliography in Process, 1977–1985," *Journal of Mormon History* 12 (January 1985): 113–27.

On Arrington and his impact on history, see Leonard J. Arrington, *Adventures of a Church Historian* (Urbana: University of Illinois Press, 1998); Gregory A. Prince, *Leonard Arrington and the Writing of Mormon History* (Salt Lake City: University of Utah Press, 2016); Davis Bitton, "Ten Years in Camelot: A Personal Memoir," *Dialogue* 16 (Autumn 1983): 9–20.

After the Historical Department was reduced, Beecher and Davis Bitton edited *New Views of Mormon History: A Collection of Essays in Honor of Leonard J. Arrington* (Salt Lake City: University of Utah Press, 1987), which included two essays by department historians: Jill Mulvay Derr, "Changing Relief Society Charity to Make Way for Welfare," 242–72, and Carol Cornwall Madsen, "Schism in the Sisterhood: Mormon Women and Partisan Politics, 1890–1900," 211–41. Madsen published "Emmeline B. Wells, 'Am I Not a Woman and a Sister,'" *BYU Studies* 22 (Spring 1982): 161–78 and a masterful dissertation on Wells, "A Mormon Woman in Victorian America" (University of Utah, 1985). Jill Mulvay Derr also focused on nineteenth-century women, publishing "Eliza R. Snow and the Woman Question," *BYU Studies* 16 (Winter 1976): 250–64 and "The Liberal Shall Be Blessed: Sarah M. Kimball," *Utah Historical Quarterly* 44 (Summer 1976): 205–21. After she left the Historical Department, Derr published with her husband, C. Brooklyn Derr, an insightful analysis of how women negotiated male authority, "Outside the Mormon Hierarchy: Alternative Aspects of Institutional Power," *Dialogue* 15 (Winter 1982): 21–43. Working with Lavina Anderson, Maureen Ursenbach Beecher edited key essays in the influential *Sisters in Spirit* (Carbondale: University of Illinois Press, 1987).

The turn toward social history, combined with a fear of producing analytical scholarship that might not be faith-promoting, led to a flourishing of oral histories during the eighties and nineties sponsored by the Charles Redd Center under the auspices of historian Jessie Embry (https://reddcenter.byu.edu/Pages/CRCOralHistoryProjects.aspx) and available in Special Collections at the BYU library. Those oral histories that include a substantial number of women include African American, Asian American, Hispanic, Polynesian, Native American, family life (monogamous Mormons living around the turn of the century), polygamy, nurses, home front World War II, and missionaries.

The discussion of the Latter-day Saint understanding of Heavenly Mother comes within a wider context of explorations of female divinity. Under the impact of psychological and then feminist thought, scholars began to translate, republish, and rethink the work of earlier writers who explored the role of mother goddesses in world religions, particularly Johann Jakob Bachofen, *Myth, Religion, and Mother Right* (1861); Jane Ellen Harrison, *Ancient Art and Ritual* (1913); Robert Graves, *The White Goddess* (1948); and Eric Neumann, *The Great Mother* (1951). Scholars then elaborated on the feminine aspects of God and the powerful roles of female saints. Key texts are Raphael Patai, *The Hebrew Goddess* (1967); Marija Gimbutas, *The Goddesses and Gods of Old Europe* (1974); Merlin Stone, *When God Was a Woman* (1976); and Marina Warner, *Alone of All Her Sex: The Myth and Cult of the Virgin Mary* (1976) and her *Joan of Arc: The Image of Female Heroism* (1981). See Cynthia Eller, "Ancient Matriarchies in Nineteenth- and Twentieth-Century Feminist Thought," in Rosemary Skinner Keller et al., eds., *The Encyclopedia of Women and Religion in North America* (Bloomington: Indiana University Press, 2006), 804–09, and her critical appraisal, *The Myth of Matriarchal Prehistory: Why an Invented Past Won't Give Women a Future* (Boston: Beacon Press, 2000).

Linda King Newell's argument about the decline of women's influence in Mormonism is supported by most scholarship from the 1980s. Vella Evans's 1985 PhD dissertation from the University of Utah, "Woman's Image in Authoritative Mormon Discourse: A Rhetorical Analysis," documented how representations of the ideal Mormon woman went from being multifaceted to being singularly focused on domesticity by the 1940s. A declension thesis was also evident in Jessie L. Embry's master's thesis (BYU, 1974) on

Relief Society wheat storage, summarized as "Grain Storage: The Balance of Power Between Priesthood Authority and Relief Society Autonomy," *Dialogue* 15 (Winter 1982): 59–66.

For a history of *Sunstone*, see Martha Sonntag Bradley, "Theological Discussion or Support Group," *Sunstone* (July 2002): 33–44.

For additional reflections on women and the priesthood from this era see Linda King Newell, "The Historical Relationship of Mormon Women and Priesthood," *Dialogue* 18 (Fall 1985): 21–32; Melodie Moench Charles, "LDS Women and Priesthood," *Dialogue* 18 (Fall 1985): 15–20; D. Michael Quinn, "Mormon Women Have Had the Priesthood Since 1843," in Maxine Hanks, ed., *Women and Authority: Re-emerging Mormon Feminism* (Salt Lake City: Signature Books, 1992), 365–85; and Margaret Toscano, "If Mormon Women Have Had the Priesthood Since 1843, Why Aren't They Using It?" *Dialogue* 27 (Summer 1994): 219–26.

For an analysis of the changing representations of Emma Smith, see Max Perry Mueller, "Changing Portraits of the Elect Lady: Emma Smith in Non-Mormon, RLDS, and LDS Historiography, 1933–2005," *Journal of Mormon History* 37 (Spring 2011): 183–214.

The story of how Mormonism developed a conservative political, theological, and social conservativism has not been fully told because of restrictions on archival material. What is available is Patrick Q. Mason, "Ezra Taft Benson and Modern (Book of) Mormon Conservatism," in *Out of Obscurity: Mormonism Since 1945* (New York: Oxford University Press, 2016), 63–80; Jan Shipps, "Ezra Taft Benson and the Conservative Turn of 'Those Amazing Mormons,'" in Randall Balmer and Jana Riess, eds., *Mormonism and American Politics* (New York; Columbia University Press, 2016); D. Michael Quinn, "Ezra Taft Benson and Mormon Political Conflicts," *Dialogue* 25 (1992): 1–87. Both Ezra Taft Benson and Boyd K. Packer were protégés of J. Reuben Clark; see D. Michael Quinn, *Elder Statesman: A Biography of J. Reuben Clark* (Salt Lake City: Signature Press, 2002).

While the rise of Mormon *conservativism* is under-researched, historians have carefully documented both global and national moves to the right, especially the role that religion played in that shift. See the five volumes edited by Martin E. Marty and Scott F. Appleby as a part of the Fundamentalism project (1991–95) as well as P. Norris and R. Inglehart, *Sacred and Secular, Religion and Politics Worldwide* (Cambridge, UK: Cambridge University Press, 2004) and Peter L. Berger, ed., *The Desecularization of the World* (Grand Rapids, MI: William B. Eerdmans, 1999). For the role that US Protestantism has played in that move, see Steve Brouwer, Paul Gifford, and Susan D. Rose, *Exporting the American Gospel* (New York: Routledge, 1996). On Catholicism, see Ian Linden, *Global Catholicism: Diversity and Change since Vatican II* (New York: Columbia University Press, 2009).

The literature on conservative American religion is vast, especially on the impact of fundamentalist and evangelicalism after 1980 on Protestantism and politics. Scholars soon found that contemporary Protestant conservativism had long historical roots, see Axel R. Schafer, *Countercultural Conservatives: American Evangelicalism from the Postwar Revival to the New Christian Right* (Madison: University of Wisconsin Press, 2011); Kenneth J. Heineman, *God Is Conservative: Religion, Politics, and Morality in Contemporary America* (New York: New York University Press, 1998); Joel Carpenter, *Revive Us Again: The Reawakening of American Fundamentalism* (New York: Oxford, 1997); and Clyde Wilcox and Carin Robinson, *Onward Christian Soldiers: The Religious Right in American Politics* ([1996]; Boulder, CO: Westview Press, 2011). An excellent regional study is Darren Dochuck, *From Bible Belt to Sun Belt: Plain-Folk Religion, Grassroots Politics and the Rise of Evangelical Conservativism* (New York: Norton, 2011). Latter-day Saint women did not play a major role in grassroots conservative politics, with the exception of the Utah chapter of the Eagle Forum and the formidable Gayle Ruzicka, who joined the organization in 1991. See Melanie Newport, "Utah Eagle Forum: Legitimizing Political Activism as Women's Work," in Jessie L. Embry, ed., *Oral History, Community, and Work in the American West* (Tucson: University of Arizona Press, 2013), 247–61. Comparable activism by Protestant women, the Independent Women's Forum and Concerned Women for America, are documented in Ronnee Schreiber, *Righting Feminism: Conservative Women and American Politics* (New York: Oxford University Press, 2008).

On the anticult movement and its impact on Mormonism, see Matthew Bowman, "The Evangelical Countercult Movement and Mormon Conservatism," in Patrick Mason and John G. Turner, eds., *Out of Obscurity: Mormonism Since 1945* (New York: Oxford University Press, 2016), 259–77. On anti-Mormonism in general see Lawrence Foster, "Apostate Believers: Jerald and Sandra Tanner's Encounter with Mormon History" in Roger D. Launius and Linda Thatcher, eds., *Differing Visions: Dissenters in Mormon History* (Urbana: University of Illinois Press, 1994), 343–365 and his "Career Apostates: Reflections on the Work of Jerald and Sandra Tanner," *Dialogue* 17 (Summer 1984): 35–60. On the Mark Hoffman bombing, see Linda Sillitoe and Allen Roberts, *Salamander: The Story of the Mormon Forgery Murders* ([1988]; Salt Lake City: Signature Press, 2006); for the church's perspective, see Richard E. Turley, Jr. *Victims: The LDS Church and the Mark Hofmann Case* (Urbana: University of Illinois Press, 1992).

Mormon women have always worked for wages, see Miriam B. Murphy, "Women in the Utah Workforce: From Statehood to World War II," *Utah Historical Quarterly* 50 (Spring 1982): 139–59. A direct confrontation of

Benson's perspective on wage labor is Vella Neil Evans, "Mormon Women and the Right to Work," *Dialogue* 23 (Winter 1990): 46–61.

A summary of the disciplinary action against the "September Six" is "Six Intellectuals Disciplined for Apostasy," *Sunstone* (November 1993): 65–73. The basic chronology of the tensions between members and the church authorities as sketched out by a dissenter is Lavina Fielding Anderson, "The LDS Intellectual Community and Church Leadership: A Contemporary Chronology," *Dialogue* 26 (Spring 1993): 7–64. Some of those who have been excommunicated or disfellowshipped have provided reflections or interviews, see Karen Marguerite Moloney, "Saints for All Seasons: Lavina Fielding Anderson and Bernard Shaw's Joan of Arc," *Dialogue* 36 (Fall 2003): 27–39 and D. Michael Quinn, "On Being a Mormon Historian (and Its Aftermath)," in George D. Smith, ed., *Faithful History* (Salt Lake City: Signature Books, 1992), 69–111. Margaret Toscano's autobiographical statement is in Ann Braude, ed., *Transforming the Faiths of Our Fathers: Women Who Changed American Religion* (New York: Palgrave McMillian, 2004), 157–71. Highly edited interview summaries of some of the excommunicated women are included in Philip Lindholm, *Latter-day Dissent: At the Crossroads of Intellectual Inquiry and Ecclesiastical Authority* (Salt Lake City: Greg Kofford, 2010).

CHAPTER 8

The growth in Mormonism needs to be understood within the context of the growth of "global" Christianity, especially in the Southern Hemisphere. While books in the 1970s and 1980s concentrated on the liberalizing movement of liberation theology in Latin America and Africa, by the 1990s the focus was on the rise of Pentecostalism. The most accessible general volume on this growth is Philip Jenkins, *The Next Christendom: The Coming of Global Christianity* (2001), now in its third edition (New York: Oxford University Press, 2011), and its sequel, *The New Faces of Christianity: Believing the Bible in the Global South* (New York: Oxford, 2006). A more theoretical approach is Robert Wuthnow, *Boundless Faith: The Global Outreach of American Churches* (Berkeley: University of California Press, 2009). Scholarly publications on global Pentecostalism are multiple, but a straightforward survey is Allan Heaton Anderson, *To the Ends of the Earth: Pentecostalism and the Transformation of World Christianity* (New York: Oxford University Press, 2013) and the more specialized essays in Donald E. Miller, Kimon Sargeant, and Richard Flory, eds., *Spirit and Power: The Growth and Global Impact of Pentecostalism* (New York: Oxford University Press, 2013), which include both classic statements and revisions.

For global expansion of Mormonism after World War II that takes into account this wider context, see Jehu J. Hanciles, "'Would that All God's People Were Prophets': Mormonism and the New Shape of Global Christianity," *Journal of Mormon History* 41 (April 2015): 35–68. Articles by sociologists temper the growth statistics that were provided by the church and popularized by Rodney Stark in 1987. See Rodney Stark, "The Basis of Mormon Success: A Theoretical Application," in Eric A. Eliason, ed., *Mormons and Mormonism: An Introduction to an American World Religion* (Urbana: University of Illinois Press, 2001); Lowell C. Bennion and Lawrence Young, "The Uncertain Dynamics of LDS Expansion, 1950–2020," *Dialogue* 29, no. 1 (1996): 8–32; Armand L. Mauss, "Identity and Boundary Maintenance: International Prospects for Mormonism at the Dawn of the Twenty-First Century," in Douglas Davies, ed., *Mormon Identities in Transition* (London: Cassell, 1996), 9–19; David Knowlton, "How Many Members Are There Really? Two Censuses and the Meaning of LDS Membership in Chile and Mexico," *Dialogue* 38 (2005): 53–78; and Rick Phillips, "Rethinking the International Expansion of Mormonism," *Nova Religio: The Journal of Alternative and Emergent Religions* 10 (August 2006): 52–68. For Utah's unique position in global Mormonism see Rick Phillips, "The 'Secularization' of Utah and Religious Competition," *Journal for the Scientific Study of Religion* 38 (March 1999): 72–82 and Rick Phillips and Ryan Cragun, "Contemporary Mormon Religiosity and the Legacy of 'Gathering,'" *Nova Religio: The Journal of Alternative and Emergent Religions* 16 (February 2013): 77–94.

I conducted fieldwork in the Johannesburg area of South Africa during the spring of 2015 and in Sicily and southern Italy in the spring of 2016. In addition, I greatly benefited from two collections of interviews of Latter-day Saint women. "The Gender, Narrative, and Religious Practice in Southern Africa Oral History Collection" contains approximately seventy interviews conducted in 2015 and is located at Special Collections, Claremont Colleges Library, Claremont, California. A more extensive collection (twenty-six boxes) contains interviews with black and white Africans that were conducted in 1988 as a part of the E. Dale LeBaron Oral History Project on Africa; it is housed at the L. Tom Perry Special Collections in the Harold B. Lee Library at BYU. Convert experiences dominate the interviews in a series of oral histories of "ethnic Mormons" (Asian Americans, Hispanic Americans, Native Americans, Polynesian Americans) conducted by the Charles Redd Center, also available in BYU's Special Collections.

For a broad overview of Christian and Mormon growth in Africa, see Philip Jenkins, "Letting Go: Understanding Mormon Growth in Africa," *Journal of Mormon History* 35 (Spring 2009): 1–25. Although missionaries came to South Africa as early as 1853, there is no published scholarly history. Most online summaries are based on the privately printed writings (three volumes) of Evan P. Wright, who served a mission there in the 1930s and went on to be Mission President (1948–53). However, Booker T. Alson's PhD dissertation "Transatlantic Latter-day Saints: Mormon Circulations Between America and South Africa (University of Cape Town, 2014) is a sophisticated study that includes the impact of the end of the priesthood ban on South African Latter-day Saints. He explores the relationship between missionary work and sports in "The Cumorah Baseball Club: Mormon Missionaries and Baseball in South Africa," *Journal of Mormon History* 40 (Summer 2014): 93–126. For an impressionistic account written shortly after Nelson Mandela became president of South Africa, see Andrew Cane, "The Fading Curse of Cain: Mormonism in South Africa," *Dialogue* 27 (Winter 1994): 41–56, which includes a brief discussion of social reformer Julia Mavimbela.

Scholarship on Latter-day Saints in Italy is deeper, mostly because of the scholarship of Michael W. Homer. Of his many articles, "LDS Prospects in Italy for the Twenty-first Century," *Dialogue* 29 (Spring 1996): 139–58 provides a historical summary but fails to take into account the transnational nature of modern Italian Mormonism. See also Eric R. Dursteler, "One Hundred Years of Solitude: Mormonism in Italy, 1867–1964," *International Journal of Mormon Studies* 4 (2011): 119–48.

Scholarship on women, religion, and the Southern Hemisphere evolved out of studies on the rise of Pentecostalism. From the 1990s onward, scholars refuted the Western feminist claim that religion supported an oppressive patriarchal structure to the detriment of women. Instead, they argued that women used Christianity, especially in its charismatic form, to transform gender relations. The classic work on Africa is Ruth Marshall, "Power in the Name of Jesus," *Review of African Political Economy* 52 (November 1991): 21–387, especially 29–32. On South America, see Elizabeth Brusco, *The Reformation of Machismo: Evangelical Protestantism and Gender in Colombia* (Austin: University of Texas Press, 1995). On Europe, see Salvatore Cucchiari, "Between Shame and Sanctification: Patriarchy and Its Transformation in Sicilian Pentecostalism," *American Ethnologist* 17 (November 1990): 687–707. More recent studies have complicated the claim of religious empowerment but not disproved it. For the African situation, see Jane E. Soothill, *Gender, Social Change and Spiritual Power: Charismatic Christianity in Ghana* (Boston: Brill, 2007); Ogbu Kalu, "Gendered Charisma: Charisma and Women in African Pentecostalism," in his *African Pentecostalism: An Introduction* (New York: Oxford University Press, 2008); and Maria Frahm-Arp, *Professional Women in South African Pentecostal Charismatic Churches* (Leiden, Netherlands: Brill, 2010). A rare study that departs from Pentecostalism to look at the Catholic world in Africa is Dorothy L. Hodgson, *The Church of Women: Gendered Encounters Between Maasai and Missionaries* (Bloomington: Indiana University Press, 2005). For Italy, see Annalisa Butticci, *African Pentecostals in Catholic Europe: The Politics of Presence in the Twenty-First Century* (Cambridge, MA: Harvard University Press, 2016) and her "African Pentecostal Churches in Italy: A Troubled Presence in a Catholic Country," *Yearbook of International Religious Demography* (Leiden, Netherlands: Brill, 2016), 107–15. Cecília Mariz argues for the similarities between Pentecostal and Catholic renewal groups in "Religion and Poverty in Brazil: A Comparison of Catholic and Pentecostal Communities," *Sociological Analysis* 53 (1992): 63–70.

As of this date, the best discussion of Gordon B. Hinckley's impact on Mormonism is J. B. Haws, *The Mormon Image in the American Mind: Fifty Years of Public Perception* (New York: Oxford University Press, 2013), 158–92, and Hugo N. Olaiz, "Gordon B. Hinckley and the Ritualization of Mormon History," *Sunstone* 149 (April 2008): 21–27. The impact of the Elaine L. Jack Relief Society administration has not yet been examined by scholars, but interviews with her as well as Aileen Clyde are available as a part of The Mormon Women's Voices Oral History Project in Special Collections, University of Utah, J. Willard Marriott. In addition to Chieko N. Okazaki's own inspirational publications, see Greg Prince, " 'There Is Always a Struggle': An Interview with Chieko N. Okazaki," *Dialogue* 45 (Spring 2012): 112–40.

A comprehensive history of Latter-day Saint missionary activity that integrates it into the wider context of Christian missiology has not been written. Gary Shepherd and Gordon Shepherd, in *Mormon Passage: A Missionary Chronicle* (Carbondale: University of Illinois Press, 1998), use their own diaries as missionaries to analyze the sociology and history of missionary work. Their chapter introductions are particularly helpful overviews. A critical account of the push toward baptisms in the 1960s is D. Michael Quinn, "I-Thou vs. I-It Conversions: The Mormon 'Baseball Baptism' Era," *Sunstone* 16, no. 7 (1993): 30–44.

This summary of race and Mormonism is drawn from Paul Reeve, *Religion of a Different Color: Race and the Mormon Struggle for Whiteness* (New York: Oxford, 2016). Earlier publications on African Americans include Newell C. Bringhurst, *Saints, Slaves, and Blacks: The Changing Place of Black People Within Mormonism* (Westport, CT: Greenwood Publishers, 1982). During a period of four years in the mid-eighties, the Charles Redd Center at BYU sponsored the LDS African American Oral History Project. Alan Cherry, an African American and Latter-day Saint, conducted 224 interviews, of which over half were of black women. Jessie L. Embry used these interviews to write *Black Saints in a White Church: Contemporary*

African American Mormons (Salt Lake: Signature Books, 1994). For a sociological perspective, see Armand L. Mauss, *All Abraham's Children: Changing Mormon Conceptions of Race and Lineage* (Carbondale: University of Illinois Press, 2003) and his "From Galatia to Ghana: The Racial Dynamic in Mormon History," *International Journal of Mormon Studies* 6 (2013): 54–73 as well as Mary Lou McNamara, "Secularization or Sacralization: The Change in LDS Church Policy on Blacks," in Marie Cornwall et al., eds., *Contemporary Mormonism: Social Science Perspectives* (Urbana: University of Illinois Press, 1994), 310–25.

On Jane Manning James, see the research by Quincy D. Newell, "The Autobiography and Interview of Jane Elizabeth Manning James," *Journal of Africana Religions* 1 (2013): 251–91; "'Is There No Blessing for Me?' Jane James's Construction of Space in Latter-day Saint History and Practice," in Quincy D. Newell and Eric F. Mason, eds., *New Perspectives in Mormon Studies: Creating and Crossing Boundaries* (Norman: University of Oklahoma Press, 2013), 41–65; and "Jane James's Agency," in Kate Holbrook and Matthew Bowman, eds., *Women and Mormonism: Historical and Contemporary Perspectives* (Salt Lake City: University of Utah Press, 2016), 136–48. For James's function in contemporary Mormonism, see Max Perry Muller, "Playing Jane: Re-presenting Black Mormon Memory Through Reenacting the Black Mormon Past," *Journal of Africana Religions* 1 (2013): 513–61. On Africans who sought to be baptized prior to church missionary work, see James B. Allen, "Would Be Saints: West Africa Before the 1978 Priesthood Revelation," *Journal of Mormon History* 17 (1991): 207–47.

The most complete survey of Protestant missionary work and women is Dana Lee Robert, *American Women in Mission: A Social History of Their Thought and Practice* (Macon, GA: Mercer University Press, 1997). Mormon missionaries are encouraged to keep diaries, and while many of them are formulaic, others are more candid. Multiple diaries of sister missionaries are deposited at the Church History Library in Salt Lake City. In the early nineties, eighty-six missionaries were interviewed for a Redd Center oral history project, and director Jessie Embry published "LDS Sister Missionaries: An Oral History Response, 1910–1971," *Journal of Mormon History* 23 (Spring 1992): 100–39 and "Oral History and Mormon Women Missionaries: The Stories Sound the Same," *Journal of Women Studies* 19 (1998): 171–88 on her findings. Original interviews are in BYU Special Collections. See also Carol Cornwall Madsen, "Mormon Missionary Wives in Nineteenth Century Polynesia" in Laurie F. Maffly-Kipp and Reid L. Neilson, eds., *Proclamation to the People: Nineteenth-Century Mormonism and the Pacific Basin Frontier* (Salt Lake City: University of Utah Press, 2008), 142–69; Tania Rands Lyon and Mary Ann Shumway

McFarland, "'Not Invited, But Welcome': The History and Impact of Church Policy on Sister Missionaries," *Dialogue* 36 (Fall 2003): 71–101; and Tally S. Payne, "'Our Wise and Prudent Women': Twentieth-Century Trends in Female Missionary Service," in Carol Cornwall Madsen, ed., *New Scholarship on Latter-day Saint Women in the Twentieth Century* (Provo, UT: BYU Press, 2005), 125–40. There are three master's theses: Calvin Kunz, "A History of Female Missionary Activity in The Church of Jesus Christ of Latter-day Saints, 1830-1898" (BYU, 1976); Alice Buehner, "The Communicational Function of Wearing Apparel for Lady Missionaries for the LDS Church" (BYU, 1982); and Kelly Lelegren, "'Real, Live Mormon Women': Understanding the Role of Early Twentieth-Century LDS Lady Missionaries" (Utah State University, 2009).

On the changes to the missionary system, see Dennis A. Wright and Janine Gallagher Doot, "Missionary Materials and Methods: A Preliminary Study," in Reid L. Nielson and Fred E. Woods, eds., *Go Ye into All the World: The Growth & Development of Mormon Missionary Work* (Provo, UT: Religious Studies Center, 2012), 91–116 (https://rsc .byu.edu/archived/go-ye-all-world/missionary-training-and-practices/ 5-missionary-materials-and-methods#_edn77) and Benjamin Hyrum White, "The History of *Preach My Gospel*," *Religious Educator* 14, no. 1 (2013): 129–58 (https://rsc.byu.edu/archived/volume-14-number-1- 2013/history-preach-my-gospel).

The cottage industry Deborah Tannen started with *You Just Don't Understand: Women and Men in Conversation* (New York: Morrow, 1990) includes her multiple academic and popular works, as well as Ruth Wodak, ed., *Gender and Discourse* (Thousand Oaks, CA: Sage, 1996); Lana F. Rakow, *Gender on the Line: Women, the Telephone, and Community Life* (Urbana: University of Illinois Press, 1992); Jennifer Coates, *Women Talk* (Oxford: Blackwell, 1996); and Sally Johnson and Ulrike Hanna Meinhof, eds., *Language and Masculinity* (Oxford: Blackwell, 1996). There also were scholars who challenged Tannen's conclusions, most notably Mary Crawford, *Talking Difference: On Gender and Language* (London: Sage, 1995).

The theatricality of conservative Protestantism has not surprisingly drawn the attention of scholars worldwide, see Eric W. Kramer, "Spectacle and the Staging of Power in Brazilian Neo-Pentecostalism," *Latin American Perspectives* 32 (January 2005): 95–120; Ann Pellegrini, "'Signaling through the Flames': Hell House Performance and Structures of Religious Feeling," *American Quarterly* 59 (2007): 911–35; and Jesse Weaver Shipley, "Comedians, Pastors, and the Miraculous Agency of Charisma in Ghana," *Cultural Anthropology* 24 (August 2009): 523–52. John Corrigan has explored religious emotion extensively in various publications, see

The Business of the Heart: Religion and Emotion in the Nineteenth Century (Berkeley: University of California Press, 2002). On tear shedding, see Gary L. Ebersole, "The Function of Ritual Weeping Revisited: Affective Expression and Moral Discourse," in John Corrigan, ed., *Religion and Emotion: Approaches and Interpretations* (New York: Oxford University Press, 2014): 185–222. Bernhard Lang developed the idea of "intellectual rituals" performed by communities centered on a sacred text. He explores the importance of clerical preaching but not discussions carried on by the laity. See "On Intellectual Ritual" in his *Sacred Games: A History of Christian Worship* (New Haven, CT: Yale University Press, 1997), 139–203.

Examinations of the "still" religious experience and expression of Latter-day Saints is far rarer. The most developed study is Tom Mould, *Still, the Small Voice: Narrative, Personal Revelation, and the Mormon Folk Tradition* (Logan: Utah State University Press, 2011). See also David Knowlton, "Belief, Metaphor, and Rhetoric: The Mormon Practice of Testimony Bearing," *Sunstone* 15 (April 1991): 20–27; and Stacy Burton, "Rethinking Religious Experience: Notes from Critical Theory, Feminism, and Real Life," *Dialogue* 28 (Winter 1995): 67–90. For a more theoretical examination, see Douglas J. Davies, "The Holy Spirit in Mormonism," *International Journal of Mormon Studies* 2 (Spring 2009): 23–41.

For a thorough examination of the history and problematics of Gospel Culture, see Wilfried Decoo, "In Search of Mormon Identity: Mormon Culture, Gospel Culture, and an American Worldwide Church," *International Journal of Mormon Studies* 6 (2013): 1–53. The evolution of standardized Mormon architecture in the United States (but not its global impact) is described in Paul F. Starrs, "Meetinghouses in the Mormon Mind: Ideology, Architecture, and Turbulent Streams of an Expanding Church," *Geographical Review*, 99, no. 3 (2009): 323–55 and Martha Sonntag Bradley, "The Church and Colonel Sanders: Mormon Standard Plan Architecture" (master's thesis, BYU, 1981). J. Michael Cleverly argues for the existence of subtle global variations in "Mormonism on the Big Mac Standard," *Dialogue* 29 (Summer 1996): 69–75. Tensions between local needs and dictates coming from "Salt Lake" are explored in Rick Phillips, "'De Facto Congregationalism' and Mormon Missionary Outreach: An Ethnographic Case Study," *Journal for the Scientific Study of Religion* 47 (2008): 638–43.

Lobola (or *lobolo*) is a changing practice throughout Africa, not simply in Latter-day Saint communities. See Sandra Burman and Nicolette van de Werff, "Rethinking Customary Law on Bridewealth," *Social Dynamics* 19 (1993): 111–27; David L. Chambers, "Civilizing the Natives: Marriage in Post-Apartheid South Africa," *Daedalus* 129 (Fall 2000): 101–24; and Janet Hinson Shope, "'Lobola Is Here to Stay,' Rural Black Women and

the Contradictory Meanings of Lobolo in Post-Apartheid South Africa,"
Agenda: Empowering Women for Gender Equity 68 (2006): 64–72.

CHAPTER 9

Unfortunately, the Relief Society General Board minutes from this period are currently closed to research, so we do not have an idea of what the
Relief Society Presidency had in mind as a response to their international
survey. For theoretical reflections on the relationship between women's
agency (e.g., the Relief Society focus groups) and patriarchy (the silencing
by the First Presidency), see Amy Hoyt, "Agency," and Caroline Kline,
"Patriarchy," both in Claudia L. Bushman and Caroline Kline, eds., *Mormon
Women Have Their Say: Essays from the Claremont Oral History Collection*
(Salt Lake City: Greg Kofford Books, 2013), 193–214, 215–34. Catherine
Brekus's 2010 plenary address to the Mormon Historical Association
is frequently called on by Latter-day Saint historians as justification for
their scholarship on religion and agency; see "Mormon Women and the
Problem of Historical Agency," in Kate Holbrook and Matthew Bowman,
eds., *Women and Mormonism: Historical and Contemporary Perspectives* (Salt
Lake City: University of Utah Press, 2016).

For the history of Latter-day Saint leadership's changing response to
homosexuality, see Ryan T. Cragun, Emily Williams, and J. E. Sumerau,
"From Sodomy to Sympathy: LDS Elites' Discursive Construction of
Homosexuality Over Time," *Journal for the Scientific Study of Religion* 54
(2015): 291–310. For members' behaviors, see D. Michael Quinn, *Same-
Sex Dynamics Among Nineteenth-Century Americans: A Mormon Example*
(Urbana: University of Illinois Press, 1996). A more impressionistic ac-
count is Rocky O'Donovan, "'The Abominable and Detestable Crime
against Nature,' A Brief History of Homosexuality and Mormonism,
1840–1980," in Brett Corcoran, ed., *Multiply and Replenish* (Salt Lake
City: Signature Books, 1994), 123–62. For a sociological study, see Rick
Phillips, *Conservative Christian Identity and Same-Sex Orientation: The Case
of Gay Mormons* (New York: Peter Lang, 2009). For a comparison with the
Community of Christ, another branch of the Mormon family, see O. Kendall
White Jr. and Daryl White, "Ecclesiastical Polity and the Challenge of
Homosexuality: Two Cases of Divergence Within the Mormon Tradition,"
Dialogue 37 (2004): 67–89.

On Latter-day Saint political involvement with same-sex marriage, especially Proposition 8, see the chronology by Utah State University professor
Richley H. Crapo, "Chronology of Mormon/LDS Involvement in Same-
Sex Marriage," *Mormon Social Science* (January 4, 2008), (https://www
.mormonsocialscience.org/2008/01/04/richley-crapo-chronology-of-

mormon-lds-involvement-in-same-sex-marriage-politics/); William N. Eskridge, "Latter-day Constitutionalism: Sexuality, Gender, and Mormons," *University of Illinois Law Review* 2016 no. 4 (2016): 1227–1286; Monica Youn, "Proposition 8 and the Mormon Church: A Case Study in Donor Disclosure," *George Washington Law Review* 81 (November 2013): 2108–54; and Neil L. Young, "Mormons and Same-Sex Marriage: From ERA to Prop 8," in Patrick Q. Mason and John G. Turner, eds., *Out of Obscurity: Mormonism Since 1945* (New York: Oxford University Press, 2016), 144–69. For more personal accounts, see Anna Terry Rolapp, "Prop 8," in Claudia L. Bushman and Caroline Kline, eds., *Mormon Women Have Their Say* (Salt Lake City: Greg Kofford Books, 2013), 286–301; Johanna Brooks, "On the 'Underground': What the Mormon 'Yes on 8' Campaign Reveals About the Future of Mormons in American Political Life," in Randall Balmer and Jana Riess, eds., *Mormonism and American Politics* (New York: Columbia University Press, 2016), 192–209; and D. Michael Quinn, "Prelude to the National 'Defense of Marriage' Campaign: Civil Discrimination Against Feared or Despised Minorities," *Dialogue* 33 (Fall 2000): 1–52.

The changing nature of the American family is a staple of sociological literature. A good overview is Barbara J. Risman, *Families as They Really Are* (New York: W. W. Norton, 2015). On societal strains on poor and working-class families, see June Carbone and Naomi Cahn, *Marriage Markets: How Inequality Is Remaking the American Family* (New York: Oxford University Press, 2014); Mitchell B. Peralstein, *Broken Bonds: What Family Fragmentation Means for America's Future* (Lanham, MD: Rowman & Littlefield, 2014); Andrew Cherlin, *Labor's Love Lost: The Rise and Fall of the Working-Class Family in America* (New York: Russell Sage Foundation, 2014), 90–175, and his earlier *The Marriage-Go-Round: The State of Marriage and the Family in America Today* (New York: Vintage, 2009).

For a Southern Baptist woman's response to family and gender dynamics, see Susan M. Shaw, *God Speaks to Us, Too: Southern Baptist Women on Church, Home, and Society* (Lexington: University Press of Kentucky, 2008). During the nineties, scholars explored how conservative religious women negotiate their position within the family, especially how they assert agency rather than submission, see Christel Manning, *God Gave Us the Right: Conservative Catholic, Evangelical Protestant, and Orthodox Jewish Women Grapple with Feminism* (New Brunswick, NJ: Rutgers University Press, 1999); Debra Kaufman, *Rachel's Daughters: Newly Orthodox Jewish Women* (New Brunswick, NJ: Rutgers University Press, 1991); Lynn Davidman, *Tradition in a Rootless World: Women Turn to Orthodox Judaism* (Berkeley: University of California Press, 1991); Brenda Brasher, *Godly Woman: Fundamentalism and Female Power* (New Brunswick, NJ: Rutgers

University Press, 1998); and R. Marie Griffith, *God's Daughters: Evangelical Women and the Power of Submission* (Berkeley: University of California Press, 1997). More recent reflections include R. Claire Snyder-Hall, "The Ideology of Wifely Submission: A Challenge for Feminism?" *Politics & Gender* 4 (2008): 563–86; Sally K. Gallagher, *Evangelical Identity and Gendered Family Life* (New Brunswick, NJ: Rutgers University Press, 2003); and John P. Bartkowski, *Remaking the Godly Marriage: Gender Negotiation in Evangelical Families* (New Brunswick, NJ: Rutgers University Press, 2001). Saba Mahood provides a comparison with Egyptian Islam in her oft-quoted *The Politics of Piety: The Islamic Revival and the Feminist Subject* (Princeton, NJ: Princeton University Press, 2012).

The theological understanding the Garden of Eden is tightly wound up in interpretations of evil. See James M. McLachan, "The Problem of Evil in Mormon Thought," in Terryl L. Givens and Philip Barlow, eds., *The Oxford Handbook of Mormonism* (New York: Oxford University Press, 2015), 276–91; Terryl Givens, "The Fall," in *Wrestling the Angel: The Foundations of Mormon Thought: Cosmos, God, Humanity* (New York: Oxford University Press, 2015), 176–98; Kathleen Flake, "Evil's Origins and Evil's End in the Joseph Smith Translation of Genesis," *Sunstone* 20 (August 1998): 24–29; and Sterling M. McMurrin, *The Theological Foundations of the Mormon Religion* (Salt Lake City: University of Utah Press, 1965), 57–67, 91–113. Between Talmage and contemporary reflections on the fall, there is a brief mention of the fall as a necessary act in John A. Widtsoe, *Evidences and Reconciliations* (Salt Lake City: Bookcraft, 1943), 168–70. On the place of Eve, see two essays by Boyd J. Petersen, "'The Greatest Glory of True Womanhood': Eve and the Construction of Mormon Gender Identity," in Gordon Shepherd, Lavina Fielding Anderson, and Gary Shepherd, eds., *Voices for Equality: Ordain Women and Resurgent Mormon Feminism* (Salt Lake City: Greg Kofford Books, 2015), 49–76, and "'Redeemed from the Curse Placed upon Her': Dialogic Discourse on Eve in the *Woman's Exponent*," *Journal of Mormon History* 40 (2014): 135–74. Jolene Edmunds Rockwood begins the feminist rethinking in "The Redemption of Eve," in *Sisters in Spirit: Mormon Women in Historical and Cultural Perspective* (Urbana: University of Illinois Press, 1987), 3–36. For theological reflections by another Latter-day Saint woman, see Beverly Campbell, *Eve and the Choice Made in Eden* (West Valley City, UT: Bookcraft Publisher, 2002) and *Eve and the Mortal Journey: Finding Wholeness, Happiness, and Strength* (Salt Lake City: Deseret Book Company, 2005).

Worries about the absence of men from families were stimulated by the "culture wars" of the 1990s and led sociologists and historians to take sides in the debate. Arguing for the essential role men played are David Blankenhorn, *Fatherless America: Confronting Our Most Urgent*

Social Problem (New York: Basic Books, 1995) and David Popenoe, *Life Without Father: Compelling New Evidence That Fatherhood and Marriage Are Indispensable for the Good of Children and Society* (New York: The Free Press, 1996). Judith Stacey, in *In the Name of the Family: Rethinking Values in the Postmodern Age* (Boston: Beacon Press, 1996) and *Brave New Families: Stories of Domestic Upheaval in Late Twentieth-Century America* (New York: Basic Books, 1990) responds that the family values campaign reflects and perpetuates gender, race, and class inequalities. For the evangelical responses, see John P. Bartkowski, *The Promise Keepers: Servants, Soldiers, and Godly Men* (New Brunswick, NJ: Rutgers University Press, 2004) and Dane S. Claussen, *The Promise Keepers: Essays on Masculinity and Christianity* (Jefferson, NC: McFarland, 2000). For responses by African American men, see Judith Lowder Newton, "Revolutionary Men: Civil Rights, Black Power, and the Reconfiguration of Black Masculine Ideals," in *From Panthers to Promise Keepers: Rethinking the Men's Movement* (Lanham, MD: Rowman & Littlefield, 2005); and Evelyn Kirkley, "Phallic Spirituality: Masculinities in Promise Keepers, the Million Man March and Sex Panic," *Theology & Sexuality* 12 (2000): 9–25.

For the history of Latter-day Saint attitudes on contraceptives, see Melissa Proctor, "Babies, Bodies and Birth Control," *Dialogue* 36 (Fall 2003): 159–75; Lester Bush, "Birth Control Among the Mormons: Introduction to an Insistent Question," *Dialogue* 10 (Autumn 1976): 12–44; and Donald W. Hastings, Charles H. Reynolds, and Ray R. Canning, "Mormonism and Birth Planning: The Discrepancy Between Church Authorities' Teachings and Lay Attitudes," *Population Studies* 26 (March 1972): 19–28. For Catholics, see Leslie Woodcock Tentler, *Catholics and Contraception: An American History* (Ithaca, NY: Cornell University Press, 2004). On the relationship between laity and church authority see the essays in Francis Oakley and Michael James, *The Crisis of Authority in Catholic Modernity* (New York: Oxford University Press, 2011), especially those by William V. D'Antonio et al., "American Catholics and Church Authority," 273–92, and Leslie Woodcock Tentler, "Souls and Bodies, The Birth Control Controversy and the Collapse of Confession," 293–316.

CHAPTER 10

On the digital revolution, see Katie Hafner and Matthew Lyon, *Where Wizards Stay Up Late: The Origins of the Internet* (New York: Simon & Schuster, 1996); Walter Isaacson, *The Innovators: How a Group of Hackers, Geniuses, and Geeks Created the Digital Revolution* (New York: Simon & Schuster, 2014); and Johnny Ryan, *A History of the Internet and the Digital Future* (London: Reaktion Books, 2010). On "e-religion," see

Gina Messina-Dysert and Rosemary Radford Ruether, eds., *Feminism and Religion in the 21st Century: Technology, Dialogue, and Expanding Borders* (New York: Routledge, 2015); Peter G. Horsfield and Paul Teusner, "Mediated Religion: Historical Perspectives on Christianity and the Internet," *Studies in World Christianity* 13 (2007): 278–95; Heidi Campbell, *Exploring Religious Community Online: We Are One in the Network* (New York: Peter Lang, 2005); Brenda E. Brasher, *Give Me That Online Religion* (San Francisco: John Wiley & Sons, 2001); and Jeffrey P. Zaleski, *The Soul of Cyberspace: How New Technology Is Changing Our Spiritual Lives* (San Francisco: HarperEdge, 1997). For the limits of the internet, see Benjamin M. Compaine, ed., *The Digital Divide* (Cambridge, MA: MIT Press, 2001) and Mark Warschauer, *Technology and Social Inclusion: Rethinking the Digital Divide* (Cambridge, MA: MIT Press, 2003).

On religion and blogging in the United States, see Monica A. Coleman, "Blogging as Religious Feminist Activism: Ministry To, Through, With, and From" and Gina Messina-Dysert, "#FemReligionFuture: The New Feminist Revolution in Religion," both in Gina Messina-Dysert and Rosemary Radford Ruether, eds., *Feminism and Religion in the 21st Century: Technology, Dialogue, and Expanding Borders* (New York: Routledge, 2015), 9–19, 20–33; Deborah Whitehead, "The Evidence of Things Unseen: Authenticity and Fraud in the Christian Mommy Blogosphere," *Journal of the American Academy of Religion* 83 (2015): 120–150; "'The Story God Is Weaving Us Into': Narrativizing Grief, Faith, and Infant Loss in US Evangelical Women's Blog Communities," *New Review of Hypermedia and Multimedia* 17 (December 2014): 1–15; and Pauline Hope Choeong, Alexander Halavais, and Kyounghee Kwon, "The Chronicles of Me: Understanding Blogging as a Religious Practice," *Journal of Media and Religion* 7 (2008): 107–31. On Mormon female bloggers, see Caroline Kline, "Mormon Feminist Blogs and Heavenly Mother: Spaces for Ambivalence and Innovation in Practice and Theology," in Gina Messina-Dysert and Rosemary Radford Ruether, eds., *Feminism and Religion in the 21st Century: Technology, Dialogue, and Expanding Borders* (New York: Routledge, 2015), 34–46; Kristine Haglund, "Blogging the Boundaries: Mormon Mommy Blogs and the Construction of Mormon Identity," in Patrick Q. Mason and John G. Turner, eds., *Out of Obscurity: Mormonism Since 1945* (New York: Oxford University Press, 2016), 234–56; Rosemary Avance, "Seeing the Light: Mormon Conversion and Deconversion Narratives in Off- and Online Worlds," *Journal of Media and Religion* 12 (2013): 16–24; and Brighton Capua, "Mommy Blogs and Rhetoric: Reading Experiences that Shape Maternal Identities" (master's thesis, BYU, 2013).

For the trend toward enhanced domesticity, see Sarah Leavitt, *From Catherine Beecher to Martha Stewart: A Cultural History of Domestic Advice*

(Chapel Hill: University of North Carolina Press, 2002); Susan Fraimen, "Bad Girls of Good Housekeeping: Dominique Browning and Martha Stewart," *American Literary History* 23 (Summer 2011): 260–82; M. J. McNaughton, "Of Art and Drudgery: Homekeeping, Martha Stewart, and Techné," *Home Cultures* 13 (2016): 39–62; and Emily Matchar, *Homeward Bound: Why Women Are Embracing the New Domesticity* (New York: Simon & Schuster, 2013). On earlier Mormon advice efforts, see Kate Holbrook, "Housework: The Problem that Does Have a Name," in Patrick Q. Mason and John G. Turner, eds., *Out of Obscurity: Mormonism Since 1945* (New York: Oxford University Press, 2016),198–213.

The question of whether homosexuality is sinful or not is the concern of most Catholic and Protestant writers on the subject. A typical Catholic theological reflection is Gerald D. Coleman, *Homosexuality: Catholic Teaching and Pastoral Practice* (New York: Paulist Press, 1995) and a more personal one is Mark D. Jordan, *The Silence of Sodom: Homosexuality in Modern Catholicism* (Chicago: University of Chicago Press, 2000). For Catholic histories that provide a wider perspective, see John Boswell, *Christianity, Social Tolerance, and Homosexuality: Gay People in Western Europe from the Beginning of the Christian Era to the Fourteenth Century* ([1980]; Chicago: University of Chicago Press, 2015) and his *Same-Sex Unions in Premodern Europe* (New York: Vintage, 1994).

Protestantism, obviously, has many perspectives. Theological and pastoral positions are discussed in Choon Leong Seow, *Homosexuality and Christian Community* (Louisville, KY: John Knox Press, 1996). For a history of mainstream Protestant responses, see Heather R. White, *Reforming Sodom: Protestants and the Rise of Gay Rights* (Chapel Hill: University of North Carolina Press, 2015). For ethnographic studies see Dawne Moon, *God, Sex, and Politics: Homosexuality and Everyday Theologies* (Chicago: University of Chicago Press, 2004) and Melissa M. Wilcox, *Coming Out in Christianity: Religion, Identity, and Community* (Bloomington: Indiana University Press, 2003). Although his title speaks of American "religions" Anthony M. Petro's focus is on Protestantism in *After the Wrath of God: AIDS, Sexuality, and American Religions* (New York: Oxford University Press, 2015). The rare exception to books that focus on homosexual men and Christianity is Melissa M. Wilcox, *Queer Women and Religious Individualism* (Bloomington: Indiana University Press, 2009).

Rosemary Avance addresses All Enlisted's "Wear Pants to Church Day" in "Constructing Religion in the Digital Age: The Internet and Modern Mormon Identities" (dissertation, University of Pennsylvania, 2015), 139–49. On Ordain Women, see the essays in Gordon Shepherd, Lavina Fielding Anderson, and Gary Shepherd, eds., *Voices for Equality: Ordain Women and*

Resurgent Mormon Feminism (Salt Lake City: Greg Kofford Books, 2015) and Margaret M. Toscano, "The Mormon 'Ordain Women' Movement: The Virtue of Virtual Activism," in Gina Messina-Dysert and Rosemary Radford Ruether, eds., *Feminism and Religion in the 21st Century: Technology, Dialogue, and Expanding Borders* (New York: Routledge, 2015), 153–166. Publishing at approximately the same time as Ordain Women was *Women and the Priesthood: What One Mormon Woman Believes* (Salt Lake: Deseret Book Company, 2013) by Deseret Book Company's president and CEO Sherri Dew.

On the Mormon Moment see Margaret M. Toscano, "Mormon Morality and Immortality in Stephenie Meyer's Twilight Series," in Melissa Click, Jennifer Stevens Aubrey, and Elizabeth Behm-Morawitz, eds., *Bitten by Twilight: Youth Culture, Media, and the Vampire Franchise* (New York: Peter Lang), 21–36; Jana Riess, "Book of Mormon Stories That Steph Meyer Tells to Me: LDS Themes in the Twilight Saga and *The Host*," *BYU Studies* 48 (2009): 141–47; Tanya D. Zuk, " 'Proud Mormon Polygamist': Assimilation, Popular Memory, and the Mormon Churches in *Big Love*," *Journal of Religion and Popular Culture* 26 (2014): 93–106; J. Michael Hunter, *Mormons and Popular Culture: The Global Influence of an American Phenomenon* (Santa Barbara, CA: Praeger, 2013); David E. Campbell, John C. Green, and J. Quinn Monson, "How Mormonism Affected Mitt; How Mitt Affected Mormonism," in *Seeking the Promised Land: Mormons and American Politics* (Cambridge, UK: Cambridge University Press, 2014), 222–52; Peggy Fletcher Stack, "Mitt, Mormonism, and the Media: An Unfamiliar Faith Takes the Stage in the 2013 U. S. Presidential Election," in Randall Balmer and Jana Riess, eds., *Mormonism and American Politics* (New York: Columbia University Press, 2016), 210–26; and J. B. Haws, *The Mormon Image in the American Mind* (New York: Oxford University Press), 236–81.

More recent discussions of Heavenly Mother have not overturned Linda Wilcox's basic historical narrative, but they have provided theological elaborations, see Terryl L. Givens, "Mother God," in *Wrestling the Angel: The Foundations of Mormon Thought: Cosmos, God, Humanity* (New York: Oxford University Press, 2015), 106–11; David Golding, "Heavenly Mother," in Claudia L. Bushman and Caroline Kline, eds., *Mormon Women Have Their Say: Essays from the Claremont Oral History Collection* (Salt Lake City: Greg Kofford Books, 2013); David L. Paulsen and Martin Pulido, "A Mother There": A Survey of Historical Teachings About Mother in Heaven," *BYU Studies* 50 (2011): 71–97; Kevin L. Barney, "How to Worship Our Mother in Heaven (Without Getting Excommunicated)," *Dialogue* 41, no. 4 (Winter 2008): 121–46; Margaret Merrill Toscano, "Is There a Place for Heavenly Mother in Mormon Theology? An Investigation into Discourses of Power," *Sunstone* 133 (July 2004): 14–22; Danny

L. Jorgensen, "The Mormon Gender-Inclusive Image of God," *Journal of Mormon History* 27 (2001): 95–126; Jill Mulvay Derr, "The Significance of 'O My Father' in the Personal Journey of Eliza R. Snow," *BYU Studies* 36 (1996–97): 84–126; Janice Allred, "Toward a Mormon Theology of God the Mother," *Dialogue* 27 (Summer 1994): 38–39; Carol Lynn Pearson, "Healing the Motherless House," Martha Pierce, "Personal Discourse on God the Mother," and "Emerging Discourse on the Divine Feminine," all in Maxine Hanks, ed., *Women and Authority: Re-emerging Mormon Feminism* (Salt Lake City: Signature Books, 1992), 231–96; and John Heeren, Donald B. Lindsey, and Marylee Mason, "The Mormon Concept of Mother in Heaven: A Sociological Account of Its Origins and Development," *Journal for the Scientific Study of Religion* 23 (1984): 396–411.

INDEX